S. S Clarke, John Hutton Balfour Browne

The Law of Usages and Customs

First American Edition

I0084123

S. S Clarke, John Hutton Balfour Browne

The Law of Usages and Customs
First American Edition

ISBN/EAN: 9783337812966

Printed in Europe, USA, Canada, Australia, Japan

Cover: Foto ©Suzi / pixelio.de

More available books at **www.hansebooks.com**

THE LAW

OF

USAGES AND CUSTOMS.

THE LAW

OF

USAGES AND CUSTOMS

A TREATISE

WHEREIN IS MORE PARTICULARLY POINTED OUT WHEN AND TO WHAT EXTENT
USAGES AND CUSTOMS MAY BE SET UP AS A DEFENCE, AND HOW, AS A
MATTER OF EVIDENCE, THEIR EXISTENCE WILL CONTROL,
VARY, OR EXPLAIN WRITINGS AND AGREEMENTS.

BY

J. H. BALFOUR BROWNE, Esq.,

REGISTRAR TO THE RAILWAY COMMISSIONERS, AUTHOR OF "THE LAW OF CARRIERS," "THE
MEDICAL JURISPRUDENCE OF INSANITY," ETC.

FIRST AMERICAN EDITION.

WITH LARGE ADDITIONS TO THE TEXT AND REFERENCES TO AMERICAN CASES.

BY

S. S. CLARKE,

COUNSELLOR-AT-LAW.

JERSEY CITY, N. J.:

FREDERICK D. LINN & CO.,

Law Publishers and Booksellers.

1881.

PREFACE.

———◆———

MR. BROWNE's work is the product of an able English lawyer, and
it exhibits upon every page a thorough knowledge of the principles
of the law pertaining to this important topic. He commences at the
very threshold of the inquiry and pursues it to the end in an accurate,
logical and exhaustive manner. I have taken his work for the basis
of mine, because our law in this particular is wholly derived from the
English. An elaborate examination of the English cases was, therefore, deemed essential, and it seemed to me that it would be better to
utilize the skillful, discriminate and practical presentation of the subject by Mr. Browne than to attempt to construct an entirely new one
from my own investigations. I have made copious additions to Mr.
Browne's text wherever in my judgment a more ample illustration of
the rules under consideration tended to better suit the requirements
and assist in the development of the American law. My great object
throughout the work has been to secure a statement of the entire law
with precision and simplicity. The attempt to perform this task has
forced upon me the careful examination and patient study of many
hundreds of volumes; and I have endeavored to give the gist of every
important case, including the facts, the conclusion reached and the
rule of law applied.

In the preparation of the index, I have especially tried to note every point, important or trivial. Generally, upon all leading questions, the name of the case covering the reference is given, so that there will be no difficulty in finding the proposition or the case that sustains it.

S. S. CLARKE.

September 5th, 1881.

TABLE OF CONTENTS.

CHAPTER I.

OF CUSTOMS GENERALLY.

CHAPTER II.

AS TO CUSTOMS OF THE COUNTRY AND THE ADMISSIBILITY OF THE PROOF OF THESE.

CHAPTER III.

THE USAGES OF TRADE AND THEIR ADMISSIBILITY AS EVIDENCE.

CHAPTER IV.

THE USAGES OF TRADE, THEIR OFFICE.

CHAPTER V.

USAGES, THEIR OFFICE IN SPECIAL INSTANCES.

CHAPTER VI.

PRIVATE USAGES, CUSTOM OF BROKERS, &C.

TABLE OF CASES CITED.

————————◆————————

A.

(xi)

C.

D.

G.

K.

L.

N.

O.

THE LAW

OF

USAGES AND CUSTOMS.

———◆———

I do not purpose to search for or in this place to expound the fundamental principles of all law, but to point out how large a portion of our law—which may be looked upon as crystallized common sense, and rational experience—was at one time, in an amorphous form of heterogeneous custom. Indeed, all laws have been in practice before they were put in words, just as every act had its origin in intention. Laws have to do with the conduct of mankind, but they are themselves the result of the conduct of men. They are the result of the enduring sentiments and protests of the good against the ephemeral backslidings of the evil. All laws float in men's minds long before they send down a precipitate of imperative words. It must have been understood by men that theft—the act of taking the property of another without his consent—was wrong before they made a law to punish the thief, with the view of preventing similar depredations. But long before men made a law they had bolts to their doors, and if they caught the robber they exercised their right by taking his booty from him and possibly even by inflicting upon him a vengeful punishment. This was not done by one man but by many, and we see in it the embryonic custom out of which the law has developed. There has been a gradual evolution of law from the nebulous justice

1 (1)

which was scattered in men's minds and found an expression in their conduct, to the Statute Book and the whole body of text-book-law. The real legislature is the people, and the legislative machinery which exists in this country, including the Queen, the Houses of Lords and Commons, and the Courts of Law, are only a means by which the will of the people may be ascertained and reduced to writing. What I here argue is, that the legislature is second in point of time to the executive, that custom went before law, and, indeed, that law is nothing but agreed upon usage. A very little consideration will convince the reader of the truth of these propositions.(a)

One of the most remarkable instances of the conversion of a custom into a law occurred in connection with the Landlord and Tenant (Ireland) Act, 1870 (33 & 34 Vict. c. 46). What is most curious in connection with that legislative act is that it legalized a custom, or a variety of customs, which vary in every county, the real nature of which is only very imperfectly understood. But the fact remains that here has been the recognition of a tangible custom however multiform, however various, by law—the confirmation of usage by act of Parliament. As an understanding of the facts connected with the custom of Ulster tenant-right will much facilitate the clear comprehension of the propositions set forth above, it may not be inexpedient to describe shortly the claim or right which was conferred upon the tenant by this custom which affected the relations of landlord and tenant in Ireland. The Irish Land Act assumes that a custom which bore upon the relations of landlord and tenant prevailed in the province of Ulster, and that it prevailed in forms varying according to local usages. There is, however, no definition of the custom to which the sanction of the law is given. Indeed, men are not agreed as

(a) *Ex non scripto jus venit, quod usus comprobavit: nam diuturni mores consensu utentium comprobati legem imitantur*, Inst. i. 2, 9; D. i. 3, 32. See *United States* v. *Arredondo*, 6 Pet. 691, 714.

to the nature or extent of the privileges it conferred. As to the character of the custom, Mr. Gladstone, in introducing the Bill, said, " The view we take of it is that it includes two elements—it includes compensation for improvements and it includes the price of good will. . . . We do not attempt to modify the custom ; we do not inquire into its varieties (it is well known to vary within certain limits) ; we do not attempt to improve it or to qualify it; we leave it to be examined as a matter of fact, and when it shall have been so ascertained the judge will have nothing to do but to enforce it."(b) The attention of the Commission of Enquiry into the Law and Practice in relation to the occupation of land in Ireland, which was issued in 1843 under the Presidency of the Earl of Devon, was of course directed to the Ulster custom, but even the report gives no very clear and distinct definition of the nature of the custom. In the preface to Lord Devon's digest which was published after the report of the Commission there are some sentences which throw a little light on the subject; he says, " the tenant claims what he calls ' tenant-right ' in the land, irrespective of any legal claim vested in him, or of any improvement effected by him," and further on : " It is difficult to deny that the effect of the system is a practical assumption by the tenant of a joint proprietorship in the land, although those landlords who acquiesce in it do not acknowledge to themselves this broad fact, and that the tendency is gradually to convert the proprietor into a mere rent-charger, having an indefinite and declining annuity, or the lord of a copyhold." . . . " It is in the great majority of cases not a reimbursement for outlay incurred or improvements effected on the land, but a mere life assurance or immunity from outrage. Hence the practice is more accurately and significantly termed ' selling the good will.' " Here, then, it is evident that the Ulster tenant-right originated in an equity

(b) Hansard's Parliamentary Debates, vol. 199, p. 365.

arising to the incoming tenant from the sanction given by
the landlord to his purchase of his farm. A fair and just
man could scarcely deprive him of the right of realizing the
sum which had been paid with his sanction, and hence arose
the obligation to permit him to sell again, and in this obligation enforced by public opinion, carried out in public
practice, consisted the whole custom of Ulster tenant-right.
In Mr. O'Connell's report upon the effect of the evidence
given before the Commission, the description of the custom
is as follows :

" That according to the practice of this right no person
can get into the occupation of a farm without paying the
previous occupier the price of his right of occupation or
good will, whether the land be held by lease or at will.
That on the ejectment of any occupying tenant he reserves
the full selling value of his tenant-right, less by any arrears
due to the landlord. That the same custom, unrecognized
as it is by law, prevents the lord who has bought the tenant-
right, or otherwise got into possession of a farm, from setting
it at such an increase of rent as to displace tenant-right.
Thus, middlemen are almost unknown, and the effect of
competition for land is principally to increase the value of
the tenant-right, not the amount of the rent. That tenant-
right exists even in unimproved land, and that five years'
purchase is an ordinary payment for the tenant-right of such
land, while fifteen or twenty years' purchase is often given
for the tenant-right of highly improved farms."

The effect of the evidence of Mr. Senior, who at one time
filled the office of Assistant Poor-Law Commissioner, before
the Townland Valuation Committee in 1844, was to the
effect that Ulster tenant-right entitled the tenant to the difference between the actual rent of his farm and the competition price which could be obtained for it, and that it did not
matter whether the difference could be referred to improvements effected by the tenant and his predecessor in title, or

to the fact that the farm was held originally at a low rent. He regarded it as an essential ingredient of the custom that the rent should not be raised on the incoming tenant, but suggested that the real difficulty in understanding the custom was to determine why the landlord did not increase the rent.(c) Here, then, we have a most curious custom which seems to have imposed restrictions upon the legal right of the landlord to raise his rents, and we see that that custom has by an act of the legislature become law. That this custom may have resulted from the fact that land increases in value, without the interposition of landlord or of tenant, an increase which some political economists have suggested should be appropriated to the use of the state, but which has in practice been found so inseparable and indistinguishable from the increased value which has resulted from improvements, which were by consent allowed to belong to the tenant, that they have not been distinguished in proprietorship, and hence the institution, it seems to us, of tenant-right and the gradual limitation of the landlord's ownership. So much for this curious experiment which possesses much interest to the student of the science of jurisprudence. We see here the transformation of custom into statute law. The usual course has been to find custom creeping into the common law through the decisions of the courts, and it may be useful to consider in this place, as preliminary to the main purpose of this work, that branch of the common laws which goes by the name of "customs," the thorough understanding of which cannot fail to throw light upon the law of usage.

(c) See also as to this subject, Mr. Isaac Butt's Treatise on the New Law of Compensation to Tenants in Ireland and the other provisions of the Landlord and Tenant Act, 1870. Dublin, 1871.

CHAPTER I.

OF CUSTOMS GENERALLY.

Of Customs Generally.

SEC. 1. Customs are said to be either, 1, General, or those which prevail throughout the whole kingdom; or, 2, Particular, those which for the most part affect only the inhabitants of a particular place, or the members of a particular class. Concerning general customs we need say little, just because so much might be said. By these, wherever they are applicable, the proceedings and determinations of the ordinary courts of justice are guided and directed as to the course in which lands descend by inheritance, the method of acquiring and transferring property, the requisites and obligations of contracts, the rules for the construction of wills, deeds and statutes, and by these also the respective remedies for civil injuries, and many other important particulars are settled and determined. The ordinary illustrations of this regulating influence are, that the eldest son alone is heir to his ancestor; that a deed is of no validity unless sealed and delivered; that wills shall be construed favorably, and deeds strictly; that money lent upon bond is recoverable by action of debt, and that breaking the public peace is an offence punishable by fine and imprisonment.

Validity Of.

SEC. 2. But it is evident that these usages have received the validity of recognition. They have been acknowledged to exist by the judges of the several courts of justice. The decisions of these judges are recognitions of prior facts, and the way that these prior facts were dealt with, that is the recognition of a custom.[1] In this way it has been held that judges are the depositories of the laws, and living oracles. They are bound by an oath to decide all cases according to the law of the land, that is, according to the customs already recognized; and hence the fitness of those for the judicial office who have derived extensive knowledge from wide experience and accurate study. These judicial decisions, then, are the most authoritative evidence of the existence of such a custom as shall form part of the common law of the land. In this way we find uncertain practice becoming certain and permanent rule, and that not on account of the opinion of any judge, but upon the accumulated recognitions of many; not upon the promulgations of a new doctrine, but on the maintenance and exposition of an old one. That this is so is proved by the fact that where the determination existing is contrary to reason, where the recognition of what was thought a custom has been a recognition extorted by false facts, or brought about by mistaken impressions, the

[1] There are various usages of trade and commerce which have been so often proved as existing facts, and have so far incorporated themselves into the general law, that the court will take judicial notice of them. Especially is this the case as to the custom of merchants. *Edie* v. *East India Co.*, 2 Burr. 1226; *Consequa* v. *Aidlings*, 1 Pet. (U. S. C. C.) 230; *United States* v. *Arredondo*, 6 Pet. (U. S.) 715; *Loper* v. *Dibble*, 1 Ld. Ray. 175; *Wilcox* v. *Wood*, 8 Wend. (N. Y.) 266; *Barnett* v. *Brunadae*, 12 Ct. r. F. 787; *Williams* v. *Williams*, Carth. 269; *Carter* v. *Dawmish*, Id. 82; *Erskine* v. *Murray*, 2 Ld. Ray. 1542, 1 Co. Lit. 89a.

judge is not to be bound by a former decision, but is to vindicate the older law of common sense and reason as manifested in conduct. Here he makes no new law in over-ruling an antecedent decision, which if it was unjust or unreasonable, was not law at all. He decides that it is not the established custom of the land, as has been erroneously determined. Thus there is a truth in the saying that what is not reason is not law.(a)

Common Law, How Evidenced.

SEC. 3. The decisions of courts of justice, then, are the evidence of what constitutes the common law. Although the circumstances of each case vary, the principles of many are the same. Were it not so there never could have been a custom, and consequently there never could have been a law. It is thus the recognition of the unity of principle in the variety of details which is the peculiar work of the lawyer and the judge. Where, however, a new case has to be decided, where analogy will not help as an authority or a guide, the lawyer must have recourse to what is called his discretion or common sense, which is, in fact, customary reason—and decide according to his knowledge of the customs of mankind—which will include considerations of what is just, what is expedient and what is sanctioned by a large experience of public policy.(b)

Evidence of General Custom.

SEC. 4. There is one other kind of evidence of general custom, as constitutive of the common law, and that is the writings of Glanville, Bracton, Britton, Fleta, Hengham, Littleton, Statham, Brooke, Fitzherbert, Staundford and Coke. The treatises by these writers are cited as authority, and as evidence that cases formerly occurred in which the points stated in these writers were determined in a certain

(a) Generally as to the authority of decided cases, see Ram's Science
    of Legal Judgment, chap. 3.
    (b) See Co. Litt. 66a.

way—points which have in many instances become established principles of English law.(c)

The Scope of this Work.

SEC. 5. The subject of general customs clearly falls beyond the scope of this work, except in so far as its consideration may serve as a useful introduction to the answering of questions which will fall under our cognizance in these pages; and except in so far as the principles which are the foundation of these may serve to illustrate the principles which will occupy our attention in connection with particular customs and usages.

Particular Customs.

SEC. 6. The particular customs which form, what text writers call, the second branch of the unwritten laws of England, which are actually laws affecting the inhabitants of a particular place or district,(d) are also beyond the scope which has been limited to us by our intention, and a mention of these will be all that will be necessary in this place. It is doubtless true that these particular customs, which are contrary to the general law of the land, are the remains of a multitude of local customs prevailing, some in one part, some in another, over the whole country, while it was divided into separate dominions. When these separate kingdoms become united under one rule, a unity of custom was the inevitable result, and this unity of custom was the cause of our uniformity of laws. The history of law is parallel to the history of race. And just as many races under one peaceful rule

(c) Sir Henry Sumner Maine has some curiously interesting speculations upon the influence which successive comments of Jurisconsult upon Jurisconsult have had in developing the law, in his work upon "Village Communities" (Sec. 2), in which he endeavors to explain how it comes about that the interpretation of written law by successive commentators, tends to improve and liberalize a system of jurisprudence more than the English method of what may be called "Natural Selection" or by decided cases. The reader may consult that able work with advantage.

(d) See Co. Litt. 110b.

will become one race—representing in a modified form the peculiarity of each—so many systems of laws—or those hypotheses of laws, or provisional laws, customs—will under one rule become one system, which will have the modified characteristics of many of the systems from which it derived its origin. But, further, just as in ethnology, we discover instances in which a race, even under the most favorable conditions, has remained distinct and separate in the midst of another race, although living under a common rule and associated in peace, in intercourse, and in commerce, so we find in the study of jurisprudence that certain customs, or systems of laws, have remained separate and distinct in the midst of a wide and uniform law, and have retained their characteristic peculiarities in spite of many conditions which favored an amalgamation and a unification of these various systems. These so-called customs have in many cases been confirmed to the districts which have the privilege of enjoying them by various Acts of Parliament.(e)

Gavelkind—Borough-English—Customs of Manors—Customs of London.

SEC. 7. Amongst these we find the custom of *Gavelkind* in Kent, and in some other parts of the kingdom (though, perhaps, it was general until the time of the Norman Conquest), by which, amongst other things, all the sons, and not the eldest only, succeed to their father's inheritance,(f) and by which, though the ancestor be attainted and hanged, the heir, nevertheless, succeeds to his estates without any escheat to the lord ;(g) and the custom which prevails in divers ancient boroughs and which is therefore called *Borough-English,* by which the youngest son inherits the estate in preference to all his elder brothers—the custom in other boroughs which entitles a widow to all her husband's lands

(e) Mag. Cart. 9 Hen. 3, c. 9 ; 1 Edw. 3, st. 2, c. 9 ; 14 Edw. 3, st. 1, c. 1 ; 2 Hen. 4, c. 1.

(f) Co. Litt. 140a.

(g) See as to Gavelkind, Sandy's *Consuetudinis Rancix.*

for her dower, instead of only one-third part, to which alone she is entitled under the common law.(*h*) Amongst these also are the special and particular customs of manors, of which every one has more or less, and which bind all the copyhold and customary tenants that hold of the said manors;(*i*) and also the many particular customs which exist within the city of London, and which have reference to trade, apprentices, orphans, widows and many other matters.(*k*) These last are conformed by Act of Parliament.(*l*)

Customs of London, How Proved.

SEC. 8. These, then, are the customs to which the term is most frequently applied, although, it seems to us, that such an exclusive application of the word is calculated to confuse and mislead. Such customs as Gavelkind and Borough-English have been noticed by law,(*m*) and there is now no need to prove the nature of such customs, but only that the lands in question are subject to them. When the customs of London, such as the custom of foreign attachment,(*n*) the custom that every shop is a market overt for goods of the same kind as are usually sold there;(*o*) the custom that married women may be sole traders;(*p*) the custom as to the distribution of the effects of intestate freemen;(*q*) and the custom which defines the nature of a liveryman's office,(*r*) are called in question at a trial, their existence is to be

(*h*) See the History of Boroughs, by Merewether and Stephens.

(*i*) See Scriven on Copyhold and Customary Freehold.

(*k*) See Pulling on The Laws and Customs of London. *Bradbee v. Christ's Hospital,* 2 D. N. S. 164; 5 Scott N. R. 79; *Arnold v. Poole,* 4 M. & G. 860; 5 Scott N. R. 761; *Bulbroke v. Goodeve,* 1 W. Bl. 569; *Lyons v. De Pass,* 3 P. & D. 177; 11 A. & E. 326; 9 C. & P. 68.

(*l*) See the *City of London's case,* 8 Rep. 126; *The King v. Bayshaw,* Cro.

Car. 347; see also Pulling on The Laws and Customs of London.

(*m*) Co. Litt. 175.

(*n*) Certified by Starkey in 22 Edw. 4. See 1 Roll. Abr. 554 (K.) 5; *Bruce v. Wait,* 1 M. & G. 39; *Crosby v. Hetherington,* 4 M. & G. 933.

(*o*) Certified by Sir E. Coke, 5 Rep. 83b, and in Moore 360. See also *Lyons v. De Pass,* 11 A. & E. 326.

(*p*) *Lavie v. Phillips,* 3 Burr. 1776.

(*q*) *Bruin v. Knott,* 12 Sim. 452.

(*r*) *King v. Clerk,* 1 Salk. 349.

decided, not by a jury, but by a certificate from the Lord
Mayor and aldermen by the mouth of their recorder,(s)
except in the case where the custom was of such a nature as
that the corporation is itself interested; under such circumstances the question is tried, not by certificate, but by a
jury, for "the law permits them not to certify on their own
behalf."(t)

Other Customs Recognized.

SEC. 9. Some other customs, such as the custom or law
of the road—viz., that horses and carriages should respectively keep on the near or left side;(u) or that ships and
steamboats on meeting should port their helms so as to pass
on the port side of each other;(v) or that steamboats navigating narrow channels should, whenever it is safe and
practicable, keep to the starboard, or right side of the fair-
way(w)—will be recognized by the judges without proof.

Customs of Merchants, When Must be Proved.

SEC. 10. Many writers exclude from the term custom
those rules relative to bills of exchange, partnership and
other mercantile matters, which have been classed under the
head "custom of merchants" by Blackstone,(x) on the ground
that their character is not local, and that their binding force
is not confined to a particular district. It has been remarked
that the Law Merchant is in truth only a part of the general
law of England,(y) and that courts of law must take notice

(s) *Appleton* v. *Loughton*. Cro. Car.
516; see also Pulling. Laws and Customs of London, p. 11; *Hartop* v.
Hoare, 1 Wils. 8; 2 Stra. 1187; *Blac-
quire* v. *Hawkins*, 1 Dough. 378;
Plummer v. *Bentham*, 1 Burr. 248;
Crosby v. *Hetherington*, 5 Scott N. R.
637; 12 L. J. C. P. 261; *Piper* v. *Chap-
pell*, 14 M. & W. 624.

(t) *Day* v. *Savadge*, Hobart's Rep.
85.

(u) See *Leame* v. *Bray*, 3 East 593;

Turley v. *Thomas*, 8 C. & P. 104, *per*
Coleridge, J.

(v) 17 & 18 Vict. c. 104, sec. 296.

(w) 17 & 18 Vict. c. 104, ss. 297,
298, 299. See *Morrison* v. *Gen. Steam
Nav. Co.*, 8 Exch. 733; *Gen. Steam
Nav. Co.* v. *Morrison*, 13 C. B. 581.

(x) 1 Com. 75.

(y) *Per* Holt, C. J., *Hussy* v. *Jacob*,
Ld. Raym. 88; *per* Forster, J., *Edie*
v. *East India Co.*, 2 Burr. 1226; 1
Bl. Rep. 299, S. C., 2 Inst. 58; *Stone*

of it as such. Doubtless where the custom of merchants is established and settled by known decisions, it is "the general law of the kingdom," and ought not to be left to a jury after it has been already settled by a judicial determination.(z) But there are some questions the decision of which depends upon the customs amongst merchants, which have not hitherto met with judicial recognition, and in such cases it is fit and proper to take the opinions of merchants thereon.(a) In former times it was not uncommon for judges to confer, touching points of mercantile law, with those persons who might be supposed to be conversant with it, and it is said that Lord Chancellor Hardwick adopted this course in the case of *Kruger* v. *Wilcox;*(b) and that Lord Mansfield followed his example in a case in which a question of some importance had arisen upon a sea policy of insurance.(c)

General and Local Usages.

SEC. 11. The mercantile law consists of general and local usages, and these are easily distinguished, although they not unfrequently pass into one another. Thus it is that many local customs which prevail at the present time in a particular market or at a particular port, may at one time have been general customs; while some of the customs that are at the present time universal in the trade and commerce of this country must have been confined to much narrower limits. A local custom may, as we shall hereafter see, by being

v. *Rawlinson*, Willes 561; see also *Benson* v. *Chapman*, 8 C. B., N. S. 967, note; see *Cookendorfer* v. *Preston*, 4 How. (U. S.) 317; and see *Magill* v. *Brown*, Bright (Penn.) 346, 365.

(z) *Per* Forster, J., 2 Burr. 1226; see also what Buller, J., said in *Lick-barrow* v. *Mason*, 2 T. R. 73.

(a) *Per* Wilmot, J., *Edie* v. *East India Co.*, 2 Burr. 1228. That judge said: "There may indeed be some questions depending upon customs amongst merchants, where if there is a doubt about the custom it may be fit and proper to take the opinion of merchants thereupon; yet that is only where the law remains doubtful, and even then the custom must be proved by facts, not by opinion only." Bing. in Adde.

(b) Ambler 252.

(c) *Vallejo* v. *Wheeler*, 1 Cowp. 143.

tacitly incorporated with a contract, be, in point of fact, a law to the parties contracting; yet, it is evident that when such a custom is relied upon it must be proved before the court will take notice of it.

General Usage.

Sec. 12. A general usage, when it has been ascertained and established, becomes a part of the Law Merchant, which courts of justice "are," in the words of Lord Campbell, "bound to know and to recognize."(d) "Such," he went on to say, "has been the invariable understanding and practice in Westminster Hall for a great many years, there is no decision or *dictum* to the contrary; and justice could not be administered if evidence were required to be given *toties quoties* to support such usage if issue might be joined upon them in each particular case."

The Name "Custom" to be Applied. When.

Sec. 13. So far, then, as the usage of merchants has been judicially ascertained and established, so far as it has become the acknowledged law of the land, it has, it seems to us, ceased to deserve the name of custom, just as much as Gavelkind or Borough-English ;(e) but where a general custom exists

(d) *Brandão* v. *Barnett*, 12 Cl. & F. 805. The words of his lordship show that the principle of utility has been at work in this natural selection of laws from a variety of customs. "Those customs," he says, "which have been universally and notoriously prevalent amongst merchants, and have been found by experience to be of public use have been adopted by it (the Law Merchant) upon a principle of convenience, and for the benefit of trade and commerce; and where so adopted it is unnecessary to plead and prove them." Thus a custom of merchants is at first proved by their testimony; but when once decisions are made thereon adopting it, it becomes thereupon a part of the law of the land of which the courts will take judicial notice. *Bank of Columbia* v. *Fitzhugh*, I H. & G. (Md.) 239; *Branch* v. *Burnley*, 1 Call (Va.) 159; *Consequa* v. *Willings, ante*. When either a custom or usage has been saved by statute, it has all the form of an express statute and will control all *affirmative* statutes in opposition to it, but it must always yield to a *negative* one. *Mitchell* v. *United States*, 9 Pet. (U. S.) 712.

(e) See an American case, *Cookendorfer* v. *Preston*, 4 How. 317, and see *Magill* v. *Brown*, Bright. 346.

amongst merchants which has not been judicially recognized, or particular usage exists in a particular market, which must be proved at Nisi Prius by the person who wishes to avail himself of it, it seems equally clear that the term custom is applicable, and that the laws of validity and rules of proof which we have to consider in this work are thoroughly apposite. But on the same principle, that the obligation of a particular custom must be confined to a particular district, it has been said that the usages of particular trades, when not restricted to some particular limits, but extended to the realm at large, cannot with propriety be considered as customs in the technical sense of that term.(f) Here also a usage of immemorial observance, which has received judicial sanction, becomes part of the general law of England, just as much as if it were incorporated in an act of Parliament it would become part of the statute law. These seem to us to be undeserving of the appellation customs, which we would reserve for law when it is being modelled in clay—so to speak—and before it has been transferred to the marble.(g) Custom seems to us to be applicable to the law before it has been recognized as law, but when it is in a condition to claim judicial sanction, whether that sanction is authenticated by judicial decision or by legislative enactment. Our object, then, in the following pages is to state the law which is applicable to such usages and customs; the rules of evidence which will enable the practitioner to determine the existence of an alleged custom; the rules of law which will enable him to determine its legality, when its existence is established; and the rules which will enable him to put the correct legal construction upon it. The importance of this

---

(f) Co. Litt. 115b.

(g) It may be known to most readers that the method of sculpture as practiced at the present time, is to mould the figure in clay, and by means of what may be called a many-jointed pair of compasses, and chisel work to transfer the outlines to the marble. The moulding is the work of the sculptor; the cutting of the marble can be accomplished by ordinary ungifted workmen.

inquiry can be measured by the frequency with which cases involving the discussion of the admissibility of parol evidence of custom or usage to vary, add incidents to, or explain the meaning of written contracts, come before courts of law.

Custom and Prescription.

SEC. 14. We purpose in the first place to set out succinctly the rules which apply to the validity of a custom, and before doing so it may be well to distinguish between custom and prescription, which are not unfrequently confounded, and the appreciation of the disparity in principle which exists between them will conduce to the better understanding of each.(*h*) Prescription seems to us to be the making of a right, custom the making of a law. Prescription has its meaning in the volition of an individual, while custom has its meaning in the wills of a large number of individuals. Prescription is creative of a right which gets its sanction from law, custom is creative of a law which gives its sanction to rights. It will be seen that these two are clearly distinguishable, and the confusion which has existed in some minds can scarcely be accounted for. The fact that it existed, and not any good grounds for its existence, has necessitated this explanation.(*i*)

(*h*) The distinction between custom and prescription, which has been drawn before, will be found to be parallel to the one given in the text. According to it, custom is a local usage not annexed to any person, whereas prescription is merely a personal usage, as that L. and his ancestors or those whose estate he has, have used time out of mind to enjoy a particular advantage or privilege. 2 Bla. Com. 263; *per* Cur., *Mayor of Lyme Regis* v. *Taylor*, 3 Lev. 160.

(*i*) A custom to take anything from the soil of another, or a *profit à prendre*, is not lawful. If such a right is available at all, it must be set up and established as a presumptive right belonging to some estate, and must be pleaded with a *que* estate. *Lufkin* v. *Haskell*, 3 Pick. (Mass.) 356; *Littlefield* v. *Maxwell*, 31 Me. 134. Thus, in an action *quare clausum fregit*, the defendant relied upon a custom that all the inhabitants of a certain town and manor, for the time being, had a right to depasture the uninclosed woodlands of individual proprietors within the town, and it was held that this was not a mere easement, but a right to take a profit, and implied a qualified possession, and that such a custom-

Validity of: Custom must be Ancient.

Sec. 15. The rules which bear upon the validity of a custom are these: 1. *It must have been used so long that the memory of man runneth not to the contrary.*(*j*) Thus, if an usage can be shown to have commenced, it is void as a custom, and that upon grounds which will recommend themselves as reasonable. Of course, every custom must have had a commencement, but if we can discover its inception, then we discover the individual by whose particular will the

ary right was void. To establish such a customary right, the court also held that the proof should be no less than that required to establish a right by prescription. "The entry or use," say the court, "must have been adverse or hostile to the true owner in its commencement, and it must have been used and enjoyed under a claim of right, and continued uninterrupted for a length of time sufficient to have an entry. *Smith* v. *Floyd*, 18 Barb. (N. Y.) 523. A custom to take fish or to take sand to mix with lime for the purpose of making mortar *in alieno solo*, is void. *Waters* v. *Lilly*, 4 Pick. (Mass.) 145; *Perley* v. *Langley*, 7 N. H. 233. Holding that a right to fish on another's land is a *profit à prendre*. See *Wickham* v. *Hawker*, 7 M. & W. 63; *Herbert* v. *Laughluyn*, Crob. Car. 492. So is a custom to pile wood on another's land. *Littlefield* v. *Maxwell*, 31 Me. 134. So is a custom for all the citizens of the State to take sea-weed thrown upon the shore of another's lands. *Kenyon* v. *Nichols*, 1 R. I. 106; *Nudd* v. *Hobbs*, 17 N. H. 524. The ground upon which the last two cases is based, is that the sea-weed, when so thrown upon the land, belongs to the owner of the soil, and in *Knowles* v. *Dow*, 22 N. H.

387, it was held that a custom for the inhabitants of a town to haul sea-weed from the margin of the water and *deposit* it upon another's land, and haul it away when convenient, is not void. But it would seem that the doctrine of this case is inconsistent with the doctrine of *Littlefield* v. *Maxwell*, *ante*, and really amounts to the establishment of the rule that a custom is admissible to justify a trespass. A license to enter on land and fish, cannot be implied by a usage or custom in the country at large, for every person to enter on such land to take fish. *Winder* v. *Blake*, 4 Jones (N. C.) L. 332. In *Codman* v. *Evans*, 5 Allen (Mass.) 308, it was held that an owner of land may maintain an action for the erection of a bay-window which extends over his line, by the adjoining owner, although that portion of his land which is covered by the bay-window has been laid out and is used as a highway; and evidence of a custom so to erect bay-windows is inadmissible.

(*j*) The time of *legal* memory has received a technical limitation, and refers to so early a date as the commencement of the reign of King Richard the First. Co. Litt. 115a.

custom had its birth; but that discovery negatives its existence as a custom which cannot have its origin in the impo-
tent act of any particular individual, but in the will of the
whole. No one man can be allowed to make a law. If,
however, all evidence of the commencement of a custom is
wanting, the proof that it has been practised for a long time,
and that it has been observed as far back as the memory
reaches, will amount to presumptive proof of its having prevailed during the whole period of legal memory.(k)   In such
cases, and from modern usage, the jury ought to be
instructed that they would be warranted in presuming that
the right is immemorial, unless there is evidence that fairly
rebuts it.[2]   And where a custom is once shown to have
existed, it is presumed that it still exists, unless there is
evidence disproving its existence.[3]   A right obtained by
custom or immemorial usage is disproved by proof that the
claimant's grantors or ancestors conveyed it away within the
statutory period;[4] but a right of this character, incident to
an estate, cannot be disproved by evidence that a tenant in
possession declared that he had no such right, because even
the tenant cannot be heard to derogate from his landlord's
title.[5]   The law, however, with reference to the principle
which requires the proof of immemoriality in support of a
custom, has been modified to a considerable extent by the
statute 2 & 3 Will. 4, c. 71, which provides as to customary
and prescriptive claims of rights to be exercised over the
land of other persons (such as the rights of common, or way,
or use of light), that they shall be considered as sufficiently
established by an uninterrupted enjoyment as of right, in

(k) Rex v. Joliffe, 2 B. & C. 54; Jenkins v. Harvey, 1 Cr. M. & R. 877;
cited Master Pilots, &c., of Newcastle-
upon-Tyne v. Bradley, 21 L. J. Q. B.

196, S. C., 2 E. & B. 428 n.; see, also,
Duke of Beaufort v. Smith, 4 Exch.
450; Simpson v. Wells, 7 L. R. Q. B.
214.

[2] Jenkins v. Harvey, 1 Gale 23; also,
2 C. M. & R. 383.

[3] Scales v. Key, 11 Ad. & El. 819.

[4] Aulcome v. Upton, 5 Moll. 398.
[5] Papendick v. Bridgewater, 5 El. &
Bl. 166.

some cases for thirty, iu others for twenty, years, and shall not be defeated (where such enjoyment can be proved) by showing that they commenced within the time of legal memory.(*l*) In this country such rights may be obtained by an adverse user for the period fixed by the statute for obtaining title by an adverse occupancy, which varies in the different States. In order to ascertain whether such a right exists or not, the question is simply, whether the right has been uninterruptedly exercised adversely for the statutory period.

Must have been Uninterrupted.

SEC. 16. 2. *A custom, in order to be valid, must have been continued.* If a custom ceased and re-commenced, its new beginning would be within the memory of man, and would be due to the will of an individual, which would exclude it from the definition of a custom, and make any usage subject to such a lapse void as a custom. But an interruption which is to prove valid as against a custom, must be an actual interruption of the usage, and not simply an interruption of the possession of the right.(*m*)

Illustration.

SEC. 17. One of the common illustrations will serve to make this clear. Thus, if the inhabitants of a parish have a customary right to water their cattle at a certain pool, a

(*l*) See, as to statute, *Shuttleworth* v. *Le Fleming*, 19 C. B. N. S. 687; 11 Jur. N. S. 840; *Hanmer* v. *Chance*, 11 Jur. N. S. 397; 34 L. J. Chanc. 413. Upon this see Mr. Shelford's notes in his edition (7th) of the Real Property Stats., pp. 2, 6.

(*m*) Co. Litt. 114. In order to be obligatory, a custom must be uniform, and always applicable in a given case, otherwise it cannot be presumed that the parties knew of and contracted in reference to it.

Oelrieks v. *Ford*, 23 How. (U. S.) 49; *Bowling* v. *Harrison*, 6 *Id.* 259; *Collings* v. *Hope*, 3 Wash. (U. S. C. C.) 149; *Trott* v. *Wood*, 1 Gall. (U. S.) 443; *McGregor* v. *Ins. Co.*, 1 Wash. (U. S. C. C.) 39; *Strong* v. *Carrington*, 11 Am. L. R. 287; *Martin* v. *Del. Ins. Co.*, 2 Wash. (U. S. C. C.) 254; *Smith* v. *Gibbs*, 44 N. H. 335; *Rapp* v. *Palmer*, 3 Watts (Penn.) 178; *Com.* v. *Malloy*, 57 Penn. St. 291; *United States* v. *Buchanan*, 8 How. (U. S.) 83.

mere discontinuance of the practice for ten years would not destroy the custom, although it would add to the difficulties of proving its existence. If, however, the right be discontinued for a single day, that would prove the non-existence of any asserted custom analogous with the right. But it must be remembered that the existence of a custom depends upon proof, and that the discontinuance of a custom, as it tends to increase the difficulties of proof, tends also, to that extent, to the abolition of the custom. It cannot be doubted that a custom can be abrogated by a custom, and that many of the usages which at present exist are built upon the ruins of forgotten customs. • That these antecedent customs which differ from our present practice or common habit must he forgotten, to render our present custom valid, is evident— otherwise the custom which is now in vogue would not have that element of antiquity and immemoriality to which we have already alluded. But as the acts of some make a law, so can the acts of some abrogate it. "A custom," said Tindal, C. J., in his judgment in *Tyson* v. *Smith*,(n) " comes at last to an agreement which has been evidenced by repeated acts of assent on both sides from the earliest times, before time of memory, and continuing down to our own times, that it has become the law of a particular place."

Analogy Between Custom and Language.

SEC. 18. There is a curious analogy between customs and language which we shall have to point out more than once with the view to elucidation and illustration. Language is for the expression of human thought, and in that it is so it is also a record of the past effort of human intelligence. Custom, which has arisen from human practice, from the factual language of transactions, is not only a record of the past conduct of men, but is at the same time a vehicle for the expression of intention to those who find usage ready to their hand. But there is a close analogy between the

(n) 9 A. & E. 406, at p. 425.

two. As language has passed from unity to diversity and variety, so has law passed from a central unity into a scattered and careless variety of custom, so that every place has its particular law of custom. "Dialects," says Grimm, "develop themselves progressively, and the more we look backward in the history of language the smaller is their number and the less definite their features. All multiplicity arises gradually from an original unity."(o)

Development of Customs—Dead Laws.

SEC. 19. Might we not apply almost the same true words to customs—which in our estimation bear an exactly similar relation to a system of law that dialects do to a language— that the great German philologist has applied to dialects, and say that customs have developed themselves progressively, and that the unity which we find in the history of jurisprudence has been developed into the variety of customs which we find at the present time. This capability of change in law is not an indication of its inferiority, but of its vitality. So long as men progress, so long as new events happen, new trades arise, new commerce floats upon hitherto unsailed seas, new manufactures change the features of our lives, and new and higher principles take the place of those which governed conduct, regulated acts and guided life, so long must we expect progressive change and almost lavish variety in our customs. When a people is dead, when there are no transactions to be governed, no rights to protect, no interests to regard, the law may remain unchanged, for the law is dead. We have indeed dead laws just as we have dead languages, and the words of Professor Max Müller, which are spoken with regard to the life of a language, are equally applicable when applied to a system of laws. "As soon," he remarks, "as a language loses its unbounded capability of change, its carelessness about what it throws away, and its readiness in always supplying instantaneously the wants of the mind and

(o) Geschichte der Deutschen Sprache, s. 833.

heart, its natural life is changed into a merely artificial existence."(*p*)   We cannot blame ourselves for this digression if
it enables the reader more thoroughly to appreciate the relation which exists between custom and law, if it enables him
to understand that customs are, as it were, the feeders of law,
and that there is always a slow process of customary regenera-
tion going on, which will be observable to the diligent student
of legal history, and which makes up for gradual decay of
law which is going on *pari passu*, and which results from
the gradual tendency that almost every fixed enactment has
to become obsolete.

Peaceable Enjoyment.

SEC. 20. *A custom must have been peaceably enjoyed and
acquiesced in to be valid.* If it has been the subject of
contention and dispute it has not recommended itself as
expedient to all, and the fact that it has proved a convenience to some is counteracted by the fact that it has also
proved an inconvenience to many.   But the non-consent of
these is as powerful as the consent of those; and as customs,
to be valid, owe their efficacy to common consent, the fact
that they have been immemorially disputed proves that that
universal consent was wanting.

(*p*) "I very much doubt," said Mr.
Disraeli in his speech on the Irish
Land Bill (33 & 34 Vict. c. 46), "the
propriety, as a general principle,
of legalizing customs. The moment
you legalize a custom you fix its particular character; but the value of a
custom is its flexibility and that it
adapts itself to all the circumstances
of the moment as of the locality.
All these qualities are lost the
moment you crystallize a custom
into legislation. Customs may not be
as wise as laws, but they are always
more popular. They array upon
their side alike the convictions and
the prejudices of men. They are
spontaneous. They grow out of
man's necessities and inventions,
and as circumstances change and
alter and die off, the custom falls
into desuetude and we get rid of it.
But if you make it into a law, circumstances alter, but the law remains
and becomes part of the obsolete
legislation which haunts our statute
book and harasses society." (Hansard's Debates, vol. 199. p. 1806,
delivered 11th March, 1870.)

It Must be Reasonable.

SEC. 21. It must be reasonable.(*q*)   Or as it is perhaps better to put it negatively, it must not be unreasonable.(*r*) We shall see hereafter that the words "not unreasonable"

(*q*) *Tanistry's case.* Sir J. Davis' Rep. 32; *Hilton* v. *Earl Granville*, 5 Q. B. 701; *Wilkes* v. *Broadbent*, 1 Wils. 63. The true office of a usage or custom is to interpret the otherwise indeterminate intentions of parties, and to ascertain the nature and extent of their contracts, arising not from express stipulation, but from mere implications and presumptions, and acts of a doubtful or equivocal character ; or to ascertain the true meaning of particular words in an instrument, where those words have various senses. Per *Story, J. The Reeside,* 2 Sum. (U. S.) 569; see, also, *Macomber* v. *Parker,* 13 Pick. (Mass.) 182; *Lawrence* v. *McGregor,* 5 Ham. (Ohio) 311; *Sampson* v. *Gazzam,* 6 Port. (Ala.) 123. In doubtful cases, usage may be recurred to in order to ascertain the meaning of the legislature. *Polk* v. *Hill,* 2 Overt (Tenn.) 157. It may be shown for the purpose of explaining a clause of doubtful construction in a policy of insurance or other contract, usage being the safest guide to the intention of the parties. But it can be resorted to only when the law is doubtful or unsettled. *Winthrop* v. *Union Ins. Co.,* 2 Wash. (U. S. C. C.) 7 ; see, also, *Harris* v. *Nicholas,* 5 Munf. (Va.) 483; *United States* v. *Macdaniel,* 7 Pet. (U. S.) 1; *Murray* v. *Hatch,* 6 Mass. 477; *Coit* v. *Commercial Ins. Co.,* 7 John. (N. Y.) 385 ; *Allegre* v. *Maryland Ins. Co.,* 2 G. & J. (Md.) 136; *Rankin* v. *American Ins. Co.,* 1 Hall (N. Y.) 619. It is not admissible to contradict or substantially vary the legal import of a written agreement; and it is never admitted for this purpose, nor considered to be of this character. *Renner* v. *Bank of Columbia,* 9 Wheat. (U. S.) 581; *Rankin* v. *American Ins. Co.,* 1 Hall (N. Y.) 619; *Sleght* v. *Rhinelander,* 1 John. (N. Y.) 192. In order to make it operative it must be certain, uniform and reasonable. Per *Washington, J. Collings* v. *Hope,* 3 Wash. (Penn.) C. C. 150; S. P. *Rapp* v. *Palmer,* 3 Watts (Penn.) 178; *Thomas* v. *Graves,* 1 Rep. Con. Ct. 308; *Thomas* v. *O'Hara,* 1 Con. Ct. (S. C.) 303; *Chastain* v. *Bowman,* 1 Hill (N. Y.) 270; *Trott* v. *Wood,* 1 Gall. 443; *Lewis* v. *Thatcher,* 15 Mass. 433; *United States* v. *Duval,* Gil. 356; *Barksdale* v. *Brown,* 1 N. & M. (S. C.) 519; *Buck* v. *Grimshaw,* 1 Edw. Ch. 147; *Smith* v. *Wright,* 1 Cai. (N. Y.) 45 ; *Somerby* v. *Thompson,* Wright (Ohio) 573; *Consequa* v. *Willings,* Pet. C. C. 230; *Touro* v. *Cassin,* 1 N. & M. (S. C.) 176 ; *Davis* v. *New Brig,* Gil. (U. S.) 486. When the custom of a particular place is established as stated, it may enter into the body of a contract without being inserted. Per *Tilghman, C. J. Stultz* v. *Dickey,* 5 Binn. (Penn.) 287; S. P. *Lodwicks* v. *Ohio Ins. Co.,* 5 Ham. (Ohio) 436; *Sewall* v. *Gibbs,* 1 Hall (N. Y.) 612; *Barber* v. *Brace,* 3 Conn. 9; 2 Pet. (U. S.) 148; *Bank of Columbia* v. *Fitzhugh,* 1 H. & G. (Md.) 239; *Haven* v. *Wentworth,* 2 N. H., 93; *United States* v. *Arredondo,* 6 Pet. (U. S.) 715; *Sampson* v. *Gazzam,* 6 Port. (Ala.) 123.

(*r*) 1 Bla. Com. 77; *Hix* v. *Gardiner,* 2 Bulstr. 195.

must be understood in a legal sense, or that in coming to a conclusion as to what customs are reasonable and what unreasonable, regard must be had to the legal decisions which have been made in times past upon cases involving a similar question. "Reasonable," says Sir Edward Coke, "is not always to be understood of every unlearned man's reason, but of the artificial and legal reason warranted by authority of law."(s)

Meaning of Reasonable—Private Interests.

SEC. 22. Thus it comes that a custom may be good, though the particular reason of it cannot be assigned; for it suffices, if no good legal reason can be assigned against it. A custom is not unreasonable merely because it is contrary to a particular rule or maxim of the common law, otherwise Gavelkind and Borough-English, which are directly contrary to the ordinary law of descent, or the custom of Kent, which is contrary to the law of escheats, would not be valid customs; indeed it is the very essence of a custom that it should vary from the common law.(t) Nor is a custom unreasonable because it is prejudicial to the interests of a private man,(u) if it be for the interests of the commonwealth; as, for instance, the custom to turn the plough up on the headland of another, which is for the good of husbandry, or to dry the nets on the land of another, which is in favor of fishing, and for the benefit of navigation.(v)

Unreasonable Customs, What Are.

SEC. 23. A custom which is injurious to the public, which is prejudicial to a class, and beneficial only to a particular individual, is repugnant to the law of reason. No such cus-

(s) Co. Litt. 62, but see as to usages, Paxton v. Courtnay, 2 F. & F. 131.

(t) Horton v. Beckman, 6 T. R. 760, at p. 764; Tyson v. Smith, 9 Ad. & El. 404, at p. 421.

(u) Fawcett v. Lowther, 2 Ves. 300;

Marquis of Salisbury v. Gladstone, 9 H. of L. cases, 692.

(v) See judgment, Tyson v. Smith, 9 Ad. & El. 421; Lord Falmouth v. George, 5 Bing. 286; Race v. Ward, 4 E. & B. 702.

tom could be capable of becoming law which is a rule for the benefit of all. (*w*)   Thus a custom in a manor that the com-

(*w*) Usages or customs that are opposed to the policy of the law, or which are unreasonable, can have no validity. Thus, a usage that permits a factor to pledge the good of his principal. *Newbold* v. *Wright*, 4 Rawle. (Penn.) 195. Or the master of a vessel to sell the cargo without necessity. *Bryant* v. *Com. Ins. Co.*, 6 Pick. (Mass.) 131; *Stillman* v. *Hunt*, 10 Lex. 109. Or to charge interest when the statute provides that none shall be charged. *Henry* v. *Risk*, 1 Dall. (Penn.) 265. Or authorizing a landlord to re-enter upon demised premises for a forfeiture incurred by a non-payment of rent in a manner different from that provided by law. *Stoever* v. *Whitman*, 6 Binn. (Penn.) 417. Or to transfer settlement rights by death-bed donations, without a will in writing. *Westfall* v. *Singleton*, 1 Wash. (Va.) 227. Or requiring 2,240 pounds as a ton when the statute provides that 2.000 pounds shall be treated as a ton, when the contract does not otherwise provide. *Evans* v. *Myers*, 25 Penn. St. 114; *Green* v. *Moffet*, 22 Mo. 529, have been held invalid because unreasonable and opposed to the policy of the law. So, too, for the same reason it is held that the custom and understanding of merchants in a particular trade to regard the barter or exchange of a promissory note, endorsed without recourse, as carrying with it no implied warranty of the past or future solvency of the payor, is inadmissible. *Beckwith* v. *Farnum*, 5 R. I. 230. So of a custom in the trade between this country and England, that the English merchant on receiving an endorsed bill

of exchange, must return it immediately to the endorser on protest, and that if he calls on the drawer for payment the endorser is discharged. *Brown* v. *Jackson*, 2 Wash. (Va.) 24. Also, of a custom that, when a seller of goods receives a note of the consignee without the buyer's endorsement, that the maker of the note is alone responsible, and that the buyer is discharged. *Prescott* v. *Hubbell*, 1 McCord. (S. C.) 94. The usages referred to *supra* are held invalid because they are opposed to the policy of the law in that they unsettle the well-established rules of commercial law established for the protection of the rights of parties, and which should only yield to the *express* terms of the contract itself. But, in the absence of well-established rules of law, evidence of usage is admissible. Thus the local custom of the place on which a bill of exchange is drawn, or where a promissory note is payable, regulates the number of the days of grace. *Renner* v. *Bank of Columbia*, 9 Wh. (U. S.) 581; *Bank of Washington* v. *Triplett*, 1 Pet. (U. S.) 25; S. P. *Fowler* v. *Brantly*, 14 Pet. 318; *Cookendorfer* v. *Preston*, 4 How. (U.S.) 317; *Wiseman* v. *Chiappella*, 23 How. (U. S.) 368; *Smith* v. *Glover*, 2 Cr. (U. S. C. C.) 384; *Bank of Columbia* v. *McKenny*, 3 Cr. (U. S. C. C.) 361. Such usage may be shown to have been subsequently changed. *Cookendorfer* v. *Preston*, 4 How. (U. S.) 317. The usage of the banks of the District of Columbia, to demand payment on the fourth day of grace, only applies to notes negotiated by them; not to notes deposited for collection. *Hill*

moner cannot turn in his cattle until the lord has put in his own is bad, for it is injurious to the multitude, and beneficial only to the lord.(x) So a custom that the lord of the manor shall have £3 for every proved breach of a stranger,(y) or that the lord of a manor may detain a distress taken upon his demesne, until fine be made for the damage, at the lord's will,(z) is bad, on the ground that it is unreasonable. In the case of *Tyson* v *Smith*,(a) which was an action in trespass for breaking and entering the plaintiff's close and erecting stalls, booths, &c., there, the defendant justified his

v. *Norvell*, 3 McL. (U. S.) 583. A party to a note discounted at a bank, is not bound by the special and particular usage of such bank, *unless upon his agreement, express or implied.* *Bank of Alexandria* v. *Deneale*, 2 Cr. (U. S. C. C.) 488. An established custom among insurance companies, as to an agent's property in lists of policies procured by him, may be introduced, to explain the contract with such agent. *Ensworth* v. *New York Life Insurance Co.*, 16 Am. L. R. 332. Every demise between landlord and tenant, in respect to matter in which the parties are silent, is open to explanation by the general usage and custom of the district ; the parties are presumed to contract with a tacit reference to such custom. *Van Ness* v. *Pacard*, 2 Pet. (U. S.) 137. A contract authorized by a well-known, long-established and universal custom, made by the master of a vessel, in the course of the usual employment of his ship, is binding, not only against himself and his owners, but against the vessel *in rem*. *The Hendrik Hudson*, 17 Law. Rep. 93. A general usage among ship-owners and underwriters, in relation to the settlement of average losses, if known to the

parties, becomes part of the contract. *Sanderson* v. *Columbian Insurance Co.*, 2 Cr. (U. S. C. C.) 218. The master of a steamboat will, in the absence of any special contract, be deemed to have been hired in accordance with a well-known custom of the port. *The Swallow*, Olc. (U. S.) 334. If a creditor directs his debtor to remit, and there be a custom proved, to send and receive money by mail, the jury may infer an authority to remit by mail. *Selman* v. *Dun*, 10 West. L. J. 459. It is not a deviation for a vessel from New Orleans to a northern port, to touch at Havana for further cargo, in accordance with a known usage of trade and navigation. *Thatcher* v. *McCulloh*, Olc. (U. S.) 365. A custom in contravention of a statute, is unreasonable and void. *Thompson* v. *Riggs*, 5 Wall. (U S.) 663. As to make a transaction within a statute against usury, obligatory. *Dunham* v. *Dey*, 13 John. (N. Y.) 40; *Bank of Utica* v. *Wager*, 7 Cow. (N. Y.) 712.

(x) Yearb. Trin. 2 Hen. 4, fol. 24, B. pl. 20.

(y) 21 H. 4. See 7 Vin. Abr. 183, Customs (F.) 7.

(z) Litt. s. 212.

(a) 9 Ad. & El. 406.

conduct under a custom that at fairs holden at certain times of the year on some part of the commons and waste of a manor, to be named by the lord of the manor (the *locus in quo* being parcel of such commons and waste, and named by the lord), every liege subject exercising the trade of a victualler might enter at the time of the fairs, and for the more conveniently carrying on his said trade erect a booth, &c., and continue the same for a reasonable time after the fairs, paying 2*d.* to the lord, it was held that the custom was reasonable, and that the plea was a good justification in trespass brought by the owner of the soil.(*b*)

Custom Contravening Law of Emblements.

SEC. 24. It has further been decided that a custom that a tenant shall have the way-going crop after the expiration of his term, is reasonable. "It is just; for he who sows ought to reap, and it is for the benefit and encouragement of agriculture. It is indeed against the general rule of law concerning emblements, which are not allowed to tenants who know when their term is to cease, because it is held to be their fault or folly to have sown when they knew their interest would expire before they could reap. But the cus-

(*b*) See further, as to observances which have been held as unreasonable, and therefore void as customs, *Clayton* v. *Corby*, 5 Q. B. 415; 14 L. J. Q. B. 364; *Rogers* v. *Brenton*, 10 Q. B. 26; 17 L. J. Q. B. 34; *Rockey* v. *Huggens*, Cro. Car. 220; *Badger* v. *Ford*, 3 B. & Ald. 153; *Mounsey* v. *Ismay*, 1 H. & C. 729; *Hilton* v. *Earl Granville*, 5 Q. B. 701; *Blackett* v. *Bradley*, 1 B. & S. 940, 954-5; *Elwood* v. *Bullock*, 6 Q. B. 383; *Gibbs* v. *Flight*, 3 C. B. 581; *Reg.* v. *Dalby*, 3 Q. B. 602. A reasonable custom, see *Sanders* v. *Jameson*, 2 C. & K. 557; *Gard* v. *Callard*, 6 M. & S. 69. A foreign custom which is bad in law cannot be set up to defeat the rights of a party. *Taylor* v. *Carpenter*, 2 Wash. (U. S.) 2. Nor one that is illegal. *Pierce* v. *U. S.*, 1 N. & H. (U. S.) 270. Nor one that is unreasonable. *United States* v. *Buchanan*, 8 Harr. (U. S.) 83. Or opposed to the provisions of a statute. *Walker* v. *Transportation Co.*, 3 Wall. (U. S.) 150; *Winter* v. *United States*, Hemp. (U. S.) 344; *The Forrester*, Newb. (U. S.) 81. In the absence of any law, an established usage among those engaged in navigating the Mississippi with steamers must be considered, in determining questions of fault or negligence in the management of the steamers on that river. *Myers* v. *Perry*, 1 La. Ann. 372.

tom of a particular place may rectify what otherwise would be imprudence or folly."(c)

Custom Must be Certain.

SEC. 25. *A custom to be valid must be certain.*(d)   This is an element which must necessarily, and by the force of reason, attach to a custom.   Any miscellaneous observances, which have no coherence of principle, are necessarily inefficacious as forming a rule of conduct.   It is only when observances have shaped themselves into a constant uniformity, only when their characteristics of the past can be a clear light for their incidents in the future, that they rise to the level of a custom, which is the stuff of which law is made. Hence it follows that there must be definiteness or certainty about a custom.   Thus it has been instanced since the days of Blackstone that a custom that lands shall descend to the most worthy of the owner's blood, is void on the ground that the custom gives no certain means for the discovery of merit, while a custom that lands shall descend to the next male of the blood, exclusive of females, is certain and good.(e)

Illustrations of Certainty—Vague Customs.

SEC. 26. In an early case it was held that no person has at common law a right to glean in the harvest-field, and that neither have the poor of a parish *legally settled* (as such) any

(c) *Wigglesworth* v. *Dallison*, Dougl. 201; 1 Smith Lea. Cas. p. 539; see also *Mousley* v. *Ludlam*, 21 L. J. Q. B. 64; *Dalby* v. *Hirst*, 1 B. & B. 224; see also *Stratup* v. *Dodderidge*, 2 Ld. Raym. 1158; *Naylor qui Tam* v. *Scott*, 2 Ld. Raym. 1558.

(d) *Tanistry's case*, Sir J. Davis, Rep. 32.   A custom in order to become part of a contract, or in any manner control the legal relations of parties, must be so far established and so far known to the parties that it must be supposed that their contract was made in reference to it. For this purpose the custom must be established and not casual, uniform and not varying, general and not personal, and known to the parties. *Sipperly* v. *Steward*, 50 Barb. (N. Y.) 62; *Duguid* v. *Edwards*. Id. 288; *Kendall* v. *Russel*, 5 Dana (Ky.) 501; *Stevens* v. *Reeves*, 9 Pick. (Mass.) 198; *Wood* v. *Hickok*, 2 Wend. (N. Y.) 501; *Martin* v. *Maynard*, 16 N. H. 165; *Wheeler* v. *Newbould*, 5 Duer (N. Y.) 29.

(e) 1 Roll. Abr. 565.

such right, on the ground that such a right would be inconsistent with the nature of property, and that no right can
exist at common law unless both the subject of it, and they
who claim it, are certain.(f) So again, to return to the most
ordinary, and possibly the best, illustrations of the validity
of a custom in its dependence upon certainty or uncertainty,
a custom to pay twopence an acre in lieu of tithes is good ;
but were it to pay sometimes twopence and sometimes three-
pence, as the occupier of the land chooses, is bad on account
of its uncertainty.(g) "Yet a custom," as Blackstone puts
it,(h) "to pay a year's improved value for a fine on a copyhold estate is good—though the value be uncertain—for the
value may at any time be ascertained, and the maxim of the
law is *id certum est, quod certum redi potest.*"(i) A custom,
therefore, that all the customary tenants of a manor having
gardens, parcels of their customary tenements respectively,
have immemorially by themselves, their tenants and occu-
piers, dug, taken and carried away from a waste within the
manor, to be used upon their customary tenements, for the
purpose of making and repairing grass-plots in the gardens,
for the improvement thereof, such turf covered with grass fit
for the pasture of cattle, at all times of the year, as often and
in such quantity as occasion hath required, was held bad, as
being indefinite and uncertain. And so, also, a custom for
the taking and applying of such turf for the purpose of
making and repairing the banks and mounds in, of, and for
the hedges and fences of such customary tenants is invalid
for a similar reason.(j) In that case it is evident that the
word "improvement" was most vague; no limitation prevented the tenants, if the custom had been good, from
completely destroying the pasture. The only limit to the
custom, as Lord Ellenborough remarked, was " caprice and

(f) *Steel* v. *Houghton*, 1 H. Bl. 51.

(g) 1 Bla. Com. 78 ; *Le case de
Tanistry*, Davys, 28 b. 35 ; *Blewett* v.
Tregouning, 3 Ad. & El. 554.

(h) 1 Bl. Com. by Stephen, p. 61.

(i) Broom's Leg. Max. 5th ed. 623.

(j) *Wilson* v. *Willes*, 7 East, 121.

fancy." The privilege was claimed as exercisable when occasion required—a most loose, vague, indefinite and limitless restriction; upon all these grounds it was impossible to regard such an observance as a custom. A custom to throw earth, stones, coals, &c., in heaps upon land *near* to certain coal pits, was held bad, on the ground that the word *near* is of great latitude, and too loose to support a custom.(*k*) On the other hand, in the case of the *Marquis of Salisbury* v. *Gladstone*,(*l*) which was in ejectment for a forfeiture by a lord against a copyholder of inheritance, for digging and taking clay from the manor of West Derby, in Lancashire, to be sold off the manor to any one, the defendant pleaded and proved a custom from time immemorial for the copyholders of inheritance, without license from the lord, to break the surface and dig clay without limit from and out of their copyhold tenements, for the purpose of making it into bricks to be sold off the manor, such a custom was held good in law. In that case it was not so much on the ground of uncertainty, for "without limit" might mean the whole, which is certain, but on the ground of the unreasonableness of such a custom that its validity was disputed. And Lord Cranworth's remarks upon this subject are not unworthy of attention. "It is true," he said, "that a custom to be valid must be reasonable. It is not easy to define the word 'reasonable' when applied to a custom regulating the relation between a lord and his copyholders. That relation must have had its origin in remote times by agreement between the lord, as absolute owner of the whole manor in fee simple, and those whom he was content to allow to occupy portions of it as his tenants at will. The rights of these tenants must have depended in their origin entirely on the will of the lord, and it is hard to say how any stipulations regulating such rights can, as between the tenant and the lord, be deemed void as being unreasonable. *Cujus est dare*

(*k*) *Wilkes* v. *Broadbent*, 1 Wils. 63.   (*l*) 9 H. of L. cases, 692.

ejus est disponere. Wherever restrictions, therefore, or conditions the lord may have imposed, or whatever rights the tenants may have demanded, all were within the competency of the lord to grant, or of the tenants to stipulate for. And if it were possible to show that from the time of legal memory any lawful arrangement had been actually come to between the lord and his tenants as to the terms on which the latter should hold their lands, and that arrangement had been constantly acted on, I do not see how it could ever be treated as being void because it was unreasonable. In truth, I believe that when it is said that a custom is void because it is unreasonable, nothing more is meant than that the unreasonable character of the alleged custom conclusively proves that the usage, even though it may have existed immemorially, must have resulted from accident or indulgence, and not from any right conferred in ancient times on the party setting up the custom."(*m*)

Custom Must be Obligatory.

SEC. 27. *A custom must be compulsory,* otherwise it loses the imperative character of a law. It is true that agreements which were founded in consent were the origin of customs; it is true that the observances which have become, as it were, acted or pictured laws, were at first matters of option; but whenever they are established customs, they must have ceased to be matters of choice, and must have an obligatory element—a binding force. Were it in the option of every man whether he would conform to a custom or not, were it a matter which might be referred for decision to his good pleasure, it is evident that it would be invalid upon the ground which we have already considered, viz., uncertainty. A custom to be binding must be current, it must be known and understood by those whose conduct is to be affected by its existence, whose transactions are to be influenced by its

(*m*) See also the *Bishop of Winchester* v. *Knight*, 1 P. Wms. 496; the   *Dean of Ely* v. *Warren*, 2 Atk. 189.

factual terms; but if its terms were alterable at the will of each man, if it was in the option of each man to be bound to-day and not bound to-morrow by the custom, any one whose conduct might have to conform to such a rule would find it impossible to shape his actions accordingly; any transactions which might have to be influenced by such a precept would be varying, indefinite, uncertain and absurd.(n) Thus, in the words of Blackstone, "a custom that all the inhabitants shall be rated towards the maintenance of a bridge will be good; but a custom that every man is to contribute thereto at his own pleasure, is idle and absurd, and indeed no custom at all."(o)

Customs Must be Consistent.

SEC. 28. Again, *customs must be consistent with each other ;* one cannot be set up in opposition to another.(p)   If two customs are contradictory, it is evident that they cannot both have been established by mutual consent.   Thus the allegation of one custom is not to be met by the allegation of another custom inconsistent with the first, but rather by the denial of the existence of the first as a custom.   This rule

(n) *Adams* v. *Otterbark*, 15 How. (U. S.) 539.   The same doctrines prevail in the law of the United States, where it has been held that a usage or custom of trade is the law of that trade, and to make such a custom at all obligatory, it must be ancient, so as to be generally known, certain and reasonable.   Therefore, a usage of such doubtful authority as to be known only to a few, or where merchants of a trade differ as to its existence, will not be regarded.   *Collins* v. *Hope*, 3 Wash. (U. S. C. C.) 149; compare *Donnell* v. *Columbian Ins. Co.*, 2 Sumn. (U. S.) 366; *Wilcocks* v. *Phillips*, 1 Wall. Jr. (U. S. C. C.) 47.

(o) 1 Bl. Com. by Stephen, 61.

(p) See *Aldred's case*, 9 Rep. 58b;

Kenchin v. *Knight*, 1 Wils. 253; *Parkin* v. *Radcliffe*, 1 Bos. & Pul. 282.   A special custom as to the power and authority of pilots at one port prevailing at the place of shipment, differing from the general custom, is not binding on persons residing elsewhere, unless there is proof that they had notice or knowledge of its existence.   *Marlatt* v. *Clary*, 20 Ark. 251.   The fact that there is a private custom in reference to certain matters, does not exclude evidence of a general custom relative to the same matter, unless it appears that such private custom was known to the parties or those under whom they claim.   *Beatty* v. *Gregory*, 17 Iowa 107.

really might fall under the first, which demands the moment of reasonableness for a custom, for the absurdity and unreasonableness of two mutually inconsistent customs is evident, and if one custom be admitted to exist, the other which is inconsistent with it violates the requisite of reasonableness, and is therefore invalid.

Customs, How Construed –Presumption.

Sec. 29. We come now to the question of the interpretation of special customs. One of the principal rules to be noted is, that customs in derogation of the common law are to be strictly construed.(*q*)   There is always a presumption against a thing while it is only in' the making, and a presumption in favor of the thing which is made.   There is a deep truth in Milton's remark, that error is only truth in the making, and consequently it is well to pronounce against a custom which is the making of law, in favor of a law which is recognized, acknowledged and made.   Now this doctrine of strict construction is a deference to this presumption. Thus it comes that, although by the custom of Gavelkind an infant of fifteen years may by a deed of feoffment convey away his lands in fee simple, this custom would not be held to entitle him to effect the same thing by any other conveyance.   Such a rule is contrary to the common law, and although it having become a rule is an indication that it must have had a reason, the fact that the rule of the common law is different proves that there was a reason for the diverse custom which is thus shown.   The rational way of dealing with such a case is to give effect as far as possible to the latent reason which is in both, and hence the rule of construction to which we have alluded.   Thus, where there is a custom that lands shall descend to the eldest sister, the courts will not extend the authority of this custom to include

(*q*) *Per* Bayley, J., *Richardson v. Walker*, 2 B. & C. 839.

3

an eldest niece. (r)   Where, however, there is a custom in a manor that a man may convey his copyhold in fee simple, that will not be held to preclude him from conveying it for life, for in such a case the lesser right must be held to be included in the greater, and it was therefore here said that, although customs must be strictly, they need not necessarily be literally construed. (s)

The Force of Customs—Usage and Statutory Enactments—Interpretation by Custom.

SEC. 30. No custom can prevail against an Act of Parliament. (t)   As we have pointed out, Acts of Parliament must be regarded as the results of custom, as recognitions of practices, and as the worded outcome of observances.   To allow a custom to contradict an act would be to suffer a violation of the seventh rule noted above, as it would be the recognition of inconsistent customs.   A custom, then, that every pound of butter sold in a particular market-town shall weigh ` eighteen ounces is bad. (u)   In the case of *The Magistrates of Dunbar* v. *The Duchess of Roxburgh,* (v) it was expressly held that long usage is of no avail against plain statutory enactments, and that such an usage can be binding on parties only as the interpreter of a doubtful law, and as affording a contemporaneous exposition.   But that where a statute is expressive as to some points, and silent as to others, usage may well supply the defects if not inconsistent with the express directions of the statute. (w)   These rules and prin-

(r) *Denn* v. *Spray*, 1 T. R. 466; see also *Miggleton* v. *Barnett*, 2 H. &. N. 653.

(s) Co. Cop. § 33. This limitation of rule is noticed in Coleridge's Blackstone, vol. i. p. 79.

(t) Co. Litt. 113a; *Noble* v. *Durell*, 3 T. R. 271.

(u) *Noble* v. *Durell*, 3 T. R. 271. See American cases, *Walker* v. *The Transportation Co.*, 3 Wall. (U. S.) 150; *Winter* v. *United States*, Hempst.

(U. S.) 344. It has been held that in doubtful cases usage may be recurred to, to ascertain the meaning of the legislature. *Dunbar Magistrates* v. *Duchess of Roxburgh*, 3 C. & F. 335; *Polk* v. *Hill*, 2 Overt. (Tenn.) 118, and see *United States* v. *McDaniel*, 7 Pet. (U. S.) 1, 14; *Commercial Bank* v. *Varnum*, 3 Lans. (N. Y.) 86, 90, note.

(v) 3 Cl. & F. 335.

(w) See D. i. 3, 37.

ciples will enable the reader to understand what may be called the law of customs in so far as the important question of validity arises in connection with them. But these very rules and principles will be more thoroughly understood after an examination of some cases in which the question has arisen, and when the relation of customs to the law of evidence has been more thoroughly explained and illustrated.

Confusion as to Meaning of "Custom"—Custom and Common Law.

SEC. 31. It is necessary to point out that there has been considerable confusion of thought in relation to the use of the word "custom," and to clear away, if possible, any dubiety which may exist. There are customs which really form a part of the common law of the land, and it is with reference to these customs that the rules of validity, which have been noted above, have been prescribed. But there are many other customs or usages which are not a part of the common law, but which, nevertheless, influence the conduct of men, and which are, it may be, on the way to become chapters of the unwritten rules of the country.(x) These are, as it were, provisional laws, but they lack the obligatory character which attaches to proved and recognized customs. These usages are proved by evidence like a fact, and when proved it is held in law to have an obligatory character in relation to certain executed transactions. Its existence will raise the presumption that the parties to a contract acted in conformity with its terms; it will not, however, necessitate any persons who may in the future enter into a similar contract to act in accordance with it, and the obligatory character of its terms may be done away with by the express wish of the parties and by its express exclusion from the contract. In this country the terms custom and usage are often used

(x) See the opinion of Nelson, J., in *Allen* v. *The Merchants Bank*, 15 Wend. (N. Y.), and note to *The Com-* *mercial Bank of Kentucky* v. *Varnum*, 3 Lans. (N. Y.) 94, 95.

synonymously, but they are by no means synonymous terms, and much confusion arises from a failure to properly discriminate between them.   A usage is a growing custom, but it does not become a custom until its origin is lost to the memory of men.   Indeed, in this country but few right customs exist, but we have a multitude of growing customs or usages which may affect the relations of parties in transactions to which they relate.

Habitual Law—Usages.

SEC. 32. There is an habitual law in conformity with which men shape their actions, but that habitual law, which is in a vague conformity with the law of the land, whether statute, common or customary, is quite insufficient to regulate all kinds of conduct, and so the very habitual practices of men introduces other rules which are sanctioned by the common sense and convenience of those who are familiar with the transactions. These laws of the people's own making are usages.   It is not absolutely necessary that a man should act exactly like his fellows, but as a fact most men in these matters do, for these usages are the results of collective sense and experience, (y) and just as in an unknown country a traveler will generally find the paths have considerable shrewdness, and have been planned with a view to ease and convenience, so it is with these customs of trade—these consensual laws.

Customs Not Common Law—Evidence.

SEC. 33. But these customs are not a part of the common law of the land. Although much of the common law of the land has passed through this novitiate in the market place—it being optional whether a person will act in conformity with such a usage—although it is incessant amongst those

(y) Earl Russell has well said that a proverb is the wisdom of many and the wit of one, and a custom might be looked on as a sort of factual proverb. It contains in it the common sense and common experience of all men, and it was invented by the ingenuity of one.

who execute like transactions, it comes to be a question in many cases whether an individual who has entered into some agreement has done so subject to this common custom or usage. With the customs themselves law has nothing to do. They may come, as we have seen, to be real laws; but while they are only, as it were, vague facts or general facts which have not been judicially recognized, they are of no more interest to the lawyer than particular facts. The only question which can interest him in connection with these is the laws which regulate the admissibility of their proof, and those which regulate the method of proof. The only questions, then, which we have, as lawyers, to deal with in relation to these usages, are questions of evidence. In recent times a good deal of weight has been given in courts of law to these rabble laws, and a great number of important decisions have been recorded in relation to them, and hence the importance of the subject as a recondite branch of the law of evidence.

CHAPTER II.

AS TO CUSTOMS OF THE COUNTRY AND THE ADMISSIBILITY OF THE PROOF OF THESE.

Evidence of Usage.

SEC. 34. One of the most important questions which falls under our consideration in connection with a study of the law of customs is, as to the admissibility of evidence of a usage for the purpose of modifying the meaning of a written contract. This question has to be practically answered upon very many occasions in modern courts of law, and the frequency with which this matter is brought under judicial notice is to be accounted for by our great commercial prosperity, which has increased the extent of our trade, and the energy of those who are employed in it, and has produced an intense vitality in relation to the various conveniences of transaction, which has resulted in many useful and admirable customs which may well become a part of the common law of the land.

Improvement of Law.

SEC. 35. Whenever a country is progressive its laws tend to improve. But there is one incident of the improvement of a jurisprudence which it is of much importance to note in this place. As a country becomes more civilized its criminal laws become less severe, but, at the same time, its laws of evidence seem to become less strict. Just as there is no necessity for heavy pains and penalties in a country where life and property are respected, where moral principle keeps the hands of the people from violence and from fraud; so in a country where truth is common, where people have become intelligent enough to presume that a lie is always a mistake, there is not the same necessity for the strictness of proof which is felt in a less civilized community. Those who look at the history of our laws of evidence will find ample illustration of the truth of this proposition; and one chapter of that history might be written in connection with the way in which evidence of custom has been admitted in courts of law to annex incident to and to explain the meaning of written instruments. It may be well to divide our subject, for the sake of convenience, into parts. The evidence of usage may annex incidents to contracts between—(1) landlord and tenant; (2) to contracts made in the course of trade; and (3) to other contracts, in transactions which have such regularity of practice as will admit of established usage, and in which, in fact, customs have prevailed.

Customs of the Country--Parol Evidence.

Sec. 36. First, then, with reference to contracts made between landlord and tentant. It is a well-known rule of the law of proof that parol evidence cannot be admitted to contradict or vary the terms of an agreement in writing.(a)

(a) *Meres* v. *Ansell*, 3 Wil. 275; *S. P. Ogilvie* v. *Foljambe*, 3 Mer. 53; *Attwood* v. *Small*, 6 C. & T. 232; *Besant* v. *Cross*, 10 C. B. 895; *Caine* v. *Horsfall*, 2 C. & K. 349; *Clifton* v. *Walmesley*, 5 T. R. 564; *Henson* v. *Cooper*, 3 Scott, N. R. 48; *Harnor* v. *Groves*, 15 C. B. 667; *Shore* v. *Wilson*, 9 C. & F. 355; 5 Scott N. R. 958. See also *Perkins* v. *Young*, 82 Mass. (16 Gray) 389; *Cocke* v. *Bailey*, 42 Miss. 81; *Kirk* v. *Hartman*, 63 Penn. St. 97; and see some earlier cases, such as *Halliday* v. *Hart*, 30 N. Y. 474; *Wolfe* v. *Myers*, 3 Sandf. (N. Y.) 7; *Erwin* v. *Saunders*, 1 Cow. (N. Y.) 249; *Van Ostrand*,

In case, however, the written agreement is ambiguous—if the ambiguity does not appear on the face of it, in which

v. *Reed*, 1 Wend. (N. Y.) 424; *Montgomery County Bank* v. *Albany City Bank*, 8 Barb. (N. Y.) 396. Evidence of usage is admissible to arrive at the intention of the parties when any doubt exists in relation thereto from the language of the contract, or when the contract is silent as to certain matters. *Eaton* v. *Smith*, 20 Pick. (Mass.) 150; *Dixon* v. *Dunham*, 13 Ill. 324; *Cooper* v. *Kane*, 19 Wend. (N. Y.) 386; *Shaw* v. *Mitchell*, 2 Met. (Mass.) 65; *Leach* v. *Beardslee*, 22 Conn. 404. So even when the contract is in writing and precise in its terms, evidence of usage is admissible to show the manner in which the business is done. *Fox* v. *Parker*, 44 Barb. (N. Y.) 541. So evidence of a usage is sometimes admissible to fix the rights of parties and give a right of action when none would otherwise exist. Thus, a custom of a particular place for the owners of adjoining lots, after giving notice to the adjoining owner to build his half of the fence and his refusal to do so, (in the absence of any statute regulating the matter) to build the whole and hold him for his share of the expense, has been held reasonable and binding, and enforceable by action. *Knox* v. *Artman*, 3 Rich. (S. C.) 283. So evidence of usage is admissible to show the terms of a contract not in writing and to corroborate witnesses. Thus, where the master of a coasting vessel, who had chartered it on shares, testified that the owners authorized him if he should leave the vessel to give it up to the mate, and that he did so under an oral contract with the mate to run the vessel on the same terms as

he had done; and the mate testified that he ran the vessel accordingly, as master, and that the owners ratified the agreement, it was held that evidence was admissible in order to show the terms of the contract between the new master and the owners, and to corroborate the witnesses, of a usage, at the port where the vessel belonged, to let such vessels to the master upon shares. *Thompson* v. *Hamilton*, 12 Pick. (Mass.) 425. Where a new and unusual word is used in a contract, or where a word is used in a technical or peculiar sense, as applicable to any trade or branch of business, or to any particular class of people, it is proper to receive evidence of usage to explain and illustrate it. *Eaton* v. *Smith*, 20 Pick. (Mass.) 150. Mercantile customs which are universally acted upon, enter into and form a part of the contract, although not mentioned or alluded to in its terms. *Munn* v. *Burch*, 25 Ill. 35; *Power* v. *Kane*, 5 Wis. 265. In a dispute in regard to the hiring of a vessel, the evidence of custom is admissible to explain the acts of the parties. *Perkins* v. *Jordan*, 35 Me. 231. So proof of a custom in the vicinity, for persons building a vessel together, each to be responsible for his own share only, is admissible to modify a written contract. *Riply* v. *Crooker*, 47 Me. 370. In the case of contracts, a usage known to both parties may be given in evidence, as tending to show the nature of the contract between them. *Loring* v. *Gurney*, 5 Pick. (Mass.) 15; *Thompson* v. *Hamilton*, 12 *Id.* 425; *Naylor* v. *Semmes*, 4 G. & J. (Md.) 274, but

case it is to be explained by the judge,(b) but is what is called in law a " latent ambiguity "—parol evidence is admissible to explain what, but for it, would be inexplicable.(c) The reasons for the admission of parol evidence under such circumstances are clear and strong, but where such an ambiguity can be explained by a reference to an existing custom, it is evident that such proof will have more authority than that which would attach to evidence of the party's intentions at the time the instrument was executed, or of his particular practice in relation to certain matters, as indicating what would probably be his intention in framing the document.   In all cases it is difficult to arrive at a man's intention ; and the only possible means of arriving at a correct conclusion with reference to his mental attitude is by a consideration of his words and actions.   These, however, are apt to be misconstrued, even if they are accurately remembered and correctly repeated or described.   On the other hand, the practice of all men is easy of proof, and there is the strongest presumption in favor of the supposition that he

no usage or custom, however general, can be put in evidence to vary or control the express terms of a contract. *Cadwell* v. *Meek*, 17 Ill. 220; *Renner* v. *Bank of Columbia*, 9 Wheat. 581 ; *Rankin* v. *American Ins. Co.* 1 Hall (N. Y.) 619; *Sleght* v. *Rhinelander*, 1 Johns. (N. Y.) 192; *Barlow* v. *Lambert*, 28 Ala.704; *Corwin* v. *Patch*, 4 Cal. 204; *Sigsworth* v. *McIntyre*, 18 Ill. 126; *Fay* v. *Strawn*, 32 Ill. 295; *Sandford* v. *Rawlings*, 43 Ill. 92; *Atkinson* v. *Allen*, 29 Ind. 375; *Randall* v. *Rotch*, 12 Pick. (Mass.) 107; *Macombre* v. *Parker*, 13 Id. 175 ; *Wheeler* v. *Nurse*, 20 N. H. 220; *George* v. *Bartlett*, 22 N. H. (2 Fost.) 496; *Wadsworth* v. *Allcott*, 6 N. Y. (2 Seld.) 64 ; *Cooper* v. *Purvis*, 1 Jones (N. C.) L. 141; *Sweet* v. *Jenkins*, 1 R. I. 147 ; *Meaher* v. *Lufkin*, 21 Tex. 383. And

before a custom or usage can be held binding in the construction of a contract, it must have, as to such transactions, the force of law. *Clamorgan* v. *Guissere*, 1 Mo. 141.

(b) *Smith* v. *Thompson*, 8 C. B. 44 ; 18 L. J. C. P. 314; *Hills* v. *London Gaslight Co.*, 27 L. J. Ex. 60. See also *Campbell* v. *Johnson*, 44 Mo. 247.

(c) *Rex* v. *Laindon*, 8 T R. 379; *Cocker* v. *Guy*, 2 B. & P. 565; *Padlock* v. *Fradley*, 1 C. & J. 90. See, as to the explanation of documents written in illegible hands, *Goblet* v. *Beechy*, 3 Sim. 24 ; *Masters* v. *Masters*, 1 P. Wms. 424; *Norman* v. *Morrell*, 4 Ves. 769; see also *Howlett* v. *Howlett*, 56 Barb. (N.Y.) 467; *Willis* v. *Fernald*, 23 N. J. L. (4 Vr.) 206; *Suffirn* v. *Butler*, 21 N. J. Eq. 410; *DeWolf* v. *Crandall*, 1 Sweeny (N. Y.) 556.

who wrote the document, the ambiguity of which has to be explained, did what every other body was doing—shaped his conduct according to the manners and usages of his time and district; and in that way, if a usage can be proved, the existence of which will explain the ambiguity, it is evidently the best means of arriving at a conclusion as to the intention of the individual, the explanation of whose agreement is in question. Thus it is that the proof of a custom in the explanation of an ambiguity in a written instrument is not only admitted, (d) but must be regarded as parol evidence of the highest authority.

The Construction of Grants by Usage.

Sec. 37. As a fact, evidence of usage has been admitted, from very early times, in explanation of ambiguous grants and charters, and it has been decided that the construction of such a grant is for the jury and not for the judge. (e)

(d) Doe d. Kinglake v. Beviss, 18 L. J. C. P. 628. A custom or usage that is inequitable or unjust cannot be sustained. Coleman v. Chadwick, 80 Penn. St. 81; Dans v. Waln, 71 Id. 69; Horner v. Watson, 79 Id. 242; Bean v. Balton, 3 Phila. (Penn.) 87. Nor one that is unreasonable. or not generally acquiesced in. McMartin v. Pennsylvania R. R. Co., 69 Penn. St. 374. Nor one that is in violation of law, religion or morality. Holmes v. Johnson, 42 Penn. St. 159. A usage or custom that is destructive of the subject of a grant or contract cannot be set up. Thus a person owning certain coal lands sold the coal under the land to the plaintiff, with certain specified privileges through his adjoining lands, and subsequently sold part of the coal on such adjoining land to the defendant. The plaintiff, in excavating his coal, removed the "ribs" composed of

coal, which supported the roof of the mine, causing the surface to crack and sink so that the water flowed into the plaintiff's mine, and thence into the defendant's mine. It was held that the consequences of this act could not be excused by showing that H., in mining his coal, pursued the approved and customary practice of mining in that region, and without negligence, nor by any custom in Pennsylvania that in mining the owner of the mine may remove the ribs and allow the surface to sink, as such a custom is unreasonable. Horner v. Watson, ante.

(e) Doe d. Kinglake v. Beviss, 18 L. J. C. P. 628; Beaufort (Duke) v. Swansea (Magistrate &c., of), 3 Exch. 413; Newcastle - on - Tyne (Master) Pilots, &c.) v. Bradley, 2 E.·& B. 428; Withnell v. Gratham, 1 Esp. 322; see also Wadley v. Bayliss, 5 Taunt. 752;

The real object of evidence under such circumstances is to place the court in the position of the parties to the instrument, and without the evidence of usage that would, in a large number of cases, be impossible. (f)

As to Leases.

SEC. 38. In farming leases it is usual for the lessee to covenant that he will manage his farm in a husbandlike manner; but it has been over and over again decided that in the absence of any such covenant the mere relation of landlord and tenant creates an implied obligation to farm according to the custom of the country. (g) Here, then, we have the terms of the custom becoming a part of or incorporated with the lease. But, as we shall see, an express covenant inconsistent with the custom will control and exclude this implication. (h) Customary rights and incidents universally

but see *Parker* v. *Ibbetson,* 4 C. B. N. S. 846. Evidence of usage is not admissible to vary the plain language of a deed, not ambiguous or equivocal. *Cortelyou* v. *Van Brandt,* 2 John. (N. Y.) 357. But usage as to the *form* of deeds cannot be disregarded. *Brown* v. *Farron,* 3 Ohio 155; *Kirkendall* v. *Mitchell,* 3 McLean (U. S.) 144.

(f) *Baird* v. *Fortune,* 7 Jur. N. S. 926; *Waterpark* (*Lord*) v. *Fennell,* 7 H. & L. Cas. 650; 7 W. R. 634.

(g) *Powley* v. *Walker,* 5 T. R. 373; *Leigh* v. *Hewitt,* 4 East, 154; *Angerstein* v. *Hanson,* 1 C. M. & R. 789; *Earl of Falmouth* v. *Thomas,* 1 Cr. & M. 89; *Halifax* v. *Chambers,* 4 M. & W. 662; *Martin* v. *Gilham,* 7 A. & E. 540; *Bickford* v. *Pearson,* 5 C. B. 920; *Wilkins* v. *Wood,* 17 L. J. Q. B. 319; *Sutton* v. *Temple,* 12 M. & W. 52. It is competent to show by parol what is considered, in the neighborhood, good husbandry in the cultivation,

&c., of lands. *Aughinbaugh* v. *Coppenheffer,* 55 Penn. St. 347.

(h) *Webb* v. *Plummer,* 2 B. & C. 746; *Clarke* v. *Roystone,* 13 M. & W. 752; *Roberts* v. *Baker,* 1 Cr. & M. 808; *Sutton* v. *Temple,* 12 M. & W. 52, at p. 63. While evidence of the custom of the country is admissible to add incidents to a lease in respect to matters in relation to which it is silent, yet it is never admissible to control the express terms of the lease. *Webb* v. *Plummer,* 2 B. & Ad. 746; *Dalby* v. *Hirst,* 1 B. & B. 224; *Senior* v. *Armitage,* Holt 197. In *Clarke* v. *Roystone,* 13 M. & W. 752, an action was brought against a tenant to recover the value of certain manure under an agreement as follows: After referring to other matters not material to be stated here, the agreement was, "Be it remembered, that the above closes of land have been only clipped or mown once, and since manured with eight

attaching to the subject-matter of the contract in the place and neighborhood where the contract was made, are impliedly

loads of rotten manure per acre, which the tenant agrees, when given up by him, to leave it in the same state, or allow a valuation to be made. As witness our hands, this 8th day of April, 1840. John Clarke, Moses Roystone." The declaration set up a breach of this agreement in that the defendant did not leave the premises in the same condition or state as when he received them. The defendant set up the custom of the country in defence, to pay on going in, and to pay nothing on going out, but the court held that the custom was excluded by the terms of the contract. *Parke, B.*, said : "This declaration is upon an executory contract, to pay to the plaintiff so much money on request, and thereupon that the defendant, the tenant, was to have a tenancy according to the custom of the country. Now what is the custom of the country? It is to pay half tillage upon coming in, and of course to receive half tillage upon going out. Then if you import these words into the alleged contract, and suppose the contract to be, that the tenant shall do that which the custom of the country requires, then the defendant is to pay so much money upon request as is equal to the half tillage. That is the nature of the contract described in the declaration. Now look at the proof. The proof is, that the defendant was to occupy these closes of land, which were manured the year before; and then there was a stipulation, that, at the end of the term mentioned in the contract, he should put the premises exactly in the same state

as to manure which they were in at the commencement of the tenancy, or submit to a valuation ; that is, that he should pay for the deterioration of the estate, according to the value put upon it by competent persons, by the want of such manure. Therefore, here is a stipulation, that the premises, upon the tenant's going out, shall be left in the same condition they were in at the time he entered, or that he shall pay for the difference at the end of the term. That excludes the idea of the payment of any money down at the time of entry, because, at the end of the term, he is to put them into the same condition, or to pay damages according to their deterioration. That is not according to the custom of the country; and it appears to me, therefore, that the allegation in the declaration is not proved; that the custom of the country is excluded by the terms of the contract. Instead of paying money down, the nature of the contract is altered altogether ; nothing is to be paid down, nothing is to be received on going out, but the premises are to be put into the same condition as they were in at the beginning of the term, or the difference in the value is to be paid." *Alderson, B.*, said : "It appears to me that the reasonable and natural construction of the agreement is, that the party is to pay nothing down, but that he is to do something when he goes out of possession, or to pay for the deterioration of the property if he does not; and that that stipulation being inconsistent with the custom of the country, the

annexed to the written language and terms of the contract, unless the custom is particularly and expressly excluded. Parol evidence of custom and usage consequently is always admissible to enable us to arrive at the real meaning of the parties who are naturally presumed to have contracted in conformity with the known and established usage.[1] Thus,

contract must prevail, and the custom of the country must be excluded." In *Wigglesworth* v. *Dallison*, 1 Doug. 201, it was held, that, even where there was no agreement under seal, the custom of the country might be looked at as annexing terms to the contract, unless they were expressly excluded by the agreement. *Lord Mansfield* says: "The custom does not alter or contradict the agreement in the lease, it only superadds a right which is consequential to the taking." The cases on this subject were all reviewed in *Hutton* v. *Warren*, 1 M. & W. 466; and *Parke, B.*, adverting to the case of *Senior* v. *Armitage*, Holt's N. P. C. 197, states the decision to have been, as appeared by a manuscript note of *Mr. Justice Bayley*, "that though there was a written contract between landlord and tenant, the custom of the country would still be binding, if not inconsistent with the terms of such written contract; and that not only all common law obligations, but those imposed by custom, were in full force where the contract did not vary them." That shows that even where there is a written agreement or deed, the custom is not excluded, unless there be something in the terms of the instrument inconsistent with the custom. In *Holding* v. *Piggott*, 7 Bing. 465, 5 M.

& P. 427, it was held, that, where the lease contained no stipulation as to the *mode* of *quitting*, the off-going tenant was entitled to his 'way-going crop according to the custom of the country, even although the terms of *holding* might be inconsistent with such a custom. In *Muncey* v. *Dennison*, 1 Ark. 216, where the tenant agreed to cultivate the farm according to the custom of the country, "and during the time to consume with stock on the farm all the hay, straw and clover grown thereon, which manure shall be used on the farm," and the landlord agreed to let the tenant occupy part of the homestead until midsummer day, after the expiration of the term, if necessary, "to end the cropping of the amount grown on the premises," it was held that the lease did not exclude the custom of the country, as which the tenant, having paid for straw on his incoming, was entitled to be paid for straw on his outgoing." The rule of law in reference to importing into the term of a tenancy the custom of the country, does not admit of evidence of the usage of a particular estate, or the property of a particular individual, however extensive it may be, unless it is shown that the tenant was aware of it. *Wormersly* v. *Dally*, 26 L. J. Exchq. 219.

[1] Parties are presumed to contract in reference to the usage of the trade

or business in question, if there is nothing in the agreement to exclude

the custom of the country in regard to the claims of an outgoing tenant of a farm will prevail, although there be a lease

the inference. *Hinton* v. *Locke*, 5 Hill (N. Y.) 437; *Outwater* v. *Nelson*, 20 Barb. (N. Y.) 29; and see *Wadsworth* v. *Allcott*, 6 N. Y. 64. Thus, in the case first cited *supra*, in an action on an agreement to pay for work at so much per day, it was held that a usage or custom that ten hours' labor was a day's work, and that twelve and a half hours' labor on one day was a day and a quarter within the meaning of the contract, is admissible. A general custom among masters of vessels on the lakes, carrying goods for forwarders, having a lien on the goods for their advances, to enforce such lien for the benefit of the forwarders, is binding on such carriers. *Lee* v. *Satter*, H. & D.'s Supp. (N. Y.) 163. Where, by the terms of a written contract, commission merchants are to charge a specified commission on sales, which is to be in full of all expenses, and at the termination of the contract by mutual consent, the goods on hand are transferred to other factors, evidence is incompetent to prove a usage of merchants to charge one-half commissions under such circumstances. *Ware* v. *Hayward Rubber Co.*, 3 Allen (Mass.) 84. In an action on an agreement to build an octagonal cellar wall at a certain price by the foot, evidence of the usage of measuring the angles of such walls, and of the proper mode of measuring the angles of rectangular walls, is reasonable and therefore admissible. *Ford* v. *Tirrell*, 9 Gray (Mass.) 401. In *Lowe* v. *Lehman*, 15 Ohio St. 179, it was held that where bricks are furnished and laid up under contract, by the thou-

sand, a local custom to estimate the number by measurement of the walls, upon a uniform rule based on the average size of bricks, and making slight additions for extra work and wastage, at points and places where they occur, is not an unreasonable custom; also, that when such contract is in writing, parol evidence of the custom does not contradict it, and may be given on the trial, although the custom is not specially pleaded; and that it is not error in such case, to instruct the jury, that if they find such custom to have been certain, uniform and generally acquiesced in, in the city where the parties resided, and where they made the contract, they may interpret the contract in the light of the custom, although the custom was of only seven years' standing, and although the plaintiff had not actual notice of its exist- . ence. A custom to deliver bills of lading only to the holders of the shipping receipts, was held to be reasonable, as tending to the protection of both the shipper and the ship owner, and evidence of it was held to be properly submitted to the jury. *Blossom* v. *Champion*, 37 Barb. (N. Y.) 554. But a custom is not legal if contrary to morality, religion and the law of the land; but is unreasonable, and therefore not compulsory. Thus in an ejectment, growing out of a disputed title to land, the claimant being a negro, born in another State, the defendant offered to prove that, in the region whence the plaintiff came, it was not customary for colored people to form legal marriages, and that the

under seal regulating the terms of the holding, but not containing stipulations as to the terms of quitting, which can exclude the custom.[2] The customary right of a tenant to the away-going crop, to compensation for work and labor, seed and materials employed in manuring, tilling and sowing the land, also the customary right of a landlord or reversioner to a heriot on the death of a tenant for life, and all customs and usages respecting the cultivation of the soil and the mode of husbandry, will impliedly prevail, if the lease is silent respecting them, and parol or oral evidence is consequently admissible to superadd the usage and customary right to the contract between the parties, such right and usage being recognized by law as incident to the subject

majority of them cohabit promiscuously, as well among free colored persons as slaves, in order to rebut the presumption of marriage and legitimacy from cohabitation. Held, that, as the testimony would have tended to establish a custom contrary to public morals and decency, the evidence was incompetent. *Holmes* v. *Johnson*, 42 Penn. St. 159. So, too, a custom is without force in opposition to a positive law. *Cranwell* v. *Fanny Fosdick*, 15 La. An. 436. Proof of particular customs to show the intent of parties in their acts or contracts, is allowable, only when the custom is so well established in the particular locality, trade, profession or business, that men transacting the business to which it relates, must be presumed to know it, and to contract in reference to it; it is therefore only in exceptional cases, that proof of an usage in one place is admissible to show its existence in another. A question to a witness, acquainted with stage business, whether "it is customary among hotel keepers to make any

difference in their charges for board, between persons employed in the stage business and others, when stages run regularly to their hotel," was held incompetent for generality, and also because it did not call for an established uniform custom, which had become the law of the business. *Walker* v. *Barron*, 6 Minn. 508. A custom in a manor, that copyholders of inheritance may without license from the lord of the manor dig and get clay from their copyhold tenements, for the purpose of making bricks to be sold by them off the manor, is good in law. *Salisbury* v. *Gladstone*, 6 H. & N. 123. A custom that underwriters are not liable, under the ordinary form of policy, for general average in respect of the jettison of goods stowed on deck, is a valid custom, and does not contradict the terms of the policy. *Miller* v. *Tetherington*, 6 H. & N. 278.

[2] *Hutton* v. *Warren*, 1 M. & W. 475, 476; Domat, liv. 1, tit. 1; Wood's Landlord and Tenant, 475-479.

matter of the contract, and consequential upon the taking of the lands.[3] The doctrine of annexing customary incidents to a lease has been recognized in several cases in this country, the lease itself being silent in respect to them. Notably is this the case in a Maryland case[4] where the doctrine of *Wigglesworth* v. *Dallison* was fully recognized and approved.[5] *But parol evidence of custom and usage is not*

[3] *Wigglesworth* v. *Dallison*, 1 Doug. 201; *Wilkins* v. *Wood*, 17 Law J. Q. B. 319.

[4] *Dorsey* v. *Eagle*, 7 H. & J. (Md.) 321.

[5] See also *Stultz* v. *Dickey*, 5 Binn. (Penn.) 285; *Foster* v. *Robinson*, 6 Ohio St. 90; also, *Stone* v. *McClay*, 1 Harr. (Del.) 520, where it was held that an incoming tenant might enter upon the demised premises under a custom to that effect before his term commenced, to fill an ice house on the premises. See, also, *Dieffendorf* v. *Jones*, 5 Binn. (Penn.) 289; *Carson* v. *Blazer*, 2 *Id.* 487. Where the term is fixed in the lease, the tenant cannot take the away-going crop under a custom. *Whitimarsh* v. *Cutting*, 10 John. (N. Y.) 360. In Pennsylvania, a custom of a particular place for a landlord to enter for breach of a condition in a manner different from that authorized by the common law, or the terms of the deed, is inadmissible. *Stoever* v. *Whitman*, 6 Binn. (Penn.) 416. The tenant's right to the away-going crop, as founded upon custom, was recognized by the Supreme Court of the United States in *Van Ness* v. *Packard*, 2 Pet. (U. S.) 137. And there it was held that a local custom in the city of Washington, for tenants to remove certain buildings erected by them, might be proved. *Id.* 148. See Woodfall's Landlord and Tenant 218; Bull. N.

P. 34. See further, Story's Confl. of Laws 226; Wood's Landlord and Tenant 474. The doctrine in the text has been recognized and acted upon in various English cases. The principal difficulty in its application has been to determine when these incidents may be regarded as excluded by the terms of the lease. The general rule seems to be, that the custom is admissible unless inconsistent with the written instrument. It need not, however, exclude it in express language, as seems to have been erroneously assumed in *Senior* v. *Armitage*. See *Hutton* v. *Warren*, 1 M. & W. 4. In *Senior* v. *Armitage*, 1 Holt's N. P. R. 197, evidence was admitted of a customary right to compensation for an away-going crop, though the instrument of demise contained an express stipulation, that all the manure made on the farm should be spent on it, or left at the end of the tenancy, without any compensation being paid. Such a stipulation certainly does not exclude, by implication, the tenant's right to receive a compensation for seed and labor. *Per curiam*, in *Hutton* v. *Warren*, *supra*. In *Webb* v. *Warren*, cited in the text, there was a claim of a customary allowance for foldage (a mode of manuring the ground), but there being an express provision for some payment on quitting, for the things covenanted to

*admitted to contradict or vary express stipulations and pro-
visions restricting or enlarging the exercise and enjoyment of*

be done, and an omission of foldage, held that the customary obligation to pay for the latter, was excluded. 2 B. & Ald. 746. In *Holding* v. *Piggott,* 7 Bing. 465, a lease contained stipulations limiting the quantity of grain that should be grown on the farm, and directing that the land should be summer-fallowed, and that the tenant should spend all the fodder, hay, straw, turnips, &c., on the premises; and held that the custom of the country, which would give the tenant a right to the away-going crop of wheat after a crop of turnips, was not excluded, though such crop had been grown in violation of the covenant to leave the land summer-fallowed. The court said these were stipulations as to the terms of holding, not as to the terms of quitting. In *Roberts* v. *Barker,* 1 C. & M. 803, the tenant claimed compensation for manure left on the farm, under a custom which bound the away-going tenant to leave the manure, and under which he was entitled to be paid for it by the landlord or the incoming tenant. The lease contained a condition, that the manure should not be sold or taken away, but should be left to be expended on the land, by the landlord or incoming tenant. *Lord Lyndhurst,* in delivering the judgment of the court that the custom of the country was excluded, said: "If the parties meant to be governed by the custom in this respect, there was no necessity for any stipulation, as, by the custom, the tenant would be bound to leave the manure, and would be entitled to be paid for it. It was altogether idle, therefore, to provide

for one part of that which was sufficiently provided for by the custom, unless it was intended to exclude the other part." *Hutton* v. *Warren,* (*supra*) was a case in which the plaintiff held under a lease of the glebe lands and tithes of a parish; the lease contained a stipulation, that the plaintiff should spend and consume three parts in four of the manure arising from the tithes, as well as from the glebe land, on the glebe, and leave on the land all the manure not spread or bestowed on the premises, for the use of the landlord, he paying a reasonable price for the same; and held that the custom of the country, giving an away-going allowance for seed and labor, was not excluded. *Parke, B.,* giving the judgment of the court, said: "The question is, whether from the terms of the lease, it can be collected that the parties intended to exclude the customary obligation for seed and labor." The court considered the stipulation, obliging the tenant to lay the manure arising from the tithes, as imposing a new obligation on the tenant, *dehors* the custom, and as qualifying the obligation by an engagement on the landlord's part to give a remuneration, by repurchasing a part of the produce in a particular way. "It is by no means," said the court, "to be inferred from this provision, that this is the only compensation which the tenant is to receive on quitting. If, indeed, there had been a covenant by the tenant to plow and sow a certain portion of the demised land in the last year, being such as the custom of the country required,

4

the customary right. Omissions may be supplied by the introduction of the custom, but the custom cannot prevail over and nullify the express provisions and stipulations of the contract.[6] If a lease, for example, contains an express provision as to the disposal of the away-going crop, or speci-

he being paid, on quitting, for the plowing; or to plow, sow and manure, he being paid for the manuring; the principle of *expressum facit cessare tacitum*, which governed the decision of *Webb* v. *Plummer*, would have applied; but this is not the case here. The custom of the country as to the obligation of the tenant to plow and sow, and the corresponding obligation of the landlord to pay for such plowing and sowing, in the last year of the term, is in no way varied. The only alteration made in the custom is, that the tenant is obliged to spend more than the produce of the farm on the premises, being paid for it in the same way as he would have been paid for that which the custom required him to spend." *Hutton* v. *Warren*, 1 M. & W. 466. In *Van Ness* v. *Packard*, 2 Pet. (U. S.) 187, proof was admitted of a usage in Washington for a tenant to remove buildings erected by him on the premises, provided they were removed before his term expired, and in *Wilcox* v. *Wood*, 9 Wend. (N. Y.) 346, it was held that proof of a local custom that a lease from May 1st of one year to May 1st of the next year, expires at noon of the last day. In *Moore* v. *Eason*, 11 Ired (N. C.) 568, where parol evidence was offered to prove a custom of a place, by which all leases expired at a certain time, it was held that the lease itself must first be proved, and then any incident to it could be proved by parol

evidence, but incidents could not be proved first, in order to establish the contract. In *Iddings* v. *Nagle*, 2 W. & S. (Penn.) 22, it was held that the right of a tenant holding under a written lease to take the straw growing upon the land, depends upon the lease itself, and cannot be varied by evidence of a custom or usage. By the custom of Pennsylvania, New Jersey and Delaware, a lessee for a term certain is entitled to the away-going crop (*i. e.*, the grain sown in the autumn, to be reaped the next harvest), though such right be not recognized in the contract; and he may enter to gather it, or may maintain trespass for it against the lessor or his vendee, after the expiration of the lease. *Stultz* v. *Dickey*, 5 Binn. (Penn.) 285; *Diffendorffer* v. *Jones*, cited 5 Binn. (Penn.) 289; 2 Binn. (Penn.) 487; *Comfort* v. *Duncan*, 1 Miles (Penn.) 231; *Biggs* v. *Brown*, 2 S. & R. (Penn.) 14; *Demi* v. *Bossler*, 1 Penn. 224; *Van Doren* v. *Everitt*, 5 N. J. L. 460; *Templeman* v. *Biddle*, 1 Harr. (Del.) 522; *Van Ness* v. *Packard*, 2 Pet. (U. S.) 148. In Delaware, where the lease is for one year, to wit, from April 1st to April 1st, the tenant is not entitled to the oat crop unless upon a special custom, which must be specially plead, and cannot be shown under the general issue. *Templeman* v. *Biddle, ante.*

[6] *Clarke* v. *Roystone*, 13 M. & W. 752; 14 Law J. Exch. 143; Taylor on Ev. p. 771; *Blackett* v. *R. Ex. Ass. Co.*, 2 C. and J. 249.

fies and regulates the particular allowances that are to be made by an incoming to an outgoing tenant, the custom in respect thereof is excluded.[7]

Usages of Trade.

SEC. 39. The known and received usage of a particular trade or profession, and the established course of every mercantile or professional dealing, are considered to be tacitly annexed to the terms of every mercantile or professional contract, if there be no words therein expressly controlling or excluding the ordinary operation of the usage, and parol evidence thereof may consequently be brought in aid of the written instrument.[8] Thus, although a bill of exchange is on the face of it payable on a day certain, yet the three additional days of grace, accorded by the known custom of merchants, are permitted to be annexed to the terms of the written instrument, and make a part of the contract. The general warranty in a policy of insurance to sail with convoy, is construed, according to the usage of merchants, to depart with convoy from the nearest customary place of rendezvous where convoys are to be had.[9] When a workman is hired for a year, to work at a particular trade, under a written agreement which says nothing as to any period of absence to be allowed to the workman, oral evidence may be given to show that it is the custom of the particular trade for the workmen employed in it to take certain holidays, and to absent themselves on such occasions from their work, without the permission of their masters.[1]

[7] Roxburghe v. Robertson, 2 Bligh. 156; Webb v. Plummer, 2 B. & Ald. 746; Roberts v. Barker, 1 C. & M. 808.
[8] Syers v. Jonas, 2 Exch. 111; Grant v. Maddox, 15 M. & W. 737; Hutton v. Warren, 1 M & W. 475; Bourne v. Gatcliffe, 3 Sc. N. R. 40; Sewall v. Gibbs, 1 Hall (N. Y.) 602; Astor v. Union Ins. Co., 7 Cow. (N. Y.) 202; Piesch v. Dixon, 1 Mas. (U. S.) 11.

[9] Lethulier's Case, 2 Salk. 443.
[1] Reg. v. Stoke-upon-Trent, 13 Law J. Q. B. 117. Usage may be resorted to where the contract contains all that is necessary to understand what the parties agreed to do, when the evidence explaining the usage is admitted. Dana v. Fiedler, 1 E. D. S. (N. Y.) 463. Where a custom exists in reference to a particular trade or

Rule in Brown v. Byrne.

SEC. 40. " In all contracts," observes Parke, B., "as to the subject-matter of which known usages prevail, parties are

business, and is shown to be *certain, uniform and notorious,* the contracts of parties engaged in the business are presumed to be made with reference to such custom, unless it is expressly excluded. *Dalton v. Daniels,* 2 Hilt. (N. Y.) 472. And it enters into the body of the contract without being inserted. *Stultz v. Dickey,* 5 Binn. (Penn.) 287, S. P.; *Lodwick v. Ohio Ins. Co.,* 5 Ohio, 436; *Sewall v. Gibbs,* 1 Hall. (N. Y.) 612; *Barber v. Brace,* 3 Conn. 9; *Bank of Columbia v. Fitzhugh,* 1 H. & G. (Md.) 289; *Haven v. Wenworth,* 2 N. H. 93; *United States v. Arredondo,* 6 Pet. (U. S.) 715; *Sampson v. Gazzam,* 6 Port. (Ala.) 123; *Inglebright v. Hammand,* 19 Ohio 337; *Hursh v. North,* 40 Penn. St. 241. The custom among the merchants of Pittsburg, of charging interest on accounts after six months, having existed for a long time, and become uniform and notorious, the courts of justice are bound to notice it as part of the law. *Watt v. Hoch,* 25 Penn. St. 411. The usage and practice of a firm, though not good as a custom, will be binding, if expressly made part of the contract, or shown to have been known and assented to by the defendant at the time; and evidence of such a contract, either direct or by proving a course of dealing between the parties, on such terms and of such frequency as to justify the inference that the transaction was on the accustomed terms, is admissible. *Hursh v. North,* 40 Penn. St. 241. However it may be as between themselves, the custom of merchants will not bind a person acting in a differ-

ent character. *Nichols v. DeWolf,* 1 R. I. 277. Evidence of the general usage of a single town is admissible. *Gleason v. Walsh,* 43 Me. 397. But a private usage, as a usage at an inn for the guests to leave their money or valuables at the bar, or with the keeper of the house, or his clerk, is not binding upon a guest, unless he has actual knowledge or notice of it; and whether he has such knowledge or notice is a question of fact for the jury. *Berkshire Woollen Co. v. Proctor,* 7 Cush. (Mass.) 417. Nor does a general custom at a particular store, for the customers to allow interest on open accounts after a certain time, have the effect of an agreement on the part of a party dealing at such store, to pay such interest, unless expressly or impliedly sanctioned by such party. *Searson v. Heyward,* 1 Spears (S. C.) 249. Nor will the custom of a creditor to compute interest on monthly rests bind his debtor, if it does not appear that the latter knew of such custom. *Goodnow v. Parsons,* 36 Vt. 46. Proof of particular customs to. show the intent of parties in their acts or contracts, is allowable only when the custom is so well established in the particular locality, trade, profession or business, that men transacting the business to which it relates must be presumed to know it, and to contract in reference to it. *Walker v. Barron,* 6 Minn. 508; *Martin v. Hall,* 26 Mo. 386; *Joyce v. Leighton,* 22 N. H. 71; *Saint v. Smith,* 1 Coldw. (Tenn.) 51. If a party to an action attempts to rebut evidence tending to show fraud on his part, by show-

found to proceed with the tacit assumption of these usages; they commonly reduce into writing the special particulars of their agreement, but omit to specify these known usages which are included, however, as of course, by mutual understanding; evidence, therefore, of such incidents is receivable. The contract, in truth, is partly express and in writing, partly implied or understood and unwritten. But the evidence received must not be of a particular which is repugnant to, or inconsistent with, the written contract."[2] "The usage," observes Wilde, C. J., "is admissible for the purpose of annexing incidents to the contract in matters upon which the contract is silent, but not to vary or contradict, either expressly or by implication, the express terms of the written instrument." Therefore, where a written memorandum of a contract for the sale of certain specified bales of wool at an ascertained price, stated that they were "to be paid for by cash in one month," it was held that the contract imported a sale upon a month's credit; that the vendor was entitled to delivery of the goods without payment of the price, and that evidence of a usage in the wool trade, that under contracts framed in similar terms, the vendors were not bound to deliver without receiving payment of the price, was inadmissible to alter the plain import of the written instrument. "We think," observes Wilde, C. J., "that the admission of the evidence would be to allow a right to be set up inconsistent with and contradictory to the terms of the contract, and to annex an incident to the subject matter, which if not expressly is clearly impliedly excluded by the contract.[3]

ing a custom or usage of trade to transact business in that manner, he must show a custom or usage *in relation to that branch* of business. *Hills* v. *Hoitt*, 18 N. H. 603. A printer of a newspaper may give evidence of a custom of the trade to continue the insertion of advertisements, when no order is given respecting the time, until directions are given to stop them. *Thomas* v. *O'Hara*, 1 Mill (S. C.) Const. 303.

[2] *Brown* v. *Byrne*, 3 Ell. & Bl. 715.
[3] *Spartali* v. *Benecke* 10 C. B. 221.

To Ascertain Meaning of Words.

SEC. 41. *Custom and usage* also influence the interpretation of contracts, and determine to a great extent the meaning of the words used therein.   If, by the known usage of trade, or by custom, a word has acquired, in respect of the subject matter of the contract, a peculiar sense and meaning different from the ordinary popular sense and meaning, parol evidence is admissible to show that the parties used the word in its customary trade acceptation, and not in the ordinary popular sense.   Thus, the word *thousand* in certain trades comprehends a larger number of units than it does in its ordinary acceptation.   In the herring trade, for example, *six* score herrings go to the hundred, and *sixty* to the thousand; and parol evidence is consequently admissible, to show that the word thousand, when applied to herrings, in the contracts of herring dealers means twelve hundred.   In a lease of a rabbit warren, parol evidence was admitted to show that by the custom of the country where the lease was made, in taking an account of the rabbits on a rabbit warren, the numbers were computed at one hundred dozen to a thousand, and the word *thousand* in a lease as applied to rabbits was consequently construed to mean one hundred dozen or twelve hundred.[4]   So, where an insurance was effected " to

---

[4] *Smith* v. *Wilson*, 3 B. & Ad. 728. The meaning of the words "in turn to deliver" in a charter party. *Robertson* v. *Jackson*, 2 C. B. 412. Also, "in regular turns of loading," may be explained by usage. *Schultz* v. *Leidman*, 14 C. B. 38. But in *Hudson* v. *Clementson*, 8 *Id.* 213, it was held that a custom showing that the defendant was excused from loading a vessel in regular turn, because his turn was to be determined by a party not named in the contract, was not admissible. The phrase, "mystery and art of tanning business," in an indenture of apprenticeship, will in-

clude the art of currying, or not, according to the general sense of the place where it is used; in Kentucky the *tanning business* includes, it seems, the entire process of making leather. *Barger* v. *Caldwell*, 2 Dana (Ky.) 130, 131. The force of usage is most fully illustrated by the cases relating to the construction of bills of lading, charter parties, policies of insurance and other contracts of a commercial nature. Parol evidence was held admissible to show that, by mercantile usage, the term *roots*, in a policy of insurance, is confined to such as are perishable

any port in the Baltic," evidence was admitted to show that

in their nature; and that, therefore, *sarsaparilla* not being perishable in this sense, though a *root* within the general meaning of the term, was not embraced by the memorandum in the policy. *Coit* v. *The Commercial Insurance Co.*, 7 John. (N. Y.) 385. The term *sea letter*, contained in a policy, may be shown by mercantile usage to mean " certificate of ownership." *Sleight* v. *Hartshorne*, 2 John. (N. Y.) 531. Whether the term " cargo," in a policy of insurance shall embrace *live stock*, may be settled by usage among insurance companies. *Allegre's Adm'r* v. *The Maryland Insurance Co.*, 2 G. & J. (Md.) 136. See *Chesapeake Insurance Co.* v. *Allegre*, *Id.* 164. Where a policy provided that in case of loss, the same was to be paid in in ninety days after "*proof and adjustment thereof;*" held, that parol evidence, showing what papers were by usage to be furnished to the insurers as proof under such a provision, was admissible. *Allegre* v. *The Maryland Insurance Co.*, 6 H. & J. (Md.) 408. An insurance was affected on a ship at London, insuring the ship from thence to the East Indies, the ship warranted to depart with convoy. It was shown that the ship went from London to the Downs, and from there with convoy, and was lost. The defendant insisted that there had been a breach of the warranty by departing from London without convoy. The clause "warranted to depart without convoy," must be construed according to the usage among merchants—*i. e.*, from such places where convoys are to be had, as the *Downs*. *Lethulier's Case*, 2 Salk. 443; see also 24 N. Y. 302; 22

N. Y. 37. If any terms in a policy of insurance have, by the known usage of trade, or by use and practice, as between insurers and insured, acquired an appropriate sense, they are to be construed accordingly. *Coit* v. *Com. Ins. Co.*, 7 Johns. (N. Y.) 385. To the same effect, 1 Duer. on Ins., 181, 196; 1 Phill. on Ins. 489; *Child* v. *Sun Mutual Ins. Co.*, 3 Sandf. (N. Y.) 26. So held in the case of an offer to show a usage that the word roots, in policies of insurance, was confined to such roots as are perishable in their own nature. *Coit* v. *Commercial Ins. Co.*, 7 Johns. (N. Y.) 385. Also of a usage that taking sea-elephants was within the scope of a "whaling voyage." *Child* v. *Sun Mutual Ins. Co.*, 3 Sandf. (N. Y.) 26. So where the words of an ancient deed are equivocal, the usage of the parties, under the deed, is admissible to explain them. 2 Inst. 282. Thus, where the deed gave the grantee the privilege of cutting timber for *building* on the premises, from the woods of the grantor, evidence of usage, with the knowledge of the grantor and his heirs, to cut timber for fencing, was held admissible to show the intention of the parties to apply the word "building" to the making of fences. *Livingston* v. *Ten Broeck*, 16 Johns. (N. Y.) 14. But where the language of a deed is unambiguous, clear and pertinent, it cannot be controlled by a different exposition derived from any usage under it. *Cortleyou* v. *Van Brandt*, 2 Johns. (N. Y.) 357; *Parsons* v. *Miller*, 15 Wend. (N. Y.) 561. Where a positive statute has declared the legal signification of a word, in reference to its use in con-

the Gulf of Finland was considered, by universal custom and

tracts generally, evidence of usage or custom is inadmissible to give the word a different meaning, but a court of equity may reform the contract. *Many* v. *Beekman Iron Co.*, 9 Paige Ch. (N Y.) 188. Various expressions in bills of lading are to be understood in reference to particular usage. A *clean bill of lading*, which imports that the goods are to be stowed *under deck*, may be construed to allow a stowage *upon deck*, or otherwise, according to the usage between the places contemplated by the contract as the *termini* of the voyage. *Cherry* v. *Holly*, 14 Wend. (N. Y.) 26; *Barber* v. *Brace*, 3 Conn. R. 9. So usage may authorize what might otherwise be considered a deviation in respect to the voyage. See *Lawrence* v. *McGregor*, 37 Penn. St. 193. But evidence of intent, as an independent fact, by declarations, &c., &c., would not be admissible; for the intent must be sought in the language of the bill of lading. See *Cherry* v. *Holly, Barber* v. *Brace*, and *Lawrence* v. *McGregor, supra ;* except so far as it is to be deemed a mere receipt. See *Wood* v. *Perry*, 37 Penn. St. 240. See also *Barrett* v. *Rogers*, 7 Mass. 297; *May* v. *Babcock*, 4 Ham. (Ohio) 334. The question whether a local usage might be resorted to, to show that the ordinary exception as to *perils of the seas*, in a bill of lading, would include an injury by rats, arose in *Aymer* v. *Astor*, 6 Cow. (N. Y.) 663. *Savage, C. J.*, expressed a very decided opinion in the affirmative. The other judges dissented, though upon what precise ground does not appear. In the case of *The Schooner Reeside*, 2 Sumn. (U. S.) 567, the bill of lading specified that the

goods were "to be delivered in good order and condition, dangers of the seas only excepted ;" and the point was, whether a local usage between New York and Boston (the *termini* of the voyage), might be admitted to influence the contract so far as to exempt the carriers from liability for all damages save what arose from their own neglect. Mr. *Justice Story* excluded the usage, on the ground that, if admitted, it would go, not to *interpret* or *explain*, but to *vary* and *contradict* the contract. The same doctrine was held in *Turney* v. *Wilson*, 7 Yerg. (Tenn.) 340. Evidence of a usage among coal shippers has been admitted to show what is meant by "immediate delivery," and to show that it means a delivery in some cases during the present month, and in some cases during the succeeding month. *Neldon* v. *Smith*, 36 N. J. L. 148. As to the requisites of such usage see *Schenck* v. *Griffen*, 38 *Id.* 463; *Stewart* v. *Scudder*, 34 *Id.* When a custom is in derogation of the common law, it must be clearly proved, and in order to apply it in a given case the case must clearly be brought within it. *Overman* v. *Hoboken Bank*, 30 N. J. L. 61; also, 32 *Id.* 563. Evidence is admissible of a well settled usage by which the words "store fixtures," in a policy of insurance, are applied to all furniture and other articles in a shop or warehouse necessary or convenient for use in the course of trade. *Whitmarsh* v. *Conway F. Ins. Co.*, 16 Gray (Mass.) 359. The phrase "British weight," in a charter party, may mean *gross weight*, or *net weight;* and evidence of usage is admissible to show which was meant. *God-*

consent amongst merchants and in mercantile contracts, to

dard v. *Bulow*, 1 N. & M. (S. C.) 45. It was expressly laid down in *Taylor* v. *Briggs*, 2 C. & P. 5˙5, that if the words "cotton in bales," used in a charter party, had acquired a particular meaning in regard to the trade between Liverpool and Alexandria, to which trade the instrument related, such meaning should apply. Various other phrases and expressions may be applied differently, according to the subject-matter, and the particular usage in reference to it, existing at the time of the contract; thus, what shall constitute a good delivery of goods at a particular place, no consignee being named, may depend upon the usage in that place. See *Galloway* v. *Hughes*, 1 Bail. (S. C.) 553. And see, as to the meaning of the term "deliver," *Furniss* v. *Hone*, 8 Wend. (N. Y.) 247. The term "coppered ship," in a written application for insurance, may have different meanings according to the usage at different places. *Hazzard* v. *The New England Marine Ins. Co.*, 1 Sum. (U. S.) 218. In *Bold* v. *Rayner*, 1 M. & W. 343, evidence of mercantile usage was admitted, that a bought note of goods to be delivered from "the Speedy or Charlotte, expected to arrive"—and a sold note of the goods "ex Speedy and Charlotte to arrive"—meant the same thing, and that the seller had the option to deliver the goods from either vessel. For other cases of usage relative to mercantile contracts, see the text: also, *Gabay* v. *Lloyd*, 3 Barn. & Cress. 793; *Blackett* v. *Royal Exchange Assurance Co.*, 2 Cromp. & J. 249. Bills of exchange and notes are no exceptions to the rule in regard to

usage. See note to *Yeates* v. *Pim*, 1 Holt 95. Accordingly, a custom among banks in the District of Columbia, to demand payment on the *fourth* day after a note became due, was allowed to be shown in an action against an endorser, and he was held liable, though by the settled rules of the common law, he would have been discharged by reason of failure to make demand on the third day. *Renner* v. *Bank of Columbia*, 9 Wheat. (U. S.) 581. See also *Bank of Columbia* v. *Magruder*, 6 H. & J. (Md.) 172, 180; *Bank of Washington* v. *Triplett*, 1 Pet. (U. S.) 25; *Mills* v. *United States Bank*, 11 Wheat. (U. S.) 431. See further as to usages at particular banks, *Kennebeck Bank* v. *Page*, 9 Mass. 155; *Kennebeck Bank* v. *Hammatt*, *Id.* 159; *Widgery* v. *Monroe*, 6 *Id.* 449; *Weld* v. *Gorham*, 10 *Id.* 366; *Blanchard* v. *Hilliard*, 11 *Id.* 85; *Wentworth* v. *Chase*, *Id.* 87, note; *Leavitt* v. *Simes*, 3 N. H. 14; *Bank of Utica* v. *Smith*, 18 John. (N. Y.) 230; *Loring* v. *Gurney*, 5 Pick. (Mass.) 16. But see *Woodruff* v. *The Merchants Bank of the City of New York*, 25 Wend. (N. Y.) 673, in which evidence was received at the trial of a usage and custom of merchants in the city of New York, that a draft upon the cashier of a bank, payable to order, and by him accepted, was a *check*, and not entitled to the days of grace allowed on promissory notes and bills of exchange. On a motion for a new trial, it was held that the evidence should not have been received. The court said, that "the effect of proof of usage, as given in this case, if sanctioned, would be to overturn the whole law on the subject of bills of exchange in the city

be within the Baltic, though the two seas were treated as distinct by geographers.[5] And in a lease of a coal mine evidence was admitted to show that the word *level* in mining districts had a meaning different from the ordinary popular meaning, and that the word was used by the parties to the

of New York. We need scarcely add, even if the witnesses were not mistaken, and the usage prevails there, as testified to, *it cannot be allowed to control the settled and acknowledged law of the state in respect to the description of paper."* And see the same case in 6 Hill (N. Y.) 174, in the Court of Errors, where the judgment of the Supreme Court was affirmed. See *Bowen* v. *Newell,* 8 (N. Y.) 190. In respect to the quality or character of a usage, admissible to influence the construction of a contract of any sort, for the rule in this respect seems to be the same whether the contract be written or verbal, sealed or unsealed, it must appear to be so well settled, so uniformly acted upon, and of so long a continuance, as to raise a fair presumption that it was known to both contracting parties, and that they contracted in reference to, and in conformity with it. See the cases *supra;* also, *Eager* v. *The Atlas Ins. Co.,* 14 Pick. (Mass.) 143, 144, per *Wilde, J.; Snowden* v. *Warder,* 3 Rawle (Penn.) 101, 107; *Smith* v. *Wright,* 1 Cain. R. 44; *Van Ness* v. *Pacard,* 2 Pet. 148; *Loring* v. *Gurney,* 5 Pick. 16; *Renner* v. *Bank of Columbia,* 9 Wheat. 581, *et seq.; Lawrence* v. *M'Gregor,* 37 Penn. St. 192; *Kendall* v. *Russell,* 5 Dana (Ky.) 501; *Barksdale* v. *Brown,* 1 N. & M. (S. C.) 517; *Barber* v. *Brace,* 3 Conn. 9; *Lawrence* v. *Stonington Bank,* 6 Conn. 529; *Paull* v. *Lewis,* 4 Watts 402; *Thomas* v. *O'Hara,* 1 Rep. Const. Ct.

(S. C.) 308; *Collins* v. *Hope,* 3 Wash. (U. S.) 149; *Hayward* v. *Middleton,* 3 McCord 121. And whether such is the case with regard to the usage in question, must generally be tried like other matters of fact, by the jury, if there be one. See *Heald* v. *Cooper,* 8 Mc. 33; *Williams* v. *Gilman,* 3 Id. 276; *Rushford* v. *Hatfield,* 7 East 224; *Gibson* v. *Culver,* 17 Wend. 306; *Van Ness* v. *Pacard, supra.* The usage need not be general, *i. e.,* extending over the whole country. It will be seen by the cases already cited, that usages of particular classes, and peculiar to certain localites, have been freely received. Many of the cases cited *infra* will be found full to this point. Indeed, the doctrine extends to the admission of usage at individual houses and offices, provided the usage is brought home to the knowledge of the parties in some way, so as to establish that they contracted in reference to it. See *Gabay* v. *Lloyd,* 3 B. & C. 793. And see the cases *supra* as to usages at banks. *Wood* v. *Hikock,* 2 Wend. 501. Its *antiquity,* moreover, is of no importance, further than as a circumstance in aid of the main point, which is to show that the parties knew of the usage and intended to adopt it as the law of their contract. *Per Cur.* in *Thompson* v. *Hamilton,* 12 Pick. 425, 428, 429; *Kendall* v. *Russell,* 5 Dana 503.

[5] *Uhde* v. *Walters,* 3 Camp. 16. See also *Brough* v. *Whitmore,* 4 T. R. 210; *Anderson* v. *Pitcher,* 2 B. & P. 168.

contract in the sense in which it is ordinarily employed by miners.[6]   But the custom and usage must be general and universal, and not the practice or course of dealing of a particular firm or house of trade.[7]

As to Terms of Art, &c.

SEC. 42. The meaning of all words and terms of art, and specifications of quantity, quality, weight and measure, are regulated and controlled by local custom, unless the terms have been selected, and a definite meaning given to them by the legislature.[8]   Evidence of general usage, in the trade to which the contract refers, is admissible to give a particular and peculiar sense to the words employed, as the parties may be presumed to have contracted in conformity with the custom, and to have used the words in their customary trade acceptation.   A memorandum of a contract of sale was in the terms following: "Sold Mr. W. S. 18 pockets of Kent hops, at 100s.;" and it was held that oral evidence was admissible to show that, by the usage of trade, a contract so worded was understood to mean £5 per cwt., and that the hops consequently were to be weighed, and the price ascertained, according to the weight of the article, and that the 100s. was not to be paid per pocket, without reference to the weight of the contents of such pocket.[9]   But to vary the meaning of plain words, the existence of the custom must be "clear, cogent and irresistible."   Two witnesses stated that the usual practice of the trade to Sydney was to consider steerage passengers as "cargo," and their passage money as "freight;" but could give no instances of such construction

[6] *Clayton* v. *Gregson,* 5 Ad. & E 302; *Hunt* v. *Otis Company,* 4 Met. (Mass.) 464; *Batterman* v. *Pierce,* 3 Hill (N. Y.) 174; *Parrot* v. *Thatcher,* 9 Pick. (Mass.) 426; *Collins* v. *Hope,* 3 Wash. (U. S.) C. C. 149; *Trott* v. *Wood,* 1 Gall. (U. S.) 443; *Dawson* v. *Kettle,* 4 Hill (N. Y.) 107.

[7] *Gabay* v. *Lloyd,* 3 B. & C. 797. [8] *Taylor* v. *Briggs,* 2 C. & P. 525; *Hutchinson* v. *Bowker,* 5 M. & W. 535. [9] See *Eyre* v. *Marine Ins. Co.,* 5 W. & S. (Penn.) 116; *Allegre* v. *Maryland Ins. Co.* 2 G. & J. (Mass.) 136; *Macy* v. *Whaling Ins. Co.,* 9 Metc. 354; *Spicer* v. *Cooper,* 1 Q. B. 424.

within their own knowledge, and it was held that the evidence was insufficient to establish a usage of trade, so as to vary the *prima facie* meaning of the words cargo and freight in a written contract.[1] A usage of trade can never be set up in contravention of a statute, or in opposition to a plain and clearly expressed intention. If there are peculiar expressions used in a contract or lease, which have in a particular place or trade a known meaning attached to them, it is for the jury to say what the meaning of those expressions was, but for the court to decide what the meaning of the contract is.[2] The import and meaning of words at length cannot be contradicted or altered by figures. Where the figures and words of a bill of exchange or a promissory note, for example, disagree, the courts will give force to the words at length, in preference to the figures, for the reason assigned by Marius, "because a man is more apt to commit an error with his pen in writing a figure than he is in writing a word."

Rule in Wigglesworth v. Dallison.

Sec. 43. In the leading case upon this branch of our subject (*Wigglesworth* v. *Dallison*)(i), which was an action of trespass for moving, carrying away and converting to the defendant's own use the corn of the plaintiff, growing in a farm, in the county of Lincoln, of which the plaintiff had been the tenant, it was pleaded by way of replication that within the parish of Hibaldstow, wherein the farm was situated, "there now is, and from time whereof the memory of man is not to the contrary, there hath been, a certain ancient and laudable custom there used and approved of, that is to say, that every tenant and farmer of any lands within the same parish for any term of years which hath expired on the first day of May in any year, hath been used

---

[1] *Lewis* v. *Marshall,* 13 Law J. C. P. 542; 8 ib. 823; *Trueman* v. *Loder,* 11
193.   Ad. & E. 599; *Sotilichos* v. *Kemp,* 3
[2] *Hutchinson* v. *Bowker,* 5 M. & W. Exch. 105.

(i) 1 Dougl. 207; 1 Smith's Lea. Cas. (sixth ed.) 539.

and accustomed, and of right ought to have, take and enjoy to his own use, and to reap, cut and carry away, when ripe and fit to be reaped and taken away, his 'way-going crop ; that is to say, all the corn growing upon the said lands, which hath before the expiration of such term been sown by such tenant upon any part of such lands not exceeding a reasonable quantity thereof in proportion to the residue of such lands, according to the course and usage of husbandry in the same parish, and which hath been left standing and growing upon such lands at the expiration of such term of years." The jury found the custom in the words stated. An arrest of judgment was afterwards moved, on the ground that such a custom was repugnant to the terms of the deed ; and a rule to show cause was granted, and three objections were urged on behalf of the defendants : 1. That the custom was unreasonable ; 2. That it was uncertain ; 3. That it was repugnant to the deed under which the plaintiff had held. There Lord Mansfield held that the custom was good, and said : " It is just, for he who sows ought to reap, and it is for the benefit and encouragement of agriculture. It is, indeed, against the general rule of law concerning emblements which are not allowed to tenants who know when their term is to cease, because it is held to be their fault or folly to have sown when they knew their interest would expire before they could reap.(k) But the custom of a particular place may rectify what otherwise would be imprudence or folly."(l)

Custom as to Course of Husbandry.

SEC. 44. In the case of *Dalby* v. *Hunt*,(m) which is next,

(k) See 14 & 15 Vict. c. 25, which gives the tenant a right to occupy until the end of the current year of his tenancy, in lieu of emblements.

(l) *Beaven* v. *Delahay*, 1 H. Bl. 5; *Boraston* v. *Green*, 16 East 71; *Caldecott* v. *Smithies*, 7 C. & P. 108; *Griffiths* v. *Puleston*, 13 M. & W. 358.

(m) 1 B. & B. 224; see also *Roberts* v. *Baker*, 1 Cr. & M. 808, where the question was whether a covenant in a lease whereby the tenant bound himself not, on quitting the land, to sell or take away the manure, but to leave it to be expended by the succeeding tenant, excluded the custom

in point of time, to that just referred to, a usage for the off-going tenant of a farm in a particular district to bestow his work, labor and expense in manuring, tilling, fallowing and sowing, according to the course of husbandry, and for the landlord to pay him a reasonable compensation in respect thereof, was held a valid and reasonable custom.(n)

Where Lease is Silent as to Time—Custom as to Allowance for Seeds—Stipulation in Lease.

SEC. 45. Again, in another case, it was held that, although the express terms of a lease cannot be controlled by the custom of the country, if the lease is entirely silent as to the time of quitting, evidence of the custom of the country may be given to fix the time.(o)   These cases indicate under what circumstances a custom may be proved to explain, vary or extend a written agreement; but the whole subject was so admirably dealt with by Baron Parke, in delivering the judgment of the Court of Exchequer in the case of *Hutton* v. *Warren*,(p) that we make no apology for using his clear words in this place.   In that case it was decided that a custom of the country, by which the tenant of a farm, cultivating it according to the course of good husbandry, is entitled on quitting to receive from the landlord or incoming tenant a reasonable allowance for seeds that are bestowed on the arable land in the last year of the tenancy, and is bound to leave the manure for the landlord if he will purchase it, was held

of the country, by which the out-going tenant was bound to leave the manure and was entitled to be paid for it. The court held that it did. In that case Lord Lyndhurst said : "It was contended that the stipulation to leave the manure was not inconsistent with the tenant's being paid for what was so left, and that the custom to pay for the manure might be engrafted on the engagement to leave it. But if the parties meant to be governed by the custom in this respect there was no necessity for any stipulation, as, by custom, the tenant would be bound to leave the manure, and would be entitled to be paid for it. It was altogether idle therefore to provide for one part of that which was sufficiently provided for by the custom unless it was intended to exclude the other part."

(n) 3 Moore, 536; 1 B. & B. 224.

(o) *Webb* v. *Plummer*, 2 B. & A. 746.

(p) 1 M. & W. 466; 2 Gale 71.

not to be excluded by a stipulation in the lease under which he held, that he will consume three-fourths of the hay and straw on the farm, and spread the manure arising therefrom, and leave such of it as shall not be so spread on the land for the use of the landlord on receiving a reasonable price for it.

As to Commercial Transactions—Principle of Admission of Custom—The Policy of This.

SEC. 46. In the course of his judgment the learned judge said :(q) " It has long been settled, that, in commercial transactions, extrinsic evidence of custom and usage is admissible to annex incidents to written contracts, in matters with respect to which they are silent.(r) The same rule has also been

(q) 1 M. & W. at p. 475.

(r) Evidence of usage and custom cannot be admitted to vary or control the express terms of a contract, but they may be admitted to determine that which, by the contract, is left undetermined. And the custom must be of such antiquity, extent and universality as to warrant the conclusion that it was known to the contracting parties, and that they made their contract with reference to it. *Dixon* v. *Dunham*, 14 Ill. 324. By antiquity, it is not meant that the usage must have existed for a period requisite to give it the character of a custom, but that it should have existed long enough to engraft itself as an incident upon the trade, business or matter to which it relates. Thus, where there is a contract for the delivery of shingles by the thousand, it may be shown that, by the general, well-established, and known custom of the trade, two bundles of a certain size represent a thousand; and when such custom is shown, the parties will be presumed to have contracted with reference to it. *Soutier* v. *Kellerman*,

18 Mo. 509. The usage must have existed long enough to warrant a presumption that it was known to those engaged in the trade. The more ancient the usage, the stronger is the presumption that it has entered into a given contract. *Townsend* v. *Whitby*, 5 Harr. (Del.) 55. That is, the value of a usage is largely regulated by the length of its existence. The rule as generally expressed is that, to make a usage obligatory it must have existed for such a period that it is generally known in the business to which it relates, and must be certain, uniform and reasonable. *Collins* v. *Hope*, 3 Wash. (Va.) 150; *Rapp* v. *Palmer*, 3 Watts (Pa.) 178; *Thomas* v. *Graves*, 1 Mill (S. C.) Const. 308; *Thomas* v. *O'Hara*, Id. 303; *Chastain* v. *Bowman*, 1 Hill (N. Y.) 270; *Trott* v. *Wood*, 1 Gall. (U. S.) 443; *Lewis* v. *Thatcher*, 15 Mass. 433; *United States* v. *Duval*, Gilp. (U. S.) 356; *Barksdale* v. *Brown*, 1 Nott & M. (S. C.) 519; *Buck* v. *Grimshaw*, 1 Edw. Ch. (N. Y.) 147; *Smith* v. *Wright*, 1 Cai. (N. Y.) 45; *Somerby* v. *Thompson*, Wright (Ohio) 573; *Consequa* v. *Willings*, Pet.

applied to contracts in other transactions in life in which
known usages have been established and prevailed, and this

(U. S.) C. Ct. 230; *Touro* v. *Cassin*, 1
Nott & M. (S. C.) 176; *Davis* v. *New
Brig*, Gilp. (U. S.) 486; *Harper* v.
Pound, 10 Ind. 32; *Foley* v. *Mason*,
6 Md. 37; *Register* v. *Spencer*, 24 Md.
520; *Shackelford* v. *New Orleans, &c.,
R. R. Co*, 37 Miss. 202; *Smith* v.
Gibbs, 44 N. H. 335. A usage *may*
be proved, though not ancient or
general. *Townsend* v. *Whitby*, 5 Harr.
(Del.) 55. Such evidence cannot be
admitted to explain a contract when
no ambiguity exists. *Wadsworth* v.
Aleott, 6 N. Y. 64. Nor if it is local
and confined to a small part of the
country in which the party sought
to or charged by it did not reside,
and about which there was nothing
to put him on inquiry. *Latimer* v.
Alexander, 14 Ga. 259. Although
custom or usage will not be admitted
to contradict a stipulation in writing,
it is admissible to add new terms
not expressed in or covered by the
writing. *Alabama and Tennessee
Rivers R. R.* v. *Kidd*, 29 Ala. 221.
An isolated instance is not sufficient
to prove a custom, nor will evidence of the custom of one person
be sufficient to establish a general
course of trade. *Burr* v. *Sickles*, 17
Ark. 428. But it may enter into and
become a part of the law of trade, or
the law be applied to the transactions of parties contracting and
doing business in view of, and in
reference to, such usage. *Power* v.
Kane, 5 Wis. 265. But in order to
establish a usage as affecting a contract, the party claiming the benefit
of it must show that it is so general
and well established that the parties
or all persons dealing in the business
to which it applies are presumed to

have knowledge of it, and to contract in reference to it. *Martin* v.
Hall, 26 Mo. 386. And a usage (not
commercial) to influence the meaning of plain words, not technical, in
a written contract, must be long
continued, uniform and generally
known; probably it should not be
confined to a county, but should be
shown to extend over the State.
Harper v. *Pound*, 10 Ind. 32. And
the fact that the words of themselves
are susceptible of an interpretation
apparently consistent with the intention of the parties, does not exclude
such proof. If the words are shown
to have acquired a well-known technical meaning, that will be taken to
be the sense in which they were
used. Thus in replevin for marble
retained by the carrier for the costs
of transportation, the question in
dispute was, whether marble in slabs
was wrought or unwrought, the
charge for the former being more
than for the latter. Evidence being
heard, the court instructed the jury
"that the terms wrought and unwrought, as applied to marble, are
words of doubtful signification, and
it was competent for the plaintiff to
show what meaning is given to them
by custom and usage; that such
custom, in order to bind the defendant, need not be universal, settled or
uniform among dealers and carriers.
If the jury believe from the evidence
that the generally prevailing usage
among manufacturers, dealers and
carriers, is to class and consider
marble in slabs as unwrought, then
the defendant can claim freight on
it only as of that class." It was
held that the jury were properly

has been done upon the principle of presumption that, in such transactions, the parties did not mean to express in writing the whole of the contract by which they intended to be bound, but to contract with reference to those known usages. (s) Whether such a relaxation of the strictness of

instructed. *Bancroft* v. *Peters*, 4 Mich. 619. Where, in the absence of any statutory provision, a rule of commercial law has been adopted, by the court of last resort, in a State, the usage will thenceforth be held to conform thereto, throughout the State, and this can only be rebutted by clear proof of a uniform and settled local usage to the contrary. *Isham* v. *Fox*, 7 Ohio St. 317. *Bank of Columbia* v. *Fitzhugh*, 1 H. & G. (Md) 289; *Branch* v. *Burnley*, 1 Cal. (Va.) 159; *Consequa* v. *Willing*, 1 Pet. (U. S. C. C.) 230. The custom and understanding of the merchants in a particular trade, cannot be received in evidence, to vary well-established rules of law applicable to their transactions in it; and hence, cannot be admitted to prove that the barter or exchange of a promissory note, endorsed without recourse, for cotton or any other species of merchandise, carries with it no implied warranty of the past or future solvency of the maker of the note. *Beckwith* v. *Farnum*, 5 R. I. 230.

(s) See *Gibson* v. *Small*, 4 H. of L. Cas. 397, *per* Parke, B. The general rule, that a contract complete on its face, in all its parts and purporting to be the exclusive expositor of the sense of the parties, shall not receive additions from parol evidence, is subject to the exception that a well-known and well-established usage may be shown to add incidents thereto, that are not inconsistent with the express terms of the con-

tract. *Dixon* v. *Dunham*, 13 Ill. 324; *Cooper* v. *Kane*, 19 Wend. (N. Y.) 386; *Leach* v. *Beardslee*, 22 Conn. 404; *Alabama R. R. Co.* v. *Kidd*, 29 Ala. 221, and as tending to show the nature of the contract and the real intention of the parties thereto. *Naylor* v. *Semmes*, 4 G. & J. (Md.) 274; *Loring* v. *Gurney*, 5 Pick. (Mass.) 15; *Thompson* v. *Hamilton*, 12 *Id.* 425, and the manner in which the business was done. *Fox* v. *Parker*, 44 Barb. (N. Y.) 541. This rule is predicated upon the principle of presumption that the parties did not mean to express the whole of the contract in writing by which they intended to be bound, but made their contract in reference to the usage, and in such cases the usage is as much a part of the contract as though it had actually been incorporated therein. *Pamer* v. *Kane*, 5 Wis. 265; *Hursh* v. *North*, 40 Penn. St. 241; *Stultz* v. *Dickey*, 5 Binn. (Penn.) 287; *Boorman* v. *Johnson*, 12 Wend. (N. Y.) 574; *Barber* v. *Brace*, 3 Conn. 9; *Ladwick* v. *Ohio Ins. Co.*, 5 Ohio 436; *Inglebright* v. *Hammond*, 19 Ohio 337; *Lampoon* v. *Gazzam*, 6 Port. (Ala.) 123; *Munn* v. *Burch*, 25 Ill. 35; *Sewall* v. *Gibbs*, 1 Hall (N. Y.) 612; *United States* v. *Arredondo*, 6 Pet. (U. S.) 715; *Bank of Columbia* v. *Fitzhugh*, 1 H. & G. (Md.) 239. This rule, however, must be understood as applying only in those cases where the usage is well established, certain, uniform and reasonable. *Wheeler* v. *Newbold*, 5 Ducr. (N. Y.)

5

the common law was wisely applied where formal instruments have been entered into, and particularly leases under seal,

29; *Sipperly* v. *Steward*, 50 Barb. (N. Y.) 62; *Martin* v. *Maynard*, 16 N. H. 165; *Haven* v. *Wentworth*, 2 Id. 93; *Dugnid* v. *Edwards*, 50 Barb. (N. Y.) 287; *Kendall* v. *Russell*, 5 Dana (Ky.) 501; *Stevens* v. *Reeves*, 9 Pick. (Mass.) 198; *Watt* v. *Haek*, 25 Penn. St. 411; *Searson* v. *Heymand*, 1 Spears, (S. C.) 249; *Goodnow* v. *Parsons*, 36 W. 46; *Clanmorgan* v. *Guisse*, 1 Mo. 141. A good illustration of this rule is to be found in the commercial usage by which grace is allowed upon a note or bill of exchange payable at a day certain. Thus, a note is made payable in *sixty* days from its date, commercial usage steps in and postpones the payment for three days, making it payable only until after the lapse of *sixty-three* days, and, in cases where this usage applies, so effective is it that a suit brought or protest made before the lapse of sixty-three days, is entirely inoperative. In these cases, the parties are supposed to contract in reference to the law as it exists at the time, and the only difference between taking that and a custom is that the latter is a binding law on particular persons, places and things; and, although there are some exceptions, yet in many cases the maxim *expressum facit. cessare tacitum*, applies as well to an *incident* sought to be annexed to a contract by the general law, as by a special custom. *Cherry* v. *Holly*, 14 Wend. (N. Y.) 26; *Boorman* v. *Johnson*, 12 Id. 566; *Barber* v. *Brace*, 3 Conn. 9; *Wilcox* v. *Wood*, 9 Wend. (N. Y.) 349; *Lawrence* v. *McGregor*, 37 Penn. St. 192; *Daggett* v. *Snowden*, 2 Black (U. S.) 225; *Heald* v. *Cooper*, 8 Me.

32; *Dana* v. *Fielder*, 1 E. D. S. (N. Y. C. P.) 463; *Crosby* v. *Wyatt*, 23 Me. 156; *Avery* v. *Stewart*, 2 Conn. O. G. As previously stated, a usage, in order to be incorporated in a contract, must not be impliedly excluded thereby, and moreover it must be uniform and general. Thus, an agreement to endorse any paper which W. may give " for purchases made " does not cover a claim for labor performed in rolling iron which had been so purchased to prepare it to be manufactured in a wire mill, unless a general usage is proved to include such labor under that term ; and evidence that in contracts of the kind in controversy, made for supplying a wire mill, such labor, according to the well-understood and general usage of the business, is a purchase, does not show a use so general as to justify the assumption that parties guaranteeing the payment of purchases intended to become liable for charges for such labor. *Schlessinger* v. *Dickinson*, 5 Allen (Mass.) 47. A written contract for the manufacture of iron articles as retorts cannot be affected by proof of a custom that, in the absence of an express agreement, founders shall not be held to warrant their castings against latent defects; or that, in case of apparent defects, they shall be entitled to have castings returned to them within a reasonable time, and to replace them with new ones. *Whitmore* v. *South Boston Iron Co.*, 2 Id. 52. And it is generally held that such usage must not conflict with the rules of law. Thus, a usage that when manufactured goods are sold

may well be doubted; but the contrary has been established by such authority, and the relations between landlord and tenant have been so long regulated upon the supposition that all customary obligations not altered by the contract are to remain in force that it is too late to pursue a contrary course, and it would be productive of much inconvenience if this practice were now to be disturbed.(*t*)

by sample, and both the goods and the sample have a latent defect which cannot be discovered by ordinary care by the purchaser, which defect when discovered makes the goods unmerchantable, except as damaged goods, the seller is to make good to the purchaser the damage occasioned by such defect, is not valid, being in conflict with the law in such cases. *Dickinson* v. *Gay*, 7 Allen (Mass.) 29. The same rule has also been held as to a custom or usage that goods sold shall be of such a quality as to be approved by the buyer or a public inspector, is an implied warranty or stipulation as to quality, and therefore contrary to the rule of law that in a contract of sale there is no such implied warranty. *Boardman* v. *Spooner*, 13 *Id.* 360. So as to the power of an agent or factor. Thus, a merchandise broker can have no implied authority, from the usage of trade, to warrant goods sold by him to be of merchantable quality; and evidence to prove such usage is inadmissible; and a memorandum made by such broker of a contract for the sale of goods is invalid and inadmissible in evidence, if he has inserted therein, without express authority, a warranty by the seller that they are of merchantable quality. *Dodd* v. *Farlow*, 11 Allen (Mass.) 426.

(*t*) A custom may be proved that

upon a sale of berries in bags by sample, the sample represents the average quality of the entire lot. *Schnitzer* v. *Oriental Paint Works*, 114 Mass. 123. But evidence is not admissible that by a local custom of merchants, not shown to be known to the buyer, there is an implied warranty that goods are not falsely or deceitfully packed. *Barnard* v. *Kellogg*, 10 Wall. 383; and see the American note to *Wigglesworth* v. *Dallison*, 1 Sm. Lead. Cas. Nor can a custom be proved limiting the time of the purchaser to examine and return the goods, unless the custom is so uniform and notorious that it must be presumed that the parties contracted in view of it. *Webster* v. *Granger*, 78 Ill. 230. In *Sturges* v. *Buckley*, 32 Conn. 265, the effect of a usage or custom of a trade, in overcoming an implied contract, was well illustrated. In that case the defendant was engaged in the business of forwarding farmers' produce by a railroad running into New York, and selling it on commission. He took of the plaintiff a quantity of cider in barrels, disposed of it with the barrels, and returned other barrels, equal in number and value. These the plaintiff refused to receive, and brought trover for the original ones. It was held that evidence was admissible of a custom existing among forwarders of pro-

Silence of Common Law—Away-Going Crop—Tenant-Right—
Custom not Inconsistent Admitted—Operation of Custom.

SEC. 47. The common law does so little to prescribe the
relative duties of landlord and tenant, since it leaves the

duce, by that and other roads and by vessels to New York, of leaving the barrels with their contents in such a case, and returning other barrels, equal in number and value. But such a custom to be binding, must be reasonable and followed in all cases, by all persons along the line of the same roads following the business of the plaintiff, and it must have been established so long that the plaintiff and all persons living in the vicinity could be presumed to have known of it, and acted in reference thereto. While evidence of a usage is not admissible to vary a special contract, yet it is admissible to show in what manner the business is done, although the contract is precise in its terms. *Fox* v. *Parker*, 44 Barb. (N. Y.) 541. In *Foley* v. *Mason*, 6 Md. 37, it was held that evidence of a usage is not admissible to overcome a general principle or rule of law, or to vary the term of a contract, but that it may be admitted to add to or explain a contract, but that in order to be admissible for that purpose, it must be certain, uniform and notorious, and that evidence of a usage "to deliver merchandise sold for cash, without receiving the cash simultaneously with the delivery, and without the vendor's thereby waiving the right to the cash," supported by testimony that "it was then, and now is, the general usage among flour dealers in the city of Baltimore," and by another witness, ".that in sales of flour for cash in the city of Baltimore, it is the general and constant

usage," is too vague and unmeaning to warrant the court to submit any proposition to the jury based upon it. Where goods are sold by an agent or commission merchant under instructions to sell for cash, evidence of a usage to treat a rule upon a short credit as a sale for cash, is not admissible, because such a usage is fully established, is unreasonable and therefore invalid. *Stewart* v. *Scudder*, 21 N. J. L. 96. But where nothing is said as to the time when goods delivered shall be paid for, evidence of a usage of trade in that respect is admissible to fix the time. Thus, in *Outwater* v. *Nelson*, 20 Barb. (N. Y.) 29, in an action on a receipt of a quantity of corn in store "on freight," it is competent for the defendant to prove a custom of the place, which had continued forty years, to pay for corn so left, after the owner had ordered it to be freighted, and not before, and that this custom was known to the plaintiff, and that he had been in the habit for many years of leaving grain at the same place, to be freighted on the same terms, and if established the custom is binding on the parties. In *Potter* v. *Murland*, 3 Cush. (Mass.) 384, it was held that where goods are consigned to an agent for sale, with general instructions to remit the proceeds, it is a sufficient compliance with such instructions, if the agent remit by a bill of exchange, without endorsing or guaranteeing it provided such is the usage at the agent's place of business, and the agent use proper

latter at liberty to pursue any course of management he pleases, provided he is not guilty of waste, that it is by no means surprising that the courts have been favorably inclined to the introduction of these regulations in the mode of cultivation which custom and usage have established in each district to be the most beneficial to all parties. "Accordingly, in *Wigglesworth* v. *Dallison*, afterwards affirmed in a writ of error, the tenant was allowed an away-going crop, though there was a formal lease under seal. There the lease was entirely silent on the subject of such a right, and Lord Mansfield said that the custom did not alter or contradict the lease, but only superadded something to it. The question subsequently came under the consideration of the Court of King's Bench, in the case of *Senior* v. *Armitage*, reported in Mr. Holt's Nisi Prius Cases.(*u*)   In that case, which was an action by a tenant against his landlord for compensation for seed and labor under the denomination of tenant-right, Mr. Justice Bayley, on its appearing that there was a written agreement between the parties, non-suited the plaintiff. The court afterwards set aside that non-suit, and held, as appears by a manuscript note of that learned judge, that though there was a written contract between landlord and tenant,

diligence and discretion in the purchase of the bill. In an action against the agent, to recover the proceeds of such a sale, proof of the usage and of a remittance accordingly is a sufficient *primâ facie* defence; and if it is established by the agent, the burden of proof is then on the principal to show that bills remitted in pursuance of the usage ought to be endorsed or guaranteed by the agent. Evidence of usage is admissible to establish a delivery of property sold. Thus, in *Putnam* v. *Lillatson*, 13 Met. (Mass.) 577, where shoes were sold to a distant purchaser, it was held that evidence was admissible to show that when shoes are ordered, it is the usage and course of the shoe business, when no special mode of conveyance is mentioned by the purchaser, for the manufacturer to take the shoes to ·Boston, at his own risk and cost, and there deliver them to some regular line of packets running to the purchaser's place of business, and take duplicate bills of lading, and forward one of them to the purchaser, by mail, and that from that time the delivery is complete, and the purchaser takes the risk of loss.

(*u*) P. 179. See also Woodfall, Landlord and Tenant, p. 989, 10th ed.

the custom of the country would still be binding if not inconsistent with the terms of such written contract; and that not only all common law obligations, but those imposed by custom, were in full force where the contract did not vary them. Mr. Holt appears to have stated the case too strongly when he said that the court held the custom to be operative 'unless the agreement in express terms excluded it;' and probably he has not been quite accurate in attributing a similar opinion to the Lord Chief Baron Thompson, who presided on the second trial. It would appear that the court held that the custom operated unless it could be collected from the instrument, either expressly or impliedly, that the parties did not mean to be governed by it.

As to Terms on which Tenant May Quit.

SEC. 48. On the determination of an agricultural or farming lease, by effluxion of time, it has been held that the custom of the country, in the absence of any express agreement to the contrary, regulates the terms on which the tenant may quit possession,[3] but if there is any express stipulation to that end, the custom of the country yields to it[4] accordingly, where a lessee covenanted that he would not during the term carry from off the premises any hay, straw, fodder, &c., but would yearly spend and use the same upon some proper part thereof, upon pain of forfeiting £3 for each load carried away; and would also at all times during the term fold his flock of sheep which he should keep upon the premises upon such parts where the same had been usually folded, upon the penalty of £3 a time for every time that the same should be folded off from the premises; and would also in the last year of the term, at the usual time, carry all the dung and manure arising on the premises in the preceding year to such parts of the fallowed lands as should be

---

[3] *Hutton* v. *Warren*, ante; *Roberts* v. *Barken*, 1 C. & M. 808; *Webb* v. *Plummer*, 2 B. & Ald. 746;   *Holding* v. *Piggott*, 7 Bing. 465.   [4] *Webb* v. *Plummer*, ante; *Hutton* v. *Warren*, ante.

appointed by the lessor, his heirs or assigns, or the next succeeding tenant or tenants, and there cast the same into a
mixen or mixens, he and they paying for fallowing such
land and carrying out the dung, but nothing for the dung
itself, and also grass in the ground, and for thrashing out
the corn, as was customary between a tenant coming in and
a tenant going out of a farm; it was held, that as certain
payments were specifically directed to be made by the
incoming tenant, but payment for foldage was not mentioned, the custom of the country which gave the outgoing
tenant a compensation for foldage was waived.[5] So, where
a tenant held under the terms of an expired lease, by which
it was stipulated that the lessee on quitting the farm should
not sell or take away the manure, but should leave it to be
expended on the land by the landlord, or his succeeding
tenant; the custom of the country requiring the tenant to
leave the manure, on payment for it by the landlord or his
succeeding tenant; it was held, that the custom was controlled by the express stipulation, and that the tenant, on
quitting, was not entitled to be paid for the manure.[6] But
where a lessee covenanted to spend and consume three parts
in four of the hay and straw arising from the glebe land
and tithes demised, upon the land, and to bestow the manure
arising therefrom upon the land, and to leave such part of
such manure as should not be so bestowed, at the determination of the term, upon the premises, for the use of the lessor,
he paying a reasonable price for the same; the custom of
the country, by which the tenant was bound to cultivate the
farm according to a certain course of husbandry, and was
entitled, on quitting, to a fair allowance for seeds and labor
on the arable land, and was bound to leave the manure on
the land, if the landlord chose to purchase it, was held not
to be excluded.[7]

---

[5] *Webb* v. *Plummer*, 2 B. & Ald. 746.   [7] *Hutton* v. *Warren*, 2 Gale 71.
[6] *Roberts* v. *Barker*, 3 Tyrw. 945.

Intention to Exclude Custom.

SEC. 49. "On the second trial,[8] the Lord Chief Baron Thompson held that the custom prevailed, although the written instrument contained an express stipulation that all the manure made on the farm should be spent on it or left at the end of the tenancy, without any compensation being paid. Such a stipulation certainly does not exclude by implication the tenant's right to receive compensation for seed and labor." After referring to the case of *Webb* v. *Plummer*, the learned judge said: "The question there is, whether, from the terms of the lease now under consideration, it can be collected that the parties intended to exclude the customary obligation to make allowances for seed and labor." And we have already seen how the court, through Baron Parke, answered the question.(*v*) Some further decisions, although they can scarcely throw more light on the subject after the quotation from Baron Parke's clear and luminous exposition, may illustrate these principles in different aspects, and indicate the extent of their applicability.

Custom of Country, when Inoperative.

SEC. 50. There is an earlier case than that of *Hutton* v. *Warren*,(*w*) which is not referred to in the judgment of the court. It appeared that a tenant by a clause in his lease was bound, "at his removal, to leave upon the land all the dung and manure of the preceding year, the value to be paid by the succeeding tenant, &c.; and at no time to sell or give away any of the hay or straw of the said farm, which shall always be spent on the ground;" and the point in dispute was whether the tenant under that contract was or was not entitled to take away or sell the straw of the last or 'waygoing crop, and whether, if the tenant threatens to sell the straw, the lessor is entitled to have letters of suspension and

---

[8] Of *Senior* v. *Armitage*, ante.

(*v*) See also judgment of Parke, B., in *Sutton* v. *Temple*, 12 M. & W.   52, at p. 63.

(*w*) 1 M. & W. 466; 2 Gale 71.

interdict. (x) It was held that the custom of the country
could have no operation in such a case, as there was a contract with provisions applicable to the point in dispute, and
consequently that letters of suspension and interdict might
be had and maintained by the lessor. (y)

Term of Holding and Operation of Custom—Reason for its Admission in this Case.

SEC. 51. If a lease contain no stipulations as to the mode
of quitting, the off-going tenant is entitled to his 'way-going
crop, according to the custom of the country even although
the terms of holding may be inconsistent with such a custom. (z) Although this might, at first sight, seem repugnant
to the doctrine stated above, it will upon examination be
found to be in strict conformity with the principle of that
doctrine, for the agreement under which the tenant held—in
the case in which the above principle was enunciated—was
silent altogether as to any terms on which the tenant should
quit, and the clause of the agreement which was inconsistent
with the custom of the country was a stipulation confined
expressly to the period of holding by the tenant.   It adverted
to nothing that was to take place at the end of the tenancy,
and spoke only of terms of holding during its continuance.
There was, therefore, nothing in such an agreement at variance with the application of a custom between landlord and
tenant which did not come into force until the expiration of
the term.   In that case, the rights of the landlord and tenant
were governed by the terms of the agreement during the
tenancy, and by the terms of the custom immediately afterwards.   It is clear that, as the agreement only referred to
the continuance of the tenancy, both the landlord and tenant
must have anticipated not only an end to the holding, but

(x) This was an appeal from a
decision of the Court of Session in
Scotland to the H. of L.

(y) *Roxburgh (Duke of)* v. *Robertson,* 2 Bligh. 156; see also *Hughes* v.

Gordon, 1 Bligh. 287; *Clinan* v. *Cooke,*
1 Sch. & Lef. 22; and *White* v. *Sayer,*
Palm. 211.

(z) *Holding* v. *Pigott,* 7 Bing. 465.

must have looked forward to a time when their mutual relations must be regulated by some other rule than that contained in the agreement. As there is nothing said as to the end, there is the ambiguity of silence which the custom of the country can be called upon to explain.

Custom of Country as to Time—Where Letting is by Deed— "Martinmas" Explained.

SEC. 52. The custom of the country has frequently been had recourse to for an explanation where the question of the time of a holding has been left in doubt by the written instrument;(a) and this is clearly within the rules which have been stated above. Thus, where a holding was general from Michaelmas, the custom of the country as to whether that shall be deemed Old or New Michaelmas was held to be admissible in evidence.(b) Evidence of the custom of the country was held admissible for the purpose of showing that a letting by parol from Lady-day meant from *Old Lady-day.*(c) In this case the court referred to the case last mentioned (*Furley* v. *Wood*), and distinguished it from *Doe* v. *Lea* on the ground that the letting was there *by deed,* " which," according to Holroyd, J., " is a solemn instrument, and *therefore* parol evidence was not admissible to explain the expression Lady-day there used, even supposing that it was equivocal." The soundness of this distinction, which seems to have been quite unnecessary in the case, as the contract was by parol, has been called in question. It is certainly difficult to see upon what principle it is founded, for the rule as to the inadmissibility of evidence to contradict or vary the terms of a contract is as applicable to contracts which have no seal as to those which have one. It has, therefore, been argued that it would be rash to infer that parol evidence would be receivable to explain a word of time

---

(a) *Martyn* v. *Clue,* 18 Q. B. 661, at p. 682; *White* v. *Nicholson,* 4 M. & G. 95.

(b) *Furley* v. *Wood,* 1 Esp. 198;

Hall v. *Benson,* 4 B. & Ald. 588; but see *Doe* v. *Lea,* 11 East 312.

(c) *Doe* v. *Benson,* 4 B. & Ald. 588.

used in a lease in writing, but not under seal.(d) In another case, where the defendant avowed the rent payable "at *Martinmas, to wit,* November 23d," the plaintiff pleaded *non tenuit,* and a holding from *Old* Martinmas having been proved, the court thought that the words after the *videlicet* must be rejected as inconsistent with the term Martinmas, which they thought themselves bound by statute to interpret November 11th, that no evidence was admissible to explain the record, and that there was therefore a fatal variance between it and the evidence.(e) In a Nisi Prius case, Erle, C. J., remarked: "The custom of the country cannot be set up against the legal presumption that Michaelmas means any other day than the 29th September. You must show by direct evidence that this was an Old Michaelmas tenancy."(f)

Custom not Excluded by Terms of Lease.

Sec. 53. In a case where a custom to pay for fallows was proved, it was held that there was therefore an implied contract on the part of the landlord, that if there be no incoming tenant, he will pay the outgoing tenant according to the custom.(g) Again, where, by the terms of a farm lease for seven years expiring at Michaelmas, the tenant agreed to cultivate the land according to the custom of the country, and "during the term to consume with stock on the farm all the hay, straw and clover grown thereon, which manure shall be used on the farm," and the landlord agreed to let the tenant occupy part of the homestead until Midsummer after the expiration of the term, if necessary, "to end the cropping of the tenant grown on the premises," it was held that the lease did not exclude the custom of the country, by which the tenant having paid for straw on his incoming was entitled to be paid for straw on his quitting.(h)

(d) Smith's L. Cas. 6th ed. p. 554.
(e) *Smith* v. *Walton,* 8 Bing. 238; see also *Kearney* v. *King,* 2 B. & Ald. 301.

(f) *Hogg* v. *Berrington,* 2 F. & F. 246.
(g) *Fariell* v. *Gaskoin,* 7 Exch. 273.
(h) *Muncey* v. *Dennis,* 1 H. & N. 216.

Agreement Excluding Proof of Custom.

SEC. 54. But where an action was brought by a landlord against an incoming tenant, and the declaration stated that, in consideration that the landlord would give up to the tenant possession of the farm, on which manure had been laid, and would permit him to have the benefit of the manure, he promised to pay the landlord for the same according to the custom of the country, and the breach alleged was non-payment, a written agreement was offered in evidence of the custom, which stated that the land had been manured with eight loads of manure per acre, and that the tenant agreed to leave the land, when given up by him, in the same state or to allow a valuation to be made. Here it was held that the written agreement excluded the custom of the country, as it was inconsistent with it.(i)

What Customs are Binding—Custom to Pay for Tillages.

SEC. 55. A custom not of the country, but prevalent between the owner and tenants of a particular landed estate, is not binding on a tenant who becomes such without notice of its existence.(k) Where the custom of the country was that the tenant should have the 'way-going crops on the regular expiration of a Lady-day tenancy, the tenant entered on Lady-day, but the tenancy was determined on the 1st of June, it was held that the custom would not operate.(l) In a case where the plaintiff was a tenant on a farm, with a right to use a certain part of premises until 25th March, after the expiration of the term, and where by the custom of the country the plaintiff was entitled, at the expiration of his term, to be paid by the landlord or the incoming tenant for certain tillages, and he gave up his farm to the defendant as incoming tenant at Michaelmas, 1870, before which date the tillages had been valued. After the defendant had

(i) *Clarke* v. *Roystone*, 13 M. & W. 752; *Wiltshear* v. *Cottrell*, 1 E. & B. 674.

(k) *Womersley* v. *Dally*, 26 L. J. Exch. 219.

(l) *Thorpe* v. *Eyre*, 1 Ad. & El. 926.

entered into possession, but before the 25th March, 1871, the landlord gave him notice that rent was due from the plaintiff, and required him to pay the amount of the valuation, which was less than the rent due to him, the landlord, and not to the plaintiff, which the defendant did, on receiving an indemnity from the landlord, and without the plaintiff's consent. The plaintiff brought his action for the value of the tillages, and was non-suited. And the court held that the non-suit was right, for that the contract to be implied between the incoming and outgoing tenant was subject to the right of the landlord to be paid arrears of rent out of the valuation.(*m*)

(*m*) *Stafford* v. *Gardner*, 7 L. R. C. P. 242.

CHAPTER III.

THE USAGES OF TRADE AND THEIR ADMISSIBILITY AS EVIDENCE.

Usages of Trade in Commercial Contracts.

SEC. 56. We come now to the consideration of the question as to the admissibility of evidence of a usage of trade for the purpose of importing terms into commercial contracts. That this is a question of paramount importance in an industrial age and a commercial country cannot be doubted; but even if there was any hesitation, a consideration of the number of the cases, involving this question, which have come before our courts, and of the deepness and importance of the interests of the litigants in those cases, would prove the assertion. The same preliminary remark which was made in reference to contracts affecting the relation of landlord and tenant as to the general rule as to the ambiguity in contracts would be in place here. That the doctrine of the law as to the admissibility of parol evidence, to explain away or clear up an ambiguity in a mercantile contract, is the same as that which applies to an ambiguity in contracts not made in the way of trade will be evident from the consideration of one or two cases.(a) That is, that such evidence is not admissible to explain a contract that is clear in all its terms and provisions, as to permit such evidence would change the legal relations of the parties and defeat their intention.(b)

(a) *Kempson* v. *Boyle*, 3 H. & C. 673; *Bold* v. *Rayner*, 1 M. & W. 343; but see as to inadmissibility, *Smith* v. *Jeffreys*, 15 M. & W. 562; 15 L. J. Exch. 325; *Ford* v. *Yates*, 2 Scott, N. R. 654; 2 M. & G. 549; see Taylor on Ev. (5th ed.) § 1053, p. 996; *Weston* v. *Emes*, 1 Taunt. 115; *Kaines* v. *Knightly*, Sken. 54; *Hoare* v. *Graham*, 3 Camp. 57; *Field* v. *Lelean*, 6 H. & N. 627; 30 L. J. Exch. 170; *Rawson* v. *Walker*, 1 Stark. 361; *Adams* v. *Wordley*, 1 M. & W. 374.

(b) Evidence of usage is not admissible to change the legal relation of parties to a transaction. Thus, such evidence is not admissible to show that a commission dealer receiving property for sale on commission is liable as a purchaser rather than in a fiduciary capacity. Thus, in *Duguid* v. *Edwards*, 50 Barb. (N. Y.) 288, the plaintiff brought an action against the defendant for the value of certain flour consigned to the defendant for sale. The plaintiff obtained an order of arrest on the ground that the money was obtained in a fiduciary capacity. The defendant, to get rid of the order, showed by affidavit that it was a custom among persons selling flour on commission to charge the owner in account with freights, commissions, &c., and to credit him with the avails of the sale, thus making such excess over the charges and expenses a mere simple debt, and not money received or held in a fiduciary capacity. The court held that the evidence was not admissible, upon the point that evidence of usage or custom is not admissible to deprive a party of his rights otherwise secured to him by law. *Woodruff* v. *Merchants' Bank*, 25 Wend. (N. Y.) 674; *Frith* v. *Baker*, 2 John. (N. Y.) 327; *Bowen* v. *Newell*, 18 Barb. (N. Y.) 391. In *Lawrence* v. *Maxwell*, 6 Lans. (N. Y. S. C.) 469, this rule was also well illustrated. In that case the plaintiff deposited with the defendant, a broker in New York City, four hundred shares of the stock of the Atlantic Steamship Company as security against loss by him for conducting for him (the plaintiff) certain transactions in the purchase and sale of gold coin to the close of the transactions, the defendant rendered an account thereof to the plaintiff by which it appeared that there was a balance of $11,600.22 due the defendant. This sum the plaintiff tendered to the defendant, and demanded a return of the stock deposited with him. The defendant had pledged the stock some time before the account was rendered, to raise money for his own use, and consequently could not return it. The action was brought for damages for the conversion of the stock. The defendant offered to show in defence as ex-

General Rules as to Oral Evidence.

SEC. 57. There are certain general principles which govern the interpretation of all writings which are dealt with at length in all works on the law of evidence. Some of these rules are obvious in their reasons, and necessary in their application. Thus, that the court must read the whole of a document, and must come to a conclusion as to the meaning of the words used by a careful examination of the context, and the estimate of the sense and weight of the same words in other parts of the instrument.(c)   Words must be understood, if they can, in their primary sense.(d)   Then

cusing the conversion an alleged custom or usage in the city of New York, authorizing brokers to sell or otherwise dispose of the securities pledged, as was done in this case, and as the broker might deem proper. The trial court rejected the evidence, and this ruling was sustained upon appeal, *Leonard, J.*, in delivering the opinion of the court upon this point, saying, " He," (the defendant) " offered evidence at the trial to prove that it was customary among brokers in New York to use the stock held by them as security, in the manner this stock was held by the defendant, and, upon objection, this evidence was excluded; also that the defendant had previously held stock of the plaintiff as security, which he had used in a similar manner without objection or complaint on the part of the plaintiff, although he knew of it. This also was excluded. The evidence offered was clearly inadmissible. Such a custom is simply a violation of the rights of the principal. A long continued course of wrongdoing or violation of law, will never establish a valid custom to continue it. (See upon this point, and to the same effect, *Coleman* v. *McMurdo*, 5

Rand. (Va.) 51; *Harris* v. *Carson*, 7 Leigh (Va.) 632; *Winder* v. *Blake*, 4 Jones (N. C.) L. 332). Brokers who use the stock of their principals relying upon any such custom, are liable to return it when called upon, if their demands or liabilities incurred on the security of the stock have been satisfied. If they cannot return it, they are liable in damages for the injury which is caused by a loss of the stock. It is a clear violation of trust, and an action as for a conversion of the stock, is clearly within the election of the principal. * * * It is no excuse or defence, that the broker has taken advantage of the possession of his principal's stock, and used it without complaint on his part on previous occasions. *On those occasions he returned or accounted for the stock so used, and no cause of complaint remained."*

(c) *Blundell* v. *Gladstone*, 11 Sim. 486; 1 Phill. 279, 388, 389, *s. c.; Bateman* v. *Lord Roden*, 8 Jones & Lat. 356; *Richardson* v. *Watson*, 4 B. & A. 798, 799, *per* Parke, J.; *Lang* v. *Gale*, 1 M. & S. 11; *Walsh* v. *Trevanion*, 15 Q. B. 733, 751.

(d) *Robertson* v. *French*, 4 East 135, 136, *per* Lord Ellenborough; *Mallan* v. *May*, 13 M. & W. 517, *per* Pollock,

comes the general rule to which we have adverted,(e) viz., that parol evidence cannot be received to contradict, vary, add to, or subtract from the terms of a valid written instrument.(f) However general a usage may be, it cannot be

C. B.; *Carr* v. *Montefiore*, 5 B. & S. 408; *Ford* v. *Ford*, 6 Hare 490, 491, *per* Wigram, V. C.; *Hicks* v. *Sallitt*, 23 L. J. Ch. 571; see also Bell's Com. Law of Scotland (7th ed.) vol. 1, p. 456.

(e) Ante, p. 40.

(f) *Goss* v. *Lord Nugent*, 5 B. & Ad. 64; see 2 Ph. on Evid. 350. So by the Scotch law, "a writing cannot be cut down or taken away by the testimony of witnesses."—Tait, Ev. 326, 327. The legislature has also adopted a similar rule, making it obligatory to use writing in evidence of certain dispositions, such as wills and other transactions, and those within the Statute of Frauds. See *Fawkes* v. *Lamb*, 31 L. J. Q. B. 98; see also *The Reeside*, 2 Sum. (U. S.) 567; *Chubb* v. *Seven thousand eight hundred bushels of oats*, 16 Law Rep. N. S. 492. Parol evidence of a custom cannot be received to show that a marine policy of insurance on goods shipped from New Orleans to Mobile, the language of which is plain and unambiguous, covers overland transportation of the goods by railroad. *Smith* v. *Mobile Navigation &c. Co.*, 30 Ala. 167. Nor in an action against the owners of a steamboat, as common carriers, for failing to deliver goods at the place specified in their bill of lading, is evidence of a custom among the steamboat men to ascend the river as high as the stage of the water in it permitted, and then to land their cargo and deposit the goods in warehouses, admissible for the defendants, be-

cause the effect of the custom is to contradict the terms of the contract and relieve a party from a liability that he has expressly assumed. *Cox* v. *Peterson*, 30 Ala. 608. But evidence *is* admissible to show that, by a custom existing on a particular river, flatboatmen are not responsible for a loss caused by dangers of the river, although the bill of lading contained no such exception, but in order to be operative, the custom, to be valid and binding, must be uniform, and so generally known and acquiesced in, and so well established, that the parties must be presumed to have contracted in reference to it. *Steele* v. *McTyer*, 31 Ala. 667. It is also held that the owner of a steamboat, when sued for the loss of goods by fire, may show by parol that the exceptive words "dangers of the river," in the bill of lading, by custom and usage include dangers by fire. *McClure* v. *Cox*, 32 Ala. 617; *Hibler* v. *McCartney*, 31 Ala. 501. But evidence is not admissible to vary the common bill of lading, by which goods are to be delivered in good order, &c., the danger of the seas only excepted, and to show a custom that the owners of packet vessels between New York and Boston are liable only for damage to goods caused by their own neglect, because such a usage is unreasonable and relieves the carrier from liabilities that he has expressly assumed. *The Reeside*, 2 Sum. (U. S.) 568. But evidence of usage, fixing a construction of the

6

given in evidence to alter or vary the express terms of a contract. As parties may exclude the rules of the general

words "inevitable dangers of the river," in a bill of lading for transportation of goods by inland navigation, is admissible, because the effect of the usage is only to explain the meaning of the terms employed by the parties, and to arrive at and give effect to their intention. *Gordon v. Little*, 8 S. & R. (Penn.) 533. Evidence of a custom of merchants, in Connecticut, that the freight of money, received on board a ship by the master, is his perquisite, and that he, and not the ship-owner, is liable on the contract, was held admissible in a suit against such owner for money taken on freight by the master at a West India island. *Halsey v. Brown*, 3 Day. (Conn.) 346. The express terms of a contract cannot be varied by usage, because the parties are presumed to have intended precisely what they say, and this presumption is irrebuttable, consequently, except in cases where fraud is shown, or accident or mistake, which a court of equity will rectify, they cannot be relieved from their liability as plainly expressed in the contract. *Sweet v. Jenkins*, 1 R. I. 147; *Meaghar v. Lufkin*, 21 Tex. 383; *Caldwell v. Meek*, 17 Ill. 220; *Cooper v. Purvis*, 1 Jones (N. C.) L. 141; *Renner v. Bank of Columbia*, 9 Wheat. (U. S.) 981; *Bradley v. Wheeler*, 44 N. Y. 495; *Collender v. Dinsmore*, 55 Id. 200; *Groat v. Gile*, 51 Id. 431; *Simmons v. Law*, 4 Abb. Dec. (N. Y.) 241; *Mercantile &c. Ins. Co. v. State Ins. Co.* 25 Barb. (N. Y.) 319; *St. Nicholas Ins. Co. v. Mercantile Ins. Co.*, 5 Bas. (N. Y.) 238; *Farmers' &c. Bank v. Logan*, 74 N. Y. 568; *Bank of Commerce v. Bissell*, 72 Id. 615;

Lawrence v. Gallagher, 10 J. & S. (N. Y.) 309; *Wadworth v. Alcott*, 6 N. Y. 64; *Sleight v. Rhinelander*, 1 John. (N. Y.) 192; *George v. Bartlett*, 22 N. H. 496; *Barlow v. Lambert*, 28 Ala. 704; *Wheeler v. Nourse*, 20 N. H. 220; *Corwin v. Patch*, 4 Cal. 204; *Fay v. Strawn*, 32 Ill. 295; *Sanford v. Rawlings*, 43 Id. 92; *Atkinson v. Allen*, 29 Ind. 375: *Randall v. Ratch*, 12 Pick. (Mass.) 107; *Macomber v. Parker*, 13 Id. 175. This rule was well illustrated in a case where the contract was for the delivery of "Rochester Mills Flour," and the defendant offered to deliver other flour of equal quality, but refused to deliver Rochester mill. In an action upon the contract, the defendants offered evidence that, by the usage of the trade, contracts to deliver flour of a specified brand, may be filled by other flour of equal quality. The court held that the evidence was inadmissible, because such a usage would excuse a party from doing what he had agreed to do, and, instead of carrying out the intention of the parties, would thwart it. *Beals v. Terry*, 2 Sandf. (N. Y.) 124. In an Alabama case it was sought to extend a marine policy of insurance on goods shipped from New Orleans to Mobile, so as to cover their transportation over land by railroad. The court held that evidence of a custom to that end was inadmissible, as the contract was express and plain, and purported only to cover a marine loss. *Smith v. Mobile Navigation &c. Co.*, 30 Ala. 167. So, in an action by the vendee for damages for the non-delivery of goods under a contract, which provided that the

law by contract, so, too, may they exclude either a custom or usage, and where the contract is express in its terms, it is treated as embracing the will of the parties and nothing can be shown to change it.[1] But such evidence is admissible

vendee should advance the freight, it was held that evidence of a general custom on the subject of paying freight on delivery of the goods, was not admissible, because the parties had made their own contract which was susceptible of easy explanation and needed no aid from custom and could not be controlled by it. *Hartje* v. *Collins*, 46 Penn. St. 268. In a New Hampshire case, where, by the express terms of a policy, a mutual fire insurance company agreed to pay the ascertained amount of loss " without any deduction therefrom," it was held that the company could not set up a custom or usage, on their part, in the case of a total loss, to deduct out of the amount of the ascertained loss two per cent. a month on the balance of the premium note, from the date of the last assessment until the expiration of the policy, because the effect of

such a usage would be to vary the plain and unequivocal terms of an express contract. *Swainscott Machine Co.* v. *Partridge*, 25 N. H. 369. See also *Hall* v. *Janson*, 4 El. & Bl. 500, where a policy contained a stipulation that freight was warranted free from average under five per cent. unless general. The interest assured was described as money advanced on account of freight of a cargo loaded on board and subject to the risk of the voyage. The insurer set up a custom of London, that insurers, on account of money advanced on freight, are not liable to make good a general average, but the court held that the custom was inadmissible, because it was inconsistent with the express terms of the policy, which expressly stipulated that the insurer should be liable to make good such a loss.

[1] *Meaghar* v. *Lufkin*, 21 Tex. 383; *Cadwell* v. *Meek*, 17 Ill. 220; *Renner* v. *Bank of Columbia*, 9 Wheat. (U. S.) 582; *Sweet* v. *Jenkins*, 1 R. I. 147; *Rankin* v. *American Ins. Co.*, 1 Hall (N. Y.) 619; *Cooper* v. *Purvis*, 1 Jones (N. C.) L. 141; *Sanford* v. *Rawlings*, 43 Ill. 92; *Wadsworth* v. *Allcott*, 6 N. Y. 64; *Barlow* v. *Lambert*, 28 Ala. 704; *George* v. *Bartlett*, 22 N. H. 496; *Atkinson* v. *Allen*, 29 Ind. 375; *Wheeler* v. *Nourse*, 20 N. H. 220; *Sleght* v. *Rhinelander*, 1 John. (N. Y.) 192; *Macomber* v. *Parker*, 13 Pick. (Mass.) 175; *Fay* v. *Strawn*, 32 Ill. 295; *Corwin* v. *Patch*, 4 Cal. 204; *Sigsworth* v. *McIntyre*, 18 Ill. 126. This

was well illustrated in a New York case, *Simmons* v. *Law*, 3 Keyes (N. Y.) 219. In that case, the plaintiff shipped a quantity of gold dust by the defendant's boats, from San Francisco to New York, which was never delivered. In an action for the loss, the defendant attempted to exempt himself from liability by proof of a usage of carriers inconsistent with the bill of lading, but which was well known by the shipper; but the evidence was rejected, the court saying, "A clear, certain and distinct contract is not subject to modification by proof of usage. Such a contract disposes of all cus-

to add incidents to the contract not inconsistent with its terms.[2] So, also, to show in what manner the business was done.[3] So, too, it is held that evidence of a usage is not admissible to contradict the legal import of a contract,[4] or to

toms by its own terms, and by its terms alone is the conduct of the parties to be regulated and their liability determined." See also *Collender* v. *Dinsmore*, 55 N. Y. 200; *Bradley* v. *Wheeler*, 44 *Id.* 495; *Groat* v. *Gile*, 51 *Id.* 431; *Astor* v. *Union &c. Ins. Co.*, 7 Cow. (N. Y.) 202; *Hone* v. *Mutual &c. Ins. Co.*, 2 N. Y. 235; *Stebbins* v. *Globe Ins. Co.*, 2 Hall (N. Y.) 632; *Stebbins* v. *Brown*, 65 Barb. (N. Y.) 274; *Main* v. *Eagle*, 1 E. D. S. (N. Y. C. P.) 619; *Beals* v. *Terry*, 2 Sandf. (N. Y.) 127. The rule is inflexible that *no custom or usage, however general, can be admitted to vary or control the express terms of a contract*, as the effect of such evidence would be to defeat the very purpose for which such evidence is ever received, to wit, to ascertain the real intention of the parties. The contract, when clearly expressed, must be treated as embodying the intention of the parties, and if it conflicts with known customs or usages, it affords irrebuttable evidence that the parties intended to exclude them. *Cadwell* v. *Meek*, 17 Ill. 220; *Renner* v. *Bank of Columbia*, 9 Wheat. 581; *Rankin* v. *American Ins. Co.*, 1 Hall (N.Y.) 619; *Sleght* v. *Rhinelander*, 1 Johns. (N. Y.) 192; *Barlow* v. *Lambert*, 28 Ala. 704; *Corwin* v. *Patch*, 4 Cal. 204; *Sigsworth* v. *McIntyre*, 18 Ill. 126; *Fay* v. *Strawn*, 32 Ill. 295; *Sanford* v. *Rawlings*, 43 Ill. 92; *Atkinson* v. *Allen*, 29 Ind. 375; *Randall* v. *Rotch*, 12 Pick. (Mass.) 107; *Macomber* v. *Parker*, 13 *Id.* 175; *Wheeler* v. *Nourse*, 20 N. H. 220;

George v. *Bartlett*, 22 N. H. (2 Fost.) 496; *Wadsworth* v. *Allcott*, 6 N. Y. (2 Seld.) 64; *Cooper* v. *Purvis*, 1 Jones (N. C.) L. 141; *Sweet* v. *Jenkins*, 1 R. I. 147; *Meaher* v. *Lufkin*, 21 Tex. 383.

[2] *Lace's case*, 4 C. H. Rec. (N. Y.) 158; *Wood* v. *Wilcox*, 9 Wend. (N. Y.) 346; *Dixon* v. *Dunham*, 13 Ill. 324; *Cooper* v. *Kane*, 19 Wend. (N. Y.) 386; *Leach* v. *Beardslee*, 22 Conn. 404; *Shaw* v. *Mitchell*, 2 Met. (Mass.) 65; *Alabama &c. R. R. Co.* v. *Kidd*, 29 Ala. 221; *Hursh* v. *North*, 40 Penn. St. 241; *Stultz* v. *Dickey*, 5 Binn. (Penn.) 287; *Inglebright* v. *Hammond*, 19 Ohio 337; *Sampson* v. *Gazzam*, 6 Port. (Ala.) 123; *Barber* v. *Brace*, 3 Conn. 9; *Haven* v. *Wentworth*, 2 N. H. 93.

[3] *Fox* v. *Parker*, 44 Barb. (N. Y.) 541; and to give effect thereto, *Mangum* v. *Farrington*, 1 Daly (N. Y. C. P.) 236; *Cooper* v. *Kane*, ante; *Dalton* v. *Daniels*, 2 Hilt. (N. Y. C. P.) 472; *Hinton* v. *Locke*, 5 Hill (N. Y.) 437; *Bissell* v. *Campbell*, 54 N. Y. 353; *Lee* v. *Salter*, Lalor's Supp. (N. Y.) 163; *Hartshorne* v. *Union Ins. Co.*, 36 N. Y. 172.

[4] *Holmes* v. *Pettingill*, 60 N. Y. 646; *Dalton* v. *Daniels*, ante; *Allen* v. *Dykers*, 7 Hill (N. Y.) 497; *Taylor* v. *Ketchum*, 5 Robt. (N. Y.) 507; *Vail* v. *Rice*, 5 N. Y. 155; *Harvey* v. *Cady*, 3 Mich. 431; *Smith* v. *Wilson*, 3 B. & Ad. 371; *Dodd* v. *Farlow*, 11 Allen (Mass.) 426; *Clark* v. *Roystone*, 13 M. & W. 756; *Cabot* v. *Winsor*, 1 Allen (Mass.) 546; *Huckin* v. *Cooke*, 4 T. R. 314; *Trueman* v. *Loder*, 11

contradict a settled rule of law, although it may be used for the purpose of explaining it.

Collateral Agreements.

SEC. 58. But this rule does not prevent the parties to the written contract from proving that either contemporaneously or as a preliminary measure they had entered into a distinct oral agreement on some collateral matter.(*g*) And, of course, parol evidence is admissible under the proper plea to show that the instrument is altogether void, or never had any legal existence either by reason of forgery or fraud,(*h*)

Ad. & El. 589; *Sanford* v. *Rawlings,* 43 Ill. 92; *Noble* v. *Durrell,* 3 T. R. 371; *Osgood* v. *McConnell,* 32 Ill. 74; *Mangum* v. *Ball,* 43 Miss. 288; *Simmons* v. *Law,* ante; *Luce* v. *Dorchester Ins. Co.,* 105 Mass. 297; *Muncey* v. *Dennis,* 1 H. & N. 216; *Satilichos* v. *Kemp,* 3 Exchq. 105; *Davis* v. *Galloupe,* 111 Mass. 121; *Marc* v. *Kupfer,* 34 Ill. 287; *Buckle* v. *Knoop,* 36 L. J. Exchq. 49; *Merchants Bank* v. *State Bank,* 10 Wall (U. S.) 604; *Willmering* v. *McGaughey,* 30 Iowa 205; *Sawtelle* v. *Drew,* 122 Mass. 228; *Ins. Co.* v. *Wright,* 1 Wall. (U. S.) 456; *Bank of Commerce* v. *Bissell,* 72 N. Y. 615; *Jackson* v. *Belling,* 22 La. An. 377; *Spears* v. *Ward,* 48 Ind. 546; *Glendale Mf'g Co.* v. *Ins. Co.,* 21 Conn. 19; *Schenck* v. *Griffin,* 38 N. J. L. 462; *Lombardo* v. *Case,* 45 Barb. (N. Y.) 45; *Raffert* v. *Scraggins,* 40 Ind. 195; *Sugart* v. *Mays,* 54 Ga. 554; *Coxe* v. *Heisley,* 19 Penn. St. 243; *Markham* v. *Jaudon,* 41 N. Y. 235; *Security Bank* v. *National Bank,* 67 Id. 458; *Farmers &c. Bank* v. *Sprague,* 52 Id.

605; *Warner* v. *Footman,* 54 Ga. 128; *Bowen* v. *Newell,* 8 N. Y. 190; *Outwater* v. *Nelson,* 20 Barb. (N. Y.) 29; *Frith* v. *Barker,* 2 John. (N. Y.) 327; *Marks* v. *Cass Co. Mill,* 43 Iowa 146; *Suse* v. *Pompe,* C. B. N. S. 538; *Spears* v. *Ward,* 48 Ind. 546, *Yeates* v. *Pym,* 6 Taunt. 466; *Doe* v. *Lee,* 11 East. 312; *Wetherell* v. *Neilson,* 20 Penn. St. 444; *Frith* v. *Barker,* ante; *Markham* v. *Jaudon,* ante; *Schiefflin* v. *Harvey,* 6 John. (N. Y.) 170; *Jones* v. *Bradner,* 10 Barb. (N. Y.) 193. In commenting upon the impolicy of extending the offices ·of the usages of trade in interpreting contracts, *Lord Denman,* in *Trueman* v. *Loder,* ante, says: " There is no inconvenience in requiring parties to write the whole of their contract; while, in mercantile affairs, no mischief can be greater than the uncertainty produced by permitting verbal statements to vary bargains committed to writing." See also remarks of *Story, J.,* in *The Schooner Reeside,* 2 Sum. (U. S.) 567.

(*g*) *Lindley* v. *Lacey,* 17 C. B. N. S. 558; see also *Brady* v. *Oastler,* 3 H. & C. 112; *Malpas* v. *London & South Western Rail. Co*, 35 L. J. C. P. 166 1 L. R. C. P. 336.

(*h*) *Collins* v. *Blantern,* 2 Wils. 341; 1 Smith's L. C. 310–339, and cases there cited in the notes. *Walker* v. *Smith,* 2 Vt. 539; *Rhodes* v. *Riseley,* 1 N. Chip. (Vt.) 52; *Branch Bank* v.

or that the contract was made in furtherance of objects for-
bidden by law,(*i*) or was obtained by duress,(*j*) or made by
persons incapable of contracting,(*k*) or that it is not binding
through failure of the consideration.(*l*)

Subsequent Oral Agreement—Rule in Goss v. Lord Nugent.

SEC. 59. Any obligation by writing, not under seal, may,
in the absence of statutory interference, be either totally or
partially dissolved before breach, by a subsequent oral agree-

Gaffney, 9 Ala. 152; *Condit* v. *Brown,*
21 Tex. 421; *Taylor* v. *Moore,* 28 Ark.
408; *Copeland* v. *Gorman,* 19 Tex.
253; *Corbin* v. *Flack,* 19 Ind. 459;
New York &c. Bank v. *Gibson,* 5 Duer
(N. Y.) 574; *Trustees* v. *Hill,* 12 Ia.
462; *Smalley* v. *Hale,* 32 Mo. 102;
Larrabee v. *Fairbanks,* 24 Me. 363;
Theurer v. *Schmidt,* 10 La. An. 293;
Thomas v. *Kennedy,* 24 La. An. 209;
Kain v. *Old,* 2 Br. C. 634; *Turner* v.
Turner, 44 Mo. 535; *Sparks* v. *Daw-
son,* 47 Tex. 138; *Battles* v. *Laudens-
langer,* 84 Penn. St. 446; *Walker* v.
Carrington, 84 Ill. 146; *Lull* v. *Cass,*
43 N. H. 62; *Montgomery* v. *Pickering,*
116 Mass. 227; *Koop* v. *Handy,* 41
Barb. (N. Y.) 454; *McLean* v. *Clark,*
47 Ga. 24; *Meyer* v. *Huncke,* 55 N. Y.
412; *Cobb* v. *Hatfield,* 46 N. Y. 533;
Wray v. *Wray,* 32 Ind. 126; *Kinney*
v *Kiernan,* 49 N. Y. 164; *Wharton* v.
Douglass, 76 Penn. St. 273; *Munte* v.
Gross, 56 Penn. St. 150.

(*i*) *Collins* v. *Blantern,* 2 Wils. 347;
1 Smith's L. C. 310–326; *Benyon* v.
Nettlefold, 3 M. & Gord. 94; see also
Briggs v. *Lawrence,* 3 T. R. 454;
Waymell v. *Reed,* 5 T. R. 600; *Nor-
man* v. *Cole,* 3 Esp. 253; and see
Martin v. *Clarke,* 8 R. J. 389; *Fer-
guson* v. *Sutphin,* 8 Ill. 547; *Totten* v.
United States, 92 U. S. 105; *Newsom*
v. *Thighen,* 30 Miss. 414; *Shackfer* v.
Newington, 46 N. H. 415; *Lazarre* v.
Jacques, 15 La. An. 598; *Wyman* v.

Fiske, 3 Allen (Mass.) 238; *Bowman*
v. *Torr,* 3 Ia. 571; *Corbin* v. *Sistrunk,*
19 Ala. 203; *Pratt* v. *Langdon,* 97
Mass. 97; *Parker* v. *Broas,* 20 La. An.
167; *McGuigin* v. *Ochiglevich,* 18 La.
An. 92; *Bigelow* v. *Woodard,* 15 Gray
(Mass.) 560; *Nelson* v. *Eaton,* 26 N.
Y. 410; *Craig* v. *Sibbett,* 15 Penn. St.
238.

(*j*) 2 Inst. 482, 483; *Olivari* v. *Men-
ger,* 39 Tex. 76; *Collins* v. *Blantern,*
2 Wils. 341; *Cook* v. *Moore,* 39 Tex.
255; *Feller* v. *Green,* 26 Mich. 70;
Hibbard v. *Mills,* 46 Vt. 243; *Bosley*
v. *Shanner,* 26 Ark. 280; *Seiber* v.
Price, 26 Mich. 518; *Spaid* v. *Barrett,*
57 Ill. 289; *Davis* v. *Fox,* 59 Mo. 125;
Davis v. *Luster,* 64 Mo. 43; *Miller* v.
Miller, 68 Penn. St. 486; *Knapp* v.
Hyde, 60 Barb. (N. Y.) 80; *Moore* v.
Rush, 30 La. An. 157; *Bane* v. *Det-
rick,* 52 Ill. 19.

(*k*) B. N. P. 172; *Barrett* v. *Buxton,*
2 Atk. 167.

(*l*) *Foster* v. *Jolly,* 1 C. M. & R. 707;
Solby v. *Hinde,* 2 C. & M. 516; see
Leppoe v. *National Union Bank,* 32
Md. 136; *Litchfield* v. *Falconer,* 2 Ala.
280; *Orth* v. *Sharkey,* 4 Ind. 642;
Jackson v. *Jackson,* 7 Ala. 791; *Sigs-
worth* v. *Coulter,* 18 Ill. 204; *Stacy* v.
Kemp, 97 Mass. 166; *Marshall* v.
Marshall, 12 B. Mon. (Ky.) 459; *Cart-
wright* v. *Clayton,* 25 Ga. 85; *Wise* v.
Neal, 39 Me. 422.

ment.(m) Although it has been argued that there is nothing contradictory in the rule that allows a written contract to be totally waived or discharged by parol proof, and that which forbids the reception of parol evidence, with the view of contradicting, varying, adding to, or subtracting from, such an instrument, we confess that it seems to us that the partial dissolution of a written contract seems to be the same thing as subtracting from it, and that the words of Lord Denman, in *Goss* v. *Lord Nugent*,(m) are contradictory, to a great extent, of the primary rule with regard to parol evidence. These words are: "After an agreement (at common law) has been reduced to writing, it is competent to the parties, at any time before breach of it, by a new contract not in writing, either altogether to waive, dissolve or annul the former agrement, or in any manner to add to, to subtract from, or vary, or qualify the terms of it, and thus to make a new contract, which is to be proved, partly by the written agreement, and partly by the subsequent verbal terms engrafted upon what will be thus left of the written agreement." We confess that we are unable to reconcile these

(m) *Goss* v. *Lord Nugent*. 5 B. & Ad. 65, *per* Lord Denman. The rule is well established that the parties to a contract may modify or extend it by parol, so as to apply it to new and kindred objects, or so as to embrace new parties, extend the time of performance, or so as to engraft new powers, duties or liabilities upon it, and such collateral agreement can be proved by parol. *Thomas* v. *Hammond*, 47 Tex. 43; *Bonney* v. *Morrill*, 57 Me. 368; *White* v. *Parkin*, 12 East 578; *Kelly* v. *Taylor*, 23 Cal. 11; *Robinson* v. *Batchelder*, 4 N. H. 40; *Polk* v. *Anderson*, 16 Kan. 243; *Morgan* v. *Griffith*, L. R. C. Exchq. 70; *Ingersoll* v. *Truebody*, 40 Cal. 603; *Buzzell* v. *Willard*, 44 Vt. 44; *Fields* v. *Munn*, 42 *Id.* 61; *Weaver* v. *Fletcher*, 27 Ark. 510; *Hartford Ins. Co.* v. *Wilcox*, 57 Ill. 186; *Courtinay* v. *Fuller*, 65 Me. 156; *Dixon* v. *Cook*, 47 Miss. 220; *Tusting* v. *Sullivan*, 41 Md. 170; *Gilbert* v. *Duncan*, 29 N. J. L. 133; *Raymond* v. *Sellick*, 10 Conn. 480; *Smith* v. *Richards*, 29 *Id.* 232. Indeed, it may be said to be well settled that parol evidence is admissible to prove any collateral independent fact about which the agreement is silent. *Bladen* v. *Wells*, 30 Md. 582; *Malone* v. *Dougherty*, 79 Penn. St. 46; *Lindley* v. *Lacey*, L. R., 1 C. P. 336; *Tusting* v. *Sullivan*, 41 Md. 169; *Phillips* v. *Preston*, 5 How. (U. S.) 278; *Forster* v. *McGraw*, 64 Penn. St. 464; *Fullerton* v. *Rundlett*, 27 Me. 31; *Cummings* v. *Putnam*, 19 N. H. 569; *Moore* v. *Davidson*, 18 Ala. 209.

two doctrines, and that, having in remembrance what Lord Coke calls "the uncertain testimony of slippery memory,"(n) we would have felt more inclined to adopt the rule of the law of Scotland, by which no written obligation whatever can be extinguished or renounced without either the creditor's oath or a writing signed by him.(o)   And we regard the prevailing rule as to the invalidity of the oral dissolution of a statutory instrument as an argument in favor of our proposition.(p)

Collateral Agreements.

SEC. 60. Of course, the rule is not infringed by proof of any collateral parol agreement, which does not interfere with the terms of the written contract, although it may relate to the subject-matter;(q) and it must be remem-

(n) 5 Rep. 26a.

(o) Tait on Evidence, 325. In Scotland a written agreement cannot be afterwards waived or varied by mere words, though a subsequent parol agreement, accompanied or followed by part performance, will suffice for that purpose. *Bargaddie Coal Co.* v. *Wark*, 3 Macq. Sc. Cas. H. of L. 467.

(p) See Taylor on Ev. § 1045 (5th ed.); *Marshall* v. *Lynn*, 6 M. & W. 116; *Emmet* v. *Dewkirst*, 21 L. J. Ch. 497; *Moore* v. *Campbell*, 10 Exch. 323; *Stowell* v. *Robinson*, 3 Bing. N. C. 928; *Stead* v. *Dawber*, 10 A. & E. 57.

(q) *White* v. *Parkin*, 12 East. 578; *Edwards* v. *Bates*, 7 M. & G. 600, 611, per Creswell, J.; *Foster* v. *Allanson*, 2 T. R. 479; *Fletcher* v. *Gillespie*, 3 Bing. 635. This and the above provisions have been introduced into the Indian Evidence Act, 1862; see sect. 92; see also The Law of Evidence in British India, by C. D. Field (2d ed. 1873), p. 316. The rule is well established that parol evidence of a *subsequent* agreement, varying the terms of the written agreement, is admissible. Thus, in one case, *Adler* v. *Friedman*, 16 Cal. 138, evidence of a parol agreement made subsequent thereto was admitted to show that it was agreed that a note which, on its face, bore *two* and one-half per cent. interest should bear but *one* and a half per cent. So, too, a parol agreement between two endorsers of a note to divide the loss between them, may be shown. *Phillips* v. *Preston*, 5 How. (U. S.) 278; *Cartwright* v. *Clayton*, 25 Ga. 85; *McDonald* v. *Stewart*, 18 La. An. 90. The *general* rule may be said to be that parol contemporaneous evidence is inadmissible to contradict or vary the terms of a valid written instrument, but a new agreement on a new consideration may be established by parol, whether it is a substitute for the old one, or only in addition to or beyond it. *Shepherd* v. *Wysong*, 3 W. Va. 46; *Heatherly* v. *Record*, 12 Tex. 49; *Flanders*

bered that the rule is applicable only to suits between the parties.(*r*)

General Principle Illustrated.

SEC. 61. The policy of the rule will be the better appreciated, and its nature and scope more thoroughly understood, from a consideration of some of the cases in which parol evidence has been rejected. In this place, any such inquiry, as it is mainly preliminary, must necessarily be short. Where, therefore, a policy of insurance was effected on goods "in ship or ships from Surinam to London," parol evidence was held inadmissible to show that a particular ship which was lost had been verbally excepted at the time of the contract.(*s*) And where a policy described the two termini of the voyage, the insurers were not allowed to prove by parol evidence that the risk was not to commence till the vessel reached an intermediate place.(*t*) So where a ship was particularly described in a written contract of sale, parol evidence of a further descriptive representation made prior to the sale was held inadmissible to charge the vendor, without proof, of actual fraud, all previous conversation being merged in the written contract.(*u*)

Rule as to Extrinsic Parol Evidence—Presumption.

SEC. 62. These and other cases(*v*) sufficiently illustrate the rule that, although extrinsic parol evidence is inadmissible to vary, add to, or subtract from the contents of a valid

v. *Fay,* 46 Vt. 316; *Marshall* v. *Baker,* 19 Me. 402; *Perry* v. *Central &c. R. R. Co.,* 5 Cald. (Tenn.) 138; *McKinstry* v. *Runk,* 12 N. J. Eq. 60; *Musselman* v. *Stoner,* 31 Penn. St. 265; *Cummings* v. *Putnam,* 19 N. H. 569; *Huckins* v. *Hebbard,* 34 N. Y. 24; *Keough* v. *McNitt,* 6 Minn. 513; *Holmes* v. *Doane,* 9 Cush. (Mass.) 135.

(*r*) 1 Poth. on Obl. 4, c. 2, art. 3, n. 766.

(*s*) *Kaines* v. *Knightly,* Skin. 54;

Leslie v. *De le Torre,* cited 12 East. 583.

(*t*) *Hoare* v. *Graham,* 3 Camp. 57; *Spartali* v. *Benecke,* 10 C. B. 212; *Besant* v. *Cross,* 10 C. B. 895; *Hanson* v. *Stetson,* 5 Pick. 506.

(*u*) *Pickering* v. *Dowson,* 4 Taunt. 779; see *The Isabella,* 2 Rob. Adm. 241; *White* v. *Wilson,* 2 B. & P. 116; *Rich* v. *Jackson,* 4 Br. C. C. 514.

(*v*) See Taylor on Evidence (5th ed.), § 1053, 1054, 1055, &c.

written instrument, on the sufficient grounds that the parties to the instrument must be presumed to have committed to writing all that was necessary to give full expression to their intentions and meaning, and that incalculable difficulty, confusion and mischief would arise if verbal testimony were received in such cases; still it may in all cases be adduced where there is doubt, with the view of explaining the written instrument, that is, for the purpose of enabling the court to understand the real nature of the contents of the writing before them, by an explication of the terms employed.(*w*)

(*w*) *Shore* v. *Wilson*, 9 Cl. & F. 355, *per* Parke, B.; 566, 567, *per* Tindal, C. J.; *Kell* v. *Charmer*, 23 Beav. 195; see also *Campbell* v. *Johnson*, 44 Mo. 247; *Perkins* v. *Young*, 82 Mass. 389; *Cocke* v. *Bailey*, 42 Miss. 81; *Ellis* v. *Crawford*, 39 Cal. 523; *Richards* v. *Schlegelmich*, 65 N. C. 150. That when a word has acquired a local or technical meaning by usage, it may be shown to ascertain the intention of the parties and the scope and meaning of the contract; see *Prather* v. *Ross*, 17 Ind. 495; *Clinen* v. *Cooke*, 1 Sch. & L. 22; *Barnard* v. *Adam*, 10 How. (U. S.) 270; *Sturgis* v. *Cary*, 2 Curtis (U. S. C. C.) 382; *Adams* v. *Packet Co.*, 5 C. B. N. S. 493; *Seymour* v. *Osborne*, 11 Wall. (U. S.) 546; *Brown* v. *Bryne*, 3 E. & B. 703. "Evidence may be given of a custom or usage," says *Allen, J.*, in *Lawrence* v. *Maxwell*, 53 N. Y. 21, "in explanation and application of particular words or phrases, and to aid in the interpretation of the contract, but not to derogate from the rights of the parties, or to import into the contract new terms and conditions or to vary the legal effect of the transaction." *Hudson* v. *Ede*, L. R., 3 Q. B. 412; *Whittemore* v. *Weiss*, 33 Mich. 348; *Robinson* v. *United States*, 13 Wall.

(U. S.) 363; *Merrick* v. *McNulty*, 26 Mich. 374; *George* v. *Joy*, 19 N. H. 544; *Myers* v. *Walker*, 24 Ill. 133; *Moran* v. *Prather*, 23 Wall. (U. S.) 499; *Lamb* v. *Klauss*, 30 Wis. 84; *Barnard* v. *Kellogg*, 10 Wall. (U. S.) 383; *Williams* v. *Woods*, 16 Md. 220; *Farrar* v. *Stackpole*, 6 Me. 154; *McMasters* v. *R. R. Co.*, 69 Penn. St. 374; *Brown* v. *Brooks*, 25 *Id.* 110; *Carey* v. *Bright*, 58 *Id.* 70; *Mieghen* v. *Bank*, 25 *Id.* 288; *Stone* v. *Bradbury*, 14 Me. 85. In *New Jersey Zinc Co.* v. *Boston Franklinite Co.* 15 N. J. Eq. 418, where a deed conveyed all the "zinc ore," evidence was admitted to show what was meant by the word "zinc," and to show that a certain vein, which the defendant claimed as "franklinite," passed under the word "zinc." In *Smith* v. *Clayton*, 29 N. J. L. 357, a lease of premises contained a provision that "should the said A. sell the last mentioned lot at any time after the said C. has planted the same, he shall have the privilege of sowing *grain* on the same." The lessor having sold the land after C. had planted the land, he sowed oats on the corn ground the succeeding spring, and the question was whether he was not restricted to the sowing of winter grain. The court held that

Usage in Relation to Ambiguity—The Meaning of Words.

SEC. 63. Here we find ourselves in a position to consider the laws relating to usage, for it is evident that in consider-

evidence of the meaning of the word "*grain*," as used in common parlance, was not admissible, but that it was the duty of the court to determine its meaning. But that parol evidence of the meaning of a word that is ambiguous or made so by the evidence, may be shown. See *Hart* v. *Hammett*, 18 Vt. 127; *Patch* v. *Ins. Co.* 44 Vt. 481; *Collender* v. *Dinsmore*, 55 N. Y. 204; *Collins* v. *Driscoll*, 34 Conn. 43; *Avery* v. *Stewart*, 2 Conn. 69; *Eaton* v. *Smith*, 20 Pick. (Mass.) 150; *Walls* v. *Bailey*, 49 N. Y. 464; *Taylor* v. *Sotolingo*, 6 La. An. 154; *Galena Ins. Co.* v. *Kupfer*, 28 Ill. 332; *Drake* v. *Gorce*, 22 Ala. 409; *Hooper* v. *R. R. Co.* 27 Wis. 81; *Soutier* v. *Kellerman*, 18 Mo. 509; *Johnson* v. *Ins. Co.* 39 Wis. 87; *Fitch* v. *Carpenter*, 43 Barb. (N. Y.) 50; *Wait* v. *Fairbanks*, Bray. (Vt.) 77; *Stewart* v. *Smith*, 28 Ill. 397; *Jenny Lind Co.* v. *Bower*, 11 Cal. 194; *Reynoulds* v. *Jourdan*, 6 Cal. 108; *Dent* v. *Steamship Co.*, 49 N. Y. 320; *Schnitzer* v. *Print Works*, 114 Mass. 123; *Page* v. *Cole*, 120 Mass. 37; *Howard* v. *Ins. Co.* 109 Mass. 387; *Murray* v. *Hatch*, 6 Mass. 465. In *Ganson* v. *Madigan*, 15 Wis. 144, usage was admitted to show what was meant by the word "team." In *Whitney* v. *Boardman*, 118 Mass. 242, to show what was meant by the words "all faults," in a contract where certain property was sold "with all faults," and generally where it is shown that a word has acquired a special or technical meaning in a certain trade it may be shown, because it is presumed that every person conducting such trade uses the language of the trade, and

makes his contracts in conformity with the sense in which such language is therein employed. *Carter* v. *Coal Co.* 77 Penn. St. 286; *Mieghan* v. *Bank*, 25 Id. 288. And the same rule prevails where words are used in a peculiar sense in a certain district or locality. *Pope* v. *Nickerson*, 3 Story (U. S.) 465; *Trimble* v. *Vignier*, 1 Bing. (N. C.) 151; *De La Vega* v. *Vianna*, 1 Br. Ad. 284; *De Wolfe* v. *Johnson*, 10 Wheat. (U. S.) 367; *Clayton* v. *Greyson*, 5 Ad. & El. 502; *Aben* v. *Carson*, 62 Mo. 207. The usage of a trade is admissible to fix the exact liability of the parties in cases where the contract is silent in that respect, and the law has fixed no definite standard. Thus, in a contract by which A. agrees to work for B. ten days, at $2.50 a day, the contract seems definite enough, but A. has really worked 120 hours, and the question is, has he worked *more* or *less* than 10 days. If he has worked *more* than that number of days, he is entitled to additional pay in the proportion that the excess bears to the price per day; if less, then B. is entitled to a proportionate deduction. The law has fixed no definite standard, therefore usage is the only instrumentality that can be brought in to solve the question, and the courts admit it. *Hinton* v. *Locke*, 5 Hill (N. Y.) 437. So to show what is meant by the words "weeks," "months," &c., in a certain class of contracts. *Grant* v. *Maddox*, 15 Moll. 737; *Jolly* v. *Young*, 1 Esp. 186. So, too, where certain work, as "plastering" a house, or "laying a cellar wall," &c., &c., is to be done at so much per

ing the meanings of the words used in any document regard must be had to their ordinary use. A dictionary is, after all, only a volume of precedents. But words have not only a common, conversational and literary meaning, they very often have a technical, a business sense, and in transactions connected with that particular trade or profession there is every probability that the Janus-faced word will be used in its technical sense, and it is there of importance, by means of witnesses conversant with the business, trade and locality, to which the document relates, to speak as to the particular conventional meaning of the words in question. (x)

square yard, evidence of the usage of plasterers, in the locality where the contract was made, has been held admissible to determine whether, in ascertaining the quantity, the whole sides of the house should be measured as solid, or whether allowances should be made for openings of windows and doors. The courts justly hold that contracts of this character are ambiguous to the extent that evidence of the usage of the trade is admissible to ascertain the true method of measurement and the number of yards, &c., that should be paid for, provided the usage is not unreasonable. *Walls* v. *Bailey,* 49 N. Y. 467 ; *Ford* v. *Tirrell,* 9 Gray (Mass.) 401; *Lowe* v. *Lehman,* 15 Ohio St. 179. It may be stated as a general rule, that *where a word or phrase used in a contract is susceptible of two or more meanings, extrinsic evidence is admissible to ascertain in which sense it was employed by the parties,* and if a usage exists by which the words, in the trade to which the contract relates, have acquired a definite meaning that is regarded as the real exponent of the true intention of the parties. *Bottomley* v. *Forbes,* 5 Bing. (N. C.) 121; *Journu* v. *Bordieu,* Park

on Ins. 245; *Mason* v. *Skurry, Id.* 245; *Mackenzie* v. *Dunlop,* 3 Macg. (S. C.) 26; *Buckle* v. *Knoop,* 2 L. R. Exchq. 125.

(x) See Bell's Com. b. 3, pt. 1, ch. 3 (7th ed.), vol. 1, p. 456; see also *per* Lord Eldon, in *Anderson* v. *Pitcher,* 2 B. & P. 164; *Cutter* v. *Powell,* 6 T. R. 320. Commercial men may be called as witnesses not only to prove the meaning of certain terms used in mercantile transactions, but also to prove any commercial usage. *Chaurand* v. *Augerstein,* Peake 43, but when decisions are made thereon it becomes the law of the land, of which not only all parties, but also the court, is bound to take notice. *Bank of Columbia* v. *Fitzhugh,* 1 H. & G. (Md.) 239; *Branch* v. *Burnley,* 1 Call. (Va.) 159; *Consequa* v. *Willing,* Pet. (U. S. C. C.) 230; *Robertson* v. *Money,* 1 Ry. & M. 75; *Uhde* v. *Walters,* 3 Camp. 16. The phrase, usage of trade, implies a restriction to that class of merchants or persons who deal in a certain article or prosecute a business to which the usage relates. *Astor* v. *Union Ins. Co.* 7 Cow. (N. Y.) 202; *Thompson* v. *Sloan,* 23 Wend. (N. Y.) 71. The fact that a particular mode

The Legal Principles and Usage as Evidence.

SEC. 64. The principles which have governed the admission of the evidence of usage in such cases have been uniform, but an important question arises as to the expediency of an indiscriminate admission of usages in explanation of written contracts, which has to do with the whole policy of the law; and as the subject is one which by its nature should be considered before entering upon a minute account of the various decisions in connection with the reception of evidence in such cases, this seems the proper place to set out one or two of the opinions which have been expressed upon the subject, and the principles which ought to guide to an answer to this important question.

As to the Extent to which Usage Should be Admitted to Vary Written Contracts—Practice of Traders.

SEC. 65. There have been many doubts expressed as to the expediency of the extension of the rule as to the admissibility of evidence of usage. That it was originally admissible only to explain written contracts, that it was used to assist in the rational construction of written instruments, is certain; but it is equally beyond doubt that in many cases it had been admitted to put a construction upon such writings at variance with that which was in the intention of the parties. There are scarcely any questions which come before

of doing a certain thing in a certain trade or business is very common, but that a few persons engaged in the trade do not do so, is not sufficient to establish a usage of that trade, because it is lacking in uniformity of application. *Castill* v. *Crawford*, 7 Ala. 635, nor generally can a custom or usage be proved by an isolated instance, nor can evidence of a usage of one person engaged in a business be operative to establish a general usage. *The Paragon*, 1 Ware (U. S.) 322; *Coke* v. *Dodd*, 13 Penn. St. 33; *Burr* v. *Sickles*, 17 Ark. 428. As a general rule the evidence of one person is not sufficient to establish a usage, but whether or not it will have that effect will depend upon the experience of the person in, and his general knowledge of, the trade and its methods. *Halmerson* v. *Cole*, 1 Speers (S. C.) 321; *Thomas* v. *Graves*, 1 Mill's (S. C.) Const. 309; *Bissell* v. *Ryan*, 23 Ill. 566; *Partridge* v. *Forsyth*, 29 Ala. 200; *Vail* v. *Rice*, 5 N. Y. 155; *Hamilton* v. *Nickerson*, 13 Allen (Mass.) 351.

courts of law so difficult of decision as those involving customs. Here the court has to deal with something which is vague and indefinite, which bears much similarity to law, but which yet comes before them in the guise of evidence, which is not definitely written in books, but lives only in the breath of the public and the vague traditions of the actions of men. It requires not only legal learning but genius to deal with such cases, and it is not to be wondered at if many of the common law judges shrink from the task of exercising such an indefinite jurisdiction. Lord Campbell, with great sagacity, has pointed out this fact.(y) "Lawyers," he says,

(y) See 7 El. & Bl. at p. 279. In many of the States in this country there is a strong tendency to exclude usage, not only where it in any measure conflicts with the terms of the contract, but also where it conflicts with the well established rules of the common law. "I am among those judges," said *Story, J.*, in *Donnell* v. *Columbia Ins. Co.*, 2 Sum. (U. S.) 367, "who think that usages among merchants should be very sparingly adopted, as rules of court, by courts of justice, as they are often founded in mere mistake, and still more often in the want of enlarged and comprehensive views of the full bearing of principles." In *Barnard* v. *Kellogg*, 10 Wall. (U. S.) 393, *Davis, J.*, in reference to the office of usages says, "Whatever tends to unsettle the law and make it different in the different communities into which the State is divided, leads to mischievous consequences, embarrasses trade, *and is against public policy. If, therefore,*" he adds, "*on a given state of facts the rights and liabilities of the parties are fixed by the general principle of the common law, they cannot be changed by any local custom of the place where the contract*

was made." In New York the rule is well established that evidence of a custom or usage cannot be received to change the legal import of a contract. *Holmes* v. *Pettingill*, 1 Hun. (N. Y.) 366, affd. 60 N. Y. 646; *Lane* v. *Bailey*, 47 Barb. (N. Y.) 395; *Vail* v. *Rice*, 5 N. Y. 155; *Dalton* v. *Davids*, 2 Hill (N. Y. C. P.) 472; *Hinton* v. *Locke*, 5 Hill (N. Y.) 437; *Allen* v. *Dykers*, 3 *Id.* 593; *Bissell* v. *Campbell*, 54 N. Y. 353; *Lawrence* v. *Maxwell*, 53 N. Y. 19; *Higgins* v. *Moore*, 34 N. Y. 417; *Taylor* v. *Ketchum*, 5 Robt. (N. Y.) 507; *Wadsworth* v. *Allcott*, 6 N. Y. 64; *Bargett* v. *Orient Ins. Co.*, 3 Bos. (N. Y.) 385; *Lombard* v. *Case*, 47 Barb. (N. Y.) 95; *Wall* v. *East River Ins. Co.*, 3 Durr. (N. Y.) 264. But the courts hold that such evidence is admissible to *explain* a rule of commercial law. *Firth* v. *Barker*, 2 John. (N. Y.) 327; *Emery* v. *Dunbar*, 1 Daly (N. Y. C. P.) 408; *Outwater* v. *Nelson*, 20 Barb. (N. Y.) 29; *Schiefflin* v. *Harvey*, 6 John. (N. Y.) 170; *Markham* v. *Jandon*, 41 (N. Y.) 235; *Gibson* v. *Culver*, 17 Wend. (N. Y.) 305; *Otsego County Bank* v. *Warren*, 18 Barb. (N. Y.) 290. It is also held in the same State that such evidence is not admissible to vary

"desire certainty, and would have a contract express all its

the terms of an express agreement. *Main* v. *Eagle*, 1 E. D. S. (N. Y. C. P.) 617; *Stebbins* v. *Brown*, 65 Barb. (N. Y.) 274; *Parsons* v. *Miller*, 15 Wend. (N. Y.) 561; *Bradley* v. *Wheeler*, 44 N. Y. 495; *Collender* v. *Dinsmore*, 55 N.Y. 200; *Groat* v. *Gile*, 51 N. Y. 431; *Mercantile Ins. Co.* v. *State Ins. Co.*, 25 Barb. (N. Y.) 319; *Simmons* v. *Law*, 3 Keyes, (N. Y.) 217. Therefore, when certain property is sold without an express warranty, it is held that evidence of a usage of trade to treat all such sales as with warranty is inadmissible. *Bierne* v. *Dord*, 5 N. Y. 95; *Hawes* v. *Lawrence*, 4 *Id.* 345. Substantially the same doctrine, in reference to all these matters, prevails in Massachusetts. *Homer* v. *Dorr*, 10 Mass. 26; *Strong* v. *Bliss*, 6 Met. (Mass.) 393; *Hoskins* v. *Warren*. 115 Mass. 514; *Dickinson* v. *Gay*, 7 Allen (Mass.) 9; *Richardson* v. *Copeland*, 6 Gray (Mass.) 536; *Rice* v. *Codman*, 1 Allen (Mass.) 377; *Mechanics Bank* v. *Merchants Bank*, 6 Met. (Mass.) 13; *Bliss* v. *Ropes*, 9 Allen (Mass.) 339. As to admissibility to affect contracts, *Brown* v. *Forster*, 113 Mass. 136; *Atkins* v. *Howe*, 18 Pick. (Mass.) 16; *Macomber* v. *Parker*, 13 *Id.* 175; *Randall* v. *Rotch*, 12 *Id.* 107; *Davis* v. *Galloupe*, 111 Mass. 121; *Snelling* v. *Hall*, 107 *Id.* 134; also, in Pennsylvania, *Bolton* v. *Colder*, 1 Watts (Penn.) 360; *Christian* v. *Dripps*, 28 Penn. St. 271; *Brown* v. *Arrott*, 6 W. & S. 402; *Coxe* v. *Heisley*, 19 Penn. St. 243; *Weaver* v. *Fegley*, 29 Penn. St. 243; *Evans* v. *Myers*, 25 *Id.* 114. But whatever the courts may say as to the introduction of evidence of a usage that conflicts with the well settled rules of law, it will be found in practice, and by a careful examination of the case, that the rule exists more in theory than in practice, and that the rule really is nothing more nor less than that, *evidence of a usage that conflicts with a well settled rule of law, must be of such a character as to afford irresistible evidence that the parties knew of, and contracted in reference to, the usage, rather than in reference to the rules of law, and that where nothing more than mere proof of a usage exists, and the parties knowledge thereof, it will be presumed that the parties contracted in reference to the law rather than the usage.* *Adams* v. *Pittsburgh Ins. Co.*, 76 Penn. St. 411; *Jones* v. *Wagner*, 66 *Id.* 429; *Barnard* v. *Kellogg*, 10 Wall. (U. S.) 383; *Overman* v. *Hoboken Bank*, 30 N. J. L. 61; *Id.*, 31 *Id.* 563. A contrary rule would be not only inconsistent, but actually absurd. It would in effect overturn a well settled rule that parties may waive the provisions of the common law, or a statute even, and contract in direct opposition thereto, unless the statute prohibits such a contract, or it is *malum in se* or opposed to the policy of the law. Therefore there can be no question but that in all cases where the parties may expressly contract in opposition to the common law or a statute, evidence of a usage may be given to show that the parties in a given case contracted in reference to it rather than in reference to the law, but in such cases the presumption will *primâ faciæ* be that the parties contracted in reference to the law, and in order to give effect to the usage, the evidence must be such as to fairly overcome this presumption. To illustrate, take the case of *Barnard* v. *Kellogg*, 10 Wall. (U. S.) 383.

terms, and desire that no parol evidence beyond it should

Suppose that in that case *both* parties had known of the usage in question, and it had been shown that for that reason the purchaser had omitted to examine *all* the wool, or that the parties had had similar transactions before, in which the usage had been recognized and acted upon, can there be any question but that in that event the usage would have been held effectual, and the sale treated as one with warranty as to quality? In this case it will be noticed that the court made the qualification that the usage could not be relied upon to establish a warranty, "*especially where the parties did not know of the custom.*" Again, suppose that by statute it is provided that interest on accounts shall be chargeable one year after it accrued, or by the common law, after a balance is struck; but a certain merchant has established a usage to charge interest on *monthly* balances, which is known to his customers, and upon which they have acted in all former transactions; can there be any doubt but that the courts, even in New York, as has been held in Massachusetts, would be compelled to hold, as the courts of Pennsylvania have, that such *usage* will prevail in all transactions between such merchant and his customers, rather than the rules of law in that regard? In other words, is not the usage in such cases tacitly annexed to contracts for credit between such parties, so as to become a law unto them? *Fisher v. Sargent*, 10 Cush. (Mass.) 250; *Loring v. Gurney*, 5 Pick. (Mass.) 15; *Watt v. Hoch*, 25 Penn. St. 411; *Adams v. Palmer*, 30 Penn. St. 346; *Koons v. Miller*, 3 W. & S. (Penn.) 271. The editors of Phillips on Evidence (Messrs. Cowen and Hill) in a note upon this subject, give the question as to the admissibility of evidence of a usage that conflicts with the general law a very careful and elaborate consideration. They say, vol. 2, p. 612, "We frequently meet with general propositions like the following: 'A usage must be reasonable, and can never be received to contradict a settled rule of law.'" *Frith v. Barker*, 2 John. (N. Y.) 335; *Eager v. Atlas Ins. Co.* 14 Pick. (Mass.) 141; *Homer v. Dorr*, 10 Mass. 26; *Henry v. Risk*, 1 Dall. (U. S.) 265; *Bowen v. Jackson*, Whart. (Penn.) 252; *Stoever v. Whitman*, 6 Binn. (Penn.) 416; *Rankin v. American Ins. Co.*, 1 Hall (N. Y.) 619; *Brown v. Jackson*, 2 Wash. (U. S. C. C.) 24; *Winthrop v. Union Ins. Co.*, 2 *Id.* 9; *Barksdale v. Brown*, 1 N. & McC. (S. C.) 517; (to which may be added, *Boardman v. Spooner*, 13 Allen (Mass.) 353; *Farnsworth v. Hemmer*, 1 *Id.* 494; *Glass Co. v. Morey*, 108 Mass. 570; *Barnard v. Kellogg*, 10 Wall. (U. S.) 383; *Evans v. Waln*, 71 Penn. St. 69; *Mears v. Waples*, 3 Houst. (Del.) 581; *Dewees v. Lockhart*, 1 Tex. 585; *Jones v. Wagner*, 66 Penn. St. 430; *Randall v. Smith*, 63 Mo. 105; *Security Bank v. Bank of the Republic*, 67 N. Y. 458. *Edie v. The East India Company*, 2 Burr. 1216, will, it is apprehended, be found the nucleus of most of this doctrine; and when considered in reference to the particular facts to which it was applied, is undoubtedly correct. There, *Lord Mansfield* had received evidence at Nisi Prius of the custom of merchants, that in a case of a bill of exchange payable to order, the indorsement was restrictive, unless

be receivable. But merchants and traders with a multi-

that also contained the word order. At the bar, on motion for a new trial, he and the other judges concurred, that the law being settled, the custom of merchants could not control it; that is to say, would not subvert the law of the land, as such; not that the parties might not make the indorsement restrictive by special agreement, or by the customary course of some particular business, making an exception in their own case, leaving the general law to take its course. But there the bill of exchange was drawn in the East Indies, and the main evidence came from bankers in London. Their opinion was allowed by Lord Mansfield to overturn a rule of law which pervaded the whole empire, and indeed the whole commercial world. The court, *Cowen, J.*, delivering the opinion. *Gibson* v. *Culver*, 17 Wend. (N. Y.) 308; *Rushforth* v. *Hadfield*, 17 East 225, lays down the true doctrine. There the court agreed that evidence of usage was admissible to enlarge the rights of carriers. The defendants claimed a lien on the goods carried, not only for the price of carrying them in particular, but for a general balance due to them for previous carriage. The law denies to carriers a claim for a general balance; but a long train of evidence was received, to show that custom and a particular course of trade, among a particular sort of carriers, had overcome the law. The jury found against the defendants, but the evidence was so imposing that they moved for a new trial. *Chambre, J.*, who tried the cause, put it to the jury, whether the usage was so general as to warrant them in pre-

suming that the parties who delivered the goods to be carried knew of it, and understood that they were contracting in conformity to it; if not, the general rule of law would entitle the plaintiffs to a verdict. All the judges concurred that a custom of this kind, which is *quoad hoc*, to supersede the general law of the land, should be clearly proved, and the interested encroachments of persons engaged in a particular trade watched with great jealousy. None of them disapproved the qualifications under which the case went to the jury; and *Lord Ellenborough, C. J.*, and *Grose, J.*, put it on the ground of a usage so general, and so uniformly acquiesced in for a length of time, that the jury would feel themselves constrained to say it entered into the minds of the parties, and made a part of the contract. But all this has nothing to do with the abstract question of competency. Usage, when it goes to change the law, is always hard to be made out; yet, if counsel propose to prove such a usage, and think they can establish it, there is, it seems, no rule of law which forbids the attempt. *Gibson* v. *Culver*, 17 Wend. (N. Y.) 305, 307, 308, 309, *et seq*. The doctrine on this subject has been considerably discussed in South Carolina. There a usage of the river trade, for the carrier of goods to look to the produce and consignee alone, for freight, was set up as a defense to the person who sent them; and it was held, that the usage might be proved. *Grant, J.*, who delivered the opinion, conceded that it would be difficult to make out the usage in such cases; but that has nothing to do with its

7

plicity of transactions pressing on them, and moving in a

competency. In respect to the unreasonableness of the usage, he said that, "although at the first blush, the custom alleged may appear unreasonable, and such as ought not to prevail, this is by no means conclusive that the usage was not a good one in law. In such cases recourse is had to artificial and legal reason; and thus considered, the usage may be shown to be beneficial to the boatmen themselves." He further observed: "It is competent for a man or a body of men to renounce a common law right, if they think proper; and if, in relation to the river trade, either from views of interest, on the part of boat owners, or other politic considerations, expediency has pointed out the propriety, and usage has sanctioned it, then it might become the law by which the contract should be expounded." *Middleton* v. *Heyward*, 2 N. & McC. (S. C.) 9. But see *Heyward* v. *Middleton*, 3 McC. (S. C.) 121. The fact of a particular thing being sanctioned by usage so general, uniform and extensive, as to raise the presumption that all who deal in reference to its subject, are presumed to have knowledge of the usage, and to contract in reference to it, would seem in itself to be very cogent evidence of its expediency and reasonableness, as it respects the class of persons among whom it prevails; and if not objectionable in any other point of view, the simple question should be, is it a *usage?* See the observations of *Cheves, J.,* in *Barksdale* v. *Brown*, 1 N. & McC. (S. C.) 521. This accords with the elementary notion as to the origin of usages and customs generally, in respect to

which it has been said, that where the people of a particular class or place "find any act to be good and beneficial, and apt and agreeable to their nature and dispositions, they use and practice it from time to time, and so by frequent iteration and repetition of the act, a custom is formed." *The Case of Tanistry*, Davies' Rep. 87. Thus the custom of gavelkind and borough English have grown up, and although contrary to the common law, are allowed to be good. *Id.* 88. A strong case for showing that a local usage is not necessarily bad because opposed to the general law, is that of *Snowdon* v. *Warder*, 3 Rawle (Penn.) 181. There a usage, in Philadelphia for vendors of cotton in that city, to be answerable for defects, without either fraud or express warranty being proved, was established, and a vendor held liable accordingly. This was virtually permitting that class of dealers to abrogate the common law, which else must have applied, and introduce the civil law principle in its stead. When a written contract for the sale of goods is definite and certain in its terms, as to the goods sold, or can be made so by showing the subject (a lot of oats) to which the parties intended it to apply, it cannot be controlled or modified in that respect by evidence of commercial usage. *Vail* v. *Rice*, 5 N. Y. 155. Nor can a usage of trade be shown, that a contract for flour of a particular brand may be satisfied by the delivery of flour of an equal or better quality. *Beals* v. *Terry*, 2 Sand. (N. Y.) 127. A usage will not be received in evidence to vary the construction of a contract, unless it was known

narrow circle and meeting each other, desire to write little

to the parties and they contracted in reference to it. *Wheeler* v. *Newbold*, 16 N. Y. 392; 5 Duer 29. But parties are presumed to contract with reference to a known usage. 5 Hill (N. Y.) 437; 20 Barb. (N. Y.) 29. Though evidence of usage cannot be shown where the terms of the contract are plain and unambiguous. *Wadworth* v. *Allcott*, 6 N. Y. 64. The result of the authorities, therefore, seems to be that a particular usage in reference to the contract in question, may be proved to influence its construction, though contrary to some rule of general law; and then it will be a question of fact, triable like other facts, whether the parties contracted in reference to the usage or not; in other words, whether they did or did not intend to adopt the usage, instead of the general law, as the rule for interpreting the contract. See *Gordon* v. *Little*, 8 S. & R. (Penn.) 533; *Snowden* v. *Warder*, 3 Rawle (Penn.) 101; *Renner* v. *Bank of Columbia*, 9 Wheat. (U. S.) 581, 584, 585; *Jones* v. *Fales*, 4 Mass. Rep. 245; *Kennebec Bank* v. *Page*, 9 Mass. 155; *Kennebec Bank* v. *Hammatt, Id.* 159; *Widgerey* v. *Monroe*, 6 *Id.* 449; *Weld* v. *Gotham*, 10 *Id.* 366; *Wood* v. *Wilcox*, 9 Wend. (N. Y.) 349; *Blanchard* v. *Hilliard*, 11 Mass. R. 85; *Middleton* v. *Heyward*, 2 N. & McCord (S. C.) 9; *Halsey* v. *Brown*, 3 Day (Conn.) 346. But see the cases in 25 Wend. and 6 Hill (N. Y.), cited *ante* in this note. Limitations upon this right, however, do undoubtedly exist; and cases may often arise where the court must adjudge the usage absolutely void in itself. If that which is thus sought to be incorporated with the contract would be void as

an express stipulation, the evidence cannot be allowed. Hence, usages sanctioning what is *malum in se* or *malum prohibitum*, are invalid. *Snowden* v. *Warder*, 3 Rawle (Penn.) 107; *Bryant* v. *The Commonwealth Ins. Co.*, 6 Pick. (Mass.) 131. Usages favoring the taking of unlawful interest, and trenching upon the policy of the statutes on that subject are bad (*Dunham* v. *Dey*, 13 John. (N. Y.) 44); though usage among bankers has been said to have sanctioned certain practices which else would have been deemed usurious. See *per* Savage, C. J., in *Bank of Utica* v. *Wager*, 2 Cow. (N. Y.) 712, 766; S. C. reversed on error, 8 *Id.* 398. Usages in restraint of trade are void, *semble*. *Williams* v. *Gillman*, 3 Me. 281. So of usages originating in and continued by violence, oppression and fraud, or contrary to the general good, and such, it has been said, are, for the most part, those usages and customs which have been adjudged void by the English courts, as "unreasonable," "against common right," "contrary to law," &c., &c. Davies' Rep. 89. A usage sanctioning what is unjust and against good morals, is bad; *e. g.*, a usage among banks, not to correct mistakes in counting money unless discovered before the person leaves the room (*Gallatin* v. *Bradford*, 1 Bibb (Ky.) 209); or a custom of mechanics to charge for materials according to a standard which would give them pay for materials never furnished. *Whitsides* v. *Meredith*, 3 Yeates (Penn.) 318. See *Kendall* v. *Russell*, 5 Dana (Ky.) 501. So of a custom to commit acts of trespass upon others' property (*Waters* v. *Lilly*, 4 Pick. (Mass.) 145; and a custom of

and leave unwritten what they may take for granted in

agents to depart from the instructions of their principal. *Barksdale* v. *Brown*, 1 N. & McC. (S. C.) 517. A custom of masters to sell the cargo of a stranded vessel, without necessity, has been characterized as a usage against "faith and common honesty," and therefore bad. *Bryant* v. *The Commonwealth Ins. Co.* 6 Pick. (Mass.) 145. *Quere*, whether a local usage, exempting proprietors of carrier vessels from all responsibility in respect to goods committed to their charge, except for injuries arising from the negligence of the master, would not be void, as contrary to the general good, and subversive of the interests of trade and navigation. See what was said by *Story, J.*, in *The Schooner Reeside*, 2 Sum. (U. S.) 574, 575; also, *per* Cowen, J., in *Cole* v. *Goodwin*, 19 Wend. (N. Y.) 272, *et seq.* It follows, from what has been said, that evidence of usage may be received to vary, in some sense, the *legal effect* of a written instrument. But see *Eager* v. *Atlas Ins. Co.*, 14 Pick. (Mass.) 144, as to what is there said, however, *quere. Prima facie*, every contract is to be understood as containing, in some sort, an implied reference to the general law; but when a state of facts is made out, which rebuts that presumption, and shows that the parties intended to adopt a particular usage as the rule of interpretation, the latter shall prevail, provided it be such a usage as the parties had a right to adopt. But it is obvious that where the contract itself manifests an intention, either directly or indirectly, to exclude the usage, no evidence of it can be received without overstepping the limits of exposition. "A custom

or usage of trade is only allowable as one mean to arrive at the intention, never to thwart or control it. If the stipulations of a contract indicate an *intention* in the obligor, variant from the usage, then should the stipulations prevail; otherwise, an obligation may be imposed contrary to the intention, though provided against by the express terms of the contract." *Per* Ewing, J., delivering the opinion of the court in *Kendall* v. *Russell*, 5 Dana (Ky.) 501, 502. See *per* Story, J., in *Schooner Reeside*, 2 Sum. (U. S.) 570. What shall be deemed such an expression of intention, inconsistent with the usage, as to exclude the latter, is many times a question of considerable difficulty. The general rule is clear; no extrinsic evidence of usage can be received to vary, add to, or contradict the plain sense of the contract when once properly ascertained. See *Mumford* v. *Hallett*, 1 John. (N. Y.) 439; *Rankin* v. *The American Ins. Co.*, 1 Hall (N.Y.) 619; *The Schooner Reeside*, 2 Sum. (U. S.) 56, and *Turney* v. *Wilson*, 7 Yerg. (Tenn) 540; *Stoever* v. *Whitman's Lessee*, 6 Binn. (Penn.) 516; *Turner* v. *Burrows*, 5 Wend. 541, 547; *Parsons* v. *Miller*, 15 *Id.* 562; *Snowden* v. *Warder*, 3 Rawle (Penn.) 107; *Yeates* v. *Pim*, 2 Marsh. 141; *Blackett* v. *Royal Exchange Ass. Co.*, 2 C. & J. 244. But the application of it depends so much upon particular forms of expression and terms in the contract, which may happen to strike different minds in different ways, as well as upon various collateral and extrinsic circumstances, that it is not extraordinary to find learned judges disagreeing some-

every contract. In spite of the lamentations of judges they

what on this point. That disagreement, as we have seen, is most strikingly apparent in those cases where usage has been invoked to supersede some rule of general law. Then the presumption that the parties contracted in reference to the general law, must be overcome before the usage can be applied; and very slight indications of intent, appearing in the instrument, have been seized upon as corroborating that presumption, to the extent of excluding the usage altogether. This is illustrated by many of the cases *supra*. In *Eager* v. *Atlas Ins. Co.* 14 Pick. (Mass.) 141, it was held to be the general law as to insurance of vessels, that in adjusting a partial loss on a ship which has been repaired, the proceeds of the old materials not used in the repairs are first to be deducted. The underwriters claimed, in virtue of a local usage at Boston (the place where the policy was made), that they had the right of deducting one-third new for old from the gross amount of the expense of repair. The policy was according to a form which had been recently adopted by all the insurance companies at Boston, and contained an express reference to certain usages of the Boston insurance companies, but none in respect to this. There were some stipulations, moreover, in the policy, touching partial losses, which, however, were aside of the point designed to be established by the usage. Another fact adverted to by the court was, that the question as to the general law had been settled in New York years before the present policy was underwritten, and for some time be-

fore had been pending in Massachusetts for decision. *Id.* 144. "From these and other circumstances," the court said, "the presumption is strong that the parties did not treat, as to the mode of adjustment on the basis of usage, but on that of the existing law, however it might be decided. When the contract refers *to the customs and rules* of insurance in Boston, and specifies how far they shall constitute part of the contract, it must be inferred that the parties did not intend that it should be affected thereby beyond the extent specified, especially as the form of the policy was no doubt settled with great care and deliberation." *Id.* 144, 145. These considerations were deemed quite sufficient to settle the question of usage, but another was added, viz. : that the contract being one of indemnity, and the mode of adjustment contended for by the underwriters being one which would deprive the insured of a full indemnity, the usage was opposed *to the essence of the contract. Id.* 145. See as to the mode of adjustment in such cases, according to the general law. *Byrnes* v. *National Ins. Co.*, 1 Cow. (N. Y.) 265; *Brooks* v. *The Oriental Ins. Co.*, 7 Pick. (Mass.) 259. See also the opinions of *Messrs. Nichols, Phillips* and *Jackson*, Amer. Jurist, vol. 5, pp. 252, 262, and vol. 6, p. 45, together with the authorities cited. Where a brickyard was let to H. by E. & L., the owners, under a contract that H. should make bricks in the yard, hire the workmen, &c., give in his time and services, and pay a certain sum for every thousand bricks made, as rent; E. & L. stipulating that they would attend to selling the

will continue to do so, and in a vast majority of cases of

bricks, purchasing the materials, collecting the bills, &c.; the parties to share the profits and loss equally, and E. & L. to have the right to retain the bricks, or money collected, in their possession, to the amount of all sums, &c., advanced by them from time to time to H.; held, that the bricks made under the contract were the joint property of the parties, and such being the plain intent expressed, evidence of a usage tending to vary the effect of it in such a way as to show that H. had no property in the bricks, but only a claim to a certain share of the profits, was inadmissible. *Macomber* v. *Parker*, 13 Pick. (Mass.) 175. In *Kendall* v. *Russell*, 5 Dana (Ky.) 501, the plaintiff sued to recover for laying brick in a building. The covenant under which he performed the work bound him to lay *as many bricks as the defendant might need to complete the building*, for which the defendant bound himself to pay a given sum *per thousand for each thousand brick laid*. On the trial the plaintiff claimed to recover according to a local custom allowing the quantity of brick laid to be ascertained by assuming, as a basis of calculation, that the whole was solid work, and not regarding openings, such as doors, windows, &c. The court held the terms of the contract plainly expressive of a different intent, viz.. that the plaintiff should be compensated only for the brick actually laid, and so the usage was inadmissible. See also *Whitesides* v. *Meredith*, 3 Yeates (Penn.) 318. There are various usages of trade and commerce which have been so often proved as matters of fact, and have so far incorporated themselves with

the general law that courts will judicially recognize them. See *Consequa* v. *Willings*, 1 Pet. C. C. (U. S.) 230; *Snowden* v. *Warder*, 3 Rawle (Penn.) 105; *Wilcox* v. *Wood*, 9 Wend. 349; *United States* v. *Arredondo*, 6 Pet. (U. S.) 715; *Thomas* v. *O'Hara*, 1 Const. Ct. S. C. 306. But particular usages, such as these of which we have been speaking, must be proved specially. And the circumstances of the usage being *primâ facie* " unreasonable," " against the general law," " restricted within very narrow limits," of comparatively " recent origin," &c., &c., always come in to enhance the difficulty of showing that the parties contracted in reference to it, and intended to make it the law of their case. See *Gibson* v. *Culver*, 17 Wend. (N. Y.) 307, 308, 309; *Wilcox* v. *Wood*, 9 *Id*. 349; *Middleton* v. *Heyward*, 2 N. & McCord (S. C.) 9; *Gordon* v. *Little*, 8 S. & R. (Penn.) 535; *Eager* v. *Atlas Ins. Co.*, 14 Pick. (Mass.) 143, 144; *Snowden* v. *Warder*, 3 Rawle (Penn.) 105; *Thomas* v. *O'Hara*, 1 R. Const. Ct. So. Car. 306; *Furniss* v. *Hone*, 8 Wend. (N. Y.) 266; *Allegre* v. *The Maryland Ins. Co.*, 2 G. & J. (Md.) 136. And perhaps this is the sense in which many cases are to be understood, which lay down the proposition that *a usage, to be obligatory, must be certain, uniform, reasonable and sufficiently ancient to be generally known, &c.* See the case of *Kendall* v. *Russell*, 5 Dana (Ky.) 501, and what is said at pp. 503, 504. When the question is of a custom or usage, and it is not known to those who, from their business and connections, have the best means of knowing it, ignorance of it is, in some sense, positive testimony of its

which courts of law hear nothing they do so without loss

non-existence. Thus, suppose the question to be as to the existence of a usage of trade in a foreign port, according to which the rights of parties are to be decided—and that there are two foreign witnesses, both merchants belonging to the place, and dealing in the same business, one of whom testifies in support of the usage and the other is ignorant of it, in such case it seems the usage cannot be said to be proved, especially if other merchants from the place are in court and not called on. *Per* Parker, C. J., in *Parrott* v. *Thatcher*, 9 Pick. (Mass.) 426, 431. The fact that the usage has been resisted by some, and those insisting upon it, or others of the same class, consenting to a qualification or abandonment of it in consequence of such resistance, may be quite material on the general inquiry. See *Kendall* v. *Russell*, 5 Dana (Ky.) 501, 503, 504. There is a distinction between inquiring of a witness for the *common understanding* as to the effect or import of a contract susceptible of a clear interpretation, and evidence of custom or usage. The latter is admissible, if at all, as a means of interpreting the sense in which the parties understood the language in question; while the former may only show the understanding of others, which is immaterial unless it be also the understanding of the parties. *Paull* v. *Lewis*, 4 Watts (Penn.) 402, 403. So, *semble*, as to the general understanding of the country in regard to the sense of particular words easily understood; *e. g.*, the word *acre*, in a land contract. *Id.* 403, 404, as to direct evidence of what a party declared he meant by a term *primâ*

facie unmeaning. A question arose at Nisi Prius as to the meaning of the word "cargo," in reference to a ship, and whether it included the whole loading; the counsel cited *Sergeant* v. *Read*, 2 Strange 1228, to show that it did; and he was referring to Entick's Dictionary when he was interrupted by *Tindal*, C. J., who said: "It is a question of mercantile construction. You had better lay aside your dictionary and appeal to the knowledge of the jury, for, after all, the dictionary is not authority." *Houghton* v. *Gilbart*, 7 C. & P. 701; *White* v. *Van Kirk*, 25 Barb. (N. Y.) 16. There is another class of cases where a more direct inquiry must be allowed as to the meaning of writings. Those hitherto considered relate mainly to instances where the judge is supposed capable of assigning to the words some signification, without the necessity of resorting to extrinsic evidence. If the contents of an instrument, however, are utterly unintelligible in themselves, either from being written in characters which are difficult to be deciphered, or in a language which the court does not understand, &c., the propriety of inquiry *aliunde* is still more apparent. In the progress of the arts, and the ever changing pursuits of mankind, new terms are daily devised among artists and others, in whose peculiar departments they are used, and when not understood there can be no rational objection to admit the evidence of persons conversant with their meaning to explain them. See *per* Chancellor, in *Sleight* v. *Hartshorne*, 2 John. (N. Y.) 542. In a case where a sculptor gave,

or inconvenience, and upon the whole they find this mode of

by his will, all his "bankers," evidence was allowed to show that "bankers" meant solid pieces of wood, on which were placed blocks of marble about to be worked. *Goblet* v. *Beechey*, 3 Sim. 24. See S. C., more fully reported, Wigram on Ext. Ev. 139, *et seq.* In the same will, the same word "mod" was found, and liberty was given for trying to ascertain its meaning by the evidence of persons generally conversant with the subject-matters to which the will related. See this case, *post*, note 516; also, see *Mechanics Bank* v. *Bank of Columbia*, 5 Wheat. 336. And, as a general rule, if a party has expressed himself in terms with which, as a member of a particular trade, he is familiar, but which are not understood by the court, the evidence of persons acquainted with the meaning of such terms is admissible. Wigram on Extr. Ev. 35; *Attorney-General* v. *The Plate Glass Co.*, 1 Anstr. 39; *Smith* v. *Wilson*, 3 B. & Ad. 728; *Richardson* v. *Watson*, 4 B. & Ad. 787. The custom of merchants will not bind a person acting in a different character. Nor will a usage at one port be taken to affect the dealings of parties at another. Thus, the captain of a vessel cannot bind the owner by signing bills of lading, unless he is clothed with express authority for that purpose, or authority implied by the usual course of employment or a subsequent assent, and proof of a practice of the captain to sign bills of lading for articles deliverable at one port, is no proof of authority to sign bills of lading for a different port. The power of a consignee to bind the owner extends only to such acts as are within the

object of the consignment. *Nichols* v. *DeWolf*, 1 R. I. 277. A usage governing a question of legal right cannot be proved by isolated instances, but should be so certain, uniform and notorious, that it must probably have been understood by the parties as entering into the contract. *Cope* v. *Dodd*, 13 Penn. St. 33. Even though evidence of custom cannot be admitted to vary a rule of law, it may be admitted to explain and give a proper effect to the contracts and acts of parties. *Inglebright* v. *Hammond*, 19 Ohio 337. In order to affect a person with a custom or usage different from the ordinary rules of law, it must be shown to be certain, uniform and so notorious as presumably to be known to the parties, and mere proof of an isolated instance where it was applied is not sufficient. *Jones* v. *Wager*, 66 Penn. St. 429; *Cope* v. *Dodd*, 13 Penn. St. 33; *Patterson* v. *Ben Franklin Ins. Co.*, 33 Leg. Int. 5; *Adams* v. *Pittsburgh Ins. Co.*, 76 Penn. St. 411; *Wheeler* v. *Newbould*, 5 Dun. (N. Y.) 29; *Martin* v. *Maynard*, 16 N. H. 165; *Sipperly* v. *Steward*, 50 Barb. (N. Y.) 62; *Duguid* v. *Edwards*, 50 *Id.* 288; *Wood* v. *Hicock*, 2 Wend. (N. Y.) 501; *Kendall* v. *Russell*, 5 Dana (Ky.) 501; *Stevens* v. *Reeves*, 9 Pick. (Mass.) 198. But parol proof of a particular local custom or usage should not be permitted to control the general law of the land. *Christian* v. *Dripps*, 28 Penn. St. 271; *Bolton* v. *Colder*, 1 Watts. (Penn.) 360; *Wetherill* v. *Neilson*, 20 Penn. St. 448; *Brown* v. *Anott*, 6 A. & S. (Penn.) 402; *Coxe* v. *Heisley*, 19 Penn. St. 243. But a local usage, if well established and ancient and uniform, may enter into and

dealing advantageous even at the risk of occasional litigation."

become a part of a contract where it does not conflict with the settled rules of law or defeat the essential terms of the contract. *Coxe* v. *Heisley*, ante; *Wetherill* v. *Neilson*, ante; *Rapp* v. *Palmer*, 3 Watts (Penn.) 178. Usage is evidence of the construction given to the law, and when it is established and uniform it regulates the rights and duties of those who act within its limits, but no change of usage can have a retrospective effect. *United States* v. *Buchanan, Crabbe* (U. S.) 563 ; *Steiner* v. *Coxe*, 4 Penn. St. 13. The usages of a department of the government, in settling its accounts, are intended for general rules in the transaction of its business, but will be disregarded by the courts, whenever they operate unjustly upon individuals. *United States* v. *McCall*, Gilp. (U. S.) 577 ; see also *United States* v. *Duval*, Gilp. (U. S.) 372. Where a transaction is within the statute against usury, the usage of trade, as to such transaction, cannot be received in evidence to show that it is not usurious. *Dunham* v. *Dey*, 13 Johns. (N. Y.) 40; 16 *Id.* 367 ; S. P. *Bank of Utica* v. *Wager*, 2 Cow. (N. Y.) 712 ; *Bank of Utica* v. *Smalley, Id.* 770; *New York Firemen's Ins. Co.* v. *Ely, Id.* 678. The general custom and usage under the statutes respecting the proof and acknowledgment of deeds, and the form and certificate of acknowledgment, have great weight in the construction of such statutes. *Meriam* v. *Harsen*, 2 Barb. (N. Y.) Ch. 232. But neither a custom or usage, however ancient, can override a statute. Thus, where a petition for a writ of *certiorari* contained the affidavit of a former assessor, setting forth the common

practice for a long course of years in taking shares of a corporation situated outside of this commonwealth, it was held that the evidence of usage was insufficient to control the legal interpretation of a statute provision. *Dwight* v. *Boston*, 12 Allen (Mass.) 316. So, too, a mere custom or usage cannot control the established principles of law. *Schieffelin* v. *Harvey*, Anth. (N. Y.) 56 ; *Strong* v. *Bliss*, 6 Met. (Mass.) 393 ; *Home* v. *Mutual &c. Ins. Co.*, 1 Sandf. (N. Y.) 137; *Dewees* v. *Lockhart*, 1 Tex. 535. In *Coleman* v. *McMurdo*, 5 Rand. (Va.) 51, it was held that the fact that a usage not sanctioned by law had prevailed for a long time, gave it no force as a rule by which to determine the rights of parties. The rights of parties are to be determined by law, and not by any local custom or usage, unless there is proof that such custom or usage is certain, general, frequent, and so ancient as to be generally known and acted upon, nor unless it is reasonable. *Leach* v. *Perkins*, 17 Me. 462; *Caldwell* v. *Dawson*, 4 Metc. (Ky.) 121. Known and settled local usages ought to be respected by courts and juries, unless they contravene the law or policy of the country. *Wilcocks* v. *Phillips*, Wall. Jr. (U. S.) 47. A mere local usage, in a small part of the country, cannot change the law, and give the plaintiffs an action against one man, when they were employed by another, nor control the legal relations of the parties, unless it was known to them and it can fairly be presumed that they contracted in reference to it. *Latimer* v. *Alexander*, 14 Ga. 259. It is a general

Attempts to Limit Scope of Custom—Written Contract to Speak.

SEC. 66. It is owing to the circumstances just alluded to that we find many attempts upon the part of judges to limit the extent of the applicability of custom as a means of explaining indefinite writings. We must consider these. In the case of *Hutton* v. *Warren,*(z) the judges, although they decided in accordance with the authorities cited, clearly indicated that in their opinion the relaxation of the common law in reference to this matter, where formal agreements had been entered into, and especially instruments under seal, was both unwise and unjust.(a) And Lord Denman, in delivering the opinion of the court in the case of *Freeman* v. *Loder,*(b) said: "If a legislator were called to consider the expediency of passing a law upon this subject, the conclusion at which he would arrive is hardly open to a doubt. He would decide at once that the written contract must speak for itself on all occasions; that nothing should be left to memory or speculation. There is no inconvenience in requiring parties making written contracts to write the whole of their contracts, while, in mercantile affairs, no mischief can be greater than the uncertainty produced by permitting verbal statements to vary bargains committed to writing.

Dangers of Explanatory Evidence.

SEC. 67. The nature of this explanatory evidence renders

rule that a custom is without force, in opposition to a positive law. *Cranwell* v. *Fanny Fosdick,* 15 La. Ann. 436. But under the laws of Mexico, custom may not only attain the force of law, in the absence of special provisions, *but may limit and qualify general legal rules, or even overturn the positive written law. Von Schmidt* v. *Huntington,* 1 Cal. 55. No usage which is disregarded in a court of law will be regarded in a court of chancery, as it can have no force as an equitable, unless it is also a competent legal rule. *Morrison* v. *Hart,* 2 Bibb. (Ky.) 4. In a doubtful case, usage may be resorted to to ascertain the meaning of the legislature. *Polk* v. *Hill,* Overt (Tenn.) 157.

(z) 1 M. & W. 475; see also *Anderson* v. *Pitcher,* 2 B. & P. 168, *per* Lord Eldon.

(a) See *Johnston* v. *Usborne,* 11 Ad. & El. 557.

(b) 11 Ad. & El. 597, 598.

it peculiarly dangerous. Those who have heard it must have been struck with the hesitating strain in which it is given by men of business, and their wish to secure the correctness of their answer by referring to the written documents. Again, what can be more difficult than to ascertain, as a matter of fact, such a prevalence of what is called a custom of trade as to justify a verdict that it forms part of every contract? Debate may also be fairly raised as to the right of binding strangers by customs probably unknown to them; a conflict may exist between the customs of two different places; and supposing all these difficulties removed, and the custom fully proved, still it will almost always remain doubtful whether the parties to the individual contract really meant that it should include the custom." And the same opinions have been expressed by the late able and learned Mr. Justice Story.(c) "I own myself," he said, "no friend to the almost indiscriminate habit of late years of setting up particular usages or customs in almost all kinds of business and trade, to control, vary, or annul the general liabilities of parties under the common law, as well as under the commercial law. It has long appeared to me that there is no small danger in admitting such loose and inconclusive usages and customs often unknown to particular parties and always liable to great misunderstandings and misrepresentations and abuses to outweigh the well-known and well-selected principles of law. And I rejoice to find that of late years the courts of law, both in England and in America, have been disposed to narrow the limits of the operation of such usages and customs, and to discountenance any further extension of them.(d) The true and appropriate office of a usage or custom is to interpret the otherwise indeterminate intentions of parties, and to ascertain the nature and extent of their contracts, arising not from express stipulations, but from mere

(c) *The Schooner Reeside*, 2 Sum. (U. S.) 567.

(d) See also *Story, J.*, in *Donnell* v. *Columbia Ins. Co.*, 2 Sum. (U. S.) 367.

implications and presumptions, and acts of a doubtful or equivocal character. It may also be admitted to ascertain the true meaning of a particular word or particular words in a given instrument, when the word or words have various senses, some common, some qualified and some technical, according to the subject-matter to which they are applied. But I apprehend that it can never be proper to resort to any usage or custom to control or vary the positive stipulations in a written contract, and *a fortiori* not in order to contradict them. An express contract of the parties is always admissible to supersede or vary or control a usage or custom, for the latter may always be waived at the will of the parties. But a written and express contract cannot be controlled or varied or contradicted by a usage or custom, for that would be not only to admit parol evidence to control, vary or contradict written contracts; but it would be to allow mere presumptions and implications properly arising in the absence of any positive expressions of intention to control, vary or contradict the most formal and deliberate declarations of the parties."(e)   As we shall see, however,

(e) When a contract is silent relative to certain matters in relation to which a usage exists, and the usage is known to the parties, or is so uniform and notorious that the parties may be presumed to have known of its existence, it may be shown to supply those matters. Thus, if a custom to fill orders *pro rata*, and in the order in which they are received, as fast as the articles can be manufactured, is well known to the vendee from his previous dealings with the vendor, the contract will be presumed to embrace the custom, and the vendee cannot complain that the articles are not sooner delivered. But if such custom is not known to the vendee, it cannot be regarded as ·forming any part of the contract and consequently affords no defence. *Blum* v. *New England Screw Co.*, 23 How. (U. S.) 420; see also *S. C.*, 4 Bl. (U. S. C. C.) 97. Where shingles are sold by the thousand, evidence of a usage to regard two bundles of a certain size as a thousand, is admissible. *Soutier* v. *Kellerman*, 18 Mo. 509. So, too, it is competent to show that by the usage of a certain trade, where goods are not sold on a cash sale, they are purchased on a six months' credit. *Farnsworth* v. *Chase*, 19 N. H. 534. So, where an advertisement is inserted in a newspaper, and no time during which it shall be continued is named, the publisher of the paper may show a custom of the trade to continue it until instructions are given to stop

there has, in more recent times than those to which Mr. Justice Story referred, been a tendency upon the part of judges to extend the office of a usage, and while they have been as unwilling to allow a usage to *rule* express words, they have allowed a usage to *supply* words and incidents to a written contract which were not inconsistent with it. They, too, looked to the intention of the parties, but they came to the conclusion that the real drift of these intentions would be better ascertained by a careful regard to the circumstances of the individual at the time of the contract than from a slavish regard only to the written words of the instrument. The circumstances which it was of most importance to bear in mind, as likely to affect the mental condition of the parties to the instrument, were those common circumstances which are classed under the head course of trade, and which are embodied in what we call usage. It was from this view that the recent extension of the functions of custom has taken

it. *Thomas* v. *O'Hara*, 1 Mill (S. C.) Const. 303. But proof of a usage in reference to matters about which the contract is specific, and which are repugnant thereto, is not admissible. *Boardman* v. *Spooner*, 13 Allen (Mass.) 353. Thus, where a stipulation, that all claims for damages must be made within three days, was a part of a contract of sale, evidence to prove that, according to the custom of trade in Boston, goods were returned by purchasers at auction, and received by the owners, and an allowance made after the expiration of three days, if within a reasonable time after the sale, was held inadmissible. *Atkins* v. *Howe*, 18 Pick. (Mass.) 16. So, too, it has been held that evidence is inadmissible to prove a usage in the port of Boston, that when a cargo of corn is sold in bulk, lying in the vessel in which it is imported, and the sale is made under a warranty, the purchaser receives and retains so much of the corn as answers the warranty, and rejects the residue, which, upon such rejection, becomes the property of the seller. *Clark* v. *Baker*, 11 Met. (Mass.) 186. So, in an action by the vendee of goods for damages for their non-delivery, under a contract which stipulated that the vendee was to advance the freight upon them, evidence of a general custom on the subject of paying freight to the carrier on the delivery of goods, was held inadmissible because the parties had made their own contract, which was susceptible of easy explanation, and needed no aid from custom and could not be controlled by it. *Hartfe* v. *Collins*, 46 Penn. St. 268; see also, on the general proposition, *Lombardo* v. *Case*, 45 Barb. (N. Y.) 95; *Beals* v. *Terry*, 2 Sandf. (N. Y.) 127.

place. Bearing, then, these weighed and careful words in mind, we proceed to the consideration of the law, as it has been laid down in various cases, which is applicable to the question. In this country, substantially the same rules prevail as to the operation of usages, as in England, and it may be stated, as a general rule, that a reasonable usage of any trade or business *known* to the parties contracting in reference to matters to which it applies, or so well established and so notorious that they ought to know of it, will control their relations, unless excluded by the express terms of the contract,[5] or it overrides a well-settled rule of law.[6] Thus, it is competent to show a usage of a certain trade or business, to add incidents to a contract in reference to matters about

[5] *Loring* v. *Gurney*, 5 Pick. (Mass.) 15; *Thompson* v. *Hamilton*, 12 *Id.* 425; *Parrott* v. *Thatcher*, 9 *Id.* 430; *Lowry* v. *Russell*, 8 *Id.* 360; *Stearns* v. *Reeves*, 9 *Id.* 198; *Cook* v. *Welch*, 9 Allen (Mass.) 350; *Porter* v. *Hills*, 114 Mass. 103; *Berkshire Woolen Co.* v. *Proctor*, 7 Cush. (Mass.) 417; *Scudder* v. *Bradbury*, 106 (Mass.) 422; *Cooper* v. *Kane*, 19 Wend. (N. Y.) 386; *Dalton* v. *Daniels*, 2 Hilt. (N. Y.) 472; *Hartshorne* v. *Ins. Co.*, 36 N. Y. 172; *Farmers' Bank* v. *Erie R. R. Co.*, 79 N. Y. 188; *Whitehouse* v. *Moore*, 13 Abb. Pr. (N. Y.) 142; *Fox* v. *Parker*, 42 Barb. (N. Y.) 541; *Miller* v. *Burke*, 68 N. Y. 615; *Bissell* v. *Campbell*, 54 N. Y. 53; *Aralls* v. *Bailey*, 49 N. Y. 464; *Eyre* v. *Marine Ins. Co.*, 5 W. & S. (Penn.) 115; *McMasters* v. *Pennsylvania R. R. Co.*, 69 Penn. St. 374; *Carter* v. *Philadelphia Coal Co.*, 77 *Id.* 286; *Coxe* v. *Heisley*, 19 *Id.* 243; *Aughinbaugh* v. *Coppenheffer*, 55 *Id.* 347; *Steward* v. *Scudder*, 24 N. J. L. 96; *Schenck* v. *Griffen*, 39 N. J. L. 463; *Barton* v. *McKelway*, 22 N. J. L. 165; *Leach* v. *Beardslee*, 22 Conn. 404; *Dixon* v. *Dunham*, 14 Ill. 324; *Consequa* v. *Willings*, Pet. (U. S. C. C.) 225; *Baxter* v. *Leland*, 1 Blatch. (U. S. C. C.) 526; *Sunday* v. *Gordon*, 1 Bl. & H. (U. S.) 569; *Wilcocks* v. *Phillips*, 1 Wall. Jr. (U. S. C. C.) 63; *Bispham* v. *Pollock*, 1 McLean. (U. S.) 411; *Brown* v. *Jackson*, 2 Wash. (U. S. C. C.) 24; *Union Bank* v. *Forrest*, 3 Cranch (U. S. C. C.) 218; *McGregor* v. *Ins. Co.*, 1 Wash. (U. S. C. C.) 39; *The Reeside*, 2 Sum. (U. S.) 567; *Cooke* v. *England*, 27 Md. 141; *Foster* v. *Robinson*, 6 Ohio St. 90; *Conner* v. *Robinson*, 2 Hill. (S. C.) 354; *Humphreysville &c. Co.* v. *Vermont &c. Co.*, 33 Vt. 92; *Pursell* v. *McQueen*, 9 Ala. 380; *Bodfish* v. *Fox*, 23 Me. 90; *Henkel* v. *Welsh*, 41 Mich. 664; *Bancroft* v. *Peters*, 4 Mich. 619; *Bush* v. *Pollock*, 41 Mich. 64; *Sumner* v. *Tyson*, 20 N. H. 384; *Lebanon* v. *Heath*, 47 N. H. 353; *Farnsworth* v. *Chase*, 19 *Id.* 534; *Soutier* v. *Kellerman*, 18 Mo. 509.

[6] *Dickinson* v. *Gay*, 7 Allen (Mass.) 9; *Haskins* v. *Warren*, 115 Mass. 514; *Barnard* v. *Kellogg*, 10 Wall. (U. S.) 383; *Bank of Commerce* v. *Bissell*, 72 N. Y. 615; *Farmers' Bank* v. *Logan*, 74 *Id.* 568.

which the contract itself is silent. Thus, where there was a written contract for a certain number of "barrels" of petroleum, at so much a gallon, it was held competent to show that, by the usages of the petroleum trade, the word "barrel" meant a vessel of a certain capacity, and not the statutory measure of quantity.[7] So where there was a written contract for the delivery of "a cargo of coal, water nine and one-half feet," and there was nothing said as to the quantity, evidence was admitted to show what number of tons usually constituted the cargo of a vessel drawing that depth of water.[8] In another Massachusetts case,[9] where there was a written contract for the manufacture and delivery of "horn chains," parol evidence was held admissible to show that chains made of horns and hoofs were intended by the parties, such chains being known in the market as "horn chains." Perhaps the most apt illustration of this rule may be found in a later Massachusetts case,[1] in which the defendant, by a written instrument, conveyed to the plaintiff a milk route in Boston, "with all the rights and privileges thereto belonging." There was also a clause as follows: "Also the right and good will of supplying twenty-six full eight-quart cans of custom, situated as above." In an action upon this contract, evidence of experts in the trade was held admissible to show that milk trade is bought and sold by the can, and that the right and good will of supplying customers has a known and recognized value in the market, and is worth eighty dollars a can; also that there was a uniform usage in the trade for the person, the right and good will of supplying custom, to furnish to the purchaser, customers whose average daily purchases amount to the number of cans sold; and that in the milk trade, the terms "right and good will of supplying custom," mean, when applied to sales of the trade, the right of supplying milk to the customers furnished

[7] *Miller* v. *Stevens*, 100 Mass. 518;
Keller v. *Webb*, 125 Mass. 88.
[8] *Rhoades* v. *Castner*, 12 Allen

(Mass.) 130.
[9] *Swett* v. *Shumway*, 102 Mass. 365.
[1] *Page* v. *Cole*, 120 Mass. 37.

and pointed out by the vendor, from those accustomed to buy milk of him. The instances in which incidents have been annexed to contracts by usage are numerous, and many of them are referred to in other parts of this work.[2] It is a rule, however, that the incident so to be incorporated, must not conflict with the express terms of the contract to which they are to be annexed.[3]

[2] See illustrating the rule, *Eldridge* v. *Smith*, 13 Allen (Mass.) 140; *Ashwell* v. *Radford*, L. R. 9 C. P. 20; *Bond* v. *Coke*, 71 N. C. 97; *Allen* v. *Pink*, 4 M. & W. 140; *Humfrey* v. *Dole*, 7 E. & B. 266; *Southwell* v. *Bowditch*, L. R. 1 C. P. 106; *Adams* v. *Morse*, 51 Me. 499; *Syers* v. *Jonas*, 2 Exch. 111; *Field* v. *Lelean*, 6 H. & N. 617; *Allan* v. *Sundias*, 1 H. & C. 123; *Baker* v. *Jordan*, 3 Ohio St. 438; *Renner* v. *Bank*, 9 Wheat. (U. S.) 581; *Backenstoss* v. *Stahler*, 33 Penn. St. 231; *Gadts* v. *Rose*, 17 C. B. 209; *Fleet* v. *Murton*, L. R. 7 Q. B. 126; *Smart* v. *Hyde*, 8 M. & W. 723; *Lucas* v. *Bristow*, E. B. & E. 907; *Bryewater* v. *Richardson*, 3 N. & M. 748; *Foster* v. *Ins. Co.*, 2 E. & B. 48; *Parker* v. *Ibbetson*, 4 C. B. N. S. 348; *Hutchinson* v. *Tatham*, L. R. 8 C. P. 482; *Reg.* v. *Stoke-Upon-Trent*, 5 Q. B. 303.

[3] *Bond* v. *Coke*, ante; *Brown* v. *Thurston*, 56 Me. 127; *Ring* v. *Billings*, 51 Ill. 475; *Central R. R. Co.* v. *Anderson*, 58 Ga. 393; *Wickersham* v. *Orr*, 9 Iowa 253; *Evans* v. *Waln*, 71 Penn. St. 69; *Austin* v. *Sawyer*, 9 Cow. (N. Y.) 40; *Haskins* v. *Warren*, 115 Mass. 514; *Brown* v. *Foster*, 113 *Id.* 136; *Macomber* v. *Parker*, 13 Pick. (Mass.) 175; *Odiorne* v. *New England Ins. Co.*, 101 Mass. 551. In *Randall* v. *Ratch*, 12 Pick. (Mass.) 107, it was held that evidence of a custom for a master cooper to send his apprentice on a whaling voyage, was not

admissible, because it was directly repugnant to the object and terms of the contract. In *Davis* v. *Galloupe*, 111 Mass. 121, the plaintiffs, who were stone cutters, entered into a written contract to furnish the defendant stone for a building, according to certain plans and specifications of an architect, and to do all the fitting and rebating necessary. In an action to recover for the patterns, it was held that evidence of a usage for stone cutters, in cutting stone for a building, to procure such patterns and recover the cost from the owner of the building, was not admissible; and generally it may be said that evidence of a usage is not admissible either to add to or detract from a contract when it conflicts with the express provisions thereof. *Snelling* v. *Hall*, 107 Mass. 134; *Boardman* v. *Spooner*, 13 Allen (Mass.) 359; *Whitmore* v. *South Boston Iron Co.*, 2 Allen (Mass.) 52; *Eagar* v. *Atlas Ins. Co.*, 14 Pick. (Mass.) 141; *Atkins* v. *Howe*, 18 *Id.* 16; *Macomber* v. *Howard Ins. Co.*, 7 Gray (Mass.) 207; *Stebbins* v. *Brown*, 65 Barb. (N. Y.) 274; *Beals* v. *Terry*, 2 Sandf. (N. Y.) 127; *Holmes* v. *Pettingill*, 60 N. Y. 646; *Lombardo* v. *Case*, 45 Barb. (N. Y.) 45; *Lane* v. *Bailey*, 47 *Id.* 395; *Spear* v. *Hart*, 3 Robt. (N. Y.) 420; *People's Bank* v. *Bogart*, 16 Hun. (N. Y.) 270; *Van Alstyne* v. *Ætna Ins. Co.*, 14 *Id.* 360; *Lawrence* v. *Gallagher*,

Evidence of Usage Indispensable, Where.

SEC. 68. Evidence of the usage of a trade, business or individual, is admissible to ascertain and carry into effect the real intention of the parties, because where such usage is established, of a character so general or notorious that a presumption of its knowledge by the parties can be raised, it is reasonable to presume that they contracted in reference to and in reliance upon it, or they would have excluded it in their contract, and, therefore, in the case of a usage *known* to the parties, or which is so general, uniform and unvarying as to warrant a presumption of its knowledge by them, forms a part of the contract, as much as though it had been expressly written

10 J. & S. (N. Y.) 309; *Farmers' &c. Bank* v. *Logan,* 74 N. Y. 568; *Bank of Commerce* v. *Bissell,* 72 *Id.* 615; *Rapp* v. *Palmer,* 3 Watts (Penn.) 178; *Hartje* v. *Collins,* 46 Penn. St. 268; *Harvey* v. *Cady,* 3 Mich. 431; *Spears* v. *Ward,* 48 Ind. 546; *Cabot* v. *Winsor,* 1 Allen (Mass.) 546; *Sanford* v. *Rawlings,* 43 Ill. 92; *Luce* v. *Ins. Co.,* 105 Mass. 297; *Marc* v. *Kupfer,* 34 Ill. 287; *Ins. Co.* v. *Wright,* 1 Wall. (U. S.) 456; *Marks* v. *Cass Co. Mill,* 43 Ia. 146; *Mangam* v. *Ball,* 43 Miss. 288; *Merchants' Bank* v. *State Bank,* 10 Wall. (U. S.) 604; *Osgood* v. *McConnell,* 32 Ill. 74; *Dodd* v. *Farlow,* 11 Allen (Mass.) 476; *Moran* v. *Prather,* 23 Wall. (U. S.) 499; *Willmering* v. *McGaughey,* 30 Ia. 205; *Sawtelle* v. *Drew,* 122 Mass. 228; *Schenck* v. *Griffin,* 38 N. J. L. 462; *Stanton* v. *Jerome,* 54 N. Y. 480; *Hackin* v. *Cooke,* 4 T. R. 314; *Muncey* v. *Dennis,* 1 H. & N. 216; *Suse* v. *Pompe,* 8 C. B. N. S. 538; *Glendale Woolen Co.* v. *Ins. Co.,* 21 Conn. 19; *The Schooner Reeside,* 2 Sum. (U. S.) 567; *Barnard* v. *Kellogg,* 10 Wall. (U. S.) 383. In the latter case, *Davis, J.,* said: "The proper

office of a custom or usage in trade is to ascertain and explain the meaning and intention of the parties to a contract, whether written or in parol, which could not be done without the aid of this extrinsic evidence. It does not go beyond this, and is used as a mode of interpretation, on the theory that the parties knew of its existence and contracted in reference to it. It is often employed to explain words or phrases in a contract of doubtful signification, or which may be understood in different senses according to the subject-matter to which they are applied. *But if it be inconsistent with the contract, or expressly or by necessary implication contradicts it,* it cannot be received in evidence to explain it." *Thompson* v. *Ashton,* 14 John. (N. Y.) 417; *Dickinson* v. *Gay,* 7 Allen (Mass.) 29; *Frith* v. *Barker,* 2 John. (N. Y.) 327; *Simmons* v. *Law,* 3 Keyes (N. Y.) 219; *Coxe* v. *Heisley,* 19 Penn. St. 243; *Wetherell* v. *Neilson,* 20 *Id.* 448; *Robinson* v. *United States,* 13 Wall. (U. S.) 365.

therein.[3] The maxim, "*in contractibus tacite veniunt ea quae sunt moris it consuetudinis*," has full application in such cases. "Experience and observation," says Storrs, J., in a case previously cited,[4] "prove that the engagements of individuals are in fact entered into with reference to the customs and usages which prevail in the community where they are made; they, therefore, tacitly agree to conform to them, and so far from doing injustice, by regarding such customs and usages, it is the only mode by which justice can be attained. The presumption is, indeed, that those who enter into contracts intend to be governed by the general principles of law. It is, however, competent for them to renounce these principles when public policy does not forbid, and to adopt another rule of action ; and the prevalence of a particular local usage on the subject, variant from those general rules, in the absence of evidence to resist it, affords a rational ground of inference that they intended to do so." But, in order to have this effect, it must either be known to the parties or be sufficiently ancient to warrant the presumption that it is generally known, and also certain, uniform and reasonable.[5] It

[3] *Sipperley* v. *Steward*, 50 Barb. (N. Y.) 62; *Wheeler* v. *Newbold*, 5 Duer (N. Y. Superior Court) 29; *Duguid* v. *Edwards*, 50 Barb. (N. Y.) 288; *Martin* v. *Maynard*, 16 N. H. 165; *Stultz* v. *Dickey*, 5 Binn. (Penn.) 287; *Hursh* v. *North*, 40 Penn. St. 241; *Haven* v. *Wentworth*, 2 N. H. 93; *Wood* v. *Hicock*, 2 Wend. (N. Y.) 501; *Kendall* v. *Russell*, 5 Dana (Ky.) 501; *Stevens* v. *Reeves*, 9 Pick. (Mass.) 198; *Inglebright* v. *Hammond*, 19 Ohio 337; *Ladwick* v. *Ohio Ins. Co.*, 5 *Id.* 436; *Sampson* v. *Gazzam*, 6 Port. (Ala.) 123; *Sewall* v. *Gibbs*, 1 Hall (N. Y. Superior Court) 612; *United States* v. *Arredondo*, 6 Pet. (U. S.) 715; *Bank of Columbia* v. *Fitzhugh*, 1 H. & G.

(Md.) 239; *Barber* v. *Bruce*, 3 Conn. 9; *Coit* v. *Commercial Ins. Co.*, 7 John. (N. Y.) 385 ; *Parr* v. *Anderson*, 6 East. 202; *Vallance* v. *Demar*, 1 Camp. 503 ; *Lethulier's case*, 2 Salk. 443; *Halsey* v. *Brown*, 3 Day (Conn.) 346; *Noble* v. *Kennoway*, 1 Doug. 510; *Palmer* v. *Kane*, 5 Wis. 265; *Munn* v. *Burch*, 25 Ill. 35.

[4] *Kilgore* v. *Bulkley*, 14 Conn. 390.

[5] *Shackelford* v. *N. O. R. R. Co.*, 37 Miss. 202; *Smith* v. *Gibbs*, 44 N. H. 335; *Collings* v. *Hope*, 3 Wash. (Va.) 150; *Register* v. *Spencer*, 24 Md. 520; *Rapp* v. *Palmer*, 3 Watts (Penn.) 178; *Foley* v. *Mason*, 6 Md. 37; *Thomas* v. *Graves*, 1 Mill (S. C.) Court 308; *Harper* v. *Pound*, 10 Ind. 32; *Chas-*

must be so well established in the particular locality, trade, profession or business to which it relates, that it must be presumed that men transacting the business, &c., know of, and contract in reference to it.[6] General or local customs become laws, from immemorial and universal application and acquiescence either in a particular locality affected, or in the entire community to be affected by it.[7]

Why Parol Evidence is Admitted—Law and Evidence—Evidence the Foundation of Law.

SEC. 69. We must bear in mind that the admission of parol evidence of usage is allowed on a principle of presumption that in many transactions the parties thought it unnecessary to express in writing the whole of the contract they were entering into, but to contract with reference to those known usages,(f) just as there is an implication that they contracted with a reference to ascertained physical laws. But these usages of trade with reference to which their contract was framed must be understood as something different from the general custom of merchants, which in so far as it is ascertained and recognized is the universal established law of the land, which is, as we have already seen,(g) to be collected from decisions, legal principles and analogies, and not from evidence. In all cases laws were matters of evidence once upon a time, but when they were proved, ascertained and acknowledged, they became not matters provable by new

tain v. Bowman, 1 Hill (S. C.) 270; Somerby v. Tappan, Wright (Ohio) 573; Trott v. Wood, 1 Gall. (U. S.) 443; Buck v. Grimshaw, 1 Edw. Ch. (N. Y.) 147.

(f) Kirchner v. Venus, 12 Moore P. C. C. 361.

(g) Per Foster, J., Edie v. East India Co., 1 Wm. Black, at p. 298; per Lord Campbell, in Brandão v. Barnett, 3 C. B. 519, at p. 530; per Byles, J., Suse v. Pomp, 8 C. B. N. S.

[6] Foye v. Leighton, 22 N. H. 71; Saint v. Smith, 1 Coldw. (Tenn.) 51; Walker v. Barron, 6 Minn. 508; Martin v. Hall, 26 Mo. 386.

[7] Com v. Maloy, 57 Penn. St. 591.

538, at p. 567; but see Haille v. Smith, 1 B. & P. 563, in which evidence of the general custom of merchants was received, and Vallejo v. Wheeler, Lofft. 631, at p. 644; see also per Nelson, J., in Allen v. The Merchants' Bank, 15 Wend. (N. Y.) 215.

evidence, but matters evidenced by past records, and these
records resided, for the most part, in the breasts of the
judges.   The right understanding of the real relation of law
and evidence seems to us to be a matter of some importance.
Evidence deals with facts, law with human principles as
applicable to facts.   But rough doing went before rules.
Practice has always preceded theory, and in some historical
senses evidence must be regarded as the foundation of law.
The analogy of language which is closely connected with
law—which might well be regarded as the grammar of conduct—will help us to understand this connection.   It has
been pointed out that men used to think of substantives in
action before they reached the abstract conception of a verb;
and that such phrases, in the mouths of the vulgar, as
"a-going" and "a-coming," at the present time, are indica-
tive of the early use of nouns in the place of verbs.   There
is an abstractness in expression of action or passion which
was only possible to a stage of considerable mental development.   But to us there seems to be a close analogy between
this relation of nouns and verbs which Hegel has expressed
by saying, "It is in names that we think," and the relation
which exists between evidence and law.   The province of
the one is, as it were, substantives of the other verbs.   The
province of the one is concrete experiences, of the other
abstract generalizations and commands.   But, further, we
would be inclined to think that just as verbs were at first
nothing but modified substantives—or substantives becoming
abstract—so laws were at first only evidence modified or
becoming abstract.   Hence it is that in our estimation custom or usage is the connecting link between law and evidence; hence, also, its importance, not only to the lawyer,
but to the scientific jurist.

Usage of Trade and Custom of Merchants to be Distinguished.

SEC. 70. Usages of trade, then, in the sense in which it is
ordinarily used, are to be discriminated from the general

custom of merchants, although in one way they may be regarded as the general custom of merchants in the making. This being so, it is not extraordinary that this distinction has not always been so clearly understood as it is at the present time, and that we find a learned judge in the year 1787 using these words. "Within the last thirty years," Mr. Justice Buller remarked,(h) "the commercial law of the country has taken a very different turn from what it did before. Before that period we find that, in courts of law, all the evidence in mercantile cases was thrown together; they were left generally to a jury, and produced no established principle. From that time we all know the great study has been to find some certain general principles which shall be known to all mankind, not only to rule the particular case then under consideration, but to serve as a guide for the future."

Particular General Customs.

SEC. 71. But the distinction which is to be drawn at the present time is clearly between general usages or customs which are laws, and particular usages or customs which are matters of evidence. When, however, they are proved, they engraft terms into a contract in much the same way that a general custom or law would.

Method of Proof.

SEC. 72. First, then, as to the principle of admissibility, and the method of proof.(i) Seeing that custom is only to be

(h) 2 T. R. p. 73.
(i) *Mackenzie* v. *Dunlop*, 3 Macq. H. of L. Cas. 22; see also *Kidson* v. *Empire Marine Co.*, 35 L. J. C. P. 250; see also *Myers* v. *Dresser*, 16 C. B. N. S. 646. Mercantile usage must be proved by the multiplication or aggregation of a great number of instances, showing a certain course of business and a general established understanding respecting it. *Burr*

v. *Sickles*, 17 Ark. 428; *Smith* v. *Floyd*, 18 Barb. (N. Y.) 392; *Knowles* v. *Dow*, 22 N. H. 387; *Chesapeake Bank* v. *Swain*, 29 Md. 483; *Mackenzie* v. *Dunlop*, 3 Macq. H. L. Cas. 22; *Walker* v. *Barron*, 6 Minn. 508; *Saint* v. *Smith*, 1 Coldw. (Tenn.) 51; *Foye* v. *Leighton*, 22 N. H. 71. In other words the rule is, that a usage, in order to become a part of a contract *must be so far established and so far*

inferred from a large number of individual acts, it is evident
that the only proof of the existence of a usage must be by

known to the parties that it must be
supposed that their contract was
made in reference to it. For this
purpose the custom *must be established and not casual, uniform and not
varying, general and not personal*, and.
known to the parties. *Wheeler* v.
Newbould, 5 Duer (N. Y.) 29; *Sipperley* v. *Steward*, 50 Barb. (N. Y.) 62;
Martin v. *Maynard*, 16 N. H. 165;
Duguid v. *Edwards*, 50 Barb. (N. Y.)
288; *Wood* v. *Hicock*, 2 Wend. (N.Y.)
501; *Kendall* v. *Russell*, 5 Dana (Ky.)
501; *Stevens* v. *Reeves*, 9 Pick. (Mass.)
198; *Watt* v. *Hock*, 25 Penn. St. 411;
Hursh v. *North*, 40 *Id.* 241; *Sampson*
v. *Gazzam*, 6 Port. (Ala.) 123; *Haven*
v. *Wentworth*, 2 N. H. 93; *Gallup* v.
Lederer, 1 Hun. (N. Y.) 282; *Mills* v.
Hallock, 2 Edw. Ch. (N. Y.) 652.
Where a custom or usage was set up
that a class of mercantile houses in
the same line of trade in New York,
generally known as "six months'
houses," by their general and uniform course of business, on a bill of
goods containing a memorandum
"six per cent. off for cash," would
understand a sale on six months'
credit, without any express agreement: it was held, that in order to
discharge the office of exposition,
and be admissible in evidence, it
must be found to be the general
usage of the whole of that class of
houses in the city of New York, and
so well established and uniformly
acquiesced in, and for such a length
of time, that the jury might fairly
infer that it was known to the contracting parties, and made by implication a part of their contract. If
such usage is not proved, it should
be laid out of the case; and an offer

of evidence of anything less should
be excluded. *Linsley* v. *Lovely*, 26
Vt. 123. But in order to establish it
neither antiquity nor that general
notoriety essential to establish a custom need be shown. It is sufficient
if it is shown to be so well known
and acquiesced in that it may be
reasonably presumed to have been
an ingredient imported into the contract by the parties. *Shackelford* v.
New Orleans R. R. Co., 37 Miss. 202;
Harper v. *Pound*, 10 Ind. 32; *Buck*
v. *Grimshaw*, 1 Edw. Ch. (N. Y.) 147;
Chastain v. *Bowman*, 1 Hill (S. C.)
276; *Collings* v. *Hope*, 3 Wash. (Va.)
150; *Juggomohun Ghore* v. *Manickchund*, 7 Moore Ind. App. 263; *Smith*
v. *Gibbs*, 44 N. H. 335; *Rapp* v. *Palmer*,
3 Watts (Penn.) 178; *Lewis* v. *Thatcher*,
15 Mass. 433, and this is the case
only when the usage is certain, reasonable and universally acquiesced
in, so that every one engaged in the
trade knows, or might have known
of it, if he had taken the trouble to
inquire. *Plain* v. *Allcock*, 4 F. & F.
1074. If it is sought to establish a
usage of a trade to control the meaning of words, it must be shown that
the words are used in that trade and
are understood in a defined sense,
and a mere habit of affixing a special
meaning to words when used in one
class of contracts does not amount
to such a usage as will justify the
presumption that they were used in
that sense in the contract in question. The proof must go further,
and show facts that lead to a convic-
tion that they were used in that case
in such sense. *Abbott* v. *Bates*, 43
L. J. C. P. 150; *Eaton* v. *Smith*, 20
Pick. (Mass.) 150; *Steward* v. *Scudder*,

the multiplication or aggregation of a great number of particular instances, but these instances must not be miscellaneous in character, but must have a principle of unity running through their variety, and that unity must show a certain course of business, and an established understanding respecting it. A usage of trade is a matter of fact, and must be proved like any other fact, and cannot be established by the mere opinion of witnesses. It may be proved by witnesses testifying to its existence and uniformity from their knowledge of it obtained by observation of what is practiced by themselves *and others* in the trade to which it relates, but the *opinions* of witnesses or their conclusions or inferences as to its effect, either upon the contract or the legal title or rights of parties, are not competent to show the force of such usage or its character.[8] As a general rule, one witness is not sufficient to establish a general usage.[9] But the question as to whether the evidence of one witness is sufficient or not,

24 N. J. L. 96. The testimony of a single witness is not generally sufficient to establish a usage of trade of which all are bound to take notice. *Wood* v. *Hicock*, 2 Wend. (N. Y.) 501; but if the witness discloses such familiarity with the trade as to satisfy the jury the evidence may be sufficient. *Robinson* v. *United States*, 13 Wall. (U. S.) 366; *Partridge* v. *Forsyth*, 29 Ala. 200; *Vail* v. *Rice*, 5 N. Y. 155. Nor is the custom of a particular house, of itself, sufficient proof of a general usage. *Weber* v. *Kingsland*, 8 Bos. (N. Y.) 415. In *Smith* v. *Floyd*, 18 Barb. (N. Y.) 523, it was held that the evidence to establish a customary right should not be less than that required to establish a prescriptive right. In

8 *Haskins* v. *Warren*, 115 Mass. 514; *Garey* v. *Meaghar*, 33 Ala. 630; *Chesapeake Bank* v. *Swain*, 29 Md. 483.

9 *Halverson* v. *Cole*, 1 Spears (S. C.)

Jewell v. *Carter*, 25 Ala. 498, it was held that where there is conflicting evidence, the question as to whether or not a usage is established should be left to the jury, and that where there is the evidence of only one witness thereto, the court should tell the jury that there is no evidence of a usage before them. See also *Boardman* v. *Spooner*, 13 Allen (Mass.) 359. But this is not the rule now generally recognized, and if a witness testifies fully and explicitly to the existence of a usage and his testimony is not contradicted, it cannot be assumed as a legal conclusion that the proof is insufficient. *Marston* v. *Mobile Bank*, 10 Ala. 284; *Robinson* v. *United States*, 13 Wall. (U. S.) 366.

321; *Thomas* v. *Graves*, 1 Mill (S. C.) Const. 309; *Bissell* v. *Ryan*, 23 Ill. 566; *Wood* v. *Hickok*, 2 Wend. (N. Y.) 501; *Halls* v. *Howell*, Harp. (S. C.) 427.

must be determined from the witnesses' means of information and acquaintance with the business.[1] While, as previously stated, usage cannot be established by the mere opinions of witnesses, yet, if the witness has derived all his knowledge of the usage from his own business, and it is shown to be sufficiently extensive and long continued to warrant the presumption that his knowledge in that respect is general, he may state his belief as to what such custom or usage is.[2] A usage must be proved by evidence of facts and instances in which it has been acted upon,[3] and in a case

[1] *Hamilton* v. *Nickerson*, 13 Allen (Mass.) 351; *Vail* v. *Rice*, 5 N. Y. 155; *Partridge* v. *Forsyth*, 29 Ala. 200; *Robinson* v. *United States*, 13 Wall. (U. S.) 365.

[2] *Hamilton* v. *Nickerson*, 13 Allen (Mass.) 351. Proof that in one instance the use by a son of his father's name, upon negotiable paper discounted at a bank, was known and acquiesced in by the father, does not authorize the introduction in evidence of subsequent similar acts, for the purpose of showing an implied authority in the son to sign his father's name, without proof that these also were known and acquiesced in by him, *Greenfield Bank* v. *Crafts*, 2 Allen (Mass.) 269. Evidence of a custom of manufacturers of iron castings to warrant the quality of the articles made by them, without an express contract to that effect, is admissible in an action founded on such supposed warranty. Evidence that such was the custom at three different establishments, without proof that a contrary usage obtained at others in the vicinity, is sufficient to authorize the jury to find such to be the general custom. *Sumner* v. *Tyson*, 20 N. H. 384. To prove a custom for all the inhabitants of

Hampton to deposit sea-weed upon the close of the plaintiffs, the defendant offered evidence that thirty of the inhabitants had done so for many years. *Held*, that this was competent evidence to be submitted to the jury to prove the custom. A plea alleged a custom in the inhabitants of Hampton to haul sea-weed upon the plaintiff's close. The evidence was, that only those inhabitants of Hampton exercised the right who lived at a convenient distance from the sea-shore. *Held*, that this was competent evidence of the custom. *Knowles* v. *Dow*, 22 N. H. 71.

[3] *Mills* v. *Hallock*, 4 Edw. Ch. (N. Y.) 652. A usage governing a question of legal right cannot be proved by isolated instances, but should be so certain, uniform and notorious, that it must probably have been understood by the parties as entering into the contract. *Cope* v. *Dodd*, 13 Penn. St. 33; *The Paragon*, 1 Ware (U. S.) 322; *Desha* v. *Holland*, 12 Ala. 513. Where the fact is material that a purchaser of land has actual knowledge of a right of way over the same, evidence that the way was used for many years, and that the purchaser lived all the time

where the question was whether a certain practice had been
tolerated to a certain extent at a custom house, the party

in the same immediate neighborhood, is properly submitted to the
jury. *Wissler* v. *Hershey,* 23 Penn.
St. 333. The fact that it is shown
that a certain method of doing business is "very common," does not
establish a usage. *Anstill* v. *Crawford,* 7 Ala. 335. To establish a shipping usage on a certain river, the
witness may state his habit and custom in shipping on all boats on the
river. *Berry* v. *Cooper,* 28 Ga. 543.
Proof of the usage of the clerks of
steamboats, to receive and carry
packages from one port to another,
without hire, in the expectation that
such boat would be preferred by the
parties in their shipments of freight,
is insufficient to bind the owners;
first, because no certain or fixed
standard of remuneration is shown,
nor that the consignee of the package would be liable to make any
return for the risk and labor incurred; and, second, because it is
not shown that such usage had
grown up with the consent of the
owners of vessels, or that it was
more than a mere accommodation
usage. *Cincinnati &c. Co.* v. *Boal,* 15
Ind. 345. Where the plaintiff relied
upon a parol acceptance of a bill of
exchange, evidence of a custom of
the defendants to accept always in
writing and make corresponding
entries on their books, was held
competent as tending to show in
this case that the bill had not been
accepted. *Smith* v. *Clark,* 12 Ia. 32.
Where there is proof of an agreed
price or compensation, or of a usage
which might affect it, or from which
an agreement might be inferred, it
would not be correct to authorize

them to judge of the reasonableness
of the charges, irrespective of such
agreement or usage; but the court
should determine whether, if proved
to the satisfaction of the jury, the
usage is reasonable or operative.
Codman v. *Armstrong,* 28 Me. 91.
The mere opinions of witnesses is
not evidence of a usage. *Garey* v.
Meagher, 33 Ala. 630. That a railroad company had been for about a
month in the habit of storing cotton
consigned to their agent, at the
warehouse of A., without any proof
that this was generally known, or
any other evidence that the shipper
had notice of it, is not sufficient to
bind him. *Alabama &c. R. R. Co.* v.
Kidd, 35 Ala. 209. An isolated instance is not sufficient to prove a
custom, nor will evidence of the
custom of one person be sufficient
to establish a general course of trade.
Burr v. *Sickles,* 17 Ark. 428. When
a special custom at the place of
shipment is proved, and the question is whether the purchaser had
knowledge of the special custom,
and contracted in reference to it, the
previous course of dealing between
the same parties—such as the order,
shipment and receipt of several invoices of goods, without any charge
for insurance—is sufficient evidence
from which the jury may infer
knowledge of the special custom.
Walsh v. *Frank,* 19 Ark. 270. Evidence that " there has always been a
custom at a certain saw-mill and
other mills in the neighborhood to
leave the slabs as belonging to the
mill, the owners of the logs never
claiming them," does not establish a
legal right in the mill as real estate,

denying the practice was held entitled to a ruling that the practice is not established if no witness can recall a specific

to the slabs sawed. *Adams* v. *Morse*, 51 Me. 497. Proof is admissible of a custom among merchants, where merchandise is sold on condition, to deliver it to the buyer before compliance with the condition, and that such change of custody is not *de facto* a waiver of the condition, and the property does not pass thereby. *Farlow* v. *Ellis*, 15 Gray (Mass.) 229. When, in a suit against a railroad company for an injury received while passing along a highway, an issue is made upon the unreasonable or negligent conduct of the company in the use of the highway at the time complained of, its usage at other times has no legitimate bearing upon this issue, and evidence respecting such usage is incompetent. *Gahagan* v. *Boston &c. R. R. Co.*, 1 Allen (Mass.) 187. No exception lies to the admission of evidence of a custom existing in a trade without direct evidence that it was known to the opposite party, if the party offering it contends that he can prove, from all the evidence in the case, that it must have been known to him, and that question is argued and submitted to the jury under proper instructions in matter of law. *Dodge* v. *Favor*, 15 Gray (Mass.) 82. In determining whether a salary or compensation paid to a director of a bridge corporation was a reasonable expense of the corporation, evidence is inadmissible of custom in sundry other corporations to pay directors no salaries as compensation for services. *Central Corp.* v. *Lowell*, 15 Gray (Mass.) 106. A general usage in any place, by which sales on commission are regulated,

may be given in evidence; for it is a reasonable and legal presumption that every man knows the usage of the place in which he traffics, whether by himself or his factor; and, if the usage is not illegal, he is bound by it. *Dwight* v. *Whitney*, 15 Pick. (Mass.) 179; *Goodenow* v. *Tyler*, 7 Mass. 36, 46. Goods being consigned to an agent for sale, with general instructions to remit the proceeds, it is a sufficient compliance with such instructions, if the agent remits by a bill of exchange, without endorsing or guaranteeing it, provided such is the usage at the agent's place of business, and the agent uses proper diligence and discretion in the purchase of the bill. In an action against the agent, to recover the proceeds of such a sale, proof of the usage and of a remittance accordingly is a sufficient *primâ facie* defence; and if it is established by the agent, the burden of proof is then on the principal to show that bills remitted in pursuance of the usage ought to be endorsed or guaranteed by the agent. *Potter* v. *Morland*, 3 Cush. (Mass.) 384. A usage may be proved by parol, whether it originates in a public written law, or not. *Drake* v. *Hudson*, 7 H. & J. (Md.) 399; see also *Livingston* v. *Maryland Ins. Co.*, 7 Cranch. (U. S.) 506. In an action for damages for the want of correspondence between tobacco bought by sample and the samples by which it was sold, evidence showing a custom of dealers in Baltimore of buying and selling in bulk, by samples prepared by the State inspectors, without insuring correspondence in

instance of it.[4] The mere fact that the evidence is conflicting, does not entitle the party, against whom the usage is invoked, to a ruling that the usage is not proved, but it is for the jury to say from *all* the evidence whether or not the usage is established.[5] But if only *one* witness testifies to the existence of a usage, and another equally competent and of equal credibility contradicts such evidence, it is not proper to leave it for the jury to say whether the usage is established or not, but they should be instructed that the evidence is insufficient.[6] Upon the question as to whether a certain

quality, is admissible. *Gunther* v. *Atwell*, 19 Md. 157. The existence of a general usage prevailing among banks must be established, as a fact, and not as a matter of judgment or opinion of witnesses deduced from the manner of dealing in a few instances in particular banks. *Chesapeake Bank* v. *Swain*, 29 Md. 483.

[4] *Chenevy* v. *Goodrich*, 106 Mass. 566.

[5] *Upton* v. *Sturbridge Cotton Mills*, 111 Mass. 446. In *Winsor* v. *Dellaway*, 4 Met. (Mass.) 221, where contradictory evidence was offered as to the existence of a usage on which the plaintiff relied to support his action, and the jury were instructed that, if it was proved that the usage existed, and the defendant knew it existed, the plaintiff was entitled to recover, and the jury thereupon returned a verdict for the defendant; it was held that the plaintiff had no cause of exception to such instruction. See also *Tunell* v. *Carter*, 25 Ala. 498, to same effect.

[6] *Parrott* v. *Thacher*, 9 Pick. (Mass.) 426. In the absence of better proof it was held that evidence of long and uninterrupted usage, reputation, the declarations and conduct of the owners of the adjoining land, and the

public acts of the town, was properly admitted to prove that an ancient corporation of proprietors, now extinct, had dedicated a certain lot to the public use, as a landing place. *Sevey's case*, 6 Me. 118. Evidence by a justice of the peace that, where called upon by parties to prepare conveyances for them, it was his habit to inquire whether they desired absolute or conditional conveyances; that he had no doubt such inquiry was made in the present instance; that he never failed to shape the paper according to the expressed object of the parties; and that he was also in the habit of reading the papers after they were written to those for whom they were prepared, and especially if they were workmen, was held inadmissible. *Pocock* v. *Hendricks*, 8 G. & J. (Md.) 421. In an action by commission merchants in Boston, to recover back money paid to the consignor of goods sold by the plaintiffs to a trader in the country, who failed to pay for them, evidence to show a usage of factors in Boston to credit the amount of sales immediately to the account of the principal, and charge back in case of the insolvency of the purchaser, in case the factor has not

usage exists or not, a witness may be asked to describe how, under the usage, a transaction like the one in question would be conducted by all the parties thereto from its inception to its conclusion.[7] It may be said that the usage of a trade must be proved by the multiplication or aggregation of a great number of particular instances, showing a given course of business, and a general, established understanding respecting it.[8] It is not necessary that there should be either the antiquity, uniformity or notoriety that is essential to establish a custom ; it is sufficient *if it is shown to be so well known and so generally acquiesced in that it may reasonably be presumed to have been imported into their contract by the parties.*[9] In a word, it must be shown that the usage is certain and reasonable, and so universally acquiesced in that every one engaged in the trade knows it, or might know it if he exercised reasonable diligence in making inquiry.[1] It

been negligent; and also to show the usage as to the credit given to city and country purchasers, was held to be admissible. *Dwight* v. *Whitney*, 15 Pick. (Mass.) 179. Witnesses may be examined to prove the *course* of a particular trade, but not to show what the law of that trade is. *Ruan* v. *Gardner*, 1 Wash. (U. S.) 145 ; *Austin* v. *Taylor*, 2 Ohio. 64. A witness, who had lived both in New York and Mobile, understood it was the custom of merchants that the employer should pay the expenses and passage of clerks who were engaged in the former place to do service in the latter place, for the whole of the ensuing business season ; that the witness, who was a merchant, had never so employed or paid a clerk, but he knew of one case, where, under a stipulation to that effect, the wages and passage money of a clerk thus employed were paid by the employer. Held, that this evidence

was inadmissible, and consequently incompetent to establish the usage or custom of trade. *Price* v. *White*, 9 Ala. 563. The plaintiff having proved that a steamboat of the defendants was engaged in carrying goods and merchandise, generally, for hire, and the general custom of boats engaged in similar business with that of the defendant, held that it was admissible for the defendant to explain the usage, by showing that no freight or compensation was ever charged or allowed upon remittance of money, unless some evidence was given by the boat of its receipt, in which event only, a charge was made. *Knox* v. *Rives*, 14 Ala. 249.

[7] *Kershaw* v. *Wright*, 115 Mass. 361.

[8] *MacKenzie* v. *Dunlop*, 3 Macq. H. L. Cas. 22.

[9] *Juggomohun Ghose* v. *Manickhund*, 7 Moore Ind. App. 263.

[1] *Place* v. *Allcock*, 4 Fr. F. 1074.

is a well-settled rule that a person dealing in a particular market is presumed to be acquainted with the usages of that market, and such is the rule in respect to any trade or business; therefore, when a usage in respect to any business is shown to be well established, persons dealing in reference to matters to which such usage relates, are presumed to know of it.[2]

The Force of Usage.

SEC. 73. The force of usage is derived from the habit of mind to expect uniformity in the actions of men, and to anticipate the same conduct under similar circumstances in the future which has been experienced in the past. Were such an anticipation unfounded, custom could have no meaning. But use is second nature, and produces a secondary law well nigh as binding on the thoughts and actions of mankind as the laws of Nature herself. The proof, therefore, of single instances in such cases is all-important, and it has been remarked that witnesses who are called to prove a custom of trade, or the general or prevailing course of business in that calling, should cause their minds to revolve over instances known to them of its having been acted on.(k)

Elements to be Attached to Usage—Growing Usage—Prevalent Usage.

SEC. 74. One important particular is to be noted in relation to the evidence given to support a mercantile usage, and that is, that it is not necessary to attach to it the elements of antiquity, uniformity or notoriety, which is necessary to the admission of a local law, or what is technically called a particular custom. Such a usage "may be still in course of

[2] *Grissell* v. *Bristowe*, L. R. 4 C. P. 36; *Bayliffe* v. *Butterworth*, 1 Exchq. 429; *Bawring* v. *Shepherd*, 49 L. J. Q. B. 129; *Pollock* v. *Staples*, 12 Q. B. 765; *Buckle* v. *Knaap*, 36 L. J. Exchq. 49; *Greaves* v. *Legg*, 2 H. & N. 210; *Dun-* *can* v. *Hill*, L. R. 6 Exchq. 25; *Hadkinson* v. *Kelly*, L. R. 6 Exchq. 496; *Noble* v. *Kenoway*, 2 Doug. 513; *Bayley* v. *Wilkins*, 7 C. B. 880; *Taylor* v. *Stray*, 2 C. B. N. S. 175; *Mackintosh* v. *Marshall*, 11 Moll. 116.

(k) *Hall* v. *Benson*, 7 C. & P. 911.

growth ;"(*l*) it may require evidence for its support in each case, but in the result it is enough if it appear to be so well known and acquiesced in that it may be reasonably presumed to have been an ingredient tacitly imported by the parties into their contract.(*m*) Thus, as we have seen, the

(*l*) *Juggomohun Ghore* v. *Manickchund*, 7 Moore Ind. App. 263, at p. 282.

(*m*) *Juggomohun Ghore* v. *Manickchund*, 7 Moore Ind. App. 263; *Legh* v. *Hewitt*, 4 East. 154, 159, *per* Ld. Ellenborough; *Dalby* v. *Hirst*, 1 B. & B. 224; 3 Moore 536; *Vallance* v. *Dewar*, 1 Camp. 508; but see *Collins* v. *Hope*, 3 Wash. (U. S. C. C.) 149; compare *Donnell* v. *Columbian Ins. Co.*, 2 Sum. (U. S.) 366; *Wilcocks* v. *Phillips*, 1 Wall. Jr. (U. S. C. C.) 47. Evidence of usage may be admissible in relation to a mercantile contract in writing, to show in what manner the business is done, although the contract is precise in its terms. *Fox* v. *Parker*, 44 Barb. (N. Y.) 541. But in order to become part of a contract must be so far established and so far known to the parties that it must be supposed that their contract was made in reference to it. For this purpose the custom must be established and not casual, uniform and not varying, general and not personal, and known to the parties. *Sipperly* v. *Steward*, 50 Barb. (N. Y.) 62; *Duguid* v. *Edwards*, *Id.* 288; *Kendall* v. *Russell*, 5 Dana (Ky.) 501; *Stevens* v. *Reeves*, 9 Pick. (Mass.) 198; *Wood* v. *Hickok*, 2 Wend. (N. Y.) 501; *Martin* v. *Maynard*, 16 N. H. 165; *Wheeler* v. *Newbould*, 5 Duer (N. Y.) 29. It may be resorted to where the contract contains all that is necessary to understand what the parties agreed to do, when the evidence explaining the usage is admitted.

Dana v. *Fiedler*, 1 E. D. S. (N. Y.) 463. Where a custom exists in reference to a particular trade or business, the contracts of parties engaged in the business are presumed to be made with reference to such custom, unless it is expressly excluded. *Dalton* v. *Daniels*, 2 Hilt. (N. Y.) 472. And when well established, it may enter into the body of a contract without being inserted. *Stultz* v. *Dickey*, 5 Binn. (Penn.) 287; S. P. *Lodwick* v. *Ohio Ins. Co.*, 5 Ohio 436; *Sewall* v. *Gibbs*, 1 Hall (N. Y.) 612; *Barber* v. *Brace*, 3 Conn. 9; 2 Pet. (U. S.) 148; *Bank of Columbia* v. *Fitzhugh*, 1 H. & G. (Md.) 239; *Haven* v. *Wentworth*, 2 N. H. 93; *United Statse* v. *Arredondo*, 6 Pet. (U. S.) 715; *Sampson* v. *Gazzam*, 6 Port. (Ala.) 123; *Inglebright* v. *Hammond*, 19 Ohio 337; *Hursh* v. *North*, 40 Penn. St. 241. And even the usage and practice of a firm, though not good as a custom, will be binding, if expressly made part of the contract, or shown to have been known and assented to by the defendant at the time; and evidence of such a contract, either direct, or by proving a course of dealing between the parties, on such terms, and of such frequency, as to justify the inference that the transaction was on the accustomed terms, is admissible. *Hursh* v. *North*, 40 Penn. St. 241. The custom among the merchants of Pittsburgh, of charging interest on accounts after six months, having existed for a long time, and become

"custom of the country" with reference to good husbandry means no more than that the tenant should conform to the existing prevalent usage of the country where the lands lie, (*n*) and the general usage of trade may be imported into a contract though the proof has been given of exceptions to such usage. (*o*)

Principle of Admission—Knowledge of Custom Presumed.

SEC. 75. Evidence of a particular usage, (*p*) to add to or

uniform and notorious, the courts of justice are bound to notice it as part of the law. *Watt* v. *Hoch*, 25 Penn. St. 411. A general custom at a particular store, for the customers to allow interest on open accounts after a certain time, cannot have the effect of an agreement, on the part of a party dealing at such store, to pay such interest, unless expressly or impliedly sanctioned by such party. *Searson* v. *Heyward*, 1 Spears (S. C.) 249. But the usage of a creditor to compute interest on monthly rests will not bind his debtor, if it does not appear that the latter knew of such custom. *Goodnow* v. *Parsons*, 36 Vt. 46.

(*n*) *Legh* v. *Hewitt*, 4 East. 154, 159, *per* Ld. Ellenborough; *Dalby* v. *Hirst*, 1 B. & B. 224, 228.

(*o*) *Vallance* v. *Dewar*, 1 Camp. 508. *per* Ld. Ellenborough.

(*p*) See *Kirchner* v. *Venus*, 12 Moore P. C. C. 361; 7 W. R. 455; *Meyer* v. *Dresser*, 16 C. B. N. S. 646; *Appleman* v. *Fisher*, 34 Md. 540; *Southwestern Freight &c. Co.* v. *Stanard*, 44 Mo. 71. Mr. Smith, in a note to *Wigglesworth* v. *Dallinson*, 1 Sm. Lead. Cas. 308*a*, reviews the cases and evolves the general rule, that evidence of usage will be received to annex incidents to written contracts with respect to matters in

reference to which they are silent. 1st. In contracts between landlord and tenant. 2d. In commercial contracts. 3d. In contracts in other transactions in reference to which known usages have been established and prevailed. Thus it has been held that evidence was admissible of a usage among brokers, that when mining shares are sold to be paid for "half in two and half in four months," but the contract is silent as to the time of delivery, that payment must be cotemporaneous with delivery. *Field* v. *Selean*, 6 H. & K. 617; *Bywater* v. *Richardson*, 1 Ad. & El. 508; *Foster* v. *Mentor &c. Co.*, 2 E. & B. 48; *Gadts* v. *Rose*, 17 C. B. 229; *Spartari* v. *Benecke*, 10 *Id.* 212. Or that a contract shall be defeasible on a month's notice by either party. *Parker* v. *Ibbettson*, 4 C. B. N. S. 348. Or to attach to bought and sold notes the incidents of a sale by sample. *Cuthbert* v. *Cumming*, 11 Exchq. 405; *Lucas* v. *Bristow*, E. B. & E. 907. Or of the sale of a horse, to annex a customary warranty. *Allen* v. *Prink*, 4 M. & W. 140. To a lease, the reservation of ripening crops. *Adams* v. *Morse*, 51 Me. 499; *Wintermute* v. *Light*, 46 Barb. (N. Y.) 283; *Backenstoss* v. *Stahler*, 38 Penn. St. 251; *Bond* v. *Coke*, 71 N. C. 97. But that such evidence is only receivable when the

in any manner affect the construction of a written contract is admitted only on the principle that the parties who

incident which it is sought to import into the contract is consistent with the terms of the written instrument. If inconsistent, the evidence is not receivable, whether such inconsistency is evidenced by the express terms of the contract, or by fair implication therefrom, or if it changes the relation of the parties to each other. Thus, such evidence is not admissible to vary the relation of a broker and customer, under an ordinary speculation contract, to that of pledgor and pledgee. *Baker* v. *Drake*, 66 N. Y. 518; *Markham* v. *Jandon*, 41 *Id*. 435. With respect to commercial contracts, it has been long established that evidence of an *usage of trade* applicable to the contract, and which the parties making it knew, or may be reasonably presumed to have known, is admissible for the purpose of importing terms into the contract respecting which the written contract is silent. The words "*usage* of trade" are to be understood as referring to a particular usage to be established by evidence, and perfectly distinct from that general custom of merchants, which is the universal established law of the land, which is to be collected from decisions, legal principles and analogies, not from evidence *in pais*, and the knowledge of which resides in the breasts of the judges. *Vallejo* v. *Wheeler*, Lofft. 631; *Eden* v. *India E. Co.*, 1 W. Bl. 299; 2 Burr. 1216; *sed vide*, *Haille* v. *Smith*, 1 B. & P. 563, in which evidence of the general custom of merchants was received. This distinction, indeed, between the general custom of merchants, which is

part of the law of the country, and the particular usages of certain particular businesses, and was not, it seems, so clearly marked in former times as it is now; thus we find *Buller, J.*, saying, 2 T. R. p. 73, that "within the last thirty years (his lordship spoke in 1787) the commercial law of this country has taken a very different turn from what it did before. Before that period we find that, in courts of law, all the evidence in mercantile cases was thrown together; they were left generally to a jury, and produced no established principle. From that time we all know the great study has been to find some certain general principles which shall be known to all mankind, not only to rule the particular case then under consideration, but to serve as a guide for the future." But with regard to particular commercial usages, evidence of them is admissible either to engraft terms into the contract, as in those cases concerning the time for which the underwriters' liability in respect of the goods shall continue after the arrival of the ship. *Noble* v. *Kennoway*, Dougl. 510, and see the observations on this case in *Ougier* v. *Jennings*, 1 Camp. 503 n.; *Moon* v. *Guardians of Witney Union*, 3 Bing. N. C. 817; or to explain its terms, as was done *Udhe* v. *Waters*, 3 Camp. 16, by showing that the Gulf of Finland, though not so treated by geographers, is considered by mercantile men part of the Baltic, and in *Hutchinson* v. *Bowker*, 5 M. & W. 535, where it was proved that *good* barley and *fine* barley signified in mercantile usage different things; see further, *Robertson*

made the contract were both cognizant of the usage, and are presumed to have made the contract in reference to it.

v. *Clarke*, 1 Bing. 445; *Bottomly* v. *Forbes*, 5 Bing. N. C. 123; *Moxon* v. *Atkins*, 3 Camp. 200; *Vallance* v. *Dewar*, 1 Camp. 403; *Cochran* v. *Retburg*, 3 Esp. 121; *Birch* v. *Depeyster*, 1 Stark. 210; 4 Camp. 385; *Donaldson* v. *Forster*, Abb. on Shipp. part 3, cap. 1; *Baker* v. *Payne*, 1 Ves. Jr. 459; *Raitt* v. *Mitchell*, 4 Camp. 156; *Lethulier's case*, 2 Salk. 443; *Charaud* v. *Angerstein*, Peake 43; *Bold* v. *Rayner*, 1 M. & W. 446; *Powell* v. *Horton*, 2 Bing. N. C. 668; *Bowman* v. *Horsey*, 2 M. & R. 85. In mercantile transactions, and others of ordinary occurrence, evidence of established usage is admissible, not merely to explain the terms used, but to annex customary incidents, when such usage is not expressly or impliedly excluded by the tenor of the written instrument. *Parke, B.*, in *Syers* v. *Jonas*, 2 Exch. 111, 116; and, as to evidence of a usage to pay an agent, *Hutch* v. *Carrington*, 5 C. & P. 471; for a factor to sell in his own name, *Johnston* v. *Usborne*, 11 Ad. & El. 549; that "sold eighteen pockets Kent hops at 100s." means in the hop trade 100s. per cwt., *Spicer* v. *Cooper*, 1 Q. B. 424; that "in turn to deliver," in a charter-party to Algiers means at a particular spot in the port for a particular purpose, *Robertson* v. *Jackson*, 2 C. B. 412; to explain the sense in which "the word London" was employed, *Mallan* v. *May*, 13 M. & W. 511; and see *Simpson* v. *Margitson*, 11 Q. B. 23. In *Sutton* v. *Tatham*, 10 Ad. & El. 27, it was laid down that a person employing a broker on the stock exchange, impliedly gives him authority to act in accordance with the

rules there established, though the principal be himself ignorant of them. And in *Bayliffe* v. *Butterworth*, 1 Exchq. 416, *Sutton* v. *Tatham* was expressly approved of by *Parke, B.*, and *Rolfe, B.*; and *Alderson, B.*, laid down the law generally, that "a person who deals in a particular market must be taken to deal according to the custom of that market, and he who directs another to make a contract at a particular place must be taken as intending that the contract may be made according to the usage of that place." And *Parke, B.*, distinguished the cases of *Gabay* v. *Lloyd*, 3 B. & C. 793, and *Bartlett* v. *Pentland*, 10 B. & C. 760, in which the usage of Lloyd's coffee house was held not to be binding on persons who were not shown to have been cognizant of or to have assented to it, on the ground that in *Bayliffe* v. *Butterworth*, the question was as to the *authority* which the broker received. And *Bayliffe* v. *Butterworth* has since been followed in the Queen's Bench. *Pollock* v. *Stables*, 12 Q. B. 765; see also *Bayley* v. *Williams*, 7 C. B. 886. In *Steware* v. *Cauty*, 8 M. & W. 160, a rule of the Liverpool stock exchange was admitted in evidence between parties not members of it, upon a question what was a reasonable time for the completion of a sale of shares made at Liverpool through the agency of brokers. See, further, *Stewart* v. *Aberdein*, 4 M. & W. 211. So, in a case not falling within the head of mercantile contracts, evidence has been received to show that by the custom of a particular district the words "1,000 rabbits"

9

"Many contracts," said Erle, C. J., "in one case are construed by the course of business in the particular trade, or in

meant 1,200 rabbits. *Smith* v. *Wilson*, 3 B. & Ad. 728; and see *Clayton* v. *Gregson*, 5 A. & E. 302. In *Hinton* v. *Locke*, 5 Hill (N. Y.) 437, *Bronson*, *J.*, said that he should feel great difficulty in subscribing to the case of *Smith* v. *Wilson*; that it was difficult to deny that the evidence in that case was a plain contradiction of the express contract of the parties; and that no usage or custom is admissible in evidence where it contradicts the agreement of the parties. But in *Macy* v. *Whaling Ins. Co.*, 9 Met. (Mass.) 354, 363, *Smith* v. *Wilson* appears to be approved; and it is remarked that evidence is admissible, to show that the contract, notwithstanding the common meaning of the language used, was in fact made in reference to the usage in the trade to which the contract relates; and see also *Brown* v. *Brown and others*, 8 *Id.* 573, 576. So, in *Reg.* *Stoke-upon-Trent*, 5 Q. B. 303, an agreement in writing "to serve B. from 11th November, 1815, to 11th November, 1817," at certain wages, "to lose no time on our own account, to do our work well, and behave ourselves in every respect as good servants," was considered capable of explanation by a usage in the particular trade for servants, under similar contracts, to have certain holidays and Sundays to themselves. See *Phillips* v. *Innes*, 4 Cl. & F. 234. Also, in *Grant* v. *Maddox*, 15 M. & W. 737, an agreement by the manager of a theatre to engage an actress "for three years, at a salary of £5, £6 and £7 per week in those years respectively," was explained by the usage of the theatrical profes-

sion to mean that the actress was to be paid only whilst the theatre was open for performance. So, again, in *Evans* v. *Pratt*, 3 Man. & Gr. 759; 4 Scott N. R. 370, S. C., in a memorandum as to a race, the run described was "four miles across a country," and evidence was admitted to show that in sporting parlance the meaning of those words is straight across, over all obstructions, without liberty to go through open gates. So, where there was a contract to pay freight on delivery, at a certain rate per pound, a custom was allowed to be shown that the ship owner, on payment, allowed three months' discount, which of course brought the sum below that agreed upon by the words of the contract. In all contracts, the court observed, "as to the subject-matter of which known usages prevail, parties are found to proceed with the tacit assumption of those usages; they commonly reduce into writing the special particulars of their agreement, but omit to specify those known usages, which are included, however, as of course, by mutual understanding. The contract is in truth partly express and in writing; partly implied or understood and unwritten." *Brown* v. *Byrne*, 3 Q. B. El. & Bl. So, if A. and B. were to agree for a lease, it would be implied from custom that the lessor should prepare and the lessee pay for it. *Grissell* v. *Robinson*, 3 Bing. N. C. 11. Although, in general, upon a sale of property, the vendee who is to bear the expense of the conveyance ought to prepare it. *Price* v. *Williams*, 1 M. & W. 6; *Poole* v. *Hill*, 6 M. & W. 835;

the particular place where they are made. . . . In the cases
where such local usages are imported into the contract, it is

Stephens v. *De Medina*, 4 Q. B. 422;
see, however, *Clarke* v. *Stillwell*, 8 Ad.
& El. 645. But the admissibility of
evidence of custom to explain the
meaning of a word used in any contract whatever, is subject to this
qualification, viz., that if an Act of
Parliament has given a definite
meaning to any particular word de-
noting weight, measure or number,
it must be understood to have been
used with that meaning, and no evidence of custom will be admissible
to attribute any other to it; *per
curiam*, in *Smith* v. *Wilson*, see also
Hockin v. *Cooke*, 4 T. R. 314; *The
Master of St. Cross* v. *Lord Howard de
Walden*, 6 T. R. 338; *Wing* v. *Erle*,
Cro. Eliz. 267; *Noble* v. *Durell*, 3 T.
R. 271. In *Doe* v. *Lea*, 11 East 312,
it was held that a lease by deed of
lands since the new style, to hold
from the feast of *St. Michael*, must
mean *New* Michaelmas, and could
not be shown by parol evidence to
refer to Old Michaelmas. In *Furley*
v. *Wood*, 1 Esp. 198, Runn. Eject. 112,
Lord Kenyon had under similar circumstances admitted parol evidence
of the custom of the country to
explain the meaning of the word
Michaelmas; and the court, in *Doe*
v. *Lea*, on hearing that case, asked
whether the holding there was *by
deed*, which it does not appear to
have been, and to which it may be
added that it appears possible that
it was not even in writing. In *Doe*
v. *Benson*, 4 B. & A. 588, evidence of
the custom of the country was held
admissible for the purpose of showing that a letting *by parol* from *Lady-
day*, meant from *Old Lady-day*. The
court referred to *Furley* v. *Wood*, and

distinguished that case from *Doe* v.
Lea, on the ground that the letting
there was *by deed*, "which," said
Holroyd, J., "is a solemn instrument; and *therefore* parol evidence
was inadmissible to explain the expression Lady-day there used, even
supposing that it was equivocal."
It is perhaps not easy to conceive a
distinction, founded on principle,
between the admissibility of evidence to explain terms used in a
deed, and terms used in a written
contract not under seal; for though,
when the terms of a deed are ascertained and understood, the doctrine
of estoppel gives them a more conclusive effect than those of an unsealed intrument; yet the rule that
parol evidence shall not be admitted
to vary the written terms of a contract seems to apply as strongly to
a contract without a seal as with
one, while, on the other hand, it
appears from the principal case of
Wigglesworth v. *Dallison*, without
going further, that in cases where
parol evidence is in other respects
admissible, the fact that the instrument is under seal forms no insuper-
able obstacle to its reception. Nor
does it seem necessary, in order to
prevent a contradiction between *Doe*
v. *Lea*, and *Doe* v. *Benson*, and *Furley*
v. *Wood*, to establish any such distinction between deeds and other
written instruments; for, in *Doe* v.
Benson, the letting seems not to have
been in writing, so that the objection
to the admission of parol evidence,
founded upon the nature of a written instrument, did not arise. In
Furley v. *Wood* the letting was perhaps also by mere parol; and though

because they tacitly form part of it like those contracts in which we find the words, 'and other usual terms.' They

the evidence was, it is true, offered to explain the notice to quit, still it may be urged that, when the holding was once settled, to commence from Old Michaelmas, the notice to quit, which probably contained the words "at the expiration of your term," or something *ejusdem generis*, must be held to have had express reference to, and to.be explained by it. We must not, therefore, it is submitted, too hastily infer that parol evidence of custom would be receivable to explain a word of time used in the lease in writing,.but not under seal. *Doe* v. *Lea* was acted upon by the Court of Common Pleas, in *Smith* v. *Walton*, 8 Bing. 238, where the defendant avowed for rent payable "at Martinmas, to wit, November 23d ;" the plaintiff pleaded *non tenuit*, and a holding from *Old* Martinmas having been proved, the court thought that words after the *videlicet* must be rejected, as inconsistent with the term Martinmas, which they thought themselves bound by statute to interpret November 11th ; that no evidence was admissible to explain the record, and that there was, therefore, a fatal variance between it and the evidence. See *Hockin* v. *Cooke*, 4 T. R. 314; *The Master of St. Cross* v. *Lord Howard de Walden*, 6 T. R. 338; *Kearney* v. *King*, 2 B. & A. 301; *Sprowle* v. *Legge*, 1 B. & C. 16. However, evidence of usage, though sometimes admissible to add to, or explain, is never so to vary or to contradict either expressly or by implication the terms of a written instrument. *Magee* v. *Atkinson*, 2 M. & W. 442; *Adams* v. *Wordley*, 1

M. & W. 374; *Truman* v. *Loder*, 11 Ad. & El. 589. Thus, in *Yeates* v. *Pym*, 6 Taunt. 445, in an action on a warranty of *prime singed bacon*, evidence was offered of an usage in the bacon trade, that a certain latitude of deterioration called "average taint," was allowed to subsist before the bacon ceased to answer the description of *prime bacon*. This evidence was held inadmissible, first at Nisi Prius, by *Heath, J.*, and afterwards by the Court of Common Pleas. In *Blackett* v. *Royal Exchange Ins. Co.*, 2 Tyrwh. 266, which was an action on a policy upon " *ship, &c., boat, and other furniture*," evidence was offered that it was not the usage of underwriters to pay for boats slung on the davits, on the larboard quarter, but was rejected at Nisi Prius, and the rejection confirmed by the Court of Exchequer. "The objection," said *Lord Lyndhurst*, delivering judgment, "to the parol evidence is, not that it was to explain any ambiguous words in the policy, or any words which might admit of doubt, or to introduce matter upon which the policy was silent, but that it was at direct variance with the words of the policy, and in plain opposition to the language it used, viz., that whereas, the policy imported to be upon ship, furniture, and apparel generally, the usage is to say, that it is not upon furniture and apparel generally, but upon part only, excluding the boat. Usage may be admissible to explain what is doubtful, but is never admissible to contradict what is plain." The language must neither add to, nor qualify, nor contradict, the written

then form part of the contract. The contract expresses what is particular to the bargain, and the usage supplies the rest."(q)   As it is only a law in growth, and not in completeness, persons are only *presumed* to be aware of it, as there was no necessity incumbent upon them of informing themselves of the whole of the customs of a trade, as there is upon every subject of becoming acquainted with the whole of the laws of a country.

May be Rebutted.

SEC. 76.   Therefore the presumption may be rebutted.(r) Thus where goods were shipped at Liverpool for Sydney, and where by bill of lading the goods were made deliverable to the shipper's order, or assigns, " he or they paying freight for the goods here as per margin," and in the margin the stated amount of freight was made payable in Liverpool to M. (who was not the shipowner), one month after the sailing of the vessel, it was held that, as against an indorsee for value of the bill of lading, the master could not detain the goods at the port of delivery on the ground of non-payment of the freight, although the jury found that by the usage of

contract, but only "ascertain by expounding" it. *Browne* v. *Byrne*, 3 Q. B. 717. In *Roberts* v. *Barker*, 1 Cr. & Mee. 808, the question was whether a covenant in a lease, whereby the tenant bound himself not, on quitting the land, to sell or take away the manure, but to leave it to be expended by the succeeding tenant, excluded the custom of the country, by which the outgoing tenadt was bound to leave the manure, and was entitled to be paid for it. The court held that it did. "It was contended," said *Lord Lyndhurst*, delivering judgment, "that the stipulation to leave the manure was not inconsistent with the tenant's being paid for what was so left, and the custom to pay for the manure might

be engrafted on the engagement to leave it. But if the parties meant to be governed by the custom in this respect, there was no necessity for any stipulation, as by the custom the tenant would be bound to leave the manure and would be entitled to be paid for it. It was altogether idle, therefore, to provide for one part of that which was sufficiently provided for by the custom, unless it was intended to exclude the other part." *Clarke* v. *Roystone*, 13 M. & W. 752; *Redding* v. *Menham*, 1 M. & R. 236; *Spartalli* v. *Bencke*, 10 Q. B. 212.

(q) *Meyer* v. *Dresser*, 16 C. B. N. S. 646, at 660.

(r) See *Southwestern Freight &c. Co.* v. *Stanard*, 44 Mo. 71.

Liverpool the shipowner does not lose his lien for the freight by making it payable at the port of shipment, and that such a local usage cannot bind a *bona fide* holder for value without notice.(s) A custom in a place from which goods are shipped, is not necessarily binding upon a consignee at another place, and from the mere fact of the existence of a certain custom at the place of shipment, a jury would not be warranted in presuming that such a usage existed at the place to which the goods were consigned. Thus, the fact that a usage existed at a city from which goods were shipped, that the bill of lading shall not be detached from the draft until the draft is paid, was held not sufficient to warrant the jury in presuming that such usage existed in a neighboring city to which the cargo was consigned.[3] In order to make such a usage valid, it must be recognized and acted upon in both cities,[4] and mere proof of its existence in

(s) *Kirchner* v. *Venus*, 12 Moore P. C. C. 361 ; 7 W. R. 455.

[3] *Mears* v. *Waples*, 3 Houst. (Del.) 581.

[4] *Mears* v. *Waples*, 4 Houst. (Del.) 62. A mere local usage is not binding upon a party unless he has notice or knowledge of its existence at the time when the contract was entered into, and the burden of establishing knowledge is on the person setting it up. *Kirchner* v. *Venus*, 12 Mo. P. C. N. S. 361 ; *Simpson* v. *Margetson*, 11 Q. B. 32 ; *The Albatross* v. *Wayne*, 16 Ohio 513 ; *Flynn* v. *Murphy*, 2 E. D. S. (N. Y. C. P.) 378 ; *Latimer* v. *Alexander*, 14 Ga. 259 ; *Barnard* v. *Kellogg*, 10 Wall. (U. S.) 383 ; *Halls* v. *Howell*, Harp. (S. C.) 427. In *Rogers* v. *Mechanics' Ins. Co.*, 1 Story (U. S.) 603, the court says, "The usage or custom of a particular port, in a particular trade, is not such a usage or custom as will, in contemplation of law, limit, control or qualify the language

of a contract of insurance. It must be some *known*, *general* usage or custom in the trade, both applicable and applied to all the ports of the State, and so notorious as to afford a presumption that all contracts of insurance in that trade are made in reference to it as a part of the policy." See also *Pittsburgh Ins. Co.* v. *Dravo*, 2 Weekly Notes Cases 194 ; *Dean* v. *Swoop*, 2 Binn. (Penn.) 72 ; *Adams* v. *Ins. Co.*, 76 Penn. St. 411 ; *Cope* v. *Dodd*, 13 *Id.* 33 ; *McMasters* v. *R. R. Co.*, 69 *Id.* 374. Indeed, any usage to be binding must be established by such clear and satisfactory evidence that a presumption naturally arises that the parties contracted in reference to it. *Bowling* v. *Harrison*, 6 How. (U. S.) 259 ; *Strong* v. *Carrington*, 11 Am. Law Reg. 287 ; *Olericks* v. *Ford*, 23 How. (U. S.) 49 ; *Collings* v. *Hope*, 3 Wash. (U. S. C. C.) 149 ; *Pierpont* v. *Fowle*, 2

one place does not warrant the inference that it exists at

W. & M. (U. S. C. C.) 24. In New York it is held that proof of a local usage is inadmissible to control the rules of law respecting a particular trade. *Higgins* v. *Moore*, 34 N. Y. 417; *Minnesota R. R. Co.* v. *Morgan*, 52 Barb. (N. Y.) 217; *Bissell* v. *Campbell*, 54 N. Y. 353. Or to vary an express agreement. *Main* v. *Eage*, 1 E. D. S. (N. Y. C. P.) 619; *Stebbins* v. *Brown*, 65 Barb. (N. Y.) 274; *Beals* v. *Terry*, 2 Sandf. (N. Y.) 127. Or add incidents thereto contrary to the rules of the general law, as to import a warranty where *caveat emptor* applies. *Hawes* v. *Lawrence*, 3 Sandf. (N. Y.) 193; also 4 N. Y. 345; *Beirne* v. *Dord*, 5 N. Y. 95. Or to qualify the plain provisions of a contract about which there is no ambiguity. *Callender* v. *Dinsmore*, 55 N. Y. 200; *Bradley* v. *Wheeler*, 44 *Id.* 495; *Mercantile &c. Ins. Co.* v. *State Ins. Co.*, 25 Barb. (N. Y.) 319; *Groat* v. *Gile*, 51 N. Y. 431; *Simmons* v. *Law*, 8 Bos. (N. Y.) 213. Or to contradict its plain legal import. *Holmes* v. *Pettingill*, 1 Hun. (N. Y.) 316; *Allen* v. *Dykers*, 3 Hill (N. Y.) 593; *Dalton* v. *Daniels*, 2 Hilt. (N. Y. C. P.) 472; *Vail* v. *Rice*, 5 N. Y. 155; *Lombardo* v. *Case*, 45 Barb. (N. Y.) 95; *Sewall* v. *Gibbs*, 1 Hall (N. Y.) 602; *Lawrence* v. *Maxwell*, 53 N. Y. 19; *Taylor* v. *Ketchum*, 35 How. Pr. (N. Y.) 289; *Wadsworth* v. *Alcott*, 6 N. Y. 64; *Spears* v. *Hart*, 3 Robt. (N. Y.) 420; *Currie* v. *Smith*, 4 Leg. Obs. (N. Y.) 343; *Lane* v. *Bailey*, 47 Barb. (N. Y.) 395; *Wall* v. *Ins. Co.*, 3 Duer (N. Y.) 264; *Bargett* v. *Oriental Ins. Co.*, 3 Bos. (N. Y.) 385; *Suydam* v. *Clark*, 2 Sandf. (N. Y.) 133. Or to overcome a settled rule of commercial law, but it may be received to explain it.

Frith v. *Barker*, 2 John. (N. Y.) 327; *Emery* v. *Dunbar*, 1 Daly (N. Y. C. P.) 408; *Bowen* v. *Newell*, 8 N. Y. 190; *Gibson* v. *Culver*, 17 Wend. (N. Y.) 305. A local usage cannot be given effect to vary a contract, as a usage for pledgees of stock to transfer it at pleasure, when the contract of pledge only provided that it might be transferred after default. *Dykers* v. *Allen*, 7 Hill (N. Y.) 497; affirming S. C., 3 *Id.* 593; *Vail* v. *Rice*, 5 N. Y. 155; *Currie* v. *Smith*, 4 Leg. Obs. (N. Y.) 343. The same rule was also applied to a usage offered to alter the legal effect of an insurance policy. *Stebbins* v. *Globe Ins. Co.*, 2 Hall (N. Y.) 632; *Mutual Safety Ins. Co.* v. *Hone*, 2 N. Y. 235. And to a usage to satisfy contracts for the sale of flour of a specified brand, by the delivery of other brands of equal or better quality. *Beals* v. *Terry*, 2 Sandf. (N. Y.) 127. Or to treat as a delivery that which is not in law a delivery. *Suydam* v. *Clark*, 2 Sandf. (N. Y.) 133; and see *Smith* v. *Lynes*, 5 N. Y. 41. A local usage can never vary the construction of a contract, unless it is clearly proved that its existence was known to the parties, and that their contract was made in reference to its terms. *Wheeler* v. *Newbould*, 5 Duer (N. Y.) 29; affd., 16 N. Y. 392. Nor if it contradicts the contract. *Sweet* v. *Jenkins*, 1 R. I. 147. A custom of a particular locality for the owner of a lot of land, after giving notice to the owner of an adjoining lot to build his half of a partition fence, and his refusal to do so, to build the whole, and hold the party refusing for his share of the expense, has been held to be a reasonable and just custom, which may be enforced.

another (*Reynolds* v. *Continental Ins. Co.*, 36 Mich. 131),

Knox v. *Artman*, 3 Rich. (S. C.) 283. A shipper of goods is chargeable with notice of an established and well known usage, existing in a particular trade, in regard to the stowage of a general ship, both as to the manner of stowing, and as to the different articles to be stowed together. And if the shipper, in such case, gives no special instructions, and his goods are stowed in conformity with such usage, he is deemed to have assented to such mode of stowage, and cannot, in case his goods are injured on the voyage, in consequence of the mode of stowage, set that up as a ground of complaint, or as a foundation for depriving the owners of their freight. *Baxter* v. *Leland*, 1 Blatch: (U. S. C. C.) 526. Where a cargo was carried by a vessel, "addressed to" the owner of the cargo, he was held to be entitled to no commissions on the freight, and any usage giving him commissions in such a case, was held to be an unreasonable one, and the shipper was allowed no deduction from the freight, because wood and water, usually stowed on deck, had been stowed below, as it appeared that the bulkheads had been so moved as to give about the same amount of room. *Jelison* v. *Lee*, 3 W. & M. (U. S. C. C.) 368. In a case before the United States Supreme Court, *Willcocks* v. *Phillips*, 1 Wall. Jr. 47, where a master and his vessel were employed near Canton, in China, in a service not strictly within their ordinary offices, and not, originally, in any way contemplated, the ship being used, by an arrangement with the agent of the owner at Canton, for twenty-two months, as an opium store-ship, and, according to usage, a sum of five dollars on each box was paid on the delivery of the opium, which was called a "kumshaw," and which was exclusive of the price paid for storage, and the "kumshaws" were paid to the master, with the acquiescence of the agent, there having been no express agreement made with respect to the same, it was held, in a suit by the owner of the vessel against the master, to recover the "kumshaws," as a part of the earnings of the vessel, that it should be left to the jury to say, whether, by the usage of the trade, the "kumshaws" belonged to the master. The court must judge of the reasonableness and validity of any usage. Thus, where there is proof of an agreed price or compensation, or of a usage which might affect it, or from which an agreement might be inferred, it would not be correct to authorize them to judge of the reasonableness of the charges, irrespective of such agreement or usage; but the court should determine whether, if proved to the satisfaction of the jury, the usage is reasonable or operative. *Codman* v. *Armstrong*, 28 Me. 91. Exercising this power, it was held by the court, in *Walker* v. *Transportation Co.*, 3 Wall. (U. S.) 150, that a local custom that ship owners shall be liable for the negligence of their agents, in cases where the statute exempts them from liability, is unreasonable and therefore invalid. So, too, in *Bliss* v. *Ropes*, 9 Allen (Mass.) 369, it was held that evidence of a custom that a master of a vessel in a particular port has no authority to bind his owners for

but when instances of its application in one place are

necessaries furnished to the vessel, is inadmissible, as it would contradict and control a settled rule of maritime law, of universal application. In *Lombardo* v. *Case*, 45 Barb. (N. Y.) 295, in an action on a contract to deliver certain railroad stock, it was held that the plaintiff would not be permitted to prove that, by the general custom of brokers and dealers in stocks in the city of New York, the words "dividends or surplus dividends," in the contract, were intended to mean dividends declared on the stock, whether they had been announced before or after the date of the contract, provided that on the day the contract was made, the stock was selling in the market "dividend on," and not "ex-dividend;" for the reason that effect could not be given to the custom, without making a new contract between the parties. It was also held, in the same case, that the words "six months from date," cannot by proof of any custom, be extended or explained to mean, or include, "a day or two before date." *Per* Sutherland, J. In *Overman* v. *Hoboken City Bank*, 30 N. J. L. 61, it was held that the holder of a check drawn upon a bank cannot avail himself of a custom by which banks belonging to an association, called the clearing house, of which the drawee was one, are bound to return checks, presented through the clearing house, and which they have no funds to pay, upon the same day, or before banking hours of the next day, under penalty of being liable for the same, and that the fact that the check was presented through the clearing house

by a bank which belonged to that association, and acted as the agent of the holder, can make no difference, as customs in derogation of the common law must be strictly pleaded, and when well pleaded, the count must show a case clearly within the usage. Therefore, an allegation of a custom that when a check is presented at the clearing house to a bank against which the check is drawn, it shall be returned within a certain time if not paid, does not cover the case of the presentment of a check to a bank which is the agent of the bank upon which it is drawn. As to the necessity of pleading a custom or usage in derogation of the common law, and its inadmissibility under the general issue, see *Govenor* v. *Withers*, 5 Gratt (Va.) 24. In an action against a railroad company by a person employed in repairing their road, to recover for injuries received while being carried by them to his work, the defendants alleged that the plaintiff was negligent in riding in the baggage car. It was held, *Strong, J.*, dissenting, that evidence that it was the custom for such workmen to ride in the baggage car was admissible. *O'Donnell* v. *Allegheny R. R. Co.*, 50 Penn. St. 490. In an action upon a contract to receive at a future day, a certain number of barrels of flour at a fixed price, evidence is not admissible to prove a custom that either party to such a contract "has a right to demand a margin to be put up, reasonably sufficient to secure the performance of the contract." *Bowie, C. J.*, dissenting. *Oehrichs* v. *Ford*, 21 Md. 489. When a special contract is proved, evi-

shown, it may be shown to exist in other places for the

dence is not admissible to show a conflicting general custom. *Exchange Bank* v. *Cookman*, 1 West Va. 69; *Detwiler* v. *Green, Ib.* 109. In an action by the payee of a note given for the purchase money of a mining claim in California, evidence of a custom there for the vendor to return a note so given if the claim proved unprofitable, as it did in this case, is not a defence without proof that the custom was known to the plaintiff, and even if the custom set up had been well established, it would be invalid because unreasonable. *Leonard* v. *Peeples*, 30 Ga. 61. Evidence of a usage with other banks organized under the same law, to discount more than the legal rate of interest, upon the acquisition of business paper, is not admissible in a suit by a bank upon the paper so discounted. *Niagara County Bank* v. *Baker*, 15 Ohio St. 68. Because a usage in violation of a statute, or which furnishes a pretext or excuse for avoiding it, is bad. *New York Fireman's Ins. Co.* v. *Ely*, 2 Cow. (N. Y.) 678; *Bank of Utica* v. *Wager*, 2 Id. 712; *Dunham* v. *Dey*, 18 John. (N.Y.) 46. Special usages are not binding, unless known to the party sought to be charged thereby. Thus, if the master of a vessel hires a berth for her at a wharf, without notice of any rule of that wharf concerning the mode of discharging cargoes different from the usage at similar wharves in the same port, a stevedore whom he employs to discharge his cargo may do so according to such usage, and, if prevented by the wharfinger, may maintain an action against him for damages. *Croucher* v. *Wilder*, 98 Mass. 322. So in an action on a

policy of insurance, evidence of a local custom amongst insurers, not communicated to the insured, nor of such notoriety as to afford any presumption of knowledge on his part, is not admissible. *Hartford Protective Insurance Co.* v. *Harmer*, 2 Ohio St. 452. But in an action on a policy of insurance, evidence is competent to prove a usage that where there has been a verbal agreement for insurance, and the terms agreed upon and entered in the books of the company, the contract for insurance is considered as valid for the insured, although the premium is not paid. *Baxter* v. *Massasoit Ins. Co.*, 13 Allen (Mass.) 320. The practical adoption and use, for a long time, of a particular route, under a right of way granted by deed without fixed and defined limits, if acquiesced in by the grantor, operate to determine the location of the way as effectually as if the same had been described in the deed, because by acquiescing in the continued use of such route the owner of the land is treated as licensing that as the way granted, and the other by using it is treated as electing to adopt it. *Bannon* v. *Angier*, 2 Allen (Mass.) 128. In an English case the defendant chartered the plaintiff's vessel to proceed to Newcastle-on-Tyne, and there be ready forthwith, "in regular turns of loading," to take on board by spout or keel, as directed, a complete cargo of four keels of coal, and the remainder coke. In an action for not loading the vessel with coke within a reasonable time, it was held that evidence was admissible to explain the meaning of the expression in the charter party, "in regular

purpose of establishing uniformity or notoriety.[5] In *Star Glass Co.* v. *Morey*, 108 Mass. 570, the rule that the usage at the place of manufacture, rather than 'that at the place of sale will prevail, was applied in a case where glass was ordered in Boston from a manufacturer of glass in Philadelphia, and the prices and sizes were designated according to the manufacturer's price cards, but the local usages as to the standard of measurement and mode of cutting to fit the corresponding sizes of sash, were different.

Incidents of a Usage Must be Reasonable.

SEC. 77. But although all the incidents which are neces-

turns of loading," by showing that there was a usage of the port of Newcastle that vessels should take in their cargoes of coke in a certain regular order or turn ; and that the question, whether the vessel was loaded within a reasonable time, ought not to be decided without reference to such usage, if proved. *Leidemann* v. *Schultz*, 14 C. B. 38. The defendant, a London merchant, employed a broker at Liverpool to purchase some wool. The broker negotiated a sale by the plaintiff to the defendant of certain bales deliverable at Odessa, " the names of the vessels to be declared as soon as the wools were shipped." In this transaction the broker acted for both plaintiff and defendant. By the custom of Liverpool, where a contract contained a stipulation that notice of an event should be given by the vendor to the vendee, it was usual for the vendor to give the notice to the broker, who communicated it to the vendee. It was held that the defendant was bound by such usage, and therefore that a notice by the plaintiff to the broker, of the names of the vessels in which the wools

were shipped, was a performance of that stipulation, although the broker omitted to communicate them to the vendee. *Greaves* v. *Legg*, 34 Eng. Law & Eq. 489. Evidence of a custom in a certain town to sell lumber without previously measuring it, is admissible, when material, if the lumber to which it is sought to be applied is not shown to have been brought into the town by water, and as such required by the statute, to be surveyed and marked. *Lee* v. *Kilburn*, 3 Gray (Mass.) 594. Where it is proved that it has been the practice, for a long series of years, for the vicars choral of a cathedral, during their year of probation, to be excluded from a share in some of the emoluments of their office, and it can be gathered from the documents in existence, that some person had the power of regulating the manner in which the vicars choral were to be maintained, it will be presumed that some regulation was made, out of which the practice originated. *Shourbridge* v. *Clark*, 22 Eng. L. & Eq. 435.

[5] *Citizens' Ins. Co.* v. *McLaughlin*, 53 Penn. St. 485; *Sumner* v. *Tyson*, 384.

sary to the recognition of a particular custom or local law are not necessary in the case of a usage of trade, still some are; it must, for instance, be reasonable to be binding, and it has been held that it is not reasonable if an honest or right-minded man would deem it unfair or unrighteous.(t) It is very evident that this is a necessary incident. Usages are the result of the experience of mankind, and have been planned with a view to their convenience. But nothing absolutely unreasonable could result from the former, or tend to produce the latter. The self-will of an individual might make dishonesty or nonsense paramount for a day, but the experience of men never could consecrate what was unrighteous, their convenience and comfort never could be subserved by what was unjust or unreasonable. Where evidence of a usage has been admitted, therefore, evidence may be given in reply, tending to show that such a supposed usage would be unreasonable.(u)

Void Usages.

SEC. 78. A usage or custom that makes a negotiable instrument transferable without endorsement, is against the policy of the law, and therefore invalid. Thus, a local custom among cotton dealers making a warehouse receipt transferable by delivery without endorsement, and such mere transfer to pass the title to the cotton unless notice is given that a receipt has been lost or got into the hands of some one not entitled to hold it, was held bad.[6] So a usage that no title passes upon an ordinary sale and delivery—no lien being reserved by contract—without actual payment of the purchase-money, is invalid.[7] In the case last cited the court took occasion to place the ground of invalidity upon the circumstance that it was an attempt by usage to engraft terms

(t) Paxton v. Courtnay, 2 F. & F. 131; see Leuckhart v. Cooper, 3 Scott 521; 3 Bing. N. C. 99; see also Southwestern

Freight &c. Co. v. Stanard, 44 Mo. 71.   (u) Bottomly v. Forbes, 5 Bing. N. C. 128.

[6] Lehman v. Marshall, 47 Ala. 362.   [7] Haskins v. Warren, 115 Mass. 514.

upon a contract inconsistent with the rules of the common law, but it would seem that the true ground of invalidity is the circumstance that such a usage is against the policy of the law. So is a usage requiring a consignee to receipt for a certain quantity of property before he has an opportunity of ascertaining whether the quantity named in the receipt has been delivered. Thus, a usage requiring a consignee to receipt for grain weighed into a delivery bin before he has taken it from the bin, or has had an opportunity, except from the other party's statement, to ascertain whether the quantity of grain receipted for is there, has been held unreasonable and therefore void.[8] In *Gallup* v. *Lederer*, 1 Hun. (N. Y.) 282, the defendant offered to show that it was the custom of merchants to sign the receipt presented by carmen with goods, without any inquiry on the part of the receiving clerk or porters as to the ownership of the goods or the place from whence they came. The evidence was excluded upon the ground that such a custom, if proved, was unreasonable and therefore invalid. "The custom," said Daniels, J., "offered to be proved, that merchants sent invoices with goods sold at the time of delivery, stating the names of the vendor and vendee, the quantity, number packages and prices of the goods, could have no effect upon the rights and obligations of the parties, even if it had been received. For, as the plaintiff did nothing which could be construed or received as an indication that the goods were owned by the broker, he could not be deprived of his property in them, or his right to the price for which they were purchased for the defendant, although the invoice delivered to the broker was fraudulently suppressed by him, and for that reason never exhibited to the defendant. The sale was made by a person known by the defendant to be a merchandise broker and speculator, and, as the goods were never placed in his possession by the plaintiff, the defendant should have ascertained

[8] *Christian* v. *First Div. St. Paul &c. R. R. Co.*, 20 Minn. 21.

that circumstance and inferred from it that he acted simply as a broker in the transaction, and not as a merchant selling his own property. The fact that the broker deceived him, and on account of such deception he failed to discover the true relation he sustained to the business, was no fault of the plaintiff, since it was practiced without his authority or knowledge, and he did nothing to render the deceit successful. The custom proposed to be proven, that merchants signed the receipts presented by carmen with goods, without any inquiry by the receiving clerk or porter, as to the ownership or the place from whence they were received, was entirely unreasonable because it placed the consequences of one person's negligence or inattention upon another, in no way connected with him, having no control over his conduct, and for whose acts he could be in no proper sense responsible. *A custom tolerating carelessness and inattention in the ordinary affairs of business,* would be inconsistent with the legal as well as social duties, which one person in those affairs owes to another. *It would be not only unreasonable, but opposed to all settled legal obligations* to maintain the validity of a custom like that the defendant proposed to prove upon this subject. In the same line of defence, the defendant was asked whether, at the time of the sale, there was a custom of brokers to sell goods in their own name and to receive pay therefor. If a custom sanctioning such a course of conduct on the part of brokers, would be valid, the inquiry was not broad enough to render the proof admissible; for it might very well have been so restricted as to time and persons as to afford no grounds for supposing that the plaintiff had any notice or knowledge of its existence. The defendant did not propose to prove a general usage upon that subject, but simply a custom of brokers that might have been unknown to all other persons. To render a custom valid and binding upon a party to a transaction included within it, the proof should show, or propose to show, if of such long continuance or general application as reasonably to warrant the conclusion that it was known to the party designed to be affected by it, or that he had actual notice or knowledge of its existence.[9] This, as well as the other offers of proof, custom was defective in this respect, and for that reason properly excluded. The effect of such a custom, so far as it extended, would be to abrogate an existing well-established rule of law, designed for the protection of persons selling their property through the agency of brokers, *and nothing less than actual or presumed assent to its application* should be allowed to render it obligatory.[1] To prove the existence of a custom, something more than the judgment or conclusion of the witness called to support it, is required. A custom is the result of usage, and can only be properly shown by proof of the usage from which it may be claimed to be derived. The inquiry in such cases is not after the opinions of traders and merchants in respect to the law upon a mercantile question, but for the evidence of a fact, to wit, the usage or practice in the course of mercantile business in the particular case."[2] So is the custom of the master of a vessel to sell the cargo of a stranded vessel without necessity;[3] or authorizing persons to charge for services never performed, or materials not furnished;[4] or an agent to violate instructions from his principal;[5] or exempting carriers from responsibility for negligence;[6] or favoring the violation of a statute;[7] or conferring a right of action

[9] *Southwestern Freight Co.* v. *Stannard*, 44 Mo. 71; *Sipperly* v. *Stewart*, 50 Barb. (N. Y.) 62; *Walls* v. *Bailey*, 49 N. Y. 464.

[1] *Rogers* v. *Mechanics' Ins. Co.*, 1 Story (U. S.) 603; *Higgins* v. *Moore*, 34 N. Y. 417; *Barnard* v. *Kellogg*, 10 Wall. (U. S.) 383.

[2] *Allen* v. *Merchants' Bank*, 22 Wend. (N. Y.) 215; *Rogers* v. *Mechanics' Ins. Co.*, ante; *Lewis* v. *Marshall*, 7 M. & G. 729.

[3] *Bryant* v. *Commonwealth Ins. Co.*,

6 Pick. (Mass.) 145. *Stillman* v. *Hurd*, 10 Tex. 107.

[4] *Whitesides* v. *Meredith*, 3 Yeates (Penn.) 318; *Kendall* v. *Russell*, 5 Dana (Ky.) 501; see *Walls* v. *Bailey*, 49 N. Y. 464.

[5] *Barksdale* v. *Brown*, 1 N. & M. (S. C.) 519; *Catlin* v. *Smith*, 24 Vt. 85.

[6] *Schooner Reeside*, 2 Sum.(U.S.) 574; *Cole* v. *Goodwin*, 19 Wend. (N.Y.) 272.

[7] *Dunham* v. *Dey*, 13 John. (N. Y.) 44; *Supervisors* v. *Van Clief*, 1 Hun. (N. Y.) 45, 47.

upon contracts void under the statute of frauds, or barred by the statute of limitations ;[8] or to transfer settlement rights by death-bed donations without a will ;[9] or for factors to pledge the goods of their principal ;[1] or to construe a contract for articles by the ton, as calling for 2,200 pounds for a ton instead of 2,000 pounds as fixed by statute ;[2] or one that is in restraint of trade ;[3] or that deprives a person of his property without compensation, as a usage of a bank not to correct mistakes in counting money unless it is discovered before the party leaves the bank ;[4] or that exempts a person from liability where he is made liable by statute, or makes him liable where he is exempt therefrom by statute ;[5] or that permits a person to commit acts of trespass upon others' property ;[6] or permits an individual to appropriate to his exclusive use,

[8] *Dunham* v. *Gould*, 13 John. (N. Y.) 367.

[9] *Westfall* v. *Singleton*, 1 Wash. (Va.) 227.

[1] *Newbold* v. *Wright*, 4 Rawle (Penn.) 195.

[2] *Evans* v. *Myers*, 25 Penn. St. 114; *Green* v. *Moffatt*, 22 Mo. 529.

[3] *Williams* v. *Gilman*, 3 Me. 281.

[4] *Gullatin* v. *Bradford*, 1 Bibl. (Ky.) 207. Where a custom for the inspector of flour to take to his own use the draft flour, drawn out to be examined, was set up, it was held that it was contrary to the policy of the law; that the statute providing certain fees for inspection, thereby impliedly forbade all other compensation; that it could not be more ancient than the inspection laws, and that they were not old enough to be immemorial, though beyond the actual memory of those then living; that though this custom had existed under the old laws, and the legislature, in remodelling them, had not expressly negatived the custom, yet that this silence was not a legislative recognition of it. And where

such inspector of flour claimed that he could not inspect by boring a half-inch hole in the head of the barrel, and that the custom allowed him to use a larger auger; the old law required him to inspect flour by a half-inch hole, while the new code required all inspectors of flour, fish, butter, &c., to inspect by a half-inch hole or in some other satisfactory manner, and required the hoops of barrels offered for inspection to be nailed. Held, that the code did not change the method of inspection established by the old law, and that it was no answer to a *mandamus* to compel the inspector to inspect a certain lot of flour by a half-inch hole, that he could not so inspect it properly, and that the custom authorized him to use a larger hole, as both the answer and the custom would be in contravention of the statute under which he held his office. *Delaplaine* v. *Cranshaw*, 15 Gratt (Va.) 457.

[5] *Walker* v. *Trans. Co.*, 3 Wall. (U. S.) 150.

[6] *Waters* v. *Lilly*, 4 Pick. (Mass.) 145.

rights which equally belong to all the public;[7] or which permits a person to take anything from another's land;[8] or that permits an intermediate carrier to deduct from back freight earned, any deficiency in the cargo as shown by a comparison of the bill of lading with the measurement of the carrier receiving it;[9] or a usage which continues the liability of common carriers after their liability is discharged by the general law;[1] or that permits an agent to warrant the quality of goods sold by him, although not authorized to do so by his principal;[2] or that seamen's wages, due under shipping articles, shall be paid to the shipping agent, to be paid by him to the boarding-house keeper bringing the seamen for their benefit;[3] or that excuses a person from liability for negligent acts;[4] or, indeed, any custom or usage that origi-

[7] *Freary* v. *Cooke,* 14 Mass. 488. In *Wadley* v. *Davis,* 63 Barb. (N. Y.) 500, it was held that a custom among persons employed to cut staves from another's bolts, should retain for his own use, not only the clippings and corner pieces, but the culls, without the owner's consent, is against public policy and void.

[8] *Perley* v. *Langley,* 7 N. H. 233. A custom to take fish, or to take sand from another's land for the purpose of making mortar, *in alieno solo,* is void. *Waters* v. *Lilly,* ante. A profit *à prendre,* is not a good custom. *Littlefield* v. *Maxwell,* 31 Me. 134; *Lupkin* v. *Haskell,* 3 Pick. (Mass.) 356.

[9] In *Strong* v. *Grand Trunk R. R. Co.,* 15 Mich. 206, such a custom was set up, but the court held that it was unreasonable and void, as it prevented the carrier from showing that there was an error in the bill of lading, and would enable the intermediate consignee to deduct for discrepancies between the bill of lading and amount delivered, which occurred owing to erroneous measurement or count when the bill was signed, and because it would deprive the carrier of his lien upon the cargo for freights to the extent of the amount thus improperly deducted.

[1] *Reed* v. *Richardson,* 98 Mass. 216.

[2] *Dadd* v. *Farlow,* 11 Allen (Mass.) 426.

[3] *Metcalf* v. *Weld,* 14 Gray (Mass.) 210.

[4] *Miller* v. *Pendleton,* 8 Gray (Mass.) 547. In *Cleaveland* v. *New Jersey Steamboat Co.,* 5 Hun. (N. Y.) 523, the defendant who was sued for injuries resulting from a failure properly to secure the gangway of its boat, offered to show that it was customary on the Hudson river on passenger boats leaving a dock at New York, to wait for departure, until the gates at the gangway are put in. The evidence was excluded, Merevin, J., saying, "Evidence of the character of a structure, either generally or as compared with similar structures used by others, and evidence of whether accidents of

nates in, or is continued by violence, oppression and fraud, or is contrary to the policy of the law, morality and religion, is void and cannot be set up either to protect rights acquired under, or defeat rights acquired in opposition to them.[5] The evidence to establish a custom must be uniform, and even an occasional practice tolerated to some extent, in a certain department of business for any given year, cannot be said to be made out without distinct proof of some specific instances during the period in question.(v)   The usage, to be binding, must be general as to place and not confined to a particular bank.(w)   We have already seen that evidence of a usage of trade is admissible to show that words used in a certain written contract were used in a peculiar, technical or local sense;(x) but we must add here, while we are speaking of the kind of evidence which is required to support a usage, that the proof of such a use must be clear and irresistible.(y)

How Proved.

SEC. 79. A usage of a trade, in order to arise to the dignity of a usage, recognized in law, must arise from a general and prevailing course of that particular business,[6] and cannot

that kind have ever happened have been sometimes admitted. But that does not reach the present point. It is in effect, an offer to show, as an excuse for its negligence, a custom of others to be equally negligent. I know of no principle to sustain it."

[5] In *Holmes* v. *Johnson*, 42 Penn. St. 159, in an action of ejectment brought to settle the disputed title to land, the claimant being a negro born in another State, the defendant offered to prove that, in the region whence the plaintiff came, it was not customary for colored people to form legal marriages, and that the majority of them cohabit promiscuously, as well among *free* colored persons as slaves, in order to rebut the presumption of marriage and legitimacy. The court rejected the evidence upon the ground that such a custom, if proved, was contrary to public morals and decency, and therefore void.

[6] Tindal, J., in *Hall* v. *Benson*, 7 C. & P. 911; *Mills* v. *Hallock*, 2 Edw. Ch. (N. Y.) 652.

(v) *Chenery* v. *Goodrich*, 106 Mass. 566; see also *per* Erle, C. J., in *Myers* v. *Dresser*, 16 C. B. N. S. 646.

(w) *Adams* v. *Otterback*, 15 How.

(U. S.) 539; but see *Vallance* v. *Dewar*, 1 Camp. 503.

(x) *Ante*, p. 47.

(y) *Lewis* v. *Marshall*, 7 M. & G. 729; 8 Scott, N. R. 477.

be proved by evidence of opinion merely, but by instances in which it has been acted upon. A witness if asked whether a certain usage exists in a particular trade, who answers yes, but is unable to give instances in which to his knowledge it has been acted upon, proves nothing.[7] It is not sufficient to show by a witness belonging to a particular trade, that he does a certain thing in a particular way, but it must also be shown that that is the usual mode adopted in the trade.[8] The course adopted by the trade should be shown,[9] and evidence of an isolated instance is insufficient.[1] But the belief of a witness in the existence of a business usage, as derived from a knowledge of the business for a long series of years, is competent to prove such usage, and it is immaterial that the knowledge is derived wholly from his own business, if that is sufficiently extensive to enable him to testify to the fact of usage.[2] It is not necessary that the witness should be engaged in a particular trade or business to make him competent to testify to a usage pertaining to it. It is sufficient if he has acquired his knowledge by dealing with those engaged in it.[3] Thus, in the case last cited, it was held that

[7] *Hall* v. *Benson,* ante ; *Cunningham* v. *Fonblanque,* 6 C. & P. 44 ; *Geary* v. *Meaghar,* 33 Ala. 630.

[8] *Pfiel* v. *Kemper,* 3 Wis. 315. In this case it was sought to fix the value of professional services by usage, and it was held not competent to ask a witness what he should have charged for the same services; but that the evidence must be either to the value of the services or the customary rate of compensation.

[9] *Ruan* v. *Gardner,* 1 Wash. 145; *Winthrop* v. *Ins. Co.,* 2 *Id.* 7 ; *Austin* v. *Williams,* 2 Ohio 64. Proof that a particular mode of selling cotton in Mobile " is very common," but that a few factors at that place would not do so, was held insufficient to estab-

lish a usage of trade. *Anstill* v. *Crawford,* 7 Ala. 385.

[1] *Burr* v. *Sickles,* 17 Ark. 428. Proof that in one instance the use by a son of his father's name upon negotiable paper discounted at a bank, was known to and acquiesced in by him, does not authorize the introduction in evidence of subsequent similar acts for the purpose of showing an implied authority in the son to sign his father's name, without proof that these also were known to and acquiesced in by the father. *Greenfield Bank* v. *Crafts,* 2 Allen (Mass.) 269.

[2] *Hamilton* v. *Nickerson,* 13 Allen (Mass.) 351.

[3] *Grippin* v. *Rice,* 1 Hills (N. Y. C. P.) 184.

the customary mode of banks in respect to certain matters, may be proved by a person who has dealt with, but was never employed by them. So the usual mode of transfering notes, drafts, &c., may be proved by a witness who has derived a knowledge thereof in any manner that enables him to testify to the facts.[4] In order to establish the existence of a general usage among banks, or, indeed, in any business, the facts must be shown ; that is, the witness must state what is done, and how, and not merely his opinion deduced from the manner of dealing in a few instances in particular banks.[5] The mere opinion of witnesses that, in certain transactions with an agent, it is customary to hold him responsible, is not such evidence of a custom in that respect as will exonerate the principal.[6] A usage may be proved by parol, whether it arises from a public written law or not,[7] and the question as to whether or not it can be established by the evidence of one witness, depends upon the extent of his experience and knowledge in that regard. But if one witness swears to the existence of a certain usage, and another, equally competent and conversant with the trade or business to which it relates, the existence of the usage is not established, especially where other witnesses could be but are not called.[8] But generally, when the evidence is conflicting, it should be submitted to the jury to determine whether the usage is established or not. But where there is only the evidence of one witness, and his testimony is not restricted to any particular time or

[4] *Commercial Bank of Pennsylvania* v. *Union Bank of New York*, 19 Barb. (N. Y.) 392.

[5] *Chesapeake Bank* v. *Swain*, 29 Md. 483.

[6] *Geary* v. *Meaghar*, 33 Ala. 630.

[7] *Drake* v. *Hudson*, 7 H. & J. (Md.) 399; *Livingston* v. *Maryland Ins. Co.*, 7 Cranch (U. S.) 506. But where it is sought to prove a usage as an incident of a written contract, the contract itself should be first produced, and then any incident to it arising from usage can be proved by parol, but incidents cannot be proved first to establish the existence of the contract, as to prove a custom of a place by which all notes expire at a certain time. *Moore* v. *Eason*, 11 *Ired.* (N.C.) L. 568.

[8] *Parrott* v. *Thacher*, 9 Pick. (Mass.) 426.

place, and tends to establish a usage in conflict with the law
or other well recognized usages, it is proper for the court to
tell the jury not to regard it.[9] A general usage in a particular place, regulating certain matters, as sales on commission, may always be shown when the usage is reasonable and
not contrary to law, and it will be presumed that every one
dealing where such usage prevails, knows of and deals in
reference to it,[1] and if the usage is not so general as to
uphold such a presumption, his knowledge thereof may be
shown by the previous course of dealing between the parties,
and this furnishes sufficient evidence from which the jury
may infer knowledge of the usage.[2] As a general rule, a
custom cannot be established from the testimony of one witness.[3] Especially is this the case when the custom sought
to be established is one in favor of a certain town or locality.
Thus, in a case where it was sought to establish a custom for
all the inhabitants of a certain town to deposit sea-weed
upon the plaintiff's land, it was held that thirty inhabitants
having testified that they had done so for many years, it
was competent evidence from which the jury might find the
custom.[4] In all cases, in order to establish a customary
right, the evidence should not be less than that required to
establish a prescriptive right.[5] The burden of proving
either a custom or usage of trade devolves upon the party
seeking the benefit of it,[6] and must be shown by facts rather
than the belief or opinion of witnesses. Thus for a witness to state that a custom or usage exists, without stating

[9] *Jewell* v. *Center*, 25 Ala. 498.

[1] *Dwight* v.*Whitney*, 15 Pick.(Mass.)
179; *Goodnow* v. *Tyler*, 7 Mass. 36.

[2] *Walsh* v. *Frank*, 19 Ark. 270.

[3] *Vait* v. *Rice*, 5 N. Y. 150; *Thomas*
v. *Graves*, 1 Mill (S. C.) Const. 309;
Wood v. *Hicock*, 2 Wend. (N. Y.) 501;
Bissell v. *Ryan*, 22 Ill. 566; *Partridge*
v. *Forsyth*, 29 Ala. 200.

[4] *Knowles* v. *Dow*, 22 N. H. 387. In
Hanmer v. *Chace*, 4 DeG. J. & S. 626,

it was held that a custom of a manor
might be proved by one instance,
and in a suit by the lord to restrain
a copyholder from digging vitreous
sand on his own tenement, evidence
of a custom to dig it for twenty-seven
years, and of a custom to dig sand
generally, was sufficient to establish
the custom.

[5] *Smith* v. *Floyd*, 18 Barb.(N.Y.)523.

[6] *Caldecott* v. *Smythies*, 7 C. & P. 808.

instances where it has been acted upon or applied, proves nothing, because the whole matter rests in his opinion or belief, but if he can speak from instances in which it has been acted upon, facts are then presented from which the jury can arrive at a conclusion.[7] While a custom or a usage, at a place distant from that in which it is sought to apply it, may be shown as tending to establish such custom or usage at the place where it is sought to give it effect, yet it has no such tendency unless instances, in which it has been acted upon, are shown at such place.[8] But proof of a single instance at the place in question, unless the effect of such evidence is antagonized by proof of similar transactions in similar establishments in which it was not acted upon.[9] To establish a custom of shippers on a certain river, it is competent for a witness to state his practice in that respect on all boats on the river.[1] The fact that a person whom it is sought to affect by a local custom or usage, lives at a great distance from the place where the custom, &c., exists, does not, if the transaction had its *situs* at such place, tend to overcome the presumption that he knew of the custom and contracts in reference to it, as it is regarded as reasonable to presume that a person knows the customs and usages of a place at which he traffics, wherever he may reside.[2] In order to establish a usage of a certain trade or business, the testimony should come from those engaged in the business, or those who are familiar with the existence and application of the usage, but the testimony of a single witness, who testifies that he knew what had been the custom of his neighbors

---

[7] *Henderson* v. *Charnock*, Peake 4.

[8] *Brown* v. *Wilkinson*, Co. Lit. 270b; *Milward* v. *Hilbert*, 3 Q. B. 120.

[9] *Citizens' Ins. Co.* v. *McLaughlin*, 53 Penn. St. 485; *Sumner* v. *Lyton*, 20 N. H. 384.

[1] *Berry* v. *Cooper*, 28 Ga. 543.

[2] *Dwight* v. *Whitney*, 15 Pick. (Mass.) 179; *Goodenow* v. *Tyler*, 7 Mass. 36. Proof of a custom among

merchants, where merchandise is sold on condition to deliver it to the buyer before the condition is complied with, and that such a change of possession is not in fact a waiver of such condition, is admissible to establish the fact that the title to the property did not pass by such delivery. *Farlow* v. *Ellis*, 15 Gray (Mass.) 229.

for several years, in relation to certain matters—as in the case cited below, the manner in which farmers received their supplies from merchants who advanced to them—is not sufficient to establish a usage.[3]

Proof Of.

SEC. 80. The evidence to establish a usage must be uniform, and even an occasional practice tolerated to a certain extent in a certain department of business for any given year, cannot be said to be made out, without distinct proof of some specific instances during the period in question.[4] Opinions or conclusions of witnesses as to the effect of a usage of trade either upon a contract or the legal rights of parties is not admissible to show either the character or force of the usage.[5] In order to disprove the application of a usage or of regulations of a board, as a Chamber of Commerce, having corporate powers, to appoint an inspector of certain classes of goods, as in the case cited below provides, one of the purposes of the rules of which is declared to be, "To establish uniformity in the commercial usages of the city," to a certain class of property, it is competent to show that certain classes of articles are specified, as subject to the rules or usage, but that the article in question is not named, and the effect of this is to show the non-existence of such usage as to the article not named.[6] When a sale is made in a place where a board of trade exists, which has established certain rules relating to the sale of certain classes of property, as cotton, and a purchaser being informed of such rules does not dissent or object to them, but proceeds with the contract, those rules become a part of the contract as much as though they had been incorporated into it, although they have not existed or been acted upon long enough to acquire the character either of a custom or usage of the trade.[7]

[3] *Smith* v. *Wright*, 56 Ala. 417.

[4] *Chenery* v. *Goodrich*, 106 Mass. 566.

[5] *Haskins* v. *Warren*, 115 Mass. 514.

[6] *Kershaw* v. *Wright*, 115 Mass. 361.

[7] *Leigh* v. *Mobile &c. R. R. Co.*, 58 Ala. 165.

CHAPTER IV.

THE USAGES OF TRADE, THEIR OFFICE.

Evidence of Collateral Customs.

SEC. 81. We come now to an important question, which must be considered in connection with the proof of a custom, and that is as to whether evidence of a custom at a different place is admissible as bearing on the question of a custom at the *locus in quo*. In one case it was distinctly laid down that to prove the manner of conducting a particular branch of trade at one place evidence may be given to show the manner in which the same branch is carried on at another place; Buller, J., remarking, "If it can be shown that the time would have been reasonable in one place that is a degree of evidence to prove that it was so in another. The effect of such evidence may be taken off by proof of a difference of circumstances. It is very true that the custom of one manor is no evidence of another, that has been determined in many cases,(a) but the point here is very different; it is a question

(a) *Anglesey (Marquis)* v. *Hatherton (Lord)*, 10 M. & W. 218.

concerning the nature of a particular branch of trade."(*b*) In another case it appeared that a plea of a custom of trade in London might be supported by proof of a custom prevailing in London and other English ports.(*c*) And in the most recent case,(*d*) in which the fact that a custom existed in the London fruit trade, that if the brokers did not give the names of their principals in the contract, they were held personally liable, evidence was given as to the existence of a similar custom in the London colonial market. The court, although it had some doubt, seeing that the case went further than *Noble* v. *Kennoway,*(*e*) decided that it was admissible, on the general principle that it would be useful in elucidating the truth,(*f*) and because, in the words of Blackburn, J., "it struck me, where the question was, does a broker in the fruit trade, if he does not disclose his principal's name, incur a personal liability in consequence? that it would be proper evidence for a jury to consider and weigh that such a custom existed in other trades, and that in those other trades the broker did incur a personal liability."(*g*) In a Pennsylvania case,[1] a policy was issued by the defendant upon a "patent leather manufactory" in Pittsburgh, Pennsylvania, belonging to the plaintiff. The policy provided that benzole, in quantities not exceeding five barrels, might be kept in a shed detached from and in the rear of the main building, *and nowhere else on said premises.* It was well known that benzole was an important and essential article in the prosecution of the business and was necessarily and universally used. The custom of the plaintiff's workmen was to carry an open bucket of it into the factory as often as wanted, and upon the morning of the fire, a workman carried an open bucket of it into the factory and set it

(*b*) *Noble* v. *Kennoway,* 2 Dougl. 510, at p. 512.

(*c*) *Milward* v. *Hibbert,* 3 Q. B. 120.

(*d*) *Fleet* v. *Murton,* 7 L. R. Q. B. 126.

(*e*) 2 Dougl. 510.

(*f*) *Per* Cockburn, C. J., 7 L. R. Q. B. at p. 130.

(*g*) 7 L. R. Q. B. at p. 134.

[1] *Citizens' Ins. Co.* v. *McLaughlin,* 53 Penn. St. 485.

down, when it almost instantly ignited, and, communicating the flames to the building, it was burned down. To prove that the method of carrying the benzole into the factory in open buckets was according to the custom of the trade, it was shown by the testimony of a witness that it was the custom in *twelve* similar factories in Newark, New Jersey, *and no evidence being introduced to show a contrary custom in Pittsburgh,* where the plaintiff's factory was located, it was held sufficient to establish the usage in Pittsburgh. Woodard, J., upon this point, said: " We think there was no error in the admission of the evidence of Harden. He gave an intelligible account of the mode of using benzole in twelve similar factories in Newark, New Jersey, and said it was brought in and used from cans and buckets. *If any other custom had been established at Pittsburgh it could have been shown, but in the absence of all other evidence on the subject, this was competent to fix the usage of the business."* Thus it will be seen that while the usage of a certain trade in one locality is not necessarily the usage of the same trade in another, yet such usage may be proved, and, unless a different usage is shown to exist in the locality to which it is sought to apply it, it will be presumed to be usage of the trade in that locality. In a New Hampshire case,[2] evidence that a custom among iron manufacturers, to warrant the quality of all the goods made by them, was held to be established by proof of such a custom in three similar establishments in the vicinity, there being no evidence of a contrary custom in any other similar establishment.

Evidence from Analogy of Customs.

SEC. 82. Again, on this question of evidence from analogy, the case of *Falkner* v. *Earle,*(*h*) may be referred to. In that case it appeared that there was a custom of Liverpool of allowing a discount of three months on freights payable on

---

[2] *Sumner* v. *Tyson,* 20 N. H. 384.

(*h*) 3 B. & S. 360; 32 L. J. Q. B. 124.

all bills of lading from ports in North America; it also appeared that when Texas was annexed to the United States of America, in 1846, the custom was in practice extended to ports in that territory, and it was held that this was evidence from which a jury might infer that the custom extended to ports in California after that country was also associated with the United States by annexation.

Effect of Custom on Written Contract—The Rule of Law—To Explain.

SEC. 83. We now come to the question as to the effect of a custom upon a written contract. We have seen that it may engraft terms upon a written contract, and that it may not contradict such a contract, and hence arises the question which we have here to consider as to what evidence is admissible in such cases, and from a consideration of the many cases which have been decided to come to a definite conclusion as to the exact meaning of the rule of law. It must be remembered that customs, such as we are dealing with here, are always questions of evidence, and hence it arises that the main question for us in this place is as to the admissibility of the evidence which is offered in their support. The rule is that evidence of particular commercial usages is admissible either to add terms to a contract, as in those cases concerning the time for which the underwriters' liability in respect of goods shall continue after the arrival of the ship,(i)

(i) *Noble* v. *Kennoway*, 2 Dougl. 510; see also *Ougier* v. *Jennings*, 1 Camp. 503, n.; see also Law of Scotland, Bell's Com. b. 3, pt. 1, ch. 3. In an action by merchants in Kentucky against commission merchants in New Orleans, for the proceeds or value of goods consigned to them for sale, on which they had made advances, and as to which there was no special agreement. Held, that it was competent for the defendants to prove that it was the custom of that city for merchants, who had made advances on goods consigned to them from other States, to ship them to foreign ports for sale; and by such proof to affect the amount of recovery, or defeat the action. *Wallace* v. *Bradshaw*, 6 Dana (Ky.) 382. A custom which authorizes an agent holding gunny bags and inspected pork, purchased for his principal, to deliver, not the specific articles but others of equal quantity and value, cannot be recognized. Under such

or to explain its terms, as was done in *Ude* v. *Walters,*(*j*) where it was shown that the Gulf of Finland, although distinguished by geographers from the Baltic, is not so distinguished by persons in trade, or as in another case, where it was proved that in mercantile usage *good* barley and *fine* barley did not mean the same thing.(*k*)

Usage Allowed to add to Contract.

SEC. 84. At first in the history of this branch of the science of evidence we find that there seems to have been some reluctance upon the part of judges to allow usage to do more than explain in cases where there was evident ambiguity. But it soon came to be understood that it was as necessary to allow usage to explain what was purposely not said as what was carelessly ill expressed, and that many persons were purposely reticent of words, as they were aware of the existence of the usage. Hence it came that it was allowed not only to explain but to add a tacitly implied incident to the contract in addition to those which were expressed. First, then, with regard to the supposed explanation of contracts by means of usage. In order to affect a person with the obligations imposed by usage or custom, it is essential to show either that *he knew* of its existence, or circumstances from which such knowledge can be presumed.[3]

a custom the property could not be identified if the agent should fail; and, after a sale in violation of orders, his interest becomes adverse to that of his employer. *Foley* v. *Bell*, 6 La. An. 760.

[3] *Boardman* v. *Gallard*, 1 Hnn. (N. Y.) 220; *Ripley* v. *Ætna Ins. Co.* 30 N. Y. 136; *Higgins* v. *Moore*, 34 *Id.* 417; *Duguid* v. *Edwards*, 50 Barb. (N. Y.) 288; *Wadley* v. *Davis*, 63 *Id.* 500; *Read* v. *Del. & Hud. Canal Co.* 3 Lans. (N. Y.) 213 ; *Boardman* v. *Volkening*, 4 T. & C. (N. Y.) 650;

(*j*) 3 Camp. 16.

(*k*) *Hutchinson* v. *Bowker*, 5 M. & W. 535; see also *Fox* v. *Parker*, 44 Barb. 541; *Collyer* v. *Collins*, 17 Abb. Pr. 467; *Wacher* v. *Quenzer*, 29 N. Y. 547.

Ohio v. *Canson*, 62 Mo. 209; *Porter* v. *Hills*, 114 Mass. 106; *Sawtelle* v. *Drew*, 122 Mass. 228; *Central R. R. Co.* v. *Anderson*, 58 Ga. 393; *Butterworth* v. *Volkenning*, 1 S. C. 450. A person who makes a contract is not bound by the usage of a particular business, unless it is so general as to furnish a

In other words, a person cannot be affected by a usage, unless he has personal knowledge of its existence, or it is shown to be so notorious, uniform and well established that he ought to have known it, and that his knowledge thereof will be conclusively presumed.[4] But when the usage is established, and circumstances that charge the parties with knowledge thereof, it will govern a contract presumed to have been made in reference to it, however partial or local

presumption of knowledge, or it is proved that he knew it. *Stevens* v. *Reeves*, 9 Pick. (Mass.) 198; *Wood* v. *Hickok*, 2 Wend. (N. Y.) 501. And in the case of a private usage, or the usages of an individual, *actual* knowledge must be shown. *Nanatuck Silk Co.* v. *Fair*, 112 Mass. 354; *Goodnow* v. *Parsons*, 36 Vt. 46; *Burger* v. *Farmers, &c., Ins. Co.*, 71 Penn. St. 422.

[4] *Walsh* v. *Mississippi Ins. Co.* 52 Mo. 434. In *Boardman* v. *Volkening, ante*, the question was, whether furniture was sold by a contract as to its price, and in order to prove that it was not, proof was offered to show that by a usage among cabinet workers they could not be employed to manufacture furniture except by the day, and the court held that a purchaser having no knowledge of the regulation could not be affected thereby. See also *Wadley* v. *Davis, ante*; *South Western Freight, &c., Co.* v. *Stannard*, 44 Mo. 71. In *Wilson* v. *Baurman*, 80 Ill. 493, the court below instructed the jury that if there was a custom among architects in a certain city at the time the contract was made, it entered into the contract, &c. This instruction was held bad because it ignored the essential element of notoriety or ancientness, and authorized the jury to act upon it, whether the parties to be affected by it knew of its existence, or could

be fairly presumed to know of it or not. A shipper of goods is chargeable with notice of an established and well known usage, existing in a particular trade, in regard to the stowage of a general ship, both as to the manner of stowing and as to the different articles to be stowed together. And if the shipper, in such case, gives no special instructions, and his goods are stowed in conformity with such usage, he is deemed to have assented to such mode of stowage, and cannot, in case his goods are injured on the voyage, in consequence of the mode of stowage, set that up as a ground of complaint or as a foundation for depriving the owners of their freight. *Baxter* v. *Leland*, 1 Blatch. (U.S. C.C.) 526. A charge of negligence in stowing goods shipped for transportation may be repelled by proof of a custom to stow such goods, for such a voyage, in the manner complained of. *Barber* v. *Brace*, 3 Conn. 9. Evidence of a custom of merchants, that the feight of money received on board a ship by the master is his perquisite, and that he, and not the ship owner, is liable on the contract, was held admissible in a suit against such owner for money taken on freight by the master at a West India island. *Halsey* v. *Brown*, 3 Day (Conn.) 346.

its application may be.[5]   The question as to whether a usage shall control or be deemed a part of a contract or not, depends upon the intention of the parties, to be determined from all the circumstances of the negotiation, and unless the usage is known to the parties, or is so general and notorious as to warrant a presumption of knowledge of it, of course an intent to be controlled by it cannot exist.[6]   In order to become a law of a trade, and make it obligatory upon those contracting in reference to matters to which it relates, it must be shown to be certain, uniform, reasonable and so generally known and of such long existence, that the parties must be presumed to have known of and contracted in reference to it, or it must be shown that the parties actually knew of its existence,[7] and the question as to whether the parties had or ought to have had knowledge of it is a question for the jury.[8]   Thus, where a usage at an inn for guests to leave their money or valuables at the bar, or with the keeper of the house, or his clerk, it was held not to be binding upon a guest unless it was shown that he had knowledge

---

[5] *Appleman* v. *Fisher,* 34 Md. 450. Usages of a particular trade are presumed to be known to those engaged in it, and to have entered into any contract therein.   *Carter* v. *Philadelphia Coal Co.,* 77 Penn. St. 286.   But a claim destructive of a contract, or the subject of a grant, cannot be set up by way of usage, 79 Penn. St. 242; *Leigh* v. *Mobile S. R. R. Co.,* 58 Ala. 165.

[6] *Carthman* v. *Salem Ins. Co.,* 14 Bush. (Ky.) 197; *Hinton* v. *Coleman,* 45 Wis. 165.

[7] *Smith* v. *Gibbs,* 44 N. H. 335; *Collings* v. *Hope,* 3 Wash. (Va.) 150; *Shackleford* v. *Mississippi N. R. R. Co.,* 37 Miss. 202; *Rapp* v. *Palmers,* 3 Watts (Penn.) 178; *Register* v. *Spencer,* 24 Md. 520; *Thomas* v. *Graves,* 1 Mills (S. C.) Const. 308; *Foley* v.

Mason, 6 Md. 608; *Trott* v. *Wood,* 1 Gall. (U. S.) 443; *Harper* v. *Pound,* 10 Ind. 32; *Christian* v. *Bowman,* 1 Hill (S. C.) 270; *Saint* v. *Smith,* 1 Cald. (Tenn.) 51; *Walker* v. *Barron,* 6 Minn. 508; *Com.* v. *Malay,* 57 Penn. St. 291; *Davis* v. *New Brig,* Gilp. (U. S.) 486; *Lewis* v. *Thatcher,* 15 Mass. 433; *Foy* v. *Leighton,* 22 N. H. 71; *Martin* v. *Hull,* 26 Mo. 386; *Tauro* v. *Cassin,* 1 N. & M. (S. C.) 176; *Thomas* v. *O'Haver,* 1 Mills (S. C.) Const. 303; *Consequa* v. *Willings,* Pet. (U. S. C. C.) 230; *Somerby* v. *Tappan,* Wright (Ohio) 573; *United States* v. *Duval,* Gilp. (U. S.) 356; *Buck* v. *Grimshaw,* 1 Edw. Ch. (N. Y.) 147; *Smith* v. *Wright,* 1 Cai. (N. Y.) 45.

[8] *Berkshire Woolen Co.* v. *Proctor,* 7 Cush. (Mass.) 417.

or actual notice of it,[9] and generally it may be said as to private or usages of individuals, they are only binding upon those who have actual knowledge thereof. Thus, the custom of a merchant to charge interest on monthly rests is not binding on a debtor unless it is shown that he knew of the custom.[1] The distinction between a custom, as such, and a

[9] *Berkshire Woolen Co. v. Proctor*, ante. Evidence of a usage among brokers to sell stock hypothecated, and return the same kind of stock on the payment of the instrument for which it was hypothecated, is inadmissible. *Allen v. Dykers*, 3 Hill (N. Y.) 593. So evidence of a custom among brokers to sell the stock of their principals upon a failure to repay advances, is not admissible to vary the terms of a contract. *Taylor v. Ketchum*, 5 Robt. (N. Y.) 507. But as to all valid usages, a person dealing with brokers is presumed to know of and contract in reference to them, and especially is this the case where the contract is expressly made subject thereto, and in such a case the broker may, where stock is purchased on a margin, sell at the stock exchange without notice to the buyer, if such is the usage on the buyer's failure to furnish a sufficient margin. *Baker v. Drake*, 66 N. Y. 518.

[1] *Goodnow v. Parsons*, 36 N. 46; *Learson v. Hayward*, 1 Spears (S. C.) 249. In *Green v. Disbrow*, 7 Lans. (N. Y. S. C.) 392, it was held that evidence as to a creditor's custom in charging interest was admissible. *Read v. McAllister*, 8 Wend. (N. Y.) 109; *Eastenly v. Cole*, 3 N. Y. 502, but that, in the particular case, it was not sufficient to charge the debtor, because it did not appear that the debtor knew of such custom before the account accrued. *Miller, P. J.*,

in commenting upon the point said, " The referee erred in allowing interest because the proof does not establish the time when the plaintiff communicated to the defendant that such was his custom. The evidence of the defendant's knowledge is very slight. The plaintiff swears that he told the defendant that his custom was to charge interest after six months, and he charged him interest on his account, and he paid it; *when* the plaintiff told him, and *when* he paid the account, is not stated. *If this was after the whole account accrued it could be of no avail.* If *before*, it should have been so stated." *Watt v. Hoch*, 25 Penn. St. 411. In *Halford v. Adams*, 2 Duer. (N. Y.) 471, the court say, "A special and particular usage of one party is not binding upon the other, without proof of actual knowledge on his part of its existence and terms." In *Magoverning v. Staples*, 7 Lans. (N. Y.) 145, the plaintiff attended a fair of the Jefferson Agricultural Society, and while quietly seated with his family upon seats established upon the grounds, he was forcibly removed by the defendant. In an action for assault and battery brought against the defendant, for forcibly ejecting the plaintiff from the fair grounds and seats, the defendant offered to show a custom of the society to charge for the use of the seats, but did not show, or offer to show, that the plaintiff knew of this custom, or

usage, in this respect, is that a custom becomes a law of a trade or business from immemorial and universal acquiescence in a neighborhood or country, and consequently must be ancient. In other words, a usage from immemorial existence ripens into a custom,[2] while a usage, if known to the parties to a transaction to which it relates, is obligatory and binding, however recent its origin ;[3] and the only object in proving its long existence, general prevalence and uniformity of application, is to raise a presumption of knowledge when actual knowledge of its existence on the part of the person to be affected by it cannot be shown.[4] The fact that in a certain trade or business certain things are always done in a certain way, furnishes the basis from which a jury has a right to presume that the parties to a contract relating to

any facts from which his knowledge thereof could be inferred, and it was held that such usage was not admissible to excuse the defendant from all liability, but that it was admissible in connection with proof that the plaintiff, while occupying the seats, was notified of the usage, and after such notice refused to leave, or upon the question of malice. *Mullin, P. J.*, upon this point said, " The court below properly excluded the custom of the society to charge for the use of the seats, the defendant not showing, or offering to show, that the plaintiff knew of the custom or was chargeable with knowledge of it. It does not appear that the plaintiff had ever before attended a fair of the society, or that he had lived in the county six months. It seems to me, however, that the offer to show that the society had established a charge of fifteen cents for the use of seats, and instructed the superintendent to collect the same, was improperly excluded. It was not admissible to charge the plaintiff with

knowledge of the regulations or of the instructions; but it was important to the defendant's defence to show that, in demanding pay of the plaintiff for the use of the seats, he was carrying into effect the instructions and regulations of the society. If there had been no authority to demand pay, it would be difficult for the defendant to find for removing the plaintiff. It lay at the very foundation of the defence." Where the plaintiff relied upon a parol acceptance of a bill of exchange, evidence of a custom of the defendants to accept always in writing and make corresponding entries on their books, was held competent as tending to show in this case that the bill had not been accepted. *Smith* v. *Clark*, 12 Ia. 32.

[2] *Commonwealth* v. *Maloy*, 57 Penn. St. 291.

[3] *Townsend* v. *Whitby*, 5 Harr. (Del.) 55.

[4] *Martin* v. *Hall*, 26 Mo. 386; *Walker* v. *Barron*, 6 Minn. 508.

such trade, within the application of such usage, had knowledge of the usage, if it affects the transaction and contracted in relation to it;[5] consequently, unless excluded by the terms of the contract, it enters into and is regarded as a part of it, as much as though it had been written therein.[6]   But, how-

[5] *White* v. *Fuller*, 4 Hun. (N. Y.) 631; *Barrett* v.*Williamson*, 4 McLean (U. S.) 597; *Myers* v. *Perry*, 1 La. An. 372; *Lebanon* v. *Heath*, 47 N. H. 353; *Clanmorgan* v. *Guisse*, 1 Mo. 141; *Perkins* v. *Jordan*, 36 Mo. 23. Witnesses may be examined to prove the course of a particular trade, but not to show what the law of that trade is. *Ruan* v. *Gardner*, 1 Wash. (U. S. C. C.) 145; *Winthrop* v. *Union Ins. Co.*, 2 Wash. (U. S. C. C.) 7; *Austin* v. *Taylor*, 2 Ham. (Ohio) 64.

[6] *Hursh* v. *North*, 40 Penn. St. 241; *Stultz* v. *Dickey*, 5 Binn. (Penn.) 287. In *Baker* v. *Squier*, 1 Hun. (N. Y.) 443, the defendant purchased a quantity of soda-ash, which was described in the contract as "225 tons Kurtz, forty-eight to fifty per cent. carbonated soda-ash." The ash was to be shipped from Liverpool to New York at the rate of twenty-five tons monthly, and each shipment was to be treated as a separate contract. The vendors notified the plaintiff of the first shipment, stating "the test is forty-eight per cent." The defendant refused to receive the property upon the ground that the test was only forty-eight per cent., when the contract called for forty-eight to fifty per cent. The plaintiff tendered the soda-ash, with a certificate of the test purporting to be issued by Hussan & Arrat, showing the test to be forty-eight. Evidence was given on the part of the plaintiff tending to show an established and universal custom of trade, by which the terms used in the contract, were understood to mean, that the soda-ash was understood to mean that the soda-ash was to be of the manufacture of one Kurtz, and was to possess at least forty-eight per cent. of alkali, which was to be according to the test of certain English chemists, recognized and known in the trade, whose certificates were attached to the invoices and received as evidence of the test; and that the test of forty-eight was understood to satisfy the contract. Messrs. Hussan & Arrat were chemists known to dealers in the article, and their certificate was recognized in the trade as a compliance with the contract. *Talcott, P. J.*, in passing upon the admissibility of this custom in evidence, said "We think the custom was properly admitted in evidence. A person engaged in a particular trade is to be presumed to be acquainted with the usages of the trade, and the contracts in reference to them; and the usage of the trade in which the contract is made may be shown to explain the meaning of a particular contract, but not to vary its *plain* terms. The figures, forty-eight to fifty per cent. convey no meaning to a person ignorant of the subject-matter of the contract, and of the usage of the trade in which it was made. And the evidence of the custom must explain the meaning of those terms or figures when used in such a contract, and did not tend to vary its import, so far as its terms were expressed." *Burnham* v. *Ayer*,

ever well established a custom or usage may be, it cannot be admitted to control or vary the express terms of a contract,[7]

30 N. H. 182; *United States* v. *Kean*, 1 McLean (U. S.) 429; *Inglebright* v. *Hammond*, 19 Ohio 337; *Ladwick* v. *Ohio Ins. Co.*, 5 *Id.* 436; *Lampson* v. *Guzzam*, 6 Part. (Ala.) 123; *United States* v. *Arredondo*, 6 Pet. (U. S.) 715. In *Steward* v. *Scudder*, 24 N. J. L. 96, it was held that to vary the ordinary meaning of plain words in a contract, as, to make the word *"cash"* mean *"credit,"* the evidence must show a special custom, *precise, definite and universal* where it exists. The rule as generally expressed is, that a usage or custom in order to be imported into a contract by inference must be so far established and so far known to the parties that it must be supposed that 'their contract was made in reference to it. For this purpose, the custom or usage must be *established,* and not casual, *uniform,* and not varying, *general,* and not personal, and must be known or presumed to be known to the parties. *Martin* v. *Maynard,* 16 N. H. 165; *Sipperly* v. *Steward,* 50 Barb. (N. Y.) 62; *Baker* v. *Squier,* 1 Hun. (N. Y.) 448; *Goodnow* v. *Parsons,* 36 N. 46; *Wood* v. *Hicock,* 2 Wend. (N. Y.) 501; *Bank of Columbia* v. *Fitzhugh,* 1 H. & G. (Md.) 239; *Barber* v. *Brace,* 3 Conn. 9; *Sewall* v. *Gibbs,* 1 Hall (N. Y.) 612; *Duguid* v. *Edwards,* 50 Barb. (N. Y.) 188; *Stevens* v. *Reeves,* 9 Pick. (Mass.) 198; *Kendall* v. *Russell,* 5 Dana (Ky.) 501; *Haven* v. *Wentworth,* 2 N. H. 193.

[7] *Holmes* v. *Pettingill,* 1 Hun. (N.Y.) 316; *Meaghar* v. *Lufkin,* 21 Tex. 383; *Sweet* v. *Jenkins,* 1 R. I. 147; *Cadwell* v. *Meek,* 17 Ill. 220; *Cooper* v. *Purvis,* 1 Jones (N. C.) L. 140; *Renner* v. *Bank of Columbia,* 9 Wheat. 581;

Wadsworth v. *Alcott,* 6 N. Y. 64; *Rankins* v. *American Ins. Co.,* 1 Hall (N. Y.) 619; *George* v. *Bartlett,* 22 N. H. 496; *Wheeler* v. *Nurse,* 20 N. H. 220; *Sleight* v. *Rhinelander,* 1 Johns. (N.Y.) 192; *Maconber* v. *Parker,* 13 Mass. 175; *Barlow* v. *Lambert,* 28 Ala. 704; *Lawrence* v. *Gallagher,* 10 J. & S. (N. Y.) 309; *Farmers' &c. Bank* v. *Logan,* 74 N. Y. 568; *Bank of Commerce* v. *Bissell,* 72 *Id.* 615; *Van Alstyne* v. *Ætna Ins. Co.,* 14 Hun. (N.Y.) 360. In the latter case the plaintiff's assignor took out a policy on a canal boat, containing a provision that the "policy shall become void if any other insurance is or shall be made upon the boat hereby insured, which, together with this insurance, shall exceed one thousand dollars." The policy permitted the boat to "navigate the inland lakes, rivers and canals of the State of New York, and the harbor of the city of New York usually navigated by vessels of this class engaged in the common carrying trade, including the North river where it forms a part of the vessel's continuous trip; also the East river as far as the southwesterly end of Blackwell's Island." There was also an indorsement on the policy as follows: "Privileged to run to Philadelphia and the waters of New Jersey." During the life of the policy the plaintiff's assignor took out a policy for $1,000 for six months on the same boat, with the same privilege as to business, except that in the body of the policy the words "also to run to Philadelphia, Fort Johnson and Elizabethport" were written. The boat was lost in the Hudson river during the life of both

or, as is said in some of the cases, to vary its legal im-

policies. To defeat the effect of the provision as to other insurance in the defendant's policy, the plaintiff introduced evidence to the effect that there is a general custom to take out what is called a "trip policy," whereby a party desiring to navigate his vessel beyond the points covered by his yearly or time policy, takes out a policy for the particular trip he desires to make; and that, according to the custom, it is supposed while the boat is outside, within those limits permitted by it, and revives again when she returns within those limits. *Talcott, C. J.*, in denying the validity of the custom, said: "According to any intelligent account of the custom, as given by the testimony, the trip policy and the time policy could not be in force at the same time: otherwise it would render the condition against further insurance ineffectual; and a usage or custom in hostility to the express provisions of a contract can be of no avail against the contract, and, so far as that contract is concerned, is void. *Mutual Safety Ins. Co. v. Hom*, 2 N. Y. 235; *Mankham v. Jandon*, 41 N. Y. 235." Upon the general proposition stated in the text, see *Atkinson v. Allen*, 29 Ind. 375; *Corwin v. Patch*, 4 Cal. 204; *Randall v. Rotch*, 12 Pick. (Mass.) 107; *Sanford v. Rawlings*, 43 Ill. 92; *Sigworth v. McIntyne*, 18 Ill. 126; *Foy v. Strawn*, 82 Ill. 295; *Stebbins v. Brown*, 65 Barb. (N. Y.) 274; *Mum v. Eage*, 1 E. D. S. (N. Y.) 619; *Beals v. Terry*, 2 Sandf. (N. Y.) 127; *Holmes v. Pettingill*, 60 N. Y. 646; *Wall v. East River Ins. Co.*, 7 *Id.* 370; *Vail v. Rice*, 5 *Id.* 155; *Haines v. Lawrence*, 4 N. Y. 345. Where the

language of a written instrument is clear and unmistakable in its terms, evidence of a usage to give it a different meaning is not admissible. Thus, where a creditor wrote to his debtor, saying, "We must request you to remit the amount," it was held that this did not authorize evidence of a local usage or understanding to give a meaning to the terms of the letter different from that which they obviously bear. *Gross v. Criss*, 3 Gratt (Va.) 262. Grain was sent by a country dealer to commission merchants in New York, with orders to sell for cash. It was sold and delivered, and a check for the amount of purchase money sent to the dealer, before it was collected of the purchaser. Within a week the purchaser failed, never having paid the money; and the merchants brought their action against the owner to recover the amount, alleging that, by the custom of trade in New York, upon a sale for cash, the purchaser has three or four days in which to pay the money. Held, that, to authorize a verdict for plaintiff, the evidence must have shown such custom to have been at the risk of the owner, and so certain, uniform, and notorious, that it must be presumed to have been understood by the parties. *Steward v. Scudder*, 24 N. J. L. 96. Though custom or usage will not be admitted to contradict a stipulation in writing, it is admissible to add new terms not expressed in or covered by the writing. *Alabama, &c. R. R. Co. v. Kidd*, 29 Ala. 221. But it may be admitted to determine that which, by the contract, is left undetermined. *Dixon v. Dunham*, 13 Ill.

port.[8] But this latter rule is subject to many exceptions, if in fact it is not altogether erroneous, for the instances are numer- · ous where evidence of usage is received to vary in some sense the legal effect of a written contract. Notably is this the case when words used in a contract have acquired a peculiar meaning, different from the sense in which they are ordinarily employed. In such cases the meaning which they have acquired by usage is admitted, in order to ascertain and carry into effect the real and true intent of the parties. Therefore it would seem that the more accurate rule is, that *proof of a*

324; *Leach* v. *Beardslee,* 22 Conn. 404; *Shaw* v. *Mitchell,* 2 Met. (Mass.) 65; *Cooper* v. *Kane,* 19 Wend. (N. Y.) 386. A contract required that a party should "clear, grub, and pile the brush, all to be done in good order on all" of a certain piece of land, in which there was a ravine. Held, that evidence was not admissible to show that the grubbing such a ravine was not usual in that neighborhood, or that the farm would be better without having it grubbed, especially if under the contract the party insists upon having such grubbing done. *Holmes* v. *Stummel,* 15 Ill. 412. In such a case the question is not what is *usual* or best to do, but what was contracted to be done.

[8] *Holmes* v. *Pettingill,* ante ; *Lawrence* v. *Maxwell,* 53 N. Y. 19; *Allen* v. *Dykens,* 3 Hill (N. Y.) 593; *Dalton* v. *Daniels,* 2 Hilt. (N. Y.) 472; *Hinton* v. *Locke,* 5 Hill (N. Y.) 437 ; *Taylor* v. *Ketchum,* 5 Robt. (N. Y.) 507 ; *Spear* v. *Hart,* 3 *Id.* 420; *Currie* v. *Smith,* 4 N. Y. Leg. Obs. 343; *Bargett* v. *Orient Ins. Co.,* 3 B. & S. (N. Y.) 385; *Vail* v. *Rice,* 5 N. Y. 155; *Suydam* v. *Clark,* 2 Sandf. (N. Y.) 133; *Wadsworth* v. *Alcott,* 6 *Id.* 64; *Lane* v. *Bailey,* 47 Barb. (N. Y.) 395; *Wall* v. *Ins. Co.,* 7 N. Y. 370; *Higgins* v.

Moore, 34 N. Y. 417; *Bissell* v. *Campbell,* 54 N. Y. 353; *Minnesota &c. R. R. Co.* v. *Morgan,* 52 Barb. (N. Y.) 217. And it is held in New York that evidence of a usage is not admissible to convert a representation into a warranty. *Stebbins* v. *Brown,* 65 Barb. (N. Y.) 274; *Beirne* v. *Dord,* 5 Sandf. (N. Y.) 95 ; *Haines* v. *Lawrence,* 4 N. Y. 345. Or to contradict a settled rule of law. *Frith* v. ‖ *Barker,* 2 Johns. (N. Y.) 327 ; *Mackenzie* v. *Smith,* 22 Am. Law Reg. 448; *Emery* v. *Dunbar,* 1 Daly (N. Y.) 408; *Schiefflin* v. *Harvey,* 6 Johns. (N. Y.) 170; *Jones* v. *Bradner,* 10 Barb. (N. Y.) 193; *Otsego Co. Bank* v. *Warren,* 18 *Id.* 290; *Outwater* v. *Nelson,* 20 *Id.* 29. And such also is the rule in Massachusetts. *Boardman* v. *Spooner,* 13 Allen (Mass.) 353. Where, by the terms of a written contract, commission merchants are to charge a specified commission on sales, which is to be in full of all expenses, and at the termination of the contract by mutual consent, the goods on hand are transferred to other factors, evidence is incompetent to prove a usage of merchants to charge one-half commission under such circumstances. *Ware* v. *Hayward Rubber Co.,* 3 Allen (Mass.) 84.

usage is never admissible to vary the plain legal import of a contract unless a latent ambiguity exists therein, or is raised by extrinsic evidence. In such cases evidence of usage, unless expressly excluded by the terms of the contract, is not only justifiable in principle, but absolutely necessary to carry into effect the real intention of the parties.[9] An apt illustration of this rule is to be found in a Connecticut case,[1] in which certain lands had been conveyed to the defendant by a deed which contained a clause as follows : " With the privilege of *deepening* the ditch leading from the premises, to drain the same over the grantor's land *as deep* as the grantee may desire." The defendant not only *deepened* but *widened* the ditch correspondingly, to keep it from caving in from the top. The plaintiff brought an action against him for the alleged trespass in widening the ditch. It appeared that the method of widening ditches at the top when they were deepened was the *usual* mode adopted in that vicinity, and that unless this was done, the defendant would have been compelled to have curbed it with stone, which would have made the expense more than the value of the land. The court held that evidence was admissible to show what the usage was in that respect, and that the parties must be treated as having contracted with reference thereto, and that if the mode adopted by the defendant was the *usual* method, he could not be held chargeable for a trespass.[2] This case

[9] Best on Evidence, (Wood's Edn.) 432; Eng. Edn. 318.

[1] *Collins* v. *Driscoll,* 34 Conn. 43.

[2] *Park, J.,* in delivering the opinion of the court in this case said, "At the time the deed was executed the ditch in question was six feet deep and six feet wide at the top, with sides sloping to two feet wide at the bottom. The deed confers authority upon the plaintiff to deepen the ditch as deep as the plaintiff may desire. The ditch was dug for the purpose of draining the premises conveyed, which was low, swampy land, adapted to the production of peat for fuel. * * Such business requires that the land should be thoroughly drained. The parties to the deed considered that the ditch already existing might be found incapable of draining the land to the extent desired, and hence, the clause in question was inserted in the deed. The defendant contends that the clause should be construed as grant-

furnishes but one of numerous instances in which the courts permit usages to control the legal effect of a contract. *All contracts tacitly refer to the circumstances under which they are made*, and it is upon this principle that courts permit evidence of particular usages and customs to be shown in aid of the interpretation of all written instruments whether ancient or modern, whenever from the nature of the case a knowledge of such usages and customs is essential in order to arrive at a correct understanding of the intention of the parties.[3] Such evidence is admissible to explain clauses of doubtful construction,[4] and show the nature of the transac-

ing the right to deepen the ditch, but as conferring no authority upon the plaintiff to widen it; that the expression is equivalent to an express prohibition against widening the ditch, however necessary it might be in deepening it. This clause would render the clause inoperative, for the ditch was but two feet wide at the bottom, and it is manifest that at that width, it could not be lowered to any practical effect, even by curbing. * * Hence, if the defendant's construction is correct, he has granted a privilege of no practical benefit, and contrary to the manifest intention of the parties. The plaintiffs claim that the defendant granted the right to deepen the ditch *in the usual mode* in similar cases, which consists in sloping the sides to an extent necessary to prevent their caving in, and render them safe from the ordinary flow of the water through the ditch. * * Some mode must have been understood by the parties, for it is easy to see that the ditch could not have been deepened without resort to some mode for protecting the sides. * * Inasmuch as the deed is silent as to the mode of deepening the

ditch, it contains a latent ambiguity, and when that is the case, extrinsic circumstances may always be shown in order to ascertain in what sense the parties intended to be understood by the terms they used. *Brower v. Brower*, 4 Conn. 269; *Sines v. Flagg*, 4 *Id.* 581; *Strong v. Benedict*, 5 *Id.* 210; *Brown v. Slater*, 16 *Id.* 192; *Baldwin v. Carter*, 17 *Id.* 201; *Ely v. Adams*, 19 John. (N. Y.) 313; *Greenleaf's* ? 288; *Swift's Dig.* 180. Should we interpret the deed by the aid of these circumstances we can have no doubt that the grantor intended to confer the right to deepen the ditch *in the usual mode.* * * If the defendant had intended to restrict the plaintiff to a mode of deepening the ditch different from the usual one, he should and would have done it specifically in his deed."

[3] *Frith v. Barker*, 2 Johns. (N. Y.) 327; *Barmen v. Newell*, 8 N. Y. 190; *Gibson v. Culver*, 17 Wend. (N. Y.) 305.

[4] *Rankin v. Am. Ins. Co.*, 1 Hall (N. Y.) 619; *Winthroop v. Union Ins. Co.*, 2 Wash. (Va.) 7; *Alleyne v. Maryland Ins. Co.*, 2 G. & J. (Md.) 136; *Harris v. Nicholas*, 5 Munf. (Va.) 483; *Coit v. Commercial Ins. Co.*, 7 Johns. (N. Y.) 385; *United States v.*

tion[5] and give effect thereto.[6] So, too, unless excluded by the terms thereof, evidence of usage *is admissible to add incidents to the contract* which are not inconsistent with its terms, and to ascertain the intention of the parties in reference to matters about which the contract is silent.[7] Proof of a usage by com-

McDaniel, 7 Pet. (U. S.) 1; *Merchants' Insurance Co.* v. *Wilson,* 2 Md. 217. The words "six per cent. off for cash," endorsed on a bill of goods, is sufficiently equivocal to render it proper to receive evidence as to how, by custom or usage among men, it is understood. *Linsley* v. *Lovely,* 26 Vt. 123. So it has been held admissible to show whether the word "cargo," in a policy of insurance, was regarded as including "live stock." *Alleyne* v. *Maryland Ins. Co., ante.* That a contract to do plastering by the square yard "justifies the plasterer to charge for the full surface of the bare walls, without deductions for cornices, baseboards or openings for doors or windows." *Walls* v. *Bailey,* 49 N. Y. 464—see *post; Outwater* v. *Nelson,* 20 Barb. (N. Y.) 29; *Markham* v. *Jordon,* 41 N. Y. 235; *Thomas* v. *O'Hara,* 1 Mill (S. C.) Const. 303; *Steward* v. *Scudder,* 24 N. J. L. 96.

[5] *Loring* v. *Gurney,* 5 Pick. (Mass.) 15; *Thompson* v. *Hamilton,* 12 *Id.* 425; *Taylor* v. *Semmes,* 4 G. & J. (Md.) 274; *Eaton* v. *Smith,* 20 Pick. (Mass.) 150.

[6] *Mangum* v. *Farrington,* 1 Daly (N.Y.) 236; *Cooper* v. *Kane,* 19 Wend. (N. Y.) 386; *Dalton* v. *Daniels,* 2 Hilt. (N. Y. C. P.) 472; *Hinton* v. *Locke,* 5 Hill (N. Y.) 437; *Stanton* v. *Small,* 3 Sandf. (N. Y.) 230; *Mackenzie* v. *Schmidt,* 22 Am. Law Reg. 448; *Bissell* v. *Campbell,* 54 N. Y. 353; *Lee* v. *Salter,* Lalor (N. Y.) 163. The rule that courts are to give construction

to contracts is frequently departed from where the contracts relate to the scientific or mechanic arts, or common words of a technical or local signification. In such cases it is common and prudent to admit the evidence of those engaged in the business to which the contract relates. *Reynolds* v. *Jordon,* 6 Cal. 108; *Myers* v. *Walker,* 24 Ill. 133; *Hart* v. *Hammett,* 18 Vt. 127; *Galma Ins. Co.* v. *Kuper,* 28 *Id.* 332; *Prather* v. *Ross,* 17 Ind. 495; *Carey* v. *Bright,* 58 Penn. St. 70; *Williams* v. *Wood,* 16 Md. 220; *Taylor* v. *Sotstings,* 6 La. An. 154; *Broadwell* v. *Broadwell,* 1 Gill. (Md.) 599; *Brown* v. *Brooks,* 25 Penn. St. 210; *Smith* v. *Clayton,* 29 N. J. L. 357; *Halbert* v. *Camer,* 37 Barb. (N. Y.) 62.

[7] *Fox* v. *Parker,* 44 Barb. (N.Y.) 541; *Cassidy* v. *Begaden,* 6 J. & S. (N. Y.) 180; *Boormen* v. *Jenkins,* 12 Wend. (N. Y.) 566. It is admissible to determine that which the contract has left undetermined. *Cooper* v. *Kane,* 19 Wend. (N. Y.) 386; *Dixon* v. *Dunham,* 14 Ill. 324; *Mitchell* v. *Mitchell,* 2 Met. (Mass.) 65; *Leach* v. *Beardslee,* 22 Conn. 404. When a contract called for trees not less than "one foot high," evidence of a usage of the dealers in that sort of trees was held admissible that the hard part of the trees between the roots and the green top was to be measured, and not the green stem, and that too, although the usage was of recent origin. *Barlow* v. *McKelway,* 22 N. J. L. 165. Proof of usage is sometimes admissible to change the char-

mission merchants, drovers, &c., to sell property left with them for sale, on approved credit, may be given when it does not impugn the clear stipulations of a contract, or is not in violation of express directions given by the owner. Thus, where a yoke of oxen was delivered to a drover to be taken to New York and sold by him on commission, and the drover took them to New York and sold them in connection with some of his own cattle, upon a credit of twenty days, to a firm that was reputed to be good, and took a note therefor covering both the price of his own and the plaintiff's cattle, and before the note became due the makers failed and became bankrupt; it was held competent for the drover to

acter of an instrument, as to show that a receipt is regarded as a bill of sale. Thus, it was held that a receipt as follows, "Rec'd of A. B. 40$\frac{10}{60}$ bushels of wheat," might be shown by parol evidence of usage to be a sale rather than a settlement. *Dawson* v. *Kittle,* 4 Hill (N. Y.) 107; *Goodyear* v. *Ogden,* 4 *Id.* 104. In *Sewall* v. *Gibbs,* 1 Hall (N. Y.) 602, it was held that a purchaser of indigo at auction which proved to be fraudulently packed, might give evidence of a custom to allow the purchaser in such case, the *actual* tare, although notice was given at the sale that the indigo would be sold subject to the usual tare. In debt against sureties on a bond conditioned for the repayment of advances made for the purchase of packed meats for shipment, and which were sent to London, evidence of usage to charge a commission on advances on shipments made to London, is admissible; and if such a usage exists, a commission is properly charged, in the absence of a special agreement to the contrary. *Turner* v. *Yates,* 16 How. (U. S.) 14. In assumpsit for goods sold, it is competent for the defendant to prove that, by the usage of dry goods jobbers in Boston, to which class the plaintiffs belonged, goods not purchased on a cash sale are purchased on a credit of six months, where the bills are not marked. *Farnsworth* v. *Chase,* 19 N. H. 534. The power of an agent to sell has been held, subject to the interpretation of usage, to mean to sell by warranty or sample. *Alexander* v. *Gibson,* 2 Camp. 555; *Dingle* v. *Hare,* 7 C. B. N. S. 145; *Randall* v. *Kehlor,* 60 Mo. 37; *Morris* v. *Bowen,* 52 N. H. 416. So, too, it has been held that a power given to an agent to sell certain species of goods, may be limited by proof of usage giving the principal the right to reject such vendees as he disapproved. *Sumner* v. *Stewart,* 69 Penn. St. 321. Where a bill of lading expresses that goods are to be carried from one port to another, a direct voyage is, *primâ facie,* intended, but this presumption may be controlled by a usage to stop at intermediate ports, or by personal knowledge on the part of the shipper that such a course is to be pursued. *Lowry* v. *Russell,* 8 Pick. (Mass.) 360.

show that in the sale of the oxen he followed the usage of the trade, not only as to the manner of sale but also as to the terms of credit, and that, if no definite instructions as to the sale were given, contrary to such usage, it operated as a full defence against the plaintiff's claim.[8] "A general usage," said Church, C. J., "affecting any branch of business, furnishes good evidence of what is regarded as right and reasonable in that respect, and when it is conformed to, negligence or misconduct cannot be imputed.[9] Proof of the general usage claimed by the defendant to exist in the city of New York, where the plaintiff intended the sale of his cattle should be made, furnished strong evidence that he not only assented, but empowered his agent, to sell on the usual credit and in the usual manner. And although commission merchants, in the absence of instructions or custom, must generally sell for cash, yet, if there is a usage modifying the course of business in this particular, or in other respects, and the sale is made in the usual and customary way, the agency is legally performed."[1] The usage offered to be proved, and which was proved, was not to contradict or control the terms of a contract definitely expressed, as it would have been if positive instructions to sell for cash down had been proved, but only to show the extent of the duty and obligation of the defendant, not thus expressed but inferable from the nature of the business in which the defendant had long been engaged, and the well known manner in which such business is usually conducted. *Usage cannot control the clear and unequivocal stipulations of a contract, but will be controlled by them.*[2] So, too, it is competent to show that by the usages of trade where certain articles are sent to commission mer-

---

[8] *Leach* v. *Beardslee,* 22 Conn. 404.

[9] *Barber* v. *Brace,* 3 Conn. 9; *Casco Mfg. Co.* v. *Dixon,* 3 Cush. (Mass.) 408.

[1] Story on Agency, §§ 60, 77, 96, 110; 2 Kent's Com. 622.

[2] *Taylor* v. *Briggs,* 2 C. & P. 525; *Smith* v. *Wilson,* 3 B. & Ad. 728; *Blackett* v. *Royal Ins. Co.,* 2 C. & J. 244; *Yates* v. *Pym,* 6 Taunt. 446; *Glendale Mfg. Co.* v. *Protection Ins. Co.,* 21 Conn. 19.

chants or others, in barrels, boxes, &c., the barrels, &c., to
be returned, it is customary to return *other* barrels, &c., equal
in number and value, in lieu of those received. Thus, in a
Connecticut case,[3] the defendant who was engaged in the
business of forwarding farmers' produce to New York and
selling it on commission, received from the plaintiff a quantity of cider in barrels, to be sold, and the barrels to be
returned. He sold the cider and barrels and returned the
plaintiff other barrels equal in number and value with those
received, which the plaintiff refused to receive, but brought
trover for the barrels in question. The defendant proved
that it was the custom of those engaged in that business to
return to shippers the same casks when practicable to do so,
but if not, to return others equal in number and value to
those received, and that the plaintiff had presumptive, if not
actual, knowledge of such custom. The court held that the
plaintiff was bound by the usage and could not recover for
the barrels. Evidence of usage and custom is admissible
whenever from the nature of the case a knowledge thereof
is essential to a right understanding of the instrument.
" The law," says an eminent law writer,[4] " is not so unreasonable as to deny to the reader of any instrument the same
light that the writer enjoyed." Consequently, if there is
not any thing upon the face of the instrument to exclude it,
and it appears that a well established usage existed in reference to the subject-matter to which it relates, when the
instrument was made, and such usage does not impair the
express terms of the instrument, and is not unreasonable or
in conflict with positive law, it may always be shown,
although its effect is to add incidents to the contract or
change the ordinary sense of certain terms employed, because
a knowledge thereof is essential to give effect to the contract
according to the true intent of the parties thereto.[5]

---

[3] *Sturges* v. *Buckley*, 32 Conn. 18.   *C. J.*, in *Boorman* v. *Johnston*, 12
[4] Wigram on Extr. Ev. 57.   Wend. (N. Y.) 573, " may be given
[5] " Parol evidence," says *Savage*,   to apply the written contract to the

THE USAGES OF TRADE, THEIR OFFICE.

Usage Defining and Explaining—Meaning of Words Explained.

SEC. 85. In such cases, then, evidence of usage is admissible to define and explain the technical, peculiar or local

subject matter—in some instances to explain expressions used in a peculiar sense, *when used by particular persons and applied to particular subjects.* It is perfectly right and consistent with fair dealing *to give effect to language used in a contract as it is understood by those who make use of it.*" Story, *J.,* in *The Schooner Reeside,* 2 Sumn. (U. S.) 569, says: "The true and appropriate office of a usage is to interpret the otherwise indeterminate intentions of the parties, and to ascertain the nature and extent of their contracts, *arising, not from express stipulations, but from mere presumptions and implications and acts of a doubtful nature.* It may also be admitted to ascertain the true meaning of a particular word, in a given instrument, when the word or words have various senses— some common, some qualified and some technical, according to the subject matter to which they are applied." Usages are to be found in almost all kinds of business, in relation to their particular and peculiar conditions, and a knowledge thereof is frequently indispensable to get at the right understanding of parties contracting in relation to matters connected therewith. The usage explains and ascertains the intention of the parties, and, not being in opposition to positive law or the general policy of the law, unreasonable, or inconsistent with the express terms of the instrument, it comes in as a species of *lex loci,* and incorporates itself with the terms of the writing. The general doctrine is not restricted to mercantile trans-

actions, but extends to every department of every species of business, whether mercantile, professional, mechanical, agricultural, &c., &c. *Wait* v. *Fairbanks,* Brayt. (Vt.) 7; *Heald* v. *Cooper.* 8 Me. 33; *Sewall* v. *Gibbs,* 1 Hall (N. Y.) 602; *Williams* v. *Gilman,* 3 Me. 276; *Gibson* v. *Culver,* 17 Wend. (N. Y.) 305; *Wood* v. *Hicock,* 2 *Id.* 501; *Gordon* v. *Little,* 8 S. & R. (Penn.) 533; *De Forest* v. *Fulton Ins. Co.,* 1 Hall (N. Y.) 84; *Harris* v. *Nicholas,* 5 Munf. (Va.) 483; *Powell* v. *Horton,* 2 Bing. (N. C.) 688; *Yeaton* v. *Bank of Alexandria,* 5 Cranch. (U. S.) 492; *Van Ness* v. *Packard,* 2 Pet. (U. S.) 148; *United States* v. *Arredondo,* 6 *Id.* 715; *Yeates* v. *Pim,* 1 Holt 95; *Homer* v. *Dorr,* 10 Mass. 26; *Stultz* v. *Dickey,* 5 Binn. (Penn.) 282; *Lebanon* v. *Heath,* 47 N. H. 353; *Hursh* v. *North.* 40 Penn. St. 241; *Watt* v. *Hock,* 25 *Id.* 411; *State* v. *McClay,* 1 Harr. (Del.) 520; *Wilcox* v. *Wood,* 9 Wend. (N. Y.) 346; *Foster* v. *Robinson,* 6 Ohio St. 90; *Ludwick* v. *Ohio Ins. Co.,* 5 Ohio 436; *Inglebright* v. *Hammond,* 19 *Id.* 337; *Barber* v. *Brace,* 3 Conn. 9; *Dalton* v. *Daniels,* 2 Hilt. (N. Y.) 472; *Lampson* v. *Gazzam,* 6 Port. (Ala.) 423; *Haven* v. *Wentworth,* 2 N. H. 93; *Munn* v. *Burch,* 25 Ill. 35; *Powers* v. *Kane,* 5 Wis. 265; *Warren Bank* v. *Parker,* 8 Gray (Mass.) 221; *Crosby* v. *Wyatt,* 23 Me. 156. Fair inferences from evidence founded upon the natural and usual course of business and of human experience are as much evidence as the principal facts from which these deductions flow; and, as such, may properly be suggested to the jury by the court in

meaning of the words used, but where the word has two
meanings, one common and universal, the other technical or
local, it will be necessary to give proof of circumstances
which will raise a presumption that the parties intended
to use the words in their later rather than in their
former relation, unless the fact can be inferred from reading the instrument itself.(*l*)   Thus the words "inhabi-
tant,"(*m*) "level,"(*n*) as understood by miners; "thou-

its charge. *Austin* v. *Bingham*, 31
Vt. 577. Numerous presumptions are
drawn from the *usual course of business*, and, unless rebutted, have the
force of positive proof. Thus if a
letter, properly addressed, is deposited in the postoffice, it affords *primâ
facie* evidence that it was received
by the party to whom it was addressed. *Kufh* v. *West*, 6 E. & P. 54;
Stockton v. *Collins*, 7 M. & W. 515;
Warren v. *Warren*, 1 C. M. & R.
250; *Keiron* v. *Johnson*, 1 Stark. 109.
So where it was shown to be the
usage of a hotel to deposit all letters
left at the bar in an urn for that
purpose, whence they were sent
every fifteen minutes throughout
the day to the rooms of the different
guests to whom they were directed,
it was held to warrant the presumption that a letter addressed to one of
the guests, and left at the bar, was
received by him. *Dana* v. *Kemble*,
19 Pick. (Mass.) 112. Presumptions
of this kind are also made from the
course of business in private offices,
as merchants'. *Hagedom* v. *Reids*,
3 Camp. 379; *Hetherington* v. *Kemp*,
4 *Id.* 193; *Hawkes* v. *Salter*, 4 Bing.
715; *Pritt* v. *Fairclough*, 3 Camp. 305;
Loosey v. *Williams*, 1 M. & M. 129;
Attorneys &c. Patteshall v. *Turpond*, 3

B. & Ad. 890. In *Hine* v. *Pomeroy*,
39 Vt. 211, the question at issue was
whether the plaintiff's attorney, in a
former action, directed the officer
making an attachment to take a
certain person as receiptor. It was
held competent to ask the attorney
what his uniform habit and course
of business as an attorney was before
and at the time of issuing said writ,
not to give officers to whom writs
were delivered any instructions as to
whom they should take as receiptors.
The presumption that where a partnership shown to exist between persons, but there is no evidence as to
the extent of their interest, that they
are interested in equal amounts.
Farrar v. *Beswick*, 1 M. & R. 527.
That bills and notes are given for a
good consideration. Byles on Bills,
2 and 108. And that a bill of exchange
is presumed to have been accepted
within a reasonable time after its
date, and *before* maturity. *Roberts* v.
Bethell, 12 C. B. 778. As well as a
large class of other presumptions too
numerous to refer to, are predicated
upon and find their support in the
usual course of business. *Cunningham*
v. *Fonblanque*, 6 C. & P. 44; *Houghton* v. *Gilbart*, 7 *Id.* 701; *Carter* v.
Abbott, 1 B. & C. 444.

(*l*) *Shore* v. *Wilson*, 9 Cl. & F. 355;
see also *Att.-Gen.* v. *Drummond*, 1
Dru. & War. 353; *Drummond* v. *Att.-*

Gen. 2 H. of L. Cas. 837.
   (*m*) *R.* v. *Mashiter*, 6 A. & E 153.
   (*n*) *Clayton* v. *Greyson*, 5. A. & E. 302.

sand,"(o) as applied to rabbits on a warren ; " weeks," as used in a theatrical contract ;(p) " months," as meaning calendar months in a charter party ;(q) " days," as meaning working days in a bill of lading ;(r) " fur,"(s) " corn,"(t) " pig iron,"(u) " freight,"(v) " salt,"(w) and other words(x) and phrases, which presented at first sight no ambiguity, have been interpreted by extrinsic evidence of usage. Evidence of usage is admissible to explain and fill up terms used in commercial and other contracts,[6] policies of insurance,[7] nego-

(o) *Smith* v. *Wilson,* 3 B. & Ad. 728.

(p) *Grant* v. *Maddox,* 12 M. & W. 737 ; see *Myers* v. *Sarl,* 30 L. J. Q. B. 9 ; 3 E. & E. 306.

(q) *Jolly* v. *Young,* 1 Esp. 186, recognized in *Simpson* v. *Margitson,* 11 Q. B. 32.

(r) *Cochran* v. *Retberg,* 3 Esp. 121.

(s) *Astor* v. *Union Ins. Co.,* 7 Cowen 202.

(t) *Mason* v. *Skurry* and *Moody* v. *Surridge,* Park, Ins. 245 ; *Scott* v. *Bourdillion,* 2 N. R. 213.

(u) *Mackenzie* v. *Dunlop,* 8 Macq. Sc. Cas. H. of L. 26.

(v) *Peisch* v. *Dickson,* 1 Mason, 11, 12 ; *Gibson* v. *Young,* 2 Moo. 224.

(w) *Journée* v. *Bourdieu,* Park.Ins.245.

(x) See *Symonds* v. *Lloyd,* 6 C. B. N. S. 691 ; see *Lewis* v. *Marshall,* 7 M. & G. 729, 738 ; *Lucas* v. *Groning,* 7 Taunt. 164 ; *Robertson* v. *Jackson,* 2 C. B. 412 ; *Lethulier's case,* 2 Salk. 443 ; *Miller* v. *Tetherington,* 6 H. & N. 278 ; *Kidson* v. *The Empire Marine Ins. Co.,* 1 L. R. C. P. 535 ; 35 L. J. C. P. 250 ; *Myers* v. *Sarl,* 30 L. J. Q. B. 9 ; *Taylor* v. *Briggs,* 2 C. & P. 525 ; *Gorrissen* v. *Perrin,* 27 L. J. C. P. 29 ; *Bold* v. *Rayner,* 1 M. & W. 343 ; *Spicer* v. *Cooper,* 1 Q. B. 421 ; 1 G. & D. 52 ; *Bowman* v. *Horsey,* 2 M. & Rob. 85, per Ld. Abinger ; *Johnston* v. *Usborne,* 11 Cl. & E. 549.

[6] *Fitch* v. *Carpenter,* 43 Barb. (N. Y.) 40 ; *Hite* v. *State,* 9 Yerg. (Tenn.) 357 ; *Sampson* v. *Gazzam,* 6 Post. (Ala.) 123 ; *Ganson* v. *Madigan,* 15 Wis. 144 ; *Rugby* v. *Goodloe,* 7 La. An. 295 ; *Wait* v. *Fairbanks,* Breyt. (Vt.) 77 ; *Noyes* v. *Canfield,* 27 Vt. 79.

[7] In *Alleyne* v. *Maryland Ins. Co.,* 2 G. & J. (Md.) 136, evidence of usage was held admissible to show that the word "cargo" did not include livestock. *Rogers* v. *Mechanics' Ins. Co.,* 1 Story (U. S.) 603 ; *Lapham* v. *Atlantic Ins. Co.,* 24 Pick. (Mass.) 1. It may be shown that it is a usage among commission merchants to effect insurance upon goods con-

signed to them without express instructions from the consignors. *De Forest* v. *Fulton Ins. Co.,* 1 Hall (N. Y.) 84. In a recent case before the Pennsylvania Supreme Court not yet reported, *Adams* v. *Pittsburgh Ins. Co.,* a custom of captains of steamboats at a large river-port to insure their boats and give premium notes therefor, held to be one to which there was great necessity to give effect, the perils of navigation being so well known that a due regard for some indemnity against loss is justly recognized as a necessary precaution. If such custom has clearly and distinctly proved to have existed so

tiable instruments[8] and other contracts when the language used therein, although well understood by the parties and by all who have to act upon it in matters connected with the particular business, would nevertheless be unintelligible and meaningless to a person not familiar with the business to which they relate. The rule that courts are to give construction to contracts is necessarily departed from where the contract relates to the scientific or mechanic arts, or contain words of a technical or local signification, or which have acquired a peculiar meaning in the business in which they are used; and, in such cases, the evidence

long as to be generally known, the owners of a steamboat so insured would be liable upon the notes given for the insurance. "*Consuetudo*," said *Coke*, "is one of the main triangles of the laws of England; those laws being divided into common law, statute law and particular customs, for if it be the general custom of the realm it is part of the common law." Co. Lit. 113–15. "A custom used upon a certain reasonable cause depriveth the common law." Littleton 112, § 169. In *Vanheath* v. *Turner*, Winch. 24, *Chief Justice Hobart* said: "The custom of merchants is part of the common law of this kingdom, of which the judges ought to take notice, and if any doubt arise to them about the custom they may send for the merchants to know their custom." That a custom so general and notorious may exist as to authorize the captain of a steamboat to effect an insurance on it for the benefit of the owners without their express directions is well settled by authority. It would not be in conflict with any statute, nor would it be unreasonable or contrary to public policy. See *Vanness* v. *Pacard*, 2 Pet. (U. S.) 148; *Gordon* v.

Little, 2 S. & R. (Pa.) 353; *Eyre* v. *Marine Ins. Co.*, 5 W. & S. (Penn.) 116; *Snowden* v. *Warder*, 3 Rawl. (Pa.) 101; *McMaster* v. *Pennsylvania R. R. Co.*, 19 P. F. Smith (Pa.) 374; *Carter* v. *Philadelphia Coal Co.*, 27 Id. 286; 1 Phill. on Ins. 80, 83; *Smith* v. *Wright*, 1 Cal. 43. It was held in *Oliver* v. *Green*, 3 Mass. 134, that a part owner of a vessel who had chartered the other part with a covenant to pay the value in case of a loss, might insure the whole vessel as his property, without disclosing that he had a special property only, in a moiety thereof. In *De Forest* v. *Fulton Fire Ins. Co.*, 1 Hall (N. Y.) 94, it was held that a commission merchant might recover on a policy of insurance for goods in his possession destroyed by fire, beyond the value of his property therein, without any express orders from the consignors of the goods to effect such insurance on proof that such was the usage of commission merchants in New York, *Mercur, J.*, Nov. 1, 1880, Albany Law Journal, vol. 23, p. 418.

[8] *Avery* v. *Stewart*, 2 Conn. 69; *Bowen* v. *Newell*, 2 Duer (N. Y.) 584; *Warren Bank* v. *Parker*, 21 Pick. (Mass.) 433.

of persons familiar with the usages of the business is indispensable to enable the court to give effect to the contract according to its intent.[9] Thus, where a note was made payable in "Canada money," evidence of brokers and others at the place where the note was payable, held admissible to show what was meant by the term.[1] So the plaintiff, under a contract to furnish carpenters to work at twelve shillings a day, upon the defendant's house, was permitted to show that, by the custom of the trade, *ten* hours constituted a day's work, and that wages for a day and a quarter for each natural day during which the men worked twelve and a half hours, was properly chargeable under it.[2] So, in an action of covenant, upon a lease containing a covenant, to get all the coal lying under certain closes, not deeper or below "the level of the bottom of said mine," it was held that evidence was admissible to show that among "miners," "*level*" would be construed in the sense of geological stratum, and might therefore mean a line above or below the horizontal depth of the mine.[3] In a contract for boots, where the contract called for "good custom cowhide boots," it was held that evidence was admissible to show what constituted "*good custom cowhide*," according to the usage of the trade.[4] In an action

[9] *Hart* v. *Hammett*, 18 Vt. 127; *Reynoulds* v. *Jourdan*, 6 Cal. 108; *Carey* v. *Bright*, 58 Penn. St. 70; *Stewart* v. *Smith*, 28 Ill. 397; *Broadwell* v. *Broadwell*, 1 Gill (Md.) 599; *Galena Ins. Co.* v. *Kupper*, 28 Ill. 332; *Taylor* v. *Sototings*, 6 La. An. 154; *Brown* v. *Brooks*, 25 Penn. St. 210; *Prather* v. *Ross*, 17 Ind. 495; *Williams* v. *Wood*, 16 Md. 220; *Cowles* v. *Garrett*, 30 Ala. 341; *Drake* v. *Goree*, 22 *Id.* 409.

[1] *Thompson* v. *Sloan*, 23 Wend. (N. Y.) 71.

[2] *Hinton* v. *Locke*, 5 Hill (N. Y.) 437. See also *Barnes* v. *Ingalls*, 39 Ala. 193, where the evidence of the general custom of mechanics and artizans in a city was held admissible to show the number of hours per day of labor required by employees in their business respectively, in order to show the establishment of such a custom among ambrotypists, daguerreotypists and photographers.

[3] *Clayton* v. *Gregson*, 4 Nev. & M. 602.

[4] *Wait* v. *Fairbanks*, Breyt. (Vt.) 77. In *Fitch* v. *Carpenter*, 43 Barb. (N. Y.) 40, it was held that evidence was admissible to show what, by the usage of the trade, was regarded as "good merchantable shipping hay," used in a written contract.

against a common carrier for loss of goods, the plaintiffs were permitted to show by parol that the words "*dangers of the river*," in the bill of lading, were, by the usage and custom of merchants and others, understood to include other casualties than those arising from water.[5] So, where the trustee of a railroad contracted with parties to carry "their freight" at certain prices, it was held that evidence of the character of the plaintiff's freighting business for several years previous to the making of the contract, was admissible to show that "hay" was not included.[6] In an action upon a contract which contained a warranty that a machine furnished should be capable, "with one man and a good *team*," &c., it was held that evidence as to the sense in which the word "team" was used, was admissible and should be ascertained by evidence as to what is understood as constituting a "team," in view of the use to which it was to be applied.[7] Where a contract entered into to put up a sugar mill and engine, specifying no time when the work should be completed, it was held that parol evidence was admissible to show such facts and usages, as, coupled with the stipulations in the contract, will indicate the period which the parties, it must be presumed, contemplated, without mentioning, from a knowledge, that such incident would be supplied by equity and usage.[8] Usage has been held admissible to show what is meant by "farm" or "homestead farm,"[9] and as to the

[5] *Sampson* v. *Gazzam*, 6 Port. (Ala.) 123. But in *Boon* v. *The Belfast*, 40 Ala. 184, where goods were lost by the seizure of the steamer by armed men, and the only exception to the carrier's liability in the bill of lading was "dangers of the river," it was held that it was not competent to show that a usage existed among all persons navigating the river exempting carriers from such losses. In *Gordon* v. *Little*, 8 S. & R. (Penn.) 535, evidence of usage fixing the

meaning of "inevitable dangers of the river," was held admissible in ascertaining what was intended thereby in a bill of lading for the transportation of goods by inland navigation.

[6] *Noyes* v. *Canfield*, 27 Vr. 79.

[7] *Ganson* v. *Madigan*, 15 Wis. 144.

[8] *Ragley* v. *Goodloe*, 7 La. An. 295.

[9] *Locke* v. *Rowell*, 47 N. H. 46. So "*product*," in a contract promising to pay the *product* of hogs. *Stewart* v. *Smith*, 28 Ill. 397.

mode of engaging and paying crews of fishing vessels, in order to show the kind of voyage contemplated;[1] to show that in certain kinds of contracts any description of written instruments are regarded as bonds by the parties.[2] Where a contract was made between coopers and log dealers by which the former agreed to pay the latter three dollars for each and every thousand feet of merchantable boards that certain logs, to be cut by the latter and deposited in the Kennebec river at a given point, might be estimated to make, the plaintiffs, who were the log dealers, insisted that the contract was entered into in reference to a usage among persons in their line of business along the Kennebec river, to estimate the quantity of boards which may be realized from a log or lot of logs before they were sawed, by a scale called the *Brunswick* scale. The defendants, however, insisted that the estimate was to be made by the *Learned* scale, and claimed that the former was erroneous and the latter exact. Under these circumstances the court held that if the usage alleged by the plaintiff existed, and was so generally understood that the plaintiff in contracting must be presumed to have had reference to it, then the estimate should be made according to the Brunswick scale.[3] In a case arising under the tariff of 1816[4] as to the meaning of the words "*loaf sugar*," and whether *crushed loaf sugar* was within the term or only *sugar in the loaf*, Judge Story held that all statutes like this one must be interpreted, not according to the abstract propriety of language, *but according to their mean-*

---

[1] *Edredge* v. *Smith*, 13 Allen (Mass.) 140.

[2] *Stone* v. *Bradbury*, 14 Me. 185.

[3] *Heald* v. *Cooper*, 8 Me. 32. In Ohio, long established usage in the execution and acknowledgment of deeds will be adhered to, even though it does not follow the literal requisitions of the statute on that subject. *Brown* v. *Farron*, 3 Ham. (Ohio) 155. Indeed, except in cases where the statute expressly or by necessary implication provides that an instrument not executed in the form prescribed by it shall be inoperative, there can be no question but that, if it is executed in the manner established by long usage, it will be upheld. *Gilman* v. *Riopelle*, 18 Mich. 145; *Kirkendall* v. *Mitchell*, 3 McLean (U. S.) 144.

[4] *United States* v. *Breed*, 1 Sumn. (U. S.) 159.

ing in trade and commerce, and in buying and selling; and
that merchants, refiners, confectioners and grocers might be
examined as witnesses for the purpose of ascertaining the
commercial import of the phrase in question, and that the
jury in the light of such usage of the trade should say
whether crushed sugar was within the term "*loaf sugar*" or
not, and they having found that it was not, their verdict was
sustained. In an English case[5] in which a somewhat similar
question was involved, a contrary doctrine was held, the
court refusing to permit evidence of experts, or the usages
of a trade or business, to be shown to interpret terms used
in a statute. In that case it appeared that by an act of Parliament[6] cast plate glass was directed to be *squared* into
plates of certain dimensions, and the question was whether
certain plates were in the shape directed. The Attorney
General, at the trial, produced books explaining the process
and the terms of art in the manufacture, and the defendants
offered to prove that by usage the word "*squaring*" had
acquired a technical meaning in the trade, and what that
meaning was, to wit, *the cutting of glass into the shape in
which it is intended for the market, whatever that shape may
be.* This was refused, and upon a motion for a new trial,
Eyre, C. B., said, "In explaining an act of Parliament it is
impossible to contend that evidence should be admitted, for
that would make it a question of fact instead of a question
of law. The judge is to direct the jury as to a point of law,
and in doing so must form his judgment of the meaning of
the legislature in the same manner as if it had come before
him by demurrer, where no evidence could be admitted.
Yet on demurrer a judge may well inform himself from
dictionaries or books on the particular subjects, concerning
the meaning of any word. If he does so at Nisi Prius and
shows them to the jury they are not to be considered as
evidence, but only as the grounds on which the judge has

---

[5] *Atty.-Gen.* v. *The Cast Plate Glass   [6] 27 Geo. III., chap. 28.
Co.*, 1 Anstr. 39.

formed his opinion, as if he were to cite any authorities for the point he lays down." Without doubt the course pursued by Story, J., will commend itself to our courts as the true and reasonable course to pursue, especially in the interpretation of statutes applying to trades or businesses which employ words in technical and peculiar senses not generally known. Indeed, in our courts usages are often regarded in ascertaining the intention of the legislature.[7] The construc-

[7] *Meriam* v. *Harsen*, 2 Barb. Ch. (N. Y.) 232. In *Polk* v. *Hill*, 2 Overt (Tenn.) 157, the court held that in cases of doubt, usage may be recurred to in order to arrive at the meaning of the legislature. Where the statute fixes the fees of an officer, he cannot set up a custom or usage by which other compensation may be taken. Thus an inspector of flour, whose fees were fixed by statute, claimed that by a custom among inspectors he was entitled to the draft flour drawn out to be examined, but the court held that such a custom was against the policy of the law; that the statute providing certain fees for inspection thereby impliedly forbade all other compensation; that it could not be more ancient than the inspection laws, and that they were not old enough to be immemorial, though beyond the actual memory of those now living; that though this custom had existed under the old laws, and the legislature, in remodeling them, had not expressly negatived the custom, yet that this silence was not a legislative recognition of it. *Delaplane* v. *Crenshaw*, 15 Gratt. (Va.) 457. It was also held in the same case that where the statute provided the way in which certain duties should be discharged, a usage or custom to perform them in another or different mode, even though the mode provided by usage was much the best, was invalid. Thus the inspector claimed that he could not inspect by boring a half-inch hole in the head of the barrel, and that the custom allowed him to use a larger auger: the old law required him to inspect flour by a half-inch hole, while the new code required all inspectors of flour, fish, butter, &c., to inspect by a half-inch hole or in some other satisfactory manner, and required the hoops of barrels offered for inspection to be nailed. Held, that the code did not change the method of inspection established by the old law, and that it was no answer to a mandamus to compel the inspector to inspect a certain lot of flour by a half-inch hole, that he could not so inspect it properly, and that the custom authorized him to use a larger hole, as both the answer and the custom would be in contravention of the statute under which he held his office. An illegal usage, prevailing for however long a period, cannot ripen into a binding custom. *Pierce* v. *United States*, 1 N. & H. (U. S.) 270. The usage of the postoffice department to require a new contractor for carrying the mail to purchase the stock of the previous contractor, at a valuation, is not binding on the government. *Nye* v. *United States*, 22 Law Rep. (U. S.) 174.

tion put upon a statute by public officers for a long series of years, not in apparent conflict with its terms, is competent evidence to aid in determining the real meaning of the statute,[8] and is regarded as having almost the force of a

[8] *Eaton* v. *Pickersgill*, 55 N. Y. 310. In *Meriam* v. *Harsen*, 2 Barb. Ch. (N. Y.) 232, it was held that a general usage, under the statute respecting the proof and acknowledgment of deeds and the form and certificate of acknowledgment, was entitled to great weight. A local custom, opposed to the provisions of a statute, is not binding. *Walker* v. *Transportation Co.*, 3 Wall. (U. S.) 150; S. P. *Winter* v. *United States*, Hemp. (U. S.) 344. Custom cannot modify a statute. *The Forrester*, Newb. 81. An illegal practice prevailing among officers of the government, no matter how long continued or extensive, can never ripen into a binding usage. *Peirce* v. *United States*, 1 N. & H. (U. S.) 270. A foreign custom which is bad in law, can confer no rights on a party. *Taylor* v. *Carpenter*, 2 W. & M. (U. S.) 2. A usage of the board of directors of a bank, to permit the cashier to misapply its funds, will not exonerate his sureties. *Minor* v. *Mechanics' Bank of Alexandria*, 1 Pet. (U. S.) 46. A usage, which would require those who are in the legal use of the waters of a harbor, as a highway, to yield to others who are using them for an unlawful purpose, will not be upheld. *The Maverick*, 1 Spr. (U. S.) 23. Nor one for wharfingers to act as agents, in accepting, on behalf of consignees, goods arriving at their several wharves, *The Middlesex*, 21 Law Rep. (U. S.) 14. Nor, indeed, any usage that is unjust or opposed to the policy of the law. To estab-

blish a local custom, derogating from the general law, it is not enough to prove *that the act has been frequently done;* it must be shown to be so generally known and recognized, that a fair presumption arises, that the parties entered into their contract, with a silent reference to it. *The Paragon*, Ware (U. S.) 322. A particular local usage, in contravention of the general law merchant, is not binding on those who have entered into no contract with reference to it. *Sturgis* v. *Cary*, 2 Curt. (U. S.) 382 ; see *Bank of Columbia* v. *Lawrence*, 2 Cr. (U. S. C. C.) 510. To be binding, it must be general, and well understood. If the usage is clearly established, that the factor has a right to charge commissions on purchases, and on acceptances, when not in funds to meet drafts at maturity, such items ought to be allowed. But commissions and interest both cannot be charged on advances. *Smetz* v. *Kennedy*, Riley (S. C.) 218. The custom of railroad companies to allow their contractors the free use of their own roads, cannot be extended so as to bind a company to pay the expenses of its contractors on the road belonging to another corporation. *Colcock* v. *Louisville R. R. Co.*, 1 Strob. (S. C.) 329. The usage or custom of a particular port, in a particular trade, will not control the language of a policy of insurance. *Rogers* v. *Mechanics' Insurance Co.*, 1 Story (U. S.) 603. To have that effect, it must be some known, general usage or cus-

judicial construction. But in order to have that effect it must have been general, continued and unquestioned,[9] and according to the case last cited, and according to the fundamental principles upon which the doctrine of usages and customs rests, if the construction claimed to have been established by usage has not been uniformly consistent therewith, it cannot be invoked as having any binding force.[1] Nor, upon principle, could such a usage be invoked when clearly opposed to the plain terms of the statute. "A custom," says the court in a Louisiana case,[2] " is without force in opposition to a positive law,[3] therefore it is not competent to show that

tom in the trade, both applicable and applied to all parts of the State, and so notorious as to afford a presumption that all contracts of insurance in that trade are made with reference to it. *Id.* Where a custom is relied on as imposing a particular duty, that custom must be shown to exist at the place where the transaction to which it relates took place. *Allen* v. *Lyles*, 35 Miss 513. Proof of a custom by boats to carry money for customers to gain patronage, does not establish a custom to carry it for hire. *Chouteau* v. *Steamboat St. Anthony*, 20 Mo. 519. The custom of the merchants of Mobile to retain notes and bills of their country customers, after they are paid, until the end of the year, for settlement, may be given in evidence to explain why a paid note was not given up. *Remy* v. *Duffee*, 4 Ala. 365.

[9] *Fellows* v. *New York*, 24 N. Y. S. C. 249; *Meriam* v. *Harsen*, 2 Barb. (N. Y.) Ch. 232.

[1] *Brady, J.*, at page 254, in *Fellows* v. *New York*, ante.

[2] *Cranwell* v. *Fanny Fosdick*, 15 La. An. 436.

[3] *Dwight* v. *Barton*, 12 Allen (Mass.)

316. Where a transaction is within the statute against usury, the usage of trade, as to such transaction, cannot be received in evidence to show that it is not usurious. *Dunham* v. *Dey*, 13 Johns. (N. Y.) 40; 16 Johns. (N. Y.) 367; *Bank of Utica* v. *Wager*, 2 Cow. (N. Y.) 712; *Bank of Utica* v. *Smalley*, 2 Cow. (N. Y.) 770; *New York Firemen Insurance Company* v. *Ely*, 2 Cow. (N. Y.) 678. Nor of a usage for factors to pledge the goods of their principals is void, being against a general rule of law. *Newbold* v. *Wright*, 4 Rawle (Penn.) 195. Or of a custom of the trade of Philadelphia to allow interest on goods sold, after six months. *Henry* v. *Risk*, 1 Dall. (Penn.) 265. Or of custom, different from the law, in a particular place, to re-enter for a forfeiture incurred by the non-payment of rent. *Stoever* v. *Whitman*, 6 Binn. (Penn.) 417. Or of a custom in the trade between this country and England, that the English merchant, on receiving an indorsed bill of exchange, must return it immediately to the indorser, on protest, and that he exonerates the indorser, if he call on the drawer, for payment. *Brown* v. *Jackson*, 2 Wash. (U. S. C. C.) 24.

by the usages of trade a transaction is not usurious when it is within the statute against usury.[4] Of course, although usage cannot repeal the plain words of a statute, yet, if its meaning is doubtful, it furnishes a rational guide to its construction,[5] and where the practice under a statute has been uniform for fifty years and more, the courts will not give it a new construction under pretext of making it better,[6] and evidence is admissible to show that what otherwise might be deemed a deviation in the usage is in fact not so.[7] The words "on the steamer" in a bill of lading, may be explained by parol proof of a general usage by which steamboats have barges in tow at certain stages of the water, and load their goods on the barges, and the goods as loaded are regarded as "on the steamer."[8] And generally where the terms used in a bill of lading have acquired a peculiar meaning by usage, evidence thereof is admissible, and the parties will be presumed to have contracted in reference thereto and used it in the *usual* sense.[9] While it has been held that, as applied to inland navigation, the words "dangers of the river," and "inevitable dangers of the river," evidence of usage fixing their construction is admissible,[1] yet a contrary rule has been adopted as to the words "dangers of the sea," and

Or of the custom, in the Northern Neck of Virginia, for persons, having mere settlement rights, to transfer them by a death-bed donation, without a will in writing. *Westfall* v. *Singleton*, 1 Wash. (Va.) 227. Or of a custom that, when a seller of goods receives a note of the consignee without the buyer's indorsement, the maker of the note is alone answerable, and that the buyer is discharged. *Prescott* v. *Hubbell*, 1 McCord. (S. C.) 94.

⁴ *Dunham* v. *Dey*, 13 Johns. (N. Y.) 40; *Bank of Utica* v. *Wager*, 2 Cow. (N. Y.) 712; *New York Fireman's Ins. Co.* v. *Ely*, *Id.* 678.

⁵ *Taylor* v. *Griswold*, 3 N. J. Eq. 222; *State* v. *Jersey City*, 24 N. J. L. 108.

⁶ *Board* v. *Cronk*, 5 N. J. Eq. 119.

⁷ *Lawrence* v. *McGregor*, ante.

⁸ *McClure* v. *Cox*, 32 Ala. 617; *Hibler* v. *McCartney*, 31 *Id.* 501.

⁹ *Wayne* v. *Steamboat General Pike*, 16 Ohio 42.

¹ *Gordon* v. *Little*, 8 S. & R. (Penn.) 533; *Sampson* v. *Gazzam*, 6 Post. (Ala.) 123. But not a usage of the carriers exempting them from liability for losses arising from causes clearly not within the meaning of the term as generally applied and understood. *Boon* v. *The Belfast*, 40 Ala. 184.

when by the bill of lading the goods were to be delivered in good order, "*dangers of the sea*" excepted, it has been held not admissible to show by usage that the ordinary exception thereto would include an injury by rats.[2] In a case in the United States Court[3] it was held not admissible to show that by usage where a bill of lading provided that the goods should be delivered in good order, "the dangers of the sea only excepted," the owners of packet vessels between New York and Boston are liable only for damages to the goods caused by their own neglect. "Such evidence," said Story, J., " would go, not to *explain*, but to *vary* and *contradict* the contract.[4] The phrase " British weight," when used in a charter party has been held explainable by evidence *de hors*, as it may mean either *gross* or *nett* weight, according to usage ;[5] so the meaning of the word " deliver," or rather what constitutes a "*delivery*," by a usage of a place ;[6] and so of the words " a good delivery," when no consignee is named,[7] and generally where a new and unusual word is used, or a common word by a well settled usage of trade has acquired a peculiar or technical sense as applicable to any particular business or class of people, its meaning may be explained and illustrated by proof of its sense according to the usage.[8] "Terms," says Lord Ellenborough, in a leading case upon the construction of instruments,[9] " are to be understood in their plain, ordinary and popular sense, unless they have generally, in respect to the subject-matter, *or by the known usage*

[2] *Aymer* v. *Astor*, 6 Cow. (N. Y.) 663. But *Savage*, *C. J.*, dissented and delivered an opinion giving very decided support to the doctrine that such evidence is admissible.

[3] *The Schooner Reeside*, 2 Sum. (U.S.) 567.

[4] See also holding the same doctrine, *Turney* v. *Wilson*, 7 Yerg. (Tenn.) 340.

[5] *Goddard* v. *Bulan*, 1 N. & McCord. (S. C.) 45.

[6] *Furniss* v. *Howe*, 8 Wend. (N.Y.) 247.

[7] *Galloway* v. *Hughes*, 1 Baily (S. C.) 553.

[8] *Eaton* v. *Smith*, 20 Pick. (Mass.) 150; *Mercantile Ins. Co.* v. *State Ins. Co.*, 25 Barb. (N. Y.) 319; *St. Nicholas Ins. Co.* v. *Mercantile Ins. Co.*, 5 Bas. (N. Y.) 238 ; *Astor* v. *Ins. Co.*, 7 Cow. (N. Y.) 202; *Horn* v. *Mutual Safety Ins. Co.*, 2 N. Y. 235; *Stebbins* v. *Globe Ins. Co.*, 2 Hall (N. Y.) 632.

[9] *Robertson* v. *French*, 4 East 135.

of trade, or the like, acquired *a peculiar* sense, *distinct from the popular sense* of the same words."[1]   But such evidence is not admissible to show that words of a plain and well known signification have acquired a directly different sense, unless the usage is *precise, definite and universal* where it exists, but where the usage is established its reception in evidence is a necessity, because the parties are presumed to have contracted in reference to it, and a knowledge of it is essential to give true effect to the contract according to its intent.[2] The rule deducible from all the cases may fairly be stated as being *when an expression used in a written instrument has a technical meaning, evidence is admissible to show that it has been used in that sense, and not in its ordinary meaning in common parlance, although that may be perfectly clear and unambiguous.*   In other words, evidence may be admitted to create an ambiguity and then to explain it.[3]   But in order to warrant the technical sense to prevail, it must be distinctly proved that it has acquired the particular meaning claimed for it,[4] and whether it has or not is a question for the jury.[5]   If a mercantile instrument is insensible when read, according to the ordinary sense of the words used therein, it is a question for the jury whether the words have not acquired a definite meaning by mercantile usage.[6]   Evidence of this character has been admitted to show the meaning of "summer leazes" in a lease to the plaintiff by which he had a right to the use of cows to be depastured on lands described as "summer leazes" and "after grass" respec-

---

[1] See also *Boorman* v. *Johnson,* 12 Wend. (N. Y.) 573; *Taylor* v. *Briggs,* 2 C. & P. 525; *Outwater* v. *Nelson,* 20 Barb. (N. Y.) 29; *Goodyear* v. *Ogden,* 4 Hill (N. Y.) 104; *Blackett* v. *Royal Ins. Co.,* 2 C. & J. 249; *Dawson* v. *Kittle,* 4 Hill (N. Y.) 107.

[2] *Leach* v. *Beardslee,* 22 Conn. 404; *Dalton* v. *Daniels,* ante; *Eaton* v. *Smith,* ante; *McClure* v. *Cox,* 32 Ala. 617; *Allegre* v. *Maryland Ins. Co.,* 2

G. & J. (Md.) 136; *Linsley* v. *Lovely,* 26 Vt. 123. Evidence of usage was admissible to show what is meant by "six per cent. off for cash."

[3] *Clayton* v. *Greyson,* 5 Ad. & El. 302; *Beacon L. & F. Assurance Co.* v. *Gibb,* 7 L. T. N. S. 574.

[4] *Taylor* v. *Briggs,* 2 C. & P. 525.

[5] *Hills* v. *Evans,* 31 L. J. Ch. 457.

[6] *Ashworth* v. *Redford,* L. & R. 9, C. P. 20.

tively, from February 2d to November. Upon the trial evidence was offered of a custom that a lessor should put his own cattle on the land called "summer leazes" up to May 12th, and it was held admissible, as in effect evidence, of the technical meaning of the word, and of the rights which passed to the plaintiff under the lease.[7] So to fix the time when a bill becomes due, when by the printed terms upon the invoice it is left indefinite. Thus, where these words were printed on the invoice, "Terms—Net cash, to be paid within six to eight weeks," and the goods not having been paid for, suit was brought scarcely seven weeks after the date; the court admitted evidence of mercantile usage as to when the bill matured, and the jury having found that by such usage the credit had expired, a verdict for the plaintiff was sustained.[8] So, too, evidence has been admitted to show that by usage when it is said in a letter that a ship will sail from St. Domingo in the month of October, it is generally understood that she will not sail until the 25th of the same month.[9] In order to make evidence of a usage for any purpose admissible and binding it must be reasonable, and in determining this point the question is, whether it is such as honest and right-minded men would regard as unfair and unrighteous, and if so, it fails to stand the test requisite to give it validity,[1] *and* it must be *certain and invariable* and such as both parties know or might have known upon reasonable inquiry.[2] The question in such cases is, whether there is a well recognized practice and usage with reference to the business to which it relates, which gives a particular sense to the words employed in it, so that the parties may be supposed to have used them in that sense.[3] The evidence,

[7] *Tudgay* v. *Sampson*, 30 L. T. N. S. 262, C. P.

[8] *Ashworth* v. *Redford*, 9 L. R. C. P. 20.

[9] *Chaurande* v. *Augerstein*, Peake 43.

[1] *Paxton* v. *Courtney*, 2 F. & F. 131.

[2] *Abbott* v. *Bates*, 22 W. R. 488, C. P.

[3] *Allegre* v. *Ins. Co.*, ante; *Gordon* v. *Little*, ante; *Miller* v. *Burke*, 68 N. Y. 615; *Farmers' Bank* v. *R. R. Co.*, 72 N. Y. 188. In *Steward* v. *Scudder*, 24 N. J. L. 96, grain was sent by a country dealer to a commission merchant with orders to sell *for cash*. It

in order to be admissible, must be as to the fact of a general usage and practice prevailing in the particular trade or business, and not the judgment and opinion of the witnesses, for the contract may safely and correctly be interpreted by reference to the fact of usage, as it is presumed that they knew of it they contracted in reference thereto; but the judgment or opinion of witnesses affords no safe guide for interpretation, because it is confined to their own knowledge.[4] This species of evidence is admissible in many cases, to add incidents to contracts and create liabilities on the part of

was sold and delivered, and a check for the amount of the purchase money sent to the dealer before it was collected of the purchaser. Within a week the purchaser failed, never having paid the money, and the merchant, brought an action against the owner to recover the amount, alleging that by the custom of trade in New York, *upon a sale for cash*, the purchaser has three or four days in which to pay the money. It was held that, in order to authorize a verdict for the plaintiff, the evidence must have shown such custom to have been at the risk of the owner, "*and so certain, uniform and notorious that it must be presumed to be understood by the parties.*" In a Vermont case, *Catlin* v. *Smith*, 24 Vt. 85, where goods were consigned to a commission merchant for sale with instructions to him to "sell for cash, *or not on credit*," and the commission merchant sold them to a party who said he would pay for them in a few days, but before paying therefor failed, it was held that the commission merchant could not defeat his liability to the consignor by showing a custom by which such sales were regarded as for cash. The distinction between this case and the

New Jersey case arises from the fact that the instructions were to sell for cash, without any qualification, while in this case the dealer was specially directed *not to sell on credit*, so that evidence of a usage that a sale on credit was regarded as a *cash* sale was expressly excluded, and could not be admitted to override the positive instructions. *Barksdale* v. *Brown*, 1 N. & M. (S. C.) 519. In *Chapman* v. *Devereux*, 32 Vt. 616, it was held that a usage to regard a sale on *thirty days* credit as a *cash* sale was void, and so of a sale on *six* days credit. *Greaves* v. *Hendricks*, (N. Y.) 16 Haz. Pa. Reg. 344.

[4] *Lewis* v. *Marshall*, 7 M. & G. 729. A usage or custom must be proved by *facts* and not from mere reports. *Mills* v. *Hallock*, 2 Edw. Ch. (N. Y.) 652; *Geary* v. *Meaghar*, 33 Ala. 630; *Chesapeake Bank* v. *Swain*, 29 Md. 483. In *Goodall* v. *New England Ins. Co.*, 25 N. H. 169, it was held that the evidence of a director of the company as to the usage or practice in regard to giving consent to other insurance, that "so far as his knowledge went" a certain practice existed, was held insufficient to establish a usage binding upon the assured, who had no knowledge of it.

parties thereto not appearing on the face of the contract. Thus, in an English case[5] it was held that evidence was admissible to show that by the usage of the tobacco trade all sales were by sample, although not so expressed in the bought and sold notes, and consequently to establish an implied warranty.[6] In a Massachusetts case,[7] to an inquiry in an application for insurance upon a manufactory, "are there casks of water in each loft kept constantly full?" the answer was "there are casks of water in each *room* kept constantly full," and the court held that evidence was admissible to show that *in the general use of language among manufacturers* the whole of a loft or story appropriated to a particular department was called one room, although the same was divided by a partition with doors, and that the meaning of the word room, and whether there was any such general use of language, was for the jury; and that if there was any such general use of the word room among *manufacturers* it need not be known and general among insurers in order to affect a contract of insurance upon manufacturing property, for they must be presumed to have so understood it. In another Massachusetts case,[8] the same general doctrine was applied to the words "store fixtures" in a policy of insurance, the courts holding that it was competent to show a well settled custom by which such words are applied *to all the furniture in the store,* whether fixed or movable. "If," said Chapman, J., "the term 'store fixtures' is a term of trade commonly used among traders and insurers, and is used in such a signification as to include any or all the articles mentioned as such in the report, those were insured by this policy." In an action upon an agreement to sell a milk route and the

[5] *Syers* v. *Jones,* 2 Exchq.

[6] See also, *Snowden* v. *Warden,* 3 Rawle (Penn.) 101, where the same rule was adopted as to sales of cotton. Also, *Cassidy* v. *Begaden,* 6 J. & S. (N. Y.) 180; *Boorman* v. *Jenkins,* 12 Wend. (N. Y.) 566. But see ¿ 105,

entitled, "Proof of usage to establish a warranty."

[7] *Daniels* v. *Hud. River Ins. Co.,* 12 Cush. (Mass.) 416.

[8] *Whitmarsh* v. *Conway Ins. Co.,* 16 Gray (Mass.) 657.

good will thereof, the testimony of experts is admissible to
show a usage in the milk trade of selling such routes by the
can, and the recognized value thereof per can.[9] So in an
action on a promise to pay commissions to an insurance
agent, evidence of a usage or custom of the trade to pay
commissions only on premiums actually collected, is admis-
ble.[1] A usage among whalers, that where a boat's crew from
a vessel strikes a whale with a harpoon, and the harpoon
with the line attached to it remained in the whale, but the
line does not remain fast to the boat, the whale belongs to
the ship that first struck it with the harpoon, although a
crew from another ship pursue and finally capture it, if the
master of the first ship claims it on the spot, is valid and will
enable the owners of the first ship to recover its value of the
crew appropriating it.[2] A custom that a railroad should
deliver freight on the platform of minor stations whose business does not justify a warehouse, and that it should be
received there by the consignee on discharge from the car,
has been held to be a good custom, and sufficient to control
the common law liability of carriers in the neighborhood.[3]
A usage among depositors in certain banks to deposit a check
on or the next day after the day on which it was received,
and of the bank immediately to return any checks from the
clearing house, which the bank has not funds to cover, has
been held to be reasonable and valid.[4] A usage among
brokers to sell stocks, deposited as collateral security for a
call loan, on failure to pay on call, is valid and binding *if
known* to the person depositing the stock.[5] But such a usage
is not admissible to vary the terms of a special contract relative to the loan. In such a case the contract will contract
the usage, and not the usage the contract.[6] In logging con-

[9] *Page* v. *Cole*, 120 Mass. 37.

[1] *Miller* v. *Ins. Co.*, 1 Abb. (N. Y.)
N. C. 470.

[2] *Swift* v. *Gifford*, 2 Low. (U. S. D. C.)
110.

[3] *McMasters* v. *Penn. R. R. Co.*, 69
Penn. St. 374.

[4] *Merrett* v. *Brackett*, 60 Me. 524.

[5] *Colket* v. *Ellis*, 10 Phila. (Penn.) 375.

[6] *Taylor* v. *Ketcham*, 5 Robt. (N.Y.) 507.

tracts which provide that No. 1 logs shall be delivered and paid for at a certain rate, it is competent to show what, by the usage of the trade, are considered No. 1 logs, the contract itself not fixing the grade.[7] A mercantile usage, that, upon the proper storage of herring on receiving it, without immediate examination, the purchaser does not waive objections to its quality, or variance from the order given, is admissible.[8]

Phrases Explained by Usage.

SEC. 86. In very many cases words and phrases which, if interpreted in their ordinary dictionary sense, would cause an instrument to be ambiguous or meaningless, may be read in connection with proof of a usage, so as to make the written contract perfectly intelligible. This has been repeatedly done in courts of law. Thus the word "privilege" has been read with the meaning attached to it by the mercantile part of the nation.(y) So where a founder of a charity had, in a deed of grant, described the objects of her munificence by the words " Godly preachers of Christ's Holy Gospel," and upon the interpretation difficulty arose as to the real meaning of that designation, extrinsic evidence, to prove that at the time of the grant there was a sect who were in the habit of calling themselves by that name, was admitted.(z) " Mauritius " has been held, according to mercantile acceptation, to be an " Indian Island."(a) And "Amelia Island " was held to denominate a region in which " Tiger Island " is comprehended, and the strict sense of the word was departed from because of the looseness of the ordinary use of these

[7] *Busch* v. *Pollack*, 41 Mich. 64.   [8] *Hinkel* v. *Welsh*, 41 Mich. 664.

(y) *Birch* v. *Depeyster*, 1 Stark. 210; 4 Camp. 385.

(z) *Shore* v. *Wilson*, 9 Cl. & F. in 355, 580, *per* Ld. Cottenham; see also *Atty.-Gen.* v. *Drummond*, 1 Dru. & War. 353; and on App., 2 H. of L. 837.

(a) *Robertson* v. *Clarke*, 1 Bing.

445, at 451, n.; *Trueman* v. *Loder*, 11 A. & E. 600; *Milward* v. *Hibbert*, 3 Q. B. 135; *Vallance* v. *Dewar*, 1 Camp. 503; *Ougier* v. *Jennings*, 1 Camp. 505, 606, n.; *Kingston* v. *Knibs*, 1 Camp. 508, *per* Ld. Ellenborough; *Godts* v. *Rose*, 17 C. B. 229.

words, a use which was compared to the common and inexact employment of the words London and Westminster.(b) The phrase, "warranted to depart with convoy," was literally construed according to the usage amongst merchants.(c) "Mess pork of Scott and Co." has been held to mean mess pork manufactured by Scott and Co.(d) And in another case, the words "Received on account of Bowman and Lay for J. Mackinson," the words "for J. Mackinson," being ambiguous, were explained by the evidence of a usage of trade which was admitted at the trial.(e)   An invoice, worded to sell goods at "£2 10s. per cent. monthly," may be explained by parol evidence, showing the meaning of the words in their ordinary employment by persons in the trade.(f)   So also such evidence may be introduced to show that a person whose name appears at the head of an invoice as vendor is not in fact a contracting party.(g)

"Days"—Pitch Pine Timber.

SEC. 87. Where there was a clause in a bill of lading, that cargo should be taken out in a certain number of days, or that demurrage should be paid, evidence of usage was admitted to prove that days as used meant working days, and not running days.(h)   In another case, the phrase "pitch pine timber" was explained by usage,(i) and the same evidence was admitted in the case of *Bold* v. *Ray-*

(b) *Moxon* v. *Atkins*, 3 Camp. 200.

(c) *Lethulier's case*, 2 Salk. 443.

(d) *Powell* v. *Horton*, 2 Bing. N. C. 668.

(e) *Bowman* v. *Horsey*, 2 M. & Rob. 85.

(f) *Schreiber* v. *Horsley*, 11 Jur. N. S. 675.

(g) *Holding* v. *Elliott*, 5 H. & N. 117.

(h) *Cochran* v. *Retberg*, 3 Esp. 121. As to meaning of "loading in turn," see *Robertson* v. *Jackson*, 2 C. B. 413; see also *Schultz* v. *Leidmann*, 14 C. B.

38; *Hudson* v. *Clementson*, 18 C. B. 213. As to evidence of a usage to pay an agent. *Hutch* v. *Carrington*, 5 C. & P. 471. For a factor to sell in his own name. *Johnston* v. *Usburne*, 11 A. & E. 549. As to renewal of commission to introducing broker on every renewal of charter effected through him. *Allan* v. *Sundius*, 1 H. & C. 123; 31 L. J. Exchq. 307.

(i) *Jones* v. *Clark*, 2 H. & N. 725; see also *Vallance* v. *Dewar*, 1 Camp. 503; *Robertson* v. *French*, 4 East. 130.

ner,(*k*) to explain a variance in the bought and sold notes exchanged over the bargain.

Explanation by Usage—Lien Abrogated by.

SEC. 88. Again, in another case, where the principle of the admission of technical evidence was approved of, it was said the words "Sail from St. Domingo in the month of October," were to be understood, when taken in connection with the usage of the trade, as indicating that the ship would not sail until the 25th.(*l*) It is evident that plain words have a stronger presumption in their favor than ambiguous ones, and therefore it has been laid down that, when it is sought to vary the meaning of such words, the evidence of custom should be very strong.(*m*) A case which has interest, as it indicates the actual abrogation of a right by a custom, may be mentioned here. The court decided in that case that a shipwright in the river Thames has no lien on a ship taken into his dock to be repaired, unless there is an express agreement to that effect, credit being given by the usage of trade to the owner of the ship for the cost of the repairs.(*n*)

Usage in Relation to Bill of Lading.

SEC. 89. Where, by a bill of lading of wool from Odessa,

(*k*) 1 M. & W. 343; see also *Field* v. *Lelean,* 6 H. & N. 617; *Fawkes* v. *Lamb,* 8 Jur. N. S. 385; 31 L. J. Q. B. 98.

(*l*) *Chaurand* v. *Angerstein,* 1 Peake 61; see also *Yates* v. *Duff,* 5 C. & P. 869. It is not competent, in an action by the owner of the cargo of a coasting vessel against a purchaser of the same from the master of the vessel, he having no express authority to sell, to give evidence of a custom of masters of such vessels, laden with lumber, to make sales in the harbor of Brazos and along the southern coast of Texas, without any other authority than the fact of

their being masters or captains of the vessels. This custom, if existing, is in contravention of established law, and, in any event, it cannot be shown when the manifest repels the existence of possible authority in the captain. *Stillman* v. *Hurd,* 10 Tex. 109.

(*m*) *Lewis* v. *Marshall,* 7 M. & G. 729; 13 L. J. C. P. 193.

(*n*) *Mitchell* v. *Raitt,* 4 Camp. 146; see also *Donaldson* v. *Foster,* Abbott on Ship., pt. 4, ch. 1, s. 6. Such a usage will require to be clearly and uniformly well known and understood among the parties. *Davis* v. *New Brig,* 9 Gilp. 473.

freight was to be paid in London on delivery, at the rate of
"80s. per cwt., gross weight, tallow and other goods and
grain or seed in proportion as per London Baltic printed
rates," it was held that extrinsic evidence was admissible to
show that, by the usage of the trade, the meaning of the bill
of lading was that 80s. per cwt. of tallow was to be taken as
the standard by which the rate of freight on all other goods
was to be measured.(o)

Bills of Lading and Other Matters.

SEC. 90. Evidence of usage, as we have seen, is admissible
to explain and give the trade meaning of terms employed in
bills of lading. Thus the words, "a clean bill of lading,"
in their ordinary sense would be understood as simply refer-
ing to the condition of the bill itself, but by usage it imports
that the goods are to be "*stowed under deck*,"[9] but it may
also be shown that it includes a stowage *upon deck* or otherwise, according to the usage between the port of shipment
and the *termini* of the voyage.[1]

**Usage in Relation to Sale of Hops—Meaning of "Bale," "Wet
Oil," "About," "London."**

SEC. 91. Again, in the hop trade, "sold 18 pockets Kent
hops at 100s.," means 100s. per cwt.(p) A bale in the
gambier trade means a compressed package weighing on the
average 2 cwt.(q) And it appears that, by usage, oil is
"wet" if it contains any water, however little;(r) that
"about" so many quarters has, as used in a delivery order,
a definite connotation;(s) that "London" may be used in
various senses;(t) and that the article called "Calcutta lin-

---

[9] *Cherry* v. *Holly*, 14 Wend. (N.
Y.) 26.

[1] *Barber* v. *Brace*, 3 Conn. 9. Evidence of intent, as an independent

(o) *The Russian Steam Navigation
Co.* v. *Silva*, 13 C. B. N. S. 610.

(p) *Spicer* v. *Cooper*, 1 Q. B. 424.

(q) *Gorrissen* v. *Perrin*, 2 C. B. N.
S. 681.

fact, is not admissible. That must
be looked for in the bill itself and
the usages incident to it. *Lawrence*
v. *McGregor*, 37 Penn. St. 240.

(r) *Warde* v. *Stewart*, 1 C. B. N. S. 88.

(s) *Moore* v. *Campbell*, 10 Exch.
323.

(t) *Mallan* v. *May*, 13 M. & W.
511.

seed" may contain 15 per cent. of tares, rape and mustard, without losing its right to the appellation "Calcutta linseed," and that on the ground that, although the admixture of foreign substance is considerable, it is not sufficient to deprive it of its distinctive character, and that there is a usage that it should pass in the market under that name.

Sporting Usage—Particular Average.

SEC. 92. In a memorandum as to a race, the run described was "four miles across country," and it was proved that in sporting parlance these words did not allow the riders to go through gates.(u)   Thus custom may say that on an agreement for a lease the lessor prepares and the lessee pays for the instrument,(v) although the general rule as to the sale of property is that the vendee, who bears the expense of the conveyance, should prepare it.(w)   In the *North Staffordshire Railway Co.* v. *Peek*,(x) the majority of the court held that the terms in a letter to carriers of goods from their customers, "Please send the marbles *not insured*," were to be read "according to the understanding of the language between carriers and their customers," and in that light they were interpreted to convey a request to carry the marbles at the owner's risk.   This decision, which was upon the construction of the 7th section of the Railway and Canal Traffic Act (17 and 18 Vict. c. 31), was reversed in the House of Lords.   So usage has been allowed to show that "particular average" does not include expenses of recovering or preserving the subject-matter of insurance on the

(u) *Evans* v. *Pratt*, 3 M. & G. 759; 4 Scott N. R. 370.
(v) *Grissell* v. *Robinson*, 3 Bing. N. C. 11.
(w) *Price* v. *Williams*, 1 M. & W. 6; *Poole* v. *Hill*, 6 M. & W. 835; *Stephens* v. *De Medina*, 4 Q. B. 422; but see *The Duke of St. Albans* v. *Shore*, 1 H. Bl. 274; *Doe d. Clarke* v. *Stillwell*, 8 Ad. & El. 645; *Hallings*

v. *Counard*, Cro. Eliz. 517.   In the case of a settlement of personal property the practice is for the lady's solicitor to draw the settlement on marriage, and for the husband to pay for it.   *Helps* v. *Clayton*, 17 C. B. N. S. 553.
(x) 10 H. of L. Cas. 473; 9 Jur. N. S. 914; 8 L. T. N. S. 768.

ground that it would not contradict the express terms of the policy.(*y*)

Notes and Bills.

SEC. 93. Notes and bills are no exception to the rules in regard to usage, and, as we have seen,[2] they are in many respects subject thereto.[3] Thus, where a note is payable in "Canada money," it may be shown what is generally understood among brokers and others as to the meaning of the words at the place where the note was made.[4] So where a note was made payable in "cotton yarn at the wholesale factory prices," it was held competent to show that by a usage of manufacturers those terms meant a certain scale of prices different from the actual wholesale prices in market.[5] In a case decided by the Supreme Court of Maine,[6] it was held that where it was shown to be the custom of a New Hampshire bank to receive payments of interest on notes in advance, and suffer them to remain and still hold the sureties, and this custom was fully known to both principal and sureties, and they went into Maine to enforce a contract made in New Hampshire arising out of a note to such bank, whereon they were sureties, and interest in advance had been taken on the note, of the principal, the sureties were held not to be released by the taking of such interest in advance. In a New York case,[7] where the defendant was sued as an endorser upon a time check drawn in New York and payable at a bank in Connecticut, it was held that evidence of a usage of all the banks in that State not to allow grace on time checks, and that usage there determined the question

(*y*) *Kidson* v. *The Empire Marine Ins. Co.*, 35 L. J. C. P. 250.

[2] Ante, p. 25, (*w*).

[3] *Renner* v. *Columbia Bank*, 9 Wheat. (U. S.) 581; *Loring* v. *Gurney*, 5 Pick. (Mass.) 16; *Bank of Columbia* v. *Magruder*, 6 H. & J. (Md.) 172; *Bank of Washington* v. *Triplett*, 1 Pet. (U. S.) 25; *Mills* v. *U. S. Bank*, 1 Wheat. (U. S.) 431.

[4] *Thompson* v. *Sloan*, 23 Wend. (N. Y.) 71.

[5] *Avery* v. *Stewart*, 2 Conn. 69.

[6] *Crosby* v. *Wyatt*, 23 Me. 156.

[7] *Bowen* v. *Newell*, 2 Duer (N. Y. Sup. Ct.) 584. Reversed in Court of Appeals, 8 N. Y. 190.

whether any particular description of negotiable paper was or was not admitted, was admissible and entitled the plaintiff to recover. But as stated in the note, this ruling was reversed by the Court of Appeals, and in New York evidence of local usage is held not admissible to rob negotiable paper of its common law qualities or deprive the parties thereto of their common law rights.[8]

As to Ambiguity and Addition of Terms—Meaning of Weekly Accounts in Building Trade—How Words are to be Understood—Presumption—Peculiar Sense, how shown.

SEC. 94. It is a most difficult thing to distinguish those cases which have been decided on the ground that the usage explained the writing from those which have been looked upon as adding terms or incidents to it. Where only half a thing is expressed, there is real ambiguity in the writing, which can only be fully explained by the addition of a term or incident. Where there is palpable ambiguity, the effect is the same; the addition of a term or the explanation of the terms which are there written gives a meaning to the writing, which it did not possess without this expert evidence. One or two more cases which seem to fall under the first of these two heads may be alluded to in this place. In a case where —by a contract under seal, by which the plaintiff contracted to build for the defendant a house and premises—it was provided that "no alterations or additions should be admitted, unless directed by the defendant's architect by writing under his hand, and a weekly account of the work done thereunder should be delivered to the architect every Monday next ensuing the performance of such work," it was held that in

---

[8] *Merchants' Bank* v. *Woodruff*, 6 Hilt. (N. Y.) 174; also 25 Wend. (N. Y.) 673. In *Bowen* v. *Newell*, 8 N. Y. 190, the court held that the paper was in law a draft, and that proof of a usage among the banks in Connecticut to treat such instruments as checks was not admissible. In other words, that the legal character of an instrument cannot be changed by usage. But see *Stone* v. *Bradbury*, 14 Me. 185, where it was held admissible to show that in certain kinds of contracts, any description of written instruments were regarded as bonds.

an action on the contract, parol evidence was admissible to show that by the usage of the building trade, "weekly accounts" meant accounts of the day work only, and did not extend to extra work capable of being measured.(z)

(z) *Myers* v. *Sarl*, 30 L. J. Q. B. 9; 7 Jur. N. S. 97. In a suit for wages, there being no special contract proved, it is proper for the plaintiff to show a custom in the business that persons, employed as he was, are not to be dismissed till the end of the season, and that the end of the season by the same custom is January 1, or July 1. After the jury have found the custom, it is still for the court to decide what, if any, effect it shall have. *Given* v. *Charron*, 15 Md. 502. So in an action by a mechanic, to recover for work done by him in the village in which he resided, it is competent for him to prove the customary charge for such work by mechanics of that village, such evidence not being intended to establish a "custom or usage." *Pursell* v. *McQueen*, 9 Ala. 380. Where by a written contract for the hiring of slaves, it was expressly stipulated that the service in which they were to be employed was "to cut cord wood on the Mississippi river, at or near Mills's Point, and for no other purpose whatever," evidence of the usage or custom of wood-cutters on the Mississippi was excluded; the words of the contract negativing any reference to such usage. *Bedford* v. *Flowers*, 11 Humph. (Tenn.) 242. Evidence of a particular usage to pay, *pro rata*, on a contract of hiring, if the slave does not work the full term agreed on, cannot be received, since the usage, if proved, could not be recognized. *Petty* v. *Gayle*, 25 Ala. 472. Evidence of

usage in paying for services, unaccompanied by, and independent of, evidence to charge the plaintiff with notice of such usage, is inadmissible to affect the plaintiff's claim for services. *Flynn* v. *Murphy*, 2 E. D. Smith (N. Y.) 378. And where a contract fixes the price of work and in terms provides that no extras shall be allowed, a custom to the contrary cannot control the express stipulation of the parties. *Phillips* v. *Starr*, 26 Iowa 349. Thus where the wages of seamen appear by the shipping articles, evidence of a further compensation, by way of customary privilege, cannot be received. *Bogert* v. *Cauman*, Anth. (N. Y.) 70. On a question involving the performance of the duties of a particular service, evidence of the customary duties of such service is admissible. *Vaughn* v. *Gardner*, 7 B. Mon. (Ky.) 326. Where a usage, regulating the compensation to be paid for a particular description of personal services, has been proved, it is for the court to say, whether the usage is or is not reasonable. The true question for the consideration of the jury, in such case, is, whether the usage was so generally known and acted upon, that the parties, from that and the other facts and circumstances proved, must be presumed to have had reference to it for the compensation to be paid; as in such case it would become, as it were, a part of their agreement, and binding upon them. *Bodfish* v. *Fox*, 23 Me. 90. In an action for labor upon a vessel, built

Some important words were used in the judgment on this case by Mr. Justice Blackburn : " The decision of this case turns simply upon the point—that the words of the written contract are to be understood in that sense which the phrase has acquired in the trade with regard to which it is used. It is the *prima facie* presumption that it was the intention of the parties to use it in that sense, and having expressed

by several owners, against one of them, evidence of the usage of the place, "that the owners were not jointly liable for materials and labor for the vessel, and that no one was authorized to make contracts for materials and labor for the vessel, so as to bind the owners generally," is inadmissible. *Leach* v. *Perkins*, 17 Me. 462. A written contract for the manufacture of any species of articles, cannot be affected by proof of a custom that, in the absence of an express agreement, the manufacturers shall not be held to warrant their castings against latent defects; and that, in case of apparent defects, they shall be entitled to have the articles returned to them within a reasonable time, and to replace them with new ones. *Whitmore* v. *South Boston Iron Co.*, 2 Allen (Mass.) 52. A locator of land, without an express agreement to receive part for his services, is not entitled by the custom of the country to any part, but must resort to his remedy at law for compensation, there being no circumstances in the case to give a court of equity jurisdiction. *Watkins* v. *Eastin*, 1 A. K. Marsh. (Ky.) 402. See *Bodley* v. *Craig*, 1 T. B. Mon. (Ky.) 77. In an action on an agreement to build an octagonal cellar wall at a certain price by the foot, evidence of the usage of measuring the angles of such walls, and of the

proper mode of measuring the angles of rectangular walls, is admissible. *Ford* v. *Tirrell*, 9 Gray (Mass.) 401. A usage among printers and booksellers, that a printer, contracting to print for a bookseller a certain number of copies, shall not print with the same types, while standing, an extra number for his own use, is reasonable, and not in restraint of trade. *Williams* v. *Gilman*, 3 Me. (3 Greenl.) 276. A usage among manufacturing corporations to give an honorable discharge to an operative who has worked faithfully with them for twelve months, and has given a fortnight's notice of an intention to leave, whereby such operative may obtain employment in other mills, does not render it obligatory upon those corporations to give such discharge in all cases where the foregoing conditions are complied with ; but the giving of such discharge is a matter of discretion and judgment with the corporation. *Thornton* v. *Suffolk Manufacturing Co.*, 10 Cush. (Mass.) 376. In England by general usage a general hiring of a servant is treated as a hiring for a year, but in this country no such usage exists, and consequently the doctrine predicated thereon does not prevail. *Kansas Pacific R. R. Co.* v. *Roberson*, 3 Cal. 142 ; Wood's Law of Master and Servant, 272–274.

themselves in a written contract making use of the phrase, it is *prima facie* as a matter of construction of the contract to be taken that they used the phrase in the particular limited sense which it has acquired in the trade. That peculiar and limited sense, if such an one had been acquired, must be shown by parol evidence; and this having been shown, then the presumption is that that was the sense in which the parties making the contract used it. I do not think that in order to introduce this extrinsic evidence it is necessary that the phrase should be at all on the face of it ambiguous. It is a well settled rule of evidence that all ambiguous expressions in reference to extrinsic matters in contracts, coming under the head of *latens ambiguitas*, may be explained by parol, the court giving to the meaning so supplied its legal sense and application.[9] The object of this class of proof is to enable the court to arrive at the real intention and relation of the parties, consequently, the only office of such proof is *to explain*, and not to modify or vary the contract.[1]   But where the contract is plain in all its pro-

---

[9] *Devonshire* v. *Niell*, 2 L. R. Ir. 132; *Doe* v. *Hiscocks*, 7 M. & W. 367.

[1] *Franklin* v. *Mooney*, 2 Tex. 452; *Purcell* v. *Burns*, 39 Conn. 429; *Ellis* v. *Crawford*, 39 Cal. 523; *Thayer* v. *Torrey*, 37 N. J. L. 339; *Acker* v. *Bender*, 33 Ala. 230; *Dana* v. *Fielder*, 12 N. Y. 40; *Nelson* v. *Sun, &c., Ins. Co.* 71 N. Y. 453; *Higgins* v. *Ins. Co.* 74 Id. 6; *Myers* v. *Lathrop*, 73 *Id.* 315; *Errico* v. *Brand*, 9 Hun. (N. Y.) 654. Thus, where a written contract was made for the sale of "600 casks" of black lead, "at $170 gold, per 100 lbs." oral evidence of the size of the casks agreed upon was held admissible. *Keller* v. *Webb*, 125 Mass. 88. So where a written contract for advances on cotton, provided that for the purpose of securing the same, "I hereby create a lien in your favor, &c., on my stock of all kinds in Twiggs county," it was held that parol evidence was admissible to show what kind of stock was included in the lien. *Saulsbury* v. *Blandy*, 60 Ga. 646, and generally where a latent ambiguity exists in a contract, parol evidence is not only admissible, but indispensable to enable the court to ascertain and carry into effect the real intention of the parties. *Dunham* v. *Gannett*, 124 Mass. 151; *Tuxbury* v. *French*, 41 Mich. 7; *Kirkpatrick* v. *Brown*, 59 Ga. 450; *Clarke* v. *Adams*, 83 Penn. St. 309; *Shuetze* v. *Bailey*, 40 Mo. 69; *Hover* v. *Tenney*, 36 Iowa 80; *Paul* v. *Denings*, 32 Md. 403; *Richard* v. *Schegelmich*, 65 N. C. 150; *Rugeley* v. *Goodloe*, 7 La. An. 295; *Hartwell* v. *Camman*, 10 N. J. Eq., 128; *Wilson* v.

visions, or the ambiguity, if any exists, is patent, parol evidence is not admissible to vary or contradict any of its provisions.[2] But, this rule, from necessity, is subject to numerous exceptions. Thus, a party may show that certain parts of the contract were inserted by the fraud of one of the parties, or that certain things that were agreed upon were fraudulently omitted,[3] or that an independent or collateral agree-

Robertson, 7 J. J. Mar. (Ky.) 78; *Patrick* v. *Grant,* 14 Me. 233; *Graham* v. *Hamilton,* 5 Ired. (N. C.) L. 428; *Cooper* v. *Berry,* 21 Ga. 526; *Hall* v. *Davis,* 36 N. H. 569; *Hotckiss* v. *Barnes,* 34 Conn. 27; *Doyle* v. *Estornet,* 13 La. An. 318; *Bowen* v. *Slaughter,* 24 Ga. 338; *Williams* v. *Waters,* 36 *Id.* 454; *Masters* v. *Freeman,* 17 Ohio St. 323; *Wilson* v. *Horne,* 37 Miss. 477. A patent ambiguity exists in an instrument when, from its perusal, it plainly appears that something more must be added before a person can ascertain which, of several things, is meant. *McNair* v. *Laler,* 6 Minn. 435.

[2] *Warren* v. *Crew,* 22 Iowa 315; *Peterson* v. *Grover,* 20 Me. 363; *Beckley* v. *Munson,* 22 Conn. 299; *Albert* v. *Zeigler,* 29 Penn. St. 50; *Bradley* v. *Bentley,* 8 Vt. 243; *Huffman* v. *Hammer,* 17 N. J. Eq. 269; *Richardson* v. *Comstock,* 21 Ark. 69; *Theuner* v. *Schmidt,* 10 La. An. 125; *Robinson* v. *Magarity,* 28 Ill. 423; *Wright* v. *Deklyne,* Pet. (U. S. C. C.) 199; *Jones* v. *Parmer,* 11 Paige Ch. (N. Y.) 650; *Young* v. *Frost,* 5 Gill. (Md.) 287; *Hoxie* v. *Hodges,* 1 Oreg. 251; *West* v. *Kelly,* 19 Ala. 353; *Huse* v. *McQuade,* 52 Mo. 388; *Brandon Mfg. Co.* v. *Morse,* 48 Vt. 322; *Mitchell* v. *Universal Life Ins. Co.* 54 Ga. 289; *Corwith* v. *Culver,* 69 Ill. 502; *Fitz* v. *Comey,* 118 Mass. 100; *Succession of Guillory,* 29 La. An. 495; *Stuart* v. *Morrison,*

67 Me. 549; *Barnand* v. *Gaslin,* 23 Minn. 192; *Morgan* v. *Adrian,* 77 N. C. 83; *Dixon* v. *Clayville,* 44 Md. 573; *Oliver* v. *Shoemaker,* 35 Mich. 464; *Miller* v. *Fletcher,* 27 Gratt. (Va.) 403.

[3] *Stark* v. *Littlepage,* 4 Rand (Va.) 368; *Waddell* v. *Glassell,* 18 Ala. 561; *Baltimore Steamboat Co.* v. *Brown,* 54 Penn. St. 77; *Townsend* v. *Cawler,* 31 Ala. 428; *Hunter* v. *Bilyeu,* 30 Ill. 228; *Hunt* v. *Carr,* 3 Ia. 581; *Pierce* v. *Wilson,* 34 Ala. 596; *Holbrook* v. *Burt,* 22 Pick. (Mass.) 546; *Ledden* v. *Myers,* 20 How. (U. S.) 506. Especially in equity. *Chetwood* v. *Brittain,* 2 N. J. Eq. 438; *Phyfe* v. *Wardell,* 2 Edw. Ch. (N. Y.) 47; *Wesley* v. *Thomas,* 6 H. & J. (Md.) 24; *Elliott* v. *Connell,* 13 Mill 91; *Christ* v. *Diffenbach,* 1 S. & R. (Penn.) 464; *Mallory* v. *Leach,* 35 Vt. 156. A party may show that his signature was obtained by fraud. *Lull* v. *Cass,* 43 N. H. 62. Of course the burden of establishing the fraud is upon the party alleging it, and as the law presumes in favor of innocence and honesty, the proof must be full, complete and establish a clear preponderance, or the claim must fail. *Pierce* v. *Wilson,* 34 Ala. 376; *Davis* v. *Stern,* 15 La. An. 176; *Sanford* v. *Handy,* 23 Wend. (N. Y.) 126; *Hunter* v. *Bilyeu,* 30 Ill. 228; *Hamilton* v. *Congers,* 28 Ga. 276; *Van Buskirk* v. *Day,* 22 Ill. 260; *Farrell* v. *Bean,* 10 Md. 217; *Selden* v. *Myers,* 20 How.

ment affecting the contract was subsequently entered into,[4]

(U. S.) 506. Parol evidence is always admissible to show that the contract is illegal or contrary to the rules of sound public policy, as that it is usurious. *Fenwick* v. *Ratcliffe*, 6 T. B. Mon. (Ky.) 154; *Succession of Fletcher*, 11 La. An. 59. Or that it is without consideration. *Groesbeck* v. *Seeley*, 13 Mich. 329; *Clark* v. *Houghton*, 12 Gray (Mass.) 38; *Wynne* v. *Whisenant*, 37 Ala. 46; *Luffburrow* v. *Henderson*, 30 Ga. 482. Or what the consideration in fact was. *Beckels* v. *Cunningham*, 14 Miss. 358; *Long* v. *Davis*, 18 Ala. 801; *Herrick* v. *Bean*, 20 Me. 51; *Fay* v. *Blackstonce*, 31 Ill. 588; *Knight* v. *Knight*, 28 Ga. 165; *Newton* v. *Jackson*, 23 Ala. 535.

[4] *Ford* v. *Smith*, 25 Ga. 675; *Adler* v. *Friedman*, 16 Cal. 138; *Phillips* v. *Preston*, 5 How. (U. S.) 278; *Cartwright* v. *Clayton*, 25 Ga. 85; *McDonald* v. *Stewart*, 18 La. An. 90; *Stearns* v. *Hall*, 9 Cush. (Mass.) 31; *Rubber Co.* v. *Dunklee*, 30 Vt. 29; *Rigsbee* v. *Bowler*, 17 Ind. 167; *Dictator* v. *Heath*, 56 Penn. St. 290; *Brock* v. *Sturdevant*, 12 Me. 81. Thus it may be shown that the original contract is discharged, and that an independent contract founded on a new consideration has been made by the parties to take the place of the written contract; but it must appear that the old contract, to the extent that it is covered by the new one, has been abandoned, as new provisions cannot be engrafted upon the written contract by parol. The new contract must be entire of itself, and take the place of the old one in the particular matter to which it relates. *Adler* v. *Friedman*, 16 Cal. 138; *Flanders* v. *Fay*, 40 Vt. 316; *Marshall* v. *Baker*, 19 Me. 402. So a new and

distinct agreement on a new consideration may be shown by parol, whether it be a substitute for the written contract, or in addition to, or beyond it. *Shepherd* v. *Wysong*, 3 W. Va. 46; *Butler* v. *Smith*, 35 Miss. 457; *Hutchins* v. *Hubbard*, 34 N. Y. 24. Thus, it may be shown that, by a parol agreement between the parties to a written contract, compensation for services, in addition to that named in the instrument, has been agreed upon. *Richardson* v. *Hooper*, 13 Pick. (Mass.) 446. That a note signed by one as surety was not to be binding, unless the signature of another person was obtained thereto. *Butler* v. *Smith*, ante. That the time for the performance of a contract has been extended. *Stearns* v. *Hall*, 9 Cush. (Mass.) 31. Or any modification of a written contract made upon a good consideration. *Holmes* v. *Douw*, 9 Cush. (Mass.) 135. So it may be shown that, by a subsequent agreement, a place of payment was agreed upon, or an agent appointed to receive the money. *Cummings* v. *Putnam*, 19 N. H. 569. The rule in reference to subsequent parol agreements, changing the terms of a written contract, is that such changes are valid and admissible in evidence when predicated upon a valid consideration, and when the original contract would have been valid if made by parol; but not when there is no consideration therefor, or when the original contract would be invalid if made by parol. *Rubber Co.* v. *Dunklee*, 30 Vt. 29; *Rigsbee* v. *Bowler*, 17 Md. 167; *Brock* v. *Sturdevant*, 12 Me. 81; *Dictator* v. *Heath*, 56 Penn. St. 290. So, too, collateral and independent facts, about which

or that a part of the contract was not reduced to writing,[5]

the written contract is silent, may be shown by parol. *Ruggles* v. *Swainvick*, 6 Minn. 526; *Van Buskirk* v. *Roberts*, 31 N. Y. 661. Parol evidence is admissible to show a *waiver* of some provision of the contract. *Wood* v. *Perry*, 1 Barb. (N. Y.) 113; *Childs* v. *Jones*, 8 B. Monr. (Ky.) 51; *Willey* v. *Hall*, 8 Ia. 62; *Leathe* v. *Bullard*, 8 Gray (Mass.) 545. As that a rate of interest agreed upon in a note or contract has been reduced. *Adler* v. *Friedman*, 16 Cal. 138. Or that the time for payment or performance has been extended. *Parker* v. *Syracuse*, 31 N. Y. 376. And, generally, to show that *any* provision of the contract has been abandoned or rescinded. *Flynn* v. *McKeon*, 6 Duer (N. Y.) 203; *Parker* v. *Syracuse*, ante; *Bank* v. *Curtis*, 24 Me. 36; *Whitcher* v. *Shattuck*, 3 Allen (Mass.) 319. Or that by a subsequent agreement between the parties, predicated on a new consideration, new stipulations were added thereto, or that its terms were varied. *Leeds* v. *Fursman*, 17 La. An. 32; *Rogers* v. *Atkinson*, 1 Ga. 12.

[5] *Winn* v. *Chamberlain*, 32 Vt. 318; *Kieth* v. *Kerr*, 17 Ind. 284; *Moss* v. *Green*, 41 Mo. 389. The rule seems to be that where writing, although embodying an agreement, is manifestly incomplete, and not intended by the parties to exhibit the whole agreement, but only to define some of its terms, *the writing is conclusive as far as it goes*, but such parts of the actual contract as are not embodied within its scope may be established by parol. *The Alida*, 1 Abb. Adm. (U. S.) 173; *Webster* v. *Hodgkins*, 25 N. H. 128; *Taylor* v. *Galland*, 3 Greene (Iowa) 17; *Miller* v. *Fitch-*

thorn, 31 Penn. St. 252; *Crane* v. *Elizabeth Association*, 29 N. J. L. 302. Thus where a contract is silent as to the place of delivery, parol evidence is admissible to show that the parties agreed on a *place* of delivery. *Mussleman* v. *Stoner*, 31 Penn. St. 265. So the *time* of delivery. *Johnston* v. *McCrary*, 5 Jones (N. C.) L. 369. And generally where a contract is manifestly incomplete, although it embodies an agreement, yet when it appears upon the face of the writing itself that it only embodies a *part* of the contract between the parties, while the writing is conclusive as far as it goes, parol evidence is admissible to show what the contract between the parties was as to those matters not reduced to writing. *Winn* v. *Chamberlain*, 32 Vt. 318; *Webster* v. *Hodgkins*, 25 N. H. 128. As where A. makes a contract in writing with B. to sell him a certain amount of standing timber for a certain sum, parol evidence is admissible to show what tract the timber was to be taken from. *Pinney* v. *Thompson*, 3 Iowa 74. So where there is a reference in a written contract to a verbal agreement between the parties, parol evidence is admissible to establish the verbal agreement, even though it adds material terms and conditions to the written contract. *Ruggles* v. *Swainvick*, 6 Minn. 526. But it must be remembered that it is only in cases where the contract itself shows that it rests partly in parol that such evidence is admissible. The mere fact that the contract is defective is not enough. *Mussleman* v. *Stoner*, 31 Penn. St. 265; *Young* v. *Jacoway*, 17 Miss. 212. Where a writing does not purport

or that in some respects the terms of the contract were

to give the whole contract, and it is evident from an inspection of the instrument that it was not intended as a contract or to express all that was agreed upon between the parties, parol evidence is admissible to show an agreement *aliunde.* Thus where A. buys a horse of B., and, upon payment of the price, B. gives to A. a writing in these words: "A. bought of B. a horse for the sum of $25," signed B., this precludes A. from denying the purchase or the price agreed upon, but it does not preclude him from showing that B. warranted the horse to be sound. *Allen* v. *Pink,* 4 M. & W. 140. See also *Executor of Corbin* v. *Sergent,* 9 N. Y. S. C. 107, where it was held that an agreement for the sale of a farm might be shown, notwithstanding a bond and mortgage had been given by the purchaser in pursuance of the agreement, the court holding that the case did not fall within the rule that the contract should be shown by the written instrument, as such instrument did not purport to express the agreement. In all other cases the verbal contract between the parties is regarded as merged in the written contract, and no part of it can be shown to rest in parol. *Crane* v. *Elizabeth Association, &c.,* 29 N. J. L. 302. Thus where a contract in writing for the sale and delivery of property is silent as to the time of delivery, parol evidence is admissible to show when the property was to be delivered. *Johnston* v. *McCrary,* 5 Jones (N. C.) 369. And *where* it was to be delivered. *Mussleman* v. *Stoner,* 31 Penn. St. 265. So to show to whom credit was given when a doubt in that respect fairly arises

upon the face of the instrument. *Dessau* v. *Bourne,* 1 McAll. (U. S.) 20; *May* v. *Hewett,* 33 Ala. 161; *Smith* v. *Alexander,* 31 Mo. 193. Or to identify the parties when there are two of the same name. *Mosely* v. *Martin,* 37 Ala. 216; *Henderson* v. *Hackney,* 23 Ga. 383; *Beauvais* v. *Wall,* 14 La. Ann. 199; *State* v. *Weare,* 38 N. H. 314; *Sawyer* v. *Boyle,* 21 Tex. 28; *Tuygle* v. *McMath,* 38 Ga. 648; *Hopkins* v. *Upsher,* 20 Tex. 89. Or to identify the subject-matter of the contract when it is fairly doubtful to what it applies. *Cary* v. *Thompson,* 1 Daly (N. Y. C. P.) 35; *Mayor* v. *Butler,* 1 Barb. (N. Y.) 325; *Almyner* v. *Dulith,* 5 N. Y. 28; *Aldrich* v. *Eshleman,* 46 Penn. St. 420. To show what land is referred to in a deed or sheriff's levy. *Stewart* v. *Chadwick,* 8 Ia. 463; *Doe* v. *Roe,* 20 Ga. 689; *Hughes* v. *Sandal,* 25 Tex. 162. To identify monuments referred to in a deed. *Robinson* v. *White,* 42 Me. 209; *Afferty* v. *Conover,* 7 Ohio St. 99. To prove that an action or prosecution is brought for the same matter covered by a previous judgment. *State* v. *Clemons,* 9 Ia. 534. As that water, the rights to which have been adjudicated in a former suit, is the same that is embraced in a later one. *Walsh* v. *Harris,* 10 Cal. 391. So to locate and identify land covered by a contract to convey, or described in a deed by general descriptions as "lands now occupied by me." *Brinkerhoff* v. *Alp,* 35 Barb. (N. Y.) 27. So to identify animals or other property sold under a written contract. *Marshall* v. *Gridly,* 46 Ill. 247; *Brooks* v. *Aldrich,* 17 N. H. 443; *Milvin* v. *Fellows,* 33 N. H. 401. Or to identify wood covered by a bill of sale or

waived,[6] or upon a sufficient consideration changed.[7] So, too, parol evidence is admissible to apply a written contract to its proper subject-matter,[8] or to identify the parties thereto.[9]

mortgage. *Sargent* v. *Salberg*, 21 Wis. 132; *Rugg* v. *Hale*, 40 Vt. 138. Parol evidence of the acts and declarations of the parties to a written contract, after its execution, is admissible to show what interpretation they put upon it, as well as to show what conditions of it were waived. But such evidence is admissible for no other purpose, and cannot be used to alter, vary, enlarge or restrict the contract itself. *Barnaby* v. *Sauer*, 18 La. Ann. 148; *Knight* v. *N. E. Worsted Co.*, 2 Cush. (Mass.) 271; *Spencer* v. *Babcock*, 22 Barb. (N. Y.) 326; *French* v. *Hayes*, 43 N. H. 30; *Emery* v. *Webster*, 42 Me. 204. So when the meaning of the parties to a contract is not clear, it may be gathered from proof of extrinsic facts, such as the acts and conduct of the parties under it. *Farmers' Bank* v. *Winfield*, 24 Wend. (N. Y.) 419; *Lowry* v. *Adams*, 22 Vt. 160. As to show whether a memorandum at the foot of a contract was intended as a part of it. *Vergan* v. *McGregor*, 23 Cal. 339. Whether it was intended to bind the principal or the agent by a contract. *R. R. Co.* v. *Middleton*, 20 Ill. 629. The purpose for which a note or account was assigned. *Cousins* v. *Westcott*, 15 Ia. 253. Or that a note, deed or contract was to be held in escrow. *Beale* v. *Poule*, 27 Md. 645.

[6] *Bryan* v. *Hunt*, 4 Sneed. (Tenn.) 548; *Willey* v. *Hall*, 8 Ia. 62; *Leathe* v. *Bullard*, 8 Gray (Mass.) 545; *Wren* v. *Fargo*, 2 Oreg. 19; *Parker* v. *Syracuse*, 31 N. Y. 376.

[7] *Leeds* v. *Fossman*, 17 La. Ann. 32; *Rogers* v. *Atkinson*, 1 Ga. 12.

[8] *Handy* v. *Matthews*, 38 Mo. 121; *Robinson* v. *White*, 42 Me. 209; *Gould* v. *Lee*, 55 Penn. St. 99; *Fitch* v. *Archibald*, 29 N. J. L. 160; *Stewart* v. *Chadwick*, 8 Iowa 463; *Bennett* v. *Pierce*, 28 Conn. 315.

[9] *Beauvais* v. *Wall*, 14 La. An. 199; *Moseley* v. *Mustin*, 37 Ala. 216; *Smith* v. *Alexander*, 31 Mo. 193; *Garwood* v. *Garwood*, 29 Cal. 514; *Walker* v. *Wells*, 25 Ga. 141; *Tuygle* v. *McMath*, 38 *Id.* 648; *Hopkins* v. *Upshur*, 20 Tex. 89. Thus, it may be shown that the contract was intended for the joint benefit of the members of a firm, although made to one of them only. *Stone* v. *Aldrich*, 43 N. H. 52. That an order drawn on a third person was to be paid in a certain kind of property. *Hinneman* v. *Rosenback*, 39 N. Y. 98. But such evidence is never admissible when the intention of the parties can be gathered from the instrument itself. *Stevens* v. *Hays*, 8 Ind. 277. And unless fraud is shown, parol evidence is never admissible to alter, vary or change the terms of a written contract, as, that a promissory note should only be paid in a certain contingency. *Hatch* v. *Hyde*, 14 Vt. 25; *Adams* v. *Wilson*, 12 Metc. (Mass.) 138; *Erwin* v. *Saunders*, 1 Cow. (N. Y.) 249; *Swank* v. *Nichols*, 24 Ind. 199; *Foy* v. *Blackstone*, 31 Ill. 528; *Boody* v. *McKinney*, 23 Me. 517. Or that a draft payable, generally was to be paid at a particular bank. *Patten* v. *Newell*, 30 Ga. 271. Or that a note payable in installments was to become due on failure to pay an installment. *Blakeman* v. *Wood*, 3 Sneed (Tenn.) 512. Or that a note was renewed upon a

Without stopping to enumerate the numerous exceptions to the
general rule excluding parol evidence where it contradicts or

condition which has not been complied with. *Warren Academy* v. *Star-
rett*, 15 Me. 443. Or that a note was
intended as a receipt. *Billings* v.
Billings, 10 Cush. (Mass.) 178; *City
Bank* v. *Addins*, 45 Me. 455. Or that
payment of a note was not to be
enforced so long as the interest was
paid. *Church* v. *Stetson*, 5 Pick.
(Mass.) 506. Or that a guardian's
note was not to be paid unless there
were assets of the ward in his hands.
Aren v. *Hoffman*, 41 Miss. 616. Or
that it is payable in any thing but
money. *Larg* v. *Johnson*, 24 N. H.
302; *Bank* v. *Keep*, 13 Wis. 209;
Cockerell v. *Kirkpatrick*, 9 Mo. 697;
Woodin v. *Foster*, 16 Barb. (N. Y.)
146. Or that the value of certain
property, when ascertained, should
be credited on the note. *Feather-
stone* v. *Wilson*. 4 Ark. 154. Or that
the note was to be paid at a different
place or on a different day from that
named therein. *Brown* v. *Wiley*, 20
How. (U. S.) 442; *Eaton* v. *Emerson*,
14 Me. 335. Or to change a word or
its ordinary meaning, used in a note,
as "if" to "when." *Garten* v. *Chandler*, 2 Bibb (Ky.) 246. Or that it is
payable in any other mode than that
appearing on its face. *Field* v. *Stin-
son*, 1 Cold. (Tenn.) 40. Or that a
surety signed the note only upon the
condition that it was to be collected
promptly at maturity. *Thompson* v.
Hall, 45 Barb. (N. Y.) 214. Or that
it was only to be paid on a contingency. *Bidwell* v. *Thompson*, 25 Tex.
245. Or that the signers of a note
acted in any other capacity than
that designated by their signature
thereto. *Hyatt* v. *Simpson*, 8 Ind. 156.
Neither is it competent to vary or

alter the relations of an indorser of
a note or bill by parol proof. *Buckley*
v. *Bently*, 48 Barb. (N. Y.) 283;
Crocker v. *Getchett*, 28 Me. 392; *Mason*
v. *Graff*, 35 Penn. St. 448; *Kern* v.
Van Pheel, 7 Minn. 426; *Barry* v.
Morse, 3 N. H. 132; *Meyer* v. *Beards-
ley*, 30 N. J. 236. Or to show what is
intended by an indorser who writes
"notice of protest waived by me.".
Buckley v. *Bentley*, 42 Barb. (N. Y.)
646. Or that the note was given for
certain property which the maker
had a right to return within a certain time, and on the return of
which the note was to be given up.
Allen v. *Forbush*, 4 Gray (Mass.) 504.
Or that the note was given for land,
and that a part of the land agreed
to be conveyed was not embraced in
the deed. *Bennett* v. *Ryan*, 9 Gray
(Mass.) 204. Or that an indorser
signed only as guarantor. *Wright* v.
Morse, 9 *Id.* 337. Or that a check
was given upon the express understanding that it was to be paid in the
bills of a certain bank. *Park* v.
Thomas, 21 Miss. 11. Or upon a condition that had failed. *Rose* v.
Learned, 14 Mass. 154. Or to show
that it was agreed when the indorser
indorsed the note that he should not
be liable. *Sands* v. *Woods*, 1 Iowa
263. Or that a note was given as a
memorandum merely, which was
not to be paid except as he collected the amount of another party.
McClanahan v. *Hinds*, 2 Strobh. (S.
C.) 122. Or that a note or due bill
given on demand was not to be paid
until a certain time. *Van Allen* v.
Allen, 1 Hill (N. Y. C. P.) 524. Or
that the payee agreed to make a deduction from a note in a certain

varies the terms of a contract, it may be said that the instances given, show that the admission of evidence of usage or custom clearly comes under the head of these exceptions to the general rule, and is admissible in any or all instances where parol evidence is admissible to affect the relations of the parties under any species of contract, whether in writing or by parol, or under seal, or not, provided it is not excluded by the express terms of the contract, and that it was *known* to the parties,[1] or is so general and uniform that the parties

contingency. *Goodard* v. *Hill*, 33 Me. 582. But it has been held that when the indorsement is in blank it may be explained by parol. *Harris* v. *Pierce*, 6 Ind. 162; *Taylor* v. *Kirn*, 18 Iowa 485; *Smith* v. *Barber*, 1 Root (Conn.) 207. As that there was a verbal agreement between the indorser and indorsee that there should be no recourse to the indorser in case of non-payment. *Girard Bank* v. *Gomley*, 2 Miles (Penn.) 405. But this is restricted to actions between the indorser and indorsee, and even in such cases, the policy of the rule is doubtful and inconsistent with the general principle that parol evidence is admissible to vary the terms of a written contract. When a person indorses his name upon the back of a note, he becomes a party to the note, and a surety for its payment. If he would restrict his liability, he should do so by the terms of his indorsement, and not allow it to rest in parol. The very fact that a contract of that character, so important to the indorser, is left to rest in parol, evinces a fraudulent purpose, which the law should not tolerate or uphold. It opens the door to perjury, and enables the indorsee to foist, upon an innocent party, a contract apparently absolute upon its face, when in fact it is

transmitted with conditions that strip it of one of the most essential elements of its value. In the case of a blank indorsement, a party cannot convert the indorser into a guarantor by writing a guaranty over his signature, except upon positive proof of authority to do so. *Cottrell* v. *Conklin*, 4 Duer (N. Y.) 45. It has been held that a person who signs a note with another, joint on its face, may show that he signed it as surety simply, and that the payee knew the fact. *Emmons* v. *Overton*, 18 B. Monr. (Ky.) 643; *Riley* v. *Gregg*, 16 Wis. 666; *Pollard* v. *Stanton*, 5 Ala. 451; *Adams* v. *Flanagan*, 36 Vt. 400; *Bank* v. *Kent*, 4 N. H. 221; *Bank* v. *Mumford*, 6 Ga. 44; *Watkins* v. *Kilpatrick*, 26 N. J. 84; *Ward* v. *Stout*, 32 Ill. 399; *Lacey* v. *Lofton*, 26 Ind. 324; *Hecksher* v. *Binney*, 3 Woodb. & M. (U. S.) 333.

[1] *Thompson* v. *Hamilton*, 12 Pick. (Mass.) 425; *Loring* v. *Gurney*, 5 *Id.* 15: *Stevens* v. *Reeves*, 9 *Id.* 198. But if the usage is special, it is not binding upon him, unless the party sought to be charged therewith has actual knowledge of it. *Berkshire Woolen Co.* v. *Prastor*, 7 Cush. (Mass.) 417. In *Croucher* v. *Wilde*, 98 Mass. 322, it was attempted to charge the master of a vessel with a usage of a certain wharf on which

must be presumed to have known of and contracted in refer-

berth for it had been engaged by the consignees as to the mode of discharging the cargo, but it was held that unless it was shown that the master had knowledge or notice of such usage it was not binding upon him. *Croucher* v. *Wilde*, 98 Mass. 322. In *Stevens* v. *Reeves*, ante, it was proved to be the usage in Andover and some factories in neighboring towns that no employe should leave without giving a fortnight's notice. A weaver who did not know of the usage left without giving such notice, and it was held that he was not bound by the usage. And a similar usage, a notice of which was printed and posted up in the company's counting-room, was held not binding unless brought home to the employe's knowledge. *Collins* v. *N. E. Iron Co.*, 115 Mass. 23. In a late Massachusetts case, *Sawtelle* v. *Drew*, 122 Mass. 228, in an action for the breach of an agreement in writing to hire the plaintiff's house, where the defence was that the plaintiff failed to cleanse the house as he agreed, evidence that "a universal custom and usage prevailed in the locality in which the house was situated, by which a lessor was required to cleanse a leased house before the lessee entered into possession," was held inadmissible without evidence that the plaintiff *knew* of the usage. But proof of repeated dealings with a party who has established a certain usage in respect to his business, is competent proof of such person's knowledge of it. *Shaw* v. *Wiley*, 18 Pick. (Mass.) 558. Evidence of former transactions between the same parties is admissible to show what

meaning they put upon a certain term. *Bourne* v. *Gatliff*, 11 Cl. & F. 45. The owner of a steamboat, and a corporation engaged in the business of supplying coal to steamboats, had for some months been accustomed to deal with each other for the supply of coal required by the boat, the requisite supply for her wants upon each trip being furnished her on each arrival. Under these circumstances the owner executed a written memorandum, acknowledging that he had purchased 1,500 tons of coal at a specified price per ton, which was, however, silent as to time and mode of delivery and payment; and it was held that the previous course of dealing between the parties might be shown to establish their intention in regard to these points. And that upon this evidence the contract must be construed as intending a delivery of the coal from time to time as it might be ordered to meet the wants of the boat, and as creating an obligation to pay for each parcel of coal as delivered. *Ib*. *The Alida*, 1 Abb. Adm. (U. S.) 173. Evidence of the usage of a single bank for two years to hold a note until the fourth day after it became due, and, if that day fell upon Sunday, to demand payment and give notice of Monday, is not sufficient to change as to the notes held by that bank, the general law requiring demand, &c., in such cases to be made on Saturday. *Adams* v. *Otterback*, 15 How. (U. S.) 539. A custom of a particular port, that seamen's advance wages, due under shipping articles, shall be paid to the shipping agent, to be paid by him to the boarding-house

ence to it.   (*Lawry* v. *Russell*, 8 Pick. (Mass.) 360; *Parrott*

keeper bringing the seamen, for their benefit, is unreasonable, and does not bind the seamen, although known to them at the time of signing the articles; and, if valid, would not be sustained by evidence that the shipping agent paid the wages to the boarding-house keeper, and charged them in account with the owner of the vessel. *Metcalf* v. *Weld*, 14 Gray (Mass.) 210.   A usage of a port that in order to constitute a delivery of water-borne goods by the carrier, it is necessary for a receipt to be given by the consignee or his agent, and that until then the liability of the carrier continues, is unreasonable and illegal.   *Reed* v. *Richardson*, 98 Mass. 216.   It is not competent, in an action by the owner of the cargo of a coasting vessel against a purchaser of the same of the master of the vessel, he having no express authority to sell, to give evidence of a custom of masters of such vessels, laden with lumber, to make sales in the harbor of Brazos and along the southern coast of Texas, without any other authority, than the fact of their being masters or captains of the vessels.   This custom, if existing, is in contravention of established law, and, in any event, it cannot be shown when the manifest repels the existence of possible authority in the captain.   *Stillman* v. *Hurd*, 10 Tex. 109.   The usages of a business are important in determining whether or not certain business entrusted to a person in a given case, has been properly done.   Thus, in a case where A. shipped on board of B.'s vessel for a fishing voyage, and signed a shipping paper in which it was agreed

that A. should have a certain proportion of the fish that he should take on the voyage, or the proceeds thereof, and that B. should render to A. an account of the delivery or sales of all such fish.   Before the vessel sailed on the voyage, A. drew an order on B., requesting him to pay to C., or order, a certain sum at the end of the voyage, if he, A., should make enough to pay said sum, which order B. accepted.   In a suit against B. on this acceptance, it was held that although it was proved that B. might have sold the fish soon after the arrival of the vessel, for a sum sufficient to pay the order, and that by delaying the sale he did not obtain a sufficient sum for that purpose, yet, if he acted in good faith, and sold the fish within a reasonable time, he was not liable to the holder of the order; and that for the purpose of proving that he acted in good faith, and made the sale in a reasonable time, evidence was admissible of the custom of those employed in like fishing voyages to delay the sale of fish as long as B. had delayed in this instance.   *Bradford* v. *Drew*, 5 Met. (Mass.) 188.   In an action for shoes sold and delivered, brought by a manufacturer against a distant purchaser, held that evidence was admissible to show that when shoes are ordered, it is the usage and course of the shoe business, when no special mode of conveyance is mentioned by the purchaser, for the manufacturer to take the shoes to Boston, at his own risk and cost, and there deliver them to some regular line of packets running to the purchaser's place of business,

v. *Thacher*, 9 *Id.* 430.)   And if the party offering such evi-

and take duplicate bills of lading, and forward one of them to the purchaser, by mail, and that from that time, the delivery is complete, and the purchaser takes the risk of loss. *Putnam* v. *Tillotson*, 13 Met. (Mass.) 517. So in a suit to recover the value of goods obtained by the defendant by a purchase for cash from an agent of the plaintiffs, evidence of the agent's agreement and general course of dealing with a former firm, consisting of two of the three plaintiffs, was held admissible for the purpose of proving the agent's authority to sell and deliver the goods for cash, if there was evidence that such former agreement and dealings were referred to in his agreement with the plaintiffs, and as a part thereof. *Buckman* v. *Chaplin*, 1 Allen (Mass.) 70. Hardware merchants in England, to whom an order had been sent from New York for the purchase of goods, brought an action for the amount of their purchase. The defendant alleged that notice of the consignment of the goods was not sent him in time to insure, and that the goods were injured on the voyage. It was held that evidence that it was the custom of hardware merchants to transmit to their consignee immediate notice of having made a consignment, was inadmissible, the plaintiffs in this case having acted only as agents, and not as vendors. *Field* v. *Banker*, 9 Bosw. (N. Y.) 467. Where there was a special contract between the parties as to the price per thousand feet that should be paid to the plaintiff for drawing certain lumber over a particular route, but the parties disagreed as to what

that price was, as fixed by the contract, evidence to show what was the usual and common price paid at that time and place for similar services, and of the amount paid to one or more individuals for drawing the same kind of lumber over the same route, at the same time, was held competent. *Swain* v. *Cheney*, 41 N. H. 232. But where the price fixed by the contract is definitely ascertainable, such evidence is not admissible. *Hartie* v. *Collins*, 46 Penn. St. 268; *Edwards* v. *Goldsmith*, 16 *Id.* 43. Such evidence is also admissible for the purpose of corroborating witnesses in certain cases. Thus where the master of a coasting vessel, who had chartered it on shares, testified that the owners authorized him, if he should leave the vessel, to give it up to the mate, and that he did so under an oral contract with the mate to run the vessel on the same terms as he had done; and the mate testified that he ran the vessel accordingly, as master, and that the owners ratified the agreement. It was held that evidence was admissible in order to show the terms of the contract between the new master and the owners, and to corroborate the witnesses, of a usage, at the port where the vessel belonged, to let such vessels to the master upon shares. *Thompson* v. *Hamilton*, 12 Pick. (Mass.) 425. So, too, such evidence is admissible to show whether or not a person has been guilty of negligence in certain cases. Thus, in a suit against a ginner of cotton, for cotton lost by fire, the plaintiff may prove the usual custom of ginners as to carrying fire about their gin-houses, also

dence contends that he can prove, from all the evidence in the case, that the other party must have known of it, no exception lies to its admission.[2] Actual knowledge of a usage which is general, need not be shown ; indeed, the party sought to be charged thereby may have in fact been ignorant thereof, but if the proof is such as to show a general and uniform usage of the trade, generally known to those engaged in it, it is sufficient to charge him with notice of its existence and to render it

the custom of the witness, if it be conformable to the general custom. *Maxwell* v. *Eason*, 1 Stew. (Ala.) 514. The fact being established that a barge was improperly loaded, the owner of the barge cannot excuse his liability by showing a usage to load barges in that manner, but proof of such a usage is evidence of the fact that such method of loading is proper, and its force cannot be overcome *except by clear proof that the loading was really improper and unsafe*, and it is for the jury to say whether the method of loading was really improper. *Stephens* v. *Tuckerman*, 33 N. J. L. 543. The doctrine of *Barber* v. *Brace*, 3 Conn. 9, may be thought to be opposed to the doctrine of the New Jersey case, and it may be, but it will be seen that, in this case, the shipping receipt stated that the goods were to be transported to the place of destination " at customary freight, dangers of the sea excepted," and the court held that, in the face of the written contract, parol evidence of an agreement as to the mode of stowage was not admissible, but that, in justification of the mode of stowage, it was competent to show a well-established commercial usage in that respect in order to show the real intention of the parties, and also for the purpose of repelling any imputation of neg-

ligence. The charge of the court, which was sustained on appeal, was that, " if a custom authorizing the stowage was satisfactorily proved, it repelled the imputation of negligence and mismanagement." But this instruction was predicated upon the ground that, in the absence of a special contract as to the mode of stowage, it must be presumed that the parties contracted in reference to the usage, and consequently that negligence could not be imputed, and this doctrine admits of no exception, for, that a well-established usage as to a certain business, is evidence of the intention of the parties contracting, without special provision as to the matters covered by the usage, is well established. *Coit* v. *Commercial Ins. Co.*, 7 Johns. (N. Y.) 385; *Parr* v. *Anderson*, 6 East 202; *Lethulier's case*, 2 Salk. 443; *Stultz* v. *Dickey*, 5 Binn. (Penn.) 287; *Inglebright* v. *Hammond*, 19 Ohio 337; *Sampson* v. *Gazzam*, 6 Port. (Ala.) 123; *Lebanon* v. *Heath*, 47 N. H. 353. In *City Bank* v. *Cutter*, 3 Pick. (Mass.) 414, it was held that where a bank had established a usage to regard a certain day as a holiday, such usage was binding upon all persons dealing with the bank who *knew* of the usage. See also *Shove* v. *Wiley*, 18 *Id.* 558.

[2] *Dodge* v. *Favor*, 15 Gray (Mass.) 82.

13

applicable to a given transaction within its scope, as much as though it had in terms been embodied in the contract,[3] but where the usage is *local*, something more than its uniformity and general application in a certain trade or business must be shown to charge a person who in fact has no knowledge of it.[4] The rule may be said to be that, if a usage is general, and applicable to a certain trade or business, and is not unreasonable or in conflict with the law, it is sufficient for a party invoking its aid to show that it is fixed and established in the trade or business to which it relates, and from such proof the law presumes that the parties contracted in reference to it.[5] This rule was well illustrated in a Massachu-

[3] *Mangum* v. *Farrington*, 1 Daly (N. Y. C. P.) 236; *Cooper* v. *Kane*, 19 Wend. (N. Y.) 386; *Bissell* v. *Campbell*, 54 N. Y. 353; *Stanton* v. *Small*, 3 Sandf. (N. Y.) 230; *Hinton* v. *Locke*, 5 Hill (N. Y.) 437 ; *Mackenzie* v. *Schmidt*, 22 Am. Law Reg. 448 ; *Hartshorne* v. *Ins. Co.*, 36 N. Y. 172 ; *McCready* v. *Wright*, 5 Duer (N. Y.) 571; *Chandler* v. *Belden*, 18 Johns. (N. Y.) 357 ; *Cope* v. *Dodd*, 13 Penn. St. 33; *Adams* v. *Pittsburgh Ins. Co.*, 76 *Id.* 411; *McMasters* v. *Penn. R. R. Co.*, 69 *Id.* 374; *McCarty* v. *Erie R. R. Co.*, 30 *Id.* 247. Evidence of a *usual* custom of trade is sufficient to affect a party with notice of it. *Whitesell* v. *Crane*, 8 W. & S. (Penn.) 369; *Watt* v. *Hoch*, 25 Penn. St. 411; *Adams* v. *Palmer*, 30 *Id.* 346; *Koons* v. *Miller*, 3 W. & S. 271.

[4] *Halford* v. *Adams*, 2 Duer (N. Y.) 471; *Sipperly* v. *Stewart*, 50 Barb. (N. Y.) 62; *Duguid* v. *Edwards*, 50 *Id.* 288.

[5] *Carter* v. *Philadelphia Coal Co.*, 77 Penn. St. 286; *Lewis* v. *Marshall*, 7 M. & G. 744; *McMasters* v. *Penn. R. R. Co.*, 69 Penn. St. 374; *Collings* v. *Hope*, 3 Wash. (U. S. C. C.) 149 ; *Koons* v. *Miller*, 3 W. & S. (Penn.)

371; *Helme* v. *Ins. Co.*, 61 Penn. St. 107; *Eyre* v. *Ins. Co.*, 5 W. & S. (Penn.) 116; *Hinton* v. *Locke*, 5 Hill (N.Y.) 437. A usage must be definite, uniform and well established, and established by clear and satisfactory evidence, so that it may be presumed that the parties had reference to it in making their contract. *Bowling* v. *Harrison*, 6 How. (U. S.) 259; *Oelricks* v. *Ford*, 23 How. (U. S.) 49; *Trott* v. *Wood*, 1 Gall. (U. S.) 443 ; *Pierpont* v. *Fowle*, 2 W. & M. (U. S.) 24; *McGregor* v. *Insurance Co. of Penn.*, 1 Wash. (U. S. C. C.) 39; *Martin* v. *Delaware Ins. Co.*, 2 Wash. (U. S. C. C.) 254; *Collings* v. *Hope*, 3 Wash. (U. S. C. C.) 149; *Strong* v. *Carrington*, 11 Am. L. R. 287. When a custom is so proved as to leave no doubt of its existence, it becomes a part of the law, and the court will so declare it without requiring it to be again proved. *Consequa* v. *Willings*, Pet. (U. S. C. C.) 225. A usage or custom will be admitted to ascertain the nature and extent of contracts not arising from express stipulations, but from implications, presumptions and acts of an equivocal character. *The Reeside*, 2 Sumn.

setts case,[6] in which a contract was made in Boston with a

(U. S.) 567. And see *Sunday* v. *Gordon*, 1 Bl. & H. (U. S.) 569. Or to ascertain the true meaning of particular words in a given instrument, where those words have various senses; but it will not be admitted to control, vary or contradict a written and express contract. *McGregor* v. *Insurance Co. of Penn.*, 1 Wash. (U. S. C. C.) 39; *Union Bank* v. *Forrest*, 3 Cr. (U. S. C. C.) 218. Where an established and well-known usage exists in a particular trade, in regard to the storage of a general ship, a shipper is chargeable with notice of it, and is deemed to have assented thereto, unless he give special instructions on the subject. *Baxter* v. *Leland*, 1 Blatchf. (U. S. C. C.) 526. The local usage of a particular foreign port will govern as to the time of delivery under a bill of lading. *Higgins* v. *United States Mail Steamship Co.*, 3 Blatchf. (U. S. C. C.) 282 ; S. P. *Broadwell* v. *Butler*, 6 McLean (U. S.) 296. A charter-party for the transportation of a cargo, prescribing no mode of storage, tacitly refers to the established and known usage of the trade. *Lamb* v. *Parkman*, 1 Spr. (U. S. C. C.) 343. In *Howard* v. *Great Western Ins. Co.*, 109 Mass. 384, on the trial of an action for a loss under a policy written here, between parties residing here, upon a vessel for a voyage from Hamburgh to Cardiff and thence to Hong Kong, contained a warranty that to load more than her registered tonnage with coal, which the underwriters defended on the ground of a breach of the warranty, in that she was loaded at Cardiff beyond her registered tonnage with a substance called patent fuel, the judge refused the plaintiff's request

for a ruling that whether patent fuel was coal within the meaning of the policy was to be determined by the usage at Cardiff, and ruled that if the plaintiff relied on a commercial usage to the effect that it was not so, the usage must be shown to have been known to the parties at the time of their contract, or so generally known that it might fairly be presumed to have contracted with reference to it, and the ruling was sustained.

[6] *Star Glass Co.* v. *Morey*, 108 Mass. 576. In *Mixer* v. *Coburn*, 11 Met. (Mass.) 559, which was an action for goods sold and delivered, a usage of trade that where glass is sold in boxes the risk of broken glass is on the buyer, is competent evidence. In *Loveland* v. *Burke*, 120 Mass. 139, it was held competent for a carrier, in defence to an action for injury to goods in their delivery by the breaking of the requisite apparatus, to show a local usage that such apparatus is to be furnished by the consignee of the goods. In *Putnam* v. *Tillotson*, 13 Met. (Mass.) 517, in an action for shoes sold to a distant purchaser, evidence was held admissible to show that where shoes are ordered it is the usage and course of the shoe business, when no special mode of conveyance is named by the purchaser, for the manufacturer to take the shoes to Boston, at his' own risk and cost, and there deliver them to some regular line of packets running to the purchaser's place of business, and take duplicate bills of lading, and forward one of them to the purchaser by mail, and that from that time the delivery is complete and the purchaser takes the risk of loss.

manufacturer of window glass in Philadelphia, for the purchase of from him of glass to be by him manufactured. The
purchaser referred for a designation of the sizes of the glass,
and as the basis of prices, to printed cards, issued by the
manufacturer without special reference to the Boston market. The glass, as ordered, did not prove of the sizes desired by the purchaser, nor comply with the standard of
measurement in Boston, although it was of the sizes designated in the cards, according to the standard of measurement
in Philadelphia. The court held that the usage as to the
standard of measurement in Philadelphia must prevail in
the absence of any provision in the contract to the contrary.
A similar rule was adopted in an earlier case,[7] in which it
was held, in an action between a manufacturer of window
frames and a dealer in them, on an issue whether the former
should pay freight on frames sold and delivered by him to
the latter, that evidence of a usage between manufacturers
and dealers in the place where the goods were made and sold,
that the manufacturers should pay the freight, was admissible and controlling. A usage that has grown up under the
law may be defeated by a change in the law that affects the
subject matter of the usage. Thus, a Washington banker
received deposits from a customer, partly in "coin" and
partly in "treasury notes," at a time when both were looked
upon as currency; and the depositor, after the passage of the
legal tender act, drew for "coin" for a portion of his deposit
exceeding the coin deposited after the passage of that act, and
the check was paid in coin. He afterwards drew for "coin,"
the balance of his coin deposited before the legal tender act,
and coin was refused, and notes, made legal tender by act of
congress, tendered him instead. Suit was brought to recover
the market value of the coin drawn for; and the plaintiff
offered evidence to show "that the usage and mode of dealing uniformly used and practiced by all the banks and bank-

---

[7] *Howe* v. *Hardy*, 106 Mass. 329.

ers of the District of Columbia, was in all cases when the deposit was made in coin, to pay checks in coin, if requested, otherwise in currency." It was held that such evidence was rightly excluded.[8] In order to establish the fact that a person has taken possession of vacant land, it is competent to prove that the claimant took such measures as are *usually* taken for that purpose, as that he drove stakes, marked with his initials, around the exterior lines of the lot, and that this is the usual mode of taking possession of such lots.[9] So,

[8] *Thompson* v. *Riggs*, 5 Wall. (U. S.) 663. In some instances, where rights have grown up under a statute or charter, although the statute or charter is subsequently repealed, the rights acquired will be upheld as usages having all the force of local common law. Thus, in Massachusetts, by an ordinance of 1641 the common law was altered as to that colony, so that all proprietors adjoining the sea were vested with the title to the soil to low water mark, but not beyond that distance where the tide ebbed beyond that point. *Gray* v. *Bartlett*, 20 Pick. (Mass.) 186; Wood on Nuisances, 101 ; *Stover* v. *Freeman*, 6 Mass. 435. This ordinance was afterwards annulled, but the courts, have ever since upheld the right *as a usage having all the force of a local common law*. Wood on Nuisances, 101; *Sale* v. *Pratt*, 19 Pick. (Mass.) 191; *Austin* v. *Carter*, 1 Mass. 231; *Barker* v. *Bates*, 19 Pick. (Mass.) 255; *Com.* v. *Charleston*, 1 *Id.* 186. And this ordinance has been assumed and acted upon in Maine, upon the same ground. *Lapish* v. *Bangor Bank*, 8 Me. 85; *Emerson* v. *Taylor*, 9 *Id.* 43; *Moore* v. *Griffin*, 20 Me. 350. So, too, in these States under this ordinance and the usages that have grown up under it, is held that it is the point at which the tide

ebbs the lowest, and not the average or common tide, which is to be taken as low water mark. *Stover* v. *Freeman*, 1 Mass. 231; *Sparhawk* v. *Bullard*, 1 Met. (Mass.) 95. In Connecticut, Rhode Island, Pennsylvania and New Jersey similar local customs exist, under which the courts have upheld the rights of riparian owners to wharf out to low water mark. *Chapman* v. *Kimball*, 9 Conn. 168; *East Haven* v. *Hemingway*, 7 *Id.* 186; *Martin* v. *Waddell*, 18 N. J. L. 186; *Ball* v. *Slack*, 2 Whart. (Penn.) 539; see Wood on Nuisances, 101; also, chapter on Navigable Streams, 605–653, particularly p. 647; also, Angell on Tide Waters, 225, where the author says, "from that time (1641) to the present an *usage* has prevailed which now has the force of a local common law, that the owner of land bounded on the sea or salt water shall hold to low water mark, as provided by the terms of the ordinance," meaning the ordinance previously referred to.

[9] *Cook* v. *Rider*, 16 Pick. (Mass.) 186. In an action involving a question as to whether piers in New York are properly constructed, evidence that piers in Boston are similarly constructed is not admissible. *Hill Mfg. Co.* v. *Providence, &c., Steamship Co.*, 125 Mass. 292. Neither is evi-

where a railroad company is sued for freight lost from its warehouse, evidence that the company used such care as is usually exercised by railroad companies in the care of such freight, is admissible, not absolutely to excuse the company from liability, but as tending to show that it exercised *reasonable* care, which is all that the law requires.[1] Where a statute prescribes the rights of parties in certain cases, a usage that extends such rights is invalid. Thus, evidence that prisoners entitled to the privilege of the jail yard, in the county of Suffolk, had been accustomed, from the time when such limits were established, to go to certain places between low-water mark and the thread of the river, as being within the bounds of the fifth ward, was held incompetent to control the construction of the statute and of the return of the selectmen, all the proceedings being recent.[2] Where public officers perform similar duties, the fact that most of them perform them

dence of the practice of other towns on the issue as to whether a certain place or construction constitutes a defect. *George* v. *Haverhill*, 110 Mass. 506; *Raymond* v. *Lowell*, 6 Cush. (Mass.) 524; *Kidder* v. *Dunstable*, 11 *Id.* 342. But in an action against a town for a defect in a highway, evidence as to the ordinary condition of similar ways in other towns is admissible upon the question as to whether the *plaintiff* was in the exercise of due care when the injury occurred. *Raymond* v. *Lowell*, ante; *Packard* v. *New Bedford*, 110 Mass. 134. But in order to be admissible it must be shown that the plaintiff *knew* of such practice in other towns. *Schoonmaker* v. *Wilbraham*, 110 Mass. 134; *Hinckley* v. *Barnstable*, 109 *Id.* 126. So in an action for an injury resulting from an injury because of the breaking of a block and chain, it was held that the plaintiff might show that it is a usual thing for a block and chain on any derrick to

break when in use. *Reilley* v. *Rand*, 123 Mass. 215. But where the act is clearly negligent, the defendant cannot be allowed to excuse himself by showing that others engaged in the same business are also negligent in the same respects. *Miller* v. *Pendleton*, 8 Gray (Mass.) 547; *Lewis* v. *Smith*, 107 Mass. 334; *Bailey* v. *New Haven, &c., Co.*, 107 *Id.* 496.

[1] *Cass* v. *Boston & Lowell R. R. Co.*, 14 Allen (Mass.) 448; *Same* v. *Boston & Albany R. R. Co.*, 112 *Id.* 455. But see *Lichtenstein* v. *Boston & Prov. R. R. Co.*, 11 Cush. (Mass.) 70, where in an action against a warehouseman for the non-delivery of property which had been fraudulently taken from their custody, and no negligence on their part was claimed to exist, it was held that the plaintiff could not show that it was *usual* among other warehousemen to take a receipt for property delivered.

[2] *Trull* v. *Wheeler*, 19 Pick. (Mass.) 240.

in a certain manner does not have any tendency to show that those performing them in a different manner have not properly performed them, or that those performing them according to such usage have properly performed them.[3] As stated elsewhere, a usage that deprives a person of his property or services without compensation, is invalid. Thus, in an action against an officer for the storage of property attached by him and left on the premises of the plaintiff, it was held that the evidence of other officers was not admissible to show that in similar cases, no charge for storage had ever been made to them.[4] Where there are several tenants of a building, who have contracted to pay the taxes, it is competent for the landlord to show a usage in such cases, to apportion the taxes among the several tenants according to the amount of rent paid by each.[5] The fact that a certain act is very unusual has no tendency to show that it was not done in a particular case.[6] A usage can be invoked to interpret a contract directly contrary to the terms employed therein. Thus, a warranty in an insurance policy, that a vessel is neutral, cannot be shown by a usage to that effect, to mean that she was not so, but only pretended to be,[7] nor upon the ordinary sale and delivery of property, can it be shown by usage, that no title thereto passes without payment of the consideration within a certain number of days, as such a usage is unreasonable,[8] as also is a usage to treat a fixture as personal property.[9] So, too, a usage that the master of a vessel has no authority in a foreign port to bind his owners for necessaries

[3] *Cutter* v. *Howe,* 122 Mass. 541; *Shattuck* v. *Woods,* 1 Pick. (Mass.) 171; *Williams* v. *Powell,* 101 Mass. 467.

[4] *Fitchburgh R. R. Co.* v. *Freeman,* 12 Gray (Mass.) 401.

[5] *Codman* v. *Hall,* 9 Allen (Mass.) 335; *Amory* v. *Melvin,* 112 Mass. 83.

[6] *Rennell* v. *Kimball,* 5 Allen (Mass.) 356. Where evidence is offered of a special contract which is legal and made by competent parties, proof that it is not the custom to make such contracts is clearly incompetent. *Goodfellow* v. *Meegan,* 32 Mo. 280; *Lane* v. *Bailey,* 47 Barb. (N. Y.) 395.

[7] *Lewis* v. *Thacher,* 15 Mass. 431.

[8] *Haskins* v. *Warren,* 115 Mass. 514.

[9] *Richardson* v. *Copeland,* 6 Gray (Mass.) 436.

furnished, contradicts a well settled rule of maritime law of universal application, and is, therefore, illegal and void.[1] Shippers of goods by rail are bound to take notice of a usage to store them, and cannot excuse themselves from liability for the expenses thereof by setting up ignorance of the usage.[2] The usages of trade and their office in determining the rights and liabilities of parties, in contracts to which they are applicable, is well illustrated in a New York case.[3] In that case, the contract between the parties was in writing. By it the plaintiffs were to furnish the material for the plastering work of the defendant's house and do the work of laying it on. The defendant was to pay them for doing the work and the material a certain price per square yard. The total of the compensation was to be got at by measurement. But the parties differed as to the measurement. The plasterers claiming the right to charge for the full surface of the walls, without deduction for cornices, base boards, or openings for doors or windows, in accordance with a usage of the trade, and the court held that the usage was reasonable. Folger, J., said, " It is not to be said of this contract that it was so plain in its terms that there could be but one conclusion as to the mode of measurement by which the number of square yards should be arrived at. It is in this case as it was in *Hinton*

---

[1] *Bliss* v. *Bapes*, 9 Allen (Mass.) 339. But a usage by the owners of vessels at particular ports to pay bills drawn by masters for supplies furnished to their vessels in foreign ports, cannot bind them as acceptors of such bills. *Bowen* v. *Stoddard*, 10 Met. (Mass.) 375.

[2] *McCarty* v. *New York and Erie R. R. Co.*, 30 Penn. St. 347; *McMasters* v. *Pennsylvania R. R. Co.*, 69 *Id.* 374. In an action on a receipt of a quantity of corn in store " on freight," it is competent for the defendant to prove a custom of the place, which had continued forty years, to pay for corn so left, after the owner had ordered it to be freighted, and not before, and that this custom was known to the plaintiff, and that he had been in the habit for many years of leaving grain at the same place, to be freighted on the same terms. *Outwater* v. *Nelson*, 20 Barb. (N. Y.) 29. A local custom at one port, regulating the mode of delivering goods there, is not binding on shippers at another port, unless known to them. *The Albatross* v. *Wayne*, 16 Ohio 513.

[3] *Walls* v. *Bailey*, 49 N. Y. 467.

v. *Locke.*[4]   There, the work was done at so much per day. The parties there differed as to how many hours made a day's work—that is, what should be the measurement of the day. And there, evidence of the usage was admitted, not to control any rule of law, nor to contradict the agreement of the parties, but to explain an ambiguity in the contract. And the proof showing a usage among carpenters that the day was to be measured by the lapse of ten hours, it was held a valid usage, and the contract was interpreted in accordance with it. In *Ford* v. *Tirrill*[5] the contract was to build the wall of an octangular cellar at the rate of eleven cents a foot, and the only question was as to the measurement. The defendant contended that the *inner* surface of the wall should be the rule. The plaintiff claimed that an additional allowance should be made for the necessary work at the angles, to support the building. It was held that the agreement as to the compensation was equivocal and obscure, and that it was competent to prove a local usage of measuring cellar walls in order to interpret the meaning of the language, and to ascertain the extent of the contract. So in *Lowe* v. *Lehman,*[6] in a contract to furnish and lay up brick at so much a thousand, the controversy was as to the proper mode of counting. Evidence of a local usage to estimate by measurement of the walls and a uniform rule, based on the average size of brick, making slight addition for extra work and wastage, deducting for openings in the wall, but not for openings in chimneys, nor for caps, sills nor lintels, was admitted as not unreasonable.[7]

---

[4] *Hinton* v. *Locke,* 5 Hill (N. Y.) 437. But see *Jordan* v. *Meredith,* 3 Yeates (Penn.) 318, where such a usage was held unreasonable.

[5] *Ford* v. *Tirrill,* 9 Gray (Mass.) 401.

[6] *Lowe* v. *Lehman,* 15 Ohio St. 179.

[7] In *Jordan* v. *Meredith,* 3 Yeates (Penn.) 318, a usage of plasterers to charge for the full surface of walls, deducting *one-half* the size of the windows therein, was held unreasonable and void. But in *Pittsburgh* v. *O'Neil,* 1 Penn. St. 342, it was held that a usage to compute the number of bricks laid in a pavement by allowing so many to the square yard, was reasonable, and might be proved by the testimony of the parties. But *quere*—Cannot it be shown that the materials so estimated could not *possibly* have been used in the work? *Hill* v. *McDowell,* 14 Penn. St. 175; *Symonds* v. *Lloyd,* 6 C. B. N. S. 691.

Where a corporation has for a long period exercised certain powers that would not be lawful without the existence of a by-law conferring them, but there is no record thereof, or evidence of its existence except such as arises from such usage, the court will, from such usage, infer that such a by-law exists delegating such 'powers. Thus, the Mercers Company was one of the ancient guilds of the city of London, and by a charter of the 17 Ric. II. the commonalty of the company were empowered to elect annually four wardens out of the commonalty. From 1391 to 1463 the practice was for the outgoing wardens to appoint their successors. From 1463 to the present time, a select body had existed under the name of the court of assistants, who held their offices for life and supplied vacancies in their own body by self-election out of the whole commonalty. The court of assistants had, since 1463, always elected the wardens from the commonalty of the company, and, of late years, exclusively from among the members of their own court. No instance was to be found of wardens having ever been elected by the commonalty at large. It was held that this usage was sufficient to warrant the inference of a by-law delegating to the court of assistants the power of electing wardens; and that such a by-law was valid, notwithstanding that it limited the right of election to a select and self-elected portion of the whole body.[8] As all usages are presumed to be predicated upon honest and fair dealing, it follows as a matter of course, that a usage that is unjust, inequitable or unfair in its operations, is unreasonable and consequently void.[9] Therefore, in the absence of an agreement to that effect, where property of a specific kind is deposited with another for a special purpose, a usage that permits the bailee to sell the property and replace it by

---

[8] *Regina* v. *Powell*, 25 Eng. L. & Eq. 53.

[9] *Coleman* v. *Chadwick*, 80 Penn. St. 81; *Evans* v. *Waln*, 71 *Id.* 69; *McMasters* v. *Penn. R. R. Co.*, 69 *Id.*

374; *Horner* v. *Watson*, 79 *Id.* 242; *Holmes* v. *Johnson*, 42 *Id.* 159; *Pittsburgh Ins. Co.* v. *Dravo*, 2 W. N. C. (Penn.) 194.

other property similar in kind and quality is held to be void.
So in New York[1] it has been held that a custom to sell stocks,
&c., deposited as collateral security for a debt, upon failure
of the debtor to pay the principal debt, is unreasonable and
void. But in Pennsylvania a custom of brokers to sell stocks
deposited as collateral for a call loan, is valid ;[2] and if such
custom is uniform and well established, there can hardly be
a question but that the doctrine of the latter case is correct,
as every person who employs a broker is presumed to know
of all their *general* customs and usages, and to contract in
reference to them.[3] In fact, every person dealing in a particular trade is presumed to be familiar with its *usual* customs.[4] A custom that real estate brokers are paid a per cent-
age for their services is valid and binding.[5]

Usage Explaining Contract.

SEC. 95. In *Robertson* v. *Jackson*,(a) where it was stipulated in the charter party that the ship should be unloaded,
weather permitting, at a certain rate per diem, to reckon
from the time of the vessel being ready to unload and "in
time to deliver," it was held that the charterers had a right
to prove that the contract was entered into with reference to
a known and recognized use of the words, "in time to
deliver," among persons conversant in the trade. The principle was given effect to in another case,(b) in which, by
charter party, the defendant agreed to load on board a vessel
at Trinidad "a full and complete cargo of sugar, molasses
and
or other produce." It appeared that it was the custom at
Trinidad to load sugar in hogsheads and molasses in pun-

---

[1] *Wheeler* v. *Newbold*, 16 N. Y. 392.

[2] *Colkert* v. *Ellis*, 1 W. N. C. 246.

[3] *Whitehouse* v. *Moore*, 13 Abb. Pr.
(N. Y.) 142.

(a) *Robertson* v. *Jackson*, 2 C. B.
412; 15 L. J. C. P. 28; see also
Schultz v. *Liedemann*, 14 C. B. 38; 18

[4] *Whitesell* v. *Crane*, 8 W. & S.
(Penn.) 369.

[5] *Inslee* v. *Jones*, Bright (Penn.)
76.

Jur. 42; 23 L. J. C. P. 17.

(b) *Cuthbert* v. *Cumming*, 10 Exch.
809; affirmed 11 Exch. 405.

cheons, in which mode they were carried more conveniently and with less loss to the merchant, and that a full and complete cargo of sugar and molasses meant a cargo so packed; it was held, both in the Court of Exchequer and Exchequer Chamber, that the custom was admissible in evidence, for it was applicable to such a charter party, and did not control, but only explained the contract, which ought to be construed with reference to the usage at the port of lading; and it was further decided that the custom was reasonable and good in law.

Undefined Words in Contract—Usage Eking Out Meaning—No Ambiguity.

SEC. 96. In another case which fell within the principle of that last referred to, the plaintiffs sold to the defendant "50 tons best palm oil, expected to arrive" "per the *Chalco*," "at £40 10s. per ton," "net duty, and inferior oil, if any, at a fair allowance." The oil on arrival was found to contain only one-fifth of the best oil, and the defendant refused to accept, whereupon the plaintiff brought his action. It was a question as to what was the intention of the parties, and it was taken that in entering into the contract, they had purposely left undefined what was to be the proportion of "wet, dirty and inferior oil." As Erle, J., remarked, "They were both engaged in the palm oil trade, and would be aware that there was great doubt as to the proportions of good and inferior oil in each cargo; and, therefore, they may well have made the contract on the understanding that such portions should not be specified." There was one established usage in the palm oil trade as to what proportions would satisfy a contract to deliver "best" palm oil, and evidence of this usage was admitted to explain what was left undefined in the contract.(c) So where, by a contract made at S., between A., who resided in that place, and B., who resided in London, B. sold to A. a cargo of St. Giles Marias

(c) *Lucas* v. *Bristowe*, E. B. & E. 907.

wheat, free on board at a French port. The grain was unknown at S., but was shown to be known elsewhere in the trade to contain a mixture of barley. But, although such evidence was offered at the trial, the judge refused it, unless it could also be shown that the fact was well known at S. This ruling was held to be erroneous.(d) In all these cases we have seen usage explaining or eking out the meaning of written contracts. In all it might be presumed that the usage which was admitted in evidence was present to the minds of the parties at the time they contracted. The very nature of the contracts led to the presumption. Still there was nothing which was palpably ambiguous, and if there had been no custom the contracts could in most of the cases have been read without bringing about any absurdity in meaning, without the interpolation of the terms which these usages had the effect of adding. Thus, " pitch pine timber " might have been understood as a general term applicable to all kinds of that wood which comes from Central America, and as inclusive of that of even Darine, and not limited to the meaning that the phrase had at Savannah. " Weekly accounts " might have been understood as meaning accounts for the extra as well as the days' work, and so with the rest.

Ambiguity Introduced by Usage—Where Usage Can Arise— Unusual Contract.

SEC. 97. In most of the cases there was no patent ambiguity upon the face of the contract; it is only a knowledge of the usage which introduces the doubt as to what was really meant. Under these circumstances, we confess we scarcely understand the decision in *Cockburn* v. *Alexander*.(e) In that case it appeared that a ship was chartered to bring home a cargo of wool, tallow, bark and other legal merchandise. The bark was not to exceed 50 tons, the tallow and hides not to exceed 80 tons, and " to deliver the same on being paid freight as follows : for wool, one penny-halfpenny

(d) *Ryder* v. *Woodley*, 10 W. R. 294.   (e) 6 C. B. 791 ; 17 L. J. C. P. 74.

per pound, and one penny-halfpenny and one-eighth of a
penny per pound impressed," for the other three articles
separate rates were fixed, and the captain was to sign bills of
lading at any rate of freight without prejudice to the charter-
party.   The ship returned with a full cargo, consisting of a
small portion only of wool, and the residue tallow, bark,
hides and other legal merchandise.   Now, here it was held
that there was no ambiguity upon the face of the charter-
party to admit parol evidence for the purpose of showing
who was to pay for pressing any wool that might be shipped.
The Chief Baron (Wilde) used these words in the course of
his judgment: "There being nothing, therefore, on the face
of the contract to raise any doubt or ambiguity that requires
to be removed or explained, it is not a case in which parol
evidence was admissible."(*f*)   But might not such proof
have been written into the written contract without making
it nonsensical or inconsistent with itself, and is not that the
true test of its admissibility?   Does not the knowledge that
there was such a usage in this case, just as in the others,
introduce an ambiguity from the fact that the written contract does not say enough?   To us there seems nothing in
the nature of this contract which should have been regarded
as impliedly excluding such proof.   We can quite understand that such an implication may arise.   We know that it
is only in trades which have a settled course of business that
usages can exist; if, therefore, a transaction, even although
in the course of such a trade, deviated from the ordinary
course of that trade—if it was unusual in any of its incidents,
then the presumption that the parties had been acting in the
light of ordinary custom would not arise, but a presumption
of a contrary nature would be the ruling thought.   This
principle has been given effect to.   A., a ship broker,
engaged with a ship owner to have a full cargo for the
ship, the rates of freight for which would average 40*s*. per

(*f*) 6 C. B. 813.

ton, and at least nine cabin passengers, passage-money to average £75. The contract was fulfilled as to the cabin passengers, but the average rate of freight for goods put on board by A. amounted to 32s. only per ton; he shipped on board, however, several steerage passengers for the voyage, the passage-money paid by whom, after deducting the expense of their diet, &c., when added to the freight of the cargo properly so called, made the average earnings of the whole ship per ton amount to more than 40s. It was held that as the contract was an unusual one, the evidence was not admissible to show that the terms "cargo" and "freight" used with reference to the voyage on which the ship was engaged would, by the general usage and course of the trade, be considered to comprise steerage passengers and the net profit arising from their passage money.(g) Before leaving the subject of glossarial usages, as they might be called, we may mention the case of *Bowman* v. *Horsey*,(h) in which it was decided that evidence of usage of trade is admissible to show the meaning of ambiguous words in a packer's receipt of goods.

When Usage is Referred to in Contract.

SEC. 98. Where by the express terms of a contract a certain mode of performance is provided, but the contract also refers to and makes the usage or custom of a certain locality a part of the contract, proof of the usage or custom is admissible, although it provides another and different mode of performance from that provided by the express terms of the contract, because in such a case the usage cannot be said to be repugnant to the express terms of the contract, but rather

(g) *Lewis* v. *Marshall*, 7 M. & G. 729. In the report of the case the editors have added the following note: "In construing as *usual* mercantile contract the question would seem to be—In what sense have the terms been used in similar contracts?

In the case of an *unusual* contract— Have the terms acquired any (and what) peculiar meaning in general mercantile language or in the particular trade?" Page 745.

(h) 2 M. & Rot. 81.

to provide an alternative mode of performance, leaving it optional with the parties to take the performance according to the usage, or according to the mode named in the contract. Thus, in a Connecticut case[6] the plaintiff, as master of a whaling ship, made a voyage under shipping articles as follows : "And the owners of the ship New England hereby promise, upon the fulfilment of the above conditions, to pay the shares of the net proceeds of all that shall be obtained by the crew during the voyage, agreeably to the shares set against their respective names, *as soon after the return of the voyage as the oil,* or whatever else may be obtained, *can be sold and the voyage made up* by the owner or agent of said ship. * * * *And the parties further agree to be subject to the usages and customs of the port of New London* in reference to this agreement." The ship returned to New London May 30th, with a full cargo of whale oil and bone, but although the cargo was discharged, weighed and gauged before the 15th of June but was not sold, and was held by the owners for an increased price, and they refused to pay the petitioner his share (one-fifteenth), because the cargo was not sold, and because, under the contract, the share was not to be paid until sold, &c. August 12th following, the plaintiff brought this petition in equity, praying for an account and the payment of his share. The plaintiff claimed that by the custom of the port of New London he was entitled to be paid his share in money, estimating the unsold cargo at its market value, or to have it apportioned, and his share allotted to him as soon as the vessel was discharged and the cargo measured and weighed, and was not bound to wait until the oil was sold. The custom was found as claimed by the plaintiff. It was claimed by the defendants that evidence of the custom was not admissible, and could not control, because a different mode of settlement and payment was provided by the contract. But the court held otherwise, Storrs, C. J., in

[6] *Smith* v. *Lawrence*, 26 Conn. 467.

delivering the opinion of the court saying, " We think that the evidence adduced by the plaintiff to prove a custom and usage prevailing at the port of New London when the agreement between these parties was made * * was admissible, *and that the plaintiff is entitled to have his rights determined by it.* It was one of the stipulations of that agreement that the parties should be subject to the usages and customs of that port in reference to the subject of that agreement. It is found that originally the shipping articles for voyages like that in which the plaintiff was engaged were substantially like that in the present case, except that they did not contain any clause in reference to the payment of the captain and crew after the oil was sold, and that then it was the general practice to apportion and deliver to them respectively their share of the oil and bone specifically," and then he traces the change in the custom until it became as shown by the plaintiff. " The principal objection made as to the proof of this custom is, that it is variant from and contradictory to the clear terms of the written agreement between these parties in regard to the mode in which the plaintiff should be paid for his services. It is plain that, whether such a custom as is here shown could affect the agreement in this case if it constituted no part of the express contract between the parties, but was introduced as usages usually are, for the purpose of expounding the agreement, is a point which it is unnecessary for us to decide, because the custom here shown constitutes a part of the express contract between the parties. It is expressly referred to in the stipulation which has been mentioned respecting it, and, therefore, is to be deemed a part of that stipulation, as much as if it was set forth in terms in the written agreement. And if we suppose that the custom is recited therein in terms, all difficulty on this point vanishes. It requires no authority to show that it might be made a part of that agreement as well by reference as by recital. Now, if the custom were described in

14

terms, would it be repugnant to or inconsistent with the rest of the contract? It is only a modification or qualification of the preceding stipulation in the contract, in regard to the mode in which the plaintiff should be paid for his services, and providing for a different mode in the exercise by him of the option reserved to him on that subject,—an alternative promised to perform a certain act, or, at the option of the promisee, a certain other act, or perhaps rather, to do the same thing in one mode, or another, at the option of the promisee." But some of the courts are inclined to hold, that even where a usage is referred to and adopted as a part of the contract, it cannot be permitted to overcome the presumption that the parties contracted in reference to the general law, if there is even a slight indication of an intent appearing in the instrument corroborating such presumption. And especially is this so if the contract expressly refers to certain usages but not to the usage attempted to be enforced. In a Massachusetts case[7] it was held to be the general law that in adjusting a partial loss on a ship, which has been repaired, the proceeds of the old materials not used in the repairs, are first to be deducted. The underwriters claimed, in virtue of a local usage at Boston, where the policy was issued, that they had the right of deducting one-third new for old from the gross amount of the expense of repairs. The policy was according to a form which had been recently adopted by all the insurance companies at Boston, and contained express reference to certain usages of the Boston insurance companies, but none in respect to this. There were some stipulations in the policy touching partial losses, which, however, were aside of the point designed to be established by the usage. The question as to the general law relative to this question had been settled in New York, and for several years before the policy was issued, had been pending in the Massachusetts court. The court rejected the usage, saying,

[7] *Eagar* v. *Atlas Ins. Co.*, 14 Pick. (Mass.) 14.

" From these and other circumstances, the presumption is strong that the parties did not treat as to the mode of adjustment on the basis of usage, but on that of the existing law, however it might be decided. *When the contract refers to the customs and rules* of insurance in Boston, and specifies how far they shall constitute a part of the contract, it must be inferred that the parties did not intend it should be affected thereby, and the extent specified, especially as the form of the policy was settled with great care and deliberation." The court also added another reason why the usage should not be received, which was, that the contract being one of indemnity, the usage was opposed to the *essence* of the contract.

Ordinary Parol Evidence and Usage—Rules as to Usage.

SEC. 99. With a view of showing the distinction which exists between ordinary parol evidence and evidence of usage, we think it well to prefix two cases in which the admissibility of the former in relation to written records of transactions has been the subject of judicial decision. In an action of assumpsit by the drawer against the acceptor of two bills of exchange payable respectively six and twelve months after date, the plea set forth an agreement (not stated to be in writing) between the plaintiff and the defendant, by which, before the making of the bills, it was agreed that the defendant should be discharged from all liability in an action commenced against him by the plaintiff on a promissory note on his paying the plaintiff the costs of such action, and a certain sum of money, and accepting the bills of exchange in question—in case the plaintiff should recover in another action brought by him against another party, on a promissory note given under similar circumstances to the defendants, and that until he should so recover, or if he should not so recover, he should not call for payment of the bills of exchange, and the plea averred that the defendant accordingly paid the costs and money agreed for, and accepted the

bills of exchange in question, and that the action against
such third party was still undetermined, it was held on
demurrer that the plea was bad in as much as the defendant
could not vary the absolute contract entered into by the bills
of exchange by a contemporaneous oral contract inconsistent
with it.(*i*) Here, then, we have a direct authority, and

(*i*) *Adams* v. *Wordley*, 1 M. & W.
374; see *Menzies* v. *Lightfoot*, 19 W.
R.578; 11 L. R. Eq. 459; 4 L. J. Chan.
561. In *Wheeler* v. *Newbold*, 16 N. Y.
39, an action was brought to recover
the amount of certain notes, &c.,
deposited by the plaintiff with the
defendant as collateral security for a
loan. The defendant offered to
prove a custom for persons holding
such collaterals to sell them at private sale, within a reasonable time
after the debt became due, after
notice that such sale would be made.
The evidence was held inadmissible.
In *Higgins* v. *Moore*, 34 N. Y. 417, an
action was brought to recover the
price of grain sold by the plaintiff to
the defendant through a broker in
the city of New York. The defence
was that the defendant had paid the
broker the price, and offered evidence of a custom in the city of New
York for persons buying to pay the
broker, when the seller lives out of
the city. The Court of Appeals held
that this evidence was not admissible. "In this case," said *Peckham*,
J., "the law defined the rights and
duties of this broker as clearly as did
those of the pledges of stock in *Allen*
v. *Dykers*, 7 Hill (N. Y.) 497, or of
choses in action in *Bowen* v. *Newell*,
8 N. Y. 190, and they could no more
be controlled by usage." "It is
obvious," said *Wright, J.*, in the
same case, "that the rights of the
parties cannot be controlled or
affected by a *local* usage in a particu-

lar trade found by the referee. The
usage is invalid, and has no binding
force upon the plaintiff for various
reasons. It being the law of the
State that a broker in general has
no authority to sell in his own name,
and therefore no authority to receive
payment for goods sold by him,
*a local custom like that found by the
referee* to exist in the city of New
York was void. Such a usage, if
sanctioned, would be to overthrow
the law in the city of New York. If
it prevails there as the referee found
it, it cannot be allowed to control
the settled and acknowledged law of
the State." The position taken by
the court in this case is wholly
untenable, and without a valid
reason. The idea that because by
the common law existing in New
York a broker has no authority to
sell in his own name, and consequently no authority to receive payment for goods sold by him, a usage
that vests him with that authority is
invalid, is preposterous. Is there
any doubt but that the defendant
might have excused himself from
liability by showing that the plaintiff had recognized such usage in
numerous similar transactions with
the same broker, which were known
to the defendant? Would not the
court, under such a state of facts,
have been compelled to say that,
notwithstanding the rules of law in
that respect, the plaintiff had impliedly conferred authority upon the

although the evidence tendered in that case was not of a usage but of another contract, the rule and principle are the same in both cases. Thus, where A., a broker, employed by B. to sell certain railway shares, agreed with C., D.'s broker, to sell him fifty shares, of which A. afterwards informed his clerk at his office, who made an entry in the book as of a sale from A. to C., and a contract note to the same effect was sent to C. A. subsequently saw the entry in the book and altered it by writing the name of B. as seller. Another note was accordingly sent the same evening or the next morning to C., but C. received them both together the next morning. C. did not return the first note, nor did A. request to have it returned. In an action brought by D. against A. for breach of the agreement in not completing the sale, the learned judge who tried the cause left it to the jury to say whether the second note was a correction of a mistake in the first, and told the jury that if the defendant entered into a written contract in his own name, he could not afterwards set up that he was acting as a broker merely, and that although known to be a broker, if he signed the contract in his own name, he was liable, and it was held that this was no misdirection, and further that evidence that it was the custom in Liverpool to send in brokers' notes without disclosing the principal's name, was properly rejected.(*k*)

broker to receive pay for him? And yet, such authority is derived entirely from a private usage between the plaintiff and his broker. Now, if a uniform usage in New York city, extending to all sales by brokers, existed in this respect, and was *known* to the parties, why should not such general usage have the effect to justify the defendant in paying the broker, as well as the private usage before referred to? In other words, Why may not the rules of law be impliedly waived by a uniform and well-known usage, as well as by an individual usage? If the one is invalid, why is not the other? (*k*) *Magee* v. *Atkinson*, 2 M. & W. 440. In *Thomas* v. *O'Hara*, 1 Const. Rep. (S. C.) 303, it was held that evidence of a trade to continue the insertion of advertisements, when no order is given respecting the time during which it shall be inserted, until directions to discontinue it is given, was admissible. But, in *Thomas* v. *Graves*, 1 *Id.* 310, it was held that a usage to charge for the continuance of an advertisement long after the object of it has on the

Classification—Principle of.

Sec. 100. We come now to a consideration of those cases in which incidents or terms have been added to written contracts by proof of usage. We have pointed out that the distinction which we have here made is one rather in fancy than in reality, but no other distinction seemed to offer hope of better method. The classification of the principles of admissibility of usage on the basis of the different trades or callings in which these factual laws were formed, or on the basis of the different instruments in the interpretation of which usages were admitted, had nothing to recommend it, although it has been adopted by Mr. Fisher in his " Digest." Indeed it was wrong in principle and misleading in result. The mere fact that the usages were in themselves different would be as intelligible a ground of classification as the one alluded to. There can be no reason for differentiating usages because the one explained the meaning of a technical word in a brewer's invoice, and the other another word of doubtful meaning in the bought and sold notes of a stock exchange transaction. It is the legal principles which are to determine the admissibility or inadmissibility of these in courts of law which ought to be made the ground of their associa-

face of it ceased, merely because its discontinuance has not been ordered, was held unreasonable and void. A usage among printers and booksellers, that a printer, contracting to print for a bookseller a certain number of copies, shall not print with the same types, while standing, an extra number for his own use, is reasonable, and not in restraint of trade. *Williams* v. *Gilman*, 3 Me. 276. And such would be the rule even were there no usage to that effect. The usages of a department of the government, in settling its accounts, are intended for general rules in the transaction of its business, but will be disregarded by the courts, whenever they operate unjustly upon individuals. *United States* v. *McCall*, Gilp. (U. S.) 577 ; see also *United States* v. *Duval*, Gilp. (U. S.) 372. But a usage of the different departments of the government to allow commissions to the officers of government upon disbursements of money under a special authority, not connected with their regular official duties, may be proved, for the purpose of establishing the measure of such officers' compensation. *United States* v. *Fillebrown*, 7 Pet. (U. S.) 50.

tion in one class rather than their intrinsic difference as facts. There was therefore no really scientific classification possible. We proceed then to the statement of the principles of some of the decisions.

Usage Adding Incident—Contract Varied by.

SEC. 101. In the case of *Brown* v. *Byrne*,(*l*) which was an action for freight by a shipowner against the indorsee of a bill of lading, to whom goods had been delivered at Liverpool, and who had accepted them, the bill of lading making them deliverable, "he paying freight for them five-eighths of a penny sterling per pound, with £5 per cent. primage and average accustomed," it was held that evidence was admissible, that by the custom of Liverpool the shipowner was entitled to a deduction of three months' discount from the freight, though such custom applied only to goods coming from ports in the Southern States of America. In this case we find that a term not expressed in the bill of lading is added to it by the custom of Liverpool. Some see the apparent terms of a contract varied in *Spartali* v. *Benecke*,(*m*) where in a contract for the sale of thirty bales of goats' wool, containing the following stipulation : "Customary allowance for tare and draft to be paid for by cash in one month, less 5 per cent. discount," evidence was allowed to show that by a usage of trade vendors are not bound under similar contracts to deliver wool without payment, and it was said that such a usage sought to annex to the contract an incident not inconsistent with its terms.

Of Corporations, Acts not Conformable to Charter.

SEC. 102. A corporation which is authorized to contract in

(*l*) 3 E. & B. 708; 18 Jur. 700. Where the master of a vessel received skins to be carried from New Orleans to New York, there to be delivered in good order, dangers of the seas excepted, and the skins were injured by rats, it was held that evidence of mercantile usage and understanding that injuries by rats are considered and treated as perils of the sea, was not admissible. *Aymar* v. *Astor*, 6 Cow. (N. Y.) 266.

(*m*) 10 C. B. 212.

a certain way, by a course of practice adopted by it, render themselves liable upon instruments executed or contracts made in a different way. Thus, where the charter of an insurance company provides that "all policies signed by the president, or in his absence by the assistant, *and counter-signed by the secretary*, shall be binding on the company," and the company had adopted a practice of issuing policies without their being countersigned by the secretary, the company cannot escape liability upon that ground, for having established a usage in this respect different from that pre-scribed by law, however improper in itself, yet they cannot avail themselves of their own wrong to avoid the contract.[8] So it has been held the National and other banks, which have been accustomed to receive bonds and other valuables for safe keeping, and this is known to and acquiesced in by the directors, thereby become liable for its loss through its gross negligence or carelessness, although such deposit is not authorized by its charter.[9]

Time of Payment—Usage Vary by Time of Payment—Cases Reconciled.

SEC. 103. Again, in *Field* v. *Lelean*,(n) evidence of a usage amongst brokers that on the sales of mining shares the seller is not bound without contemporaneous payment was held admissible to show that the defendant was not enti-tled to have the shares which he had bought from the plain-tiff delivered to him before payment, although by the bought and sold notes payment of the price was to be made, half in two, half in four months, and nothing was there said as to

---

[8] *Bulkly* v. *The Derby Fishing Co.*, 2 Conn. 353.

[9] *Chattahooche National Bank* v. *Schley*, 58 Ga. 369; *Foster* v. *Essex Bank*, 17 Mass. 479; *Smith* v. *First National Bank of Westfield*, 99 Mass. 605; *Lancaster County National Bank* v. *Smith*, 62 Penn. St. 47; *Turner* v. *First National Bank of Kekokuk*, 26 Iowa 562; *First National Bank* v. *Graham*, 79 Penn. St. 106. *Contra*, see *Wiley* v. *National Bank of Brattle-boro*, 47 Vt. 546; *Whitney* v. *National Bank of Brattleboro*, 50 *Id.* 389.

(n) 30 **L. J.** Exch. 168; Exch. Cham. 6 H. & N. 617.

the time of delivery.(o) In that case it was argued that the case of *Spartali* v. *Benecke*(p) was directly in point in favor of the defendant, and Williams, J., in his judgment said, "It may be observed that in that case, although the written instrument of sale was *mutatis mutandis*, the same substantially as in the present, the usage relied on was different. In the present it was simply that the delivery is to take place at the appointed time for payment, and not before. In *Spartali* v. *Benecke*, the usage relied upon was that the delivery was to be at the option of the buyer, and that he might require it at any time before the appointed day of payment, but in no case without payment of the price. Therefore, it was a case where I apprehend that Wildè, C. J., in his judgment treated the usage as varying the time for payment expressed in the statement of the contract; inasmuch as according to that usage, the delivery intended by the contract might take place so as to give the seller a right to call for payment before the time specified in the written instrument. But according to the usage proved in the present case, no delivery can be required or is intended to take place before that time arrived. If *Spartali* v. *Benecke* cannot be distinguished in this way, I agree it ought to be overruled."

Warranty Modified by Usage.

SEC. 104. Again, where a horse had been sold by private contract at a repository with a written warranty of soundness, and the purchaser afterwards brought an action against the seller on account of the unsoundness of the horse. The defendant was permitted to show that by one of the printed regulations hung up at the repository, warranties were only to remain in force till twelve o'clock on the day after the sale, and then upon further proof that the plaintiff was aware of this regulation, and yet made no complaint within the limited time, a nonsuit was directed to be entered.(q)

(o) *See Godts* v. *Rose* 17 C. B. 229. E. 508; see *Smart* v. *Hyde*, 8 M. &
(p) 10 C. B. 212; 19 L. J. C. B. 293. W. 723; *Foster* v. *Mentor Life Assur-*
(q) *Bywater* v. *Richardson*, 1 A. & *ance Co.*, 3 E. & B. 48.

Proof of Usage to Establish a Warranty.

SEC. 105. The question as to whether or not a usage of a certain trade can be shown to establish a warranty as to the quality, soundness or condition of goods sold, without a warranty, and under such circumstances that none can be implied, has been variously decided in our courts.[1] But, whatever may formerly have been held in this respect, it may be regarded as reasonably well settled that *a warranty cannot be imported into a contract upon the sale of property, by proof of a mere local usage of the trade, when the effect would be to contravene or override a well-settled rule of law,* unless it was known by both parties and the contract was made in reference thereto. This question is quite important, and it may be advisable to review the cases briefly. In an early New York case[2] the question was as to the effect of a

---

[1] In *Boorman* v. *Jenkins*, 12 Wend. (N. Y.) 566, a contrary doctrine was apparently held. See also *Cassidy* v. *Begoden*, 6 J. & Sp. (N. Y. Superior Ct.) 180. But it will be observed that these cases merely hold that evidence of a usage among cotton dealers is admissible to show that a sale by sample implies a warranty, and in this respect there is no conflict with the rules of law. In *Lebanon* v. *Heath*, 47 N. H. 453, evidence of a usage of a plan that substitute brokers were understood as warranting that the substitute was not a deserter, of which usage the defendant knew, was held admissible, and sufficient to support an implied warranty that the substitute was not a deserter. The doctrine of this case cannot be said to conflict with the rule stated in the text, as the doctrine of *caveat emptor* did not apply to the contract. So in *Sumner* v. *Tyson*, 20 N. H. 384, a doctrine in opposition to that stated in the text was held. In that case it was held

that evidence of a usage of manufacturers of iron castings to warrant the quality of the articles made by them, without an express contract to that effect, is admissible, and if established is sufficient to uphold an action for a breach of warranty. In an early Pennsylvania case—*Snowden* v. *Warden*, 3 Rawles (Penn.) 110—it was held that evidence of a usage among cotton dealers in Philadelphia, to regard a sale of cotton as accompanied with a warranty against latent defects, although there was neither a warranty or fraud in the sale. But the judgment in this case was dissented from by *Gibson, J.,* and in later cases before the same court a contrary doctrine has been held. *Coxe* v. *Heisley*, 19 Penn. St. 243; *Wetherell* v. *Neilson*, 20 Id. 448.

[2] *Thompson* v. *Ashton*, 14 Johns. 316. In *Bogert* v. *People's Bank*, 16 Hun. (N. Y.) 270, it was held that proof of a usage or custom as to what acceptances were understood to be in the commercial community

local usage, or the usage of a certain trade, upon a contract for the sale of goods without a warranty. In that case the plaintiff purchased a quantity of crockery of the defendants, in New York city, and upon trial he offered to show, to establish a warranty, that it was the custom of merchants engaged in the purchase and sale of crockery to sell on the invoice without an examination of the contents of the crates in which it was packed, and that it was the uniform understanding that the exhibition of the invoice amounted to an undertaking on the part of the sellers that the wares were good and merchantable. The court rejected the evidence and nonsuited the plaintiff, and upon a motion to set aside the nonsuit the court held that no custom in the sale of any particular description of goods can be admitted to control the general rules of law applicable to such contracts. In a later case a similar doctrine was held by the Court of Appeals. In that case the transaction also arose in New York city, and the action was brought to recover for an alleged breach of warranty[3] in the sale of a quantity of blankets. The plaintiff offered evidence to show that there was a custom among those dealing in blankets to sell by sample, without opening the bales; but if, upon opening the bales, the blankets were found defective, it was usual for the seller either to make an allowance to the purchaser or take them back. The court held that the doctrine of the case of *Thompson* v. *Ashton*, ante, applied in this case, and that a warranty could not be established by a usage of trade, contrary to the general rules of law. In Massachusetts this question has been before the court upon several occasions, and the rule previously stated adopted. In one case[4] a quantity of satinets was sold in cases. The sale was made by sample, and both in the sample and the goods sold there

of New York was inadmissible to establish an implied warranty, the acceptances being valid and no express warranty having been made

in reference to them.
  [3] *Bierne* v. *Dodd*, 5 N. Y. 95.
  [4] *Dickinson* v. *Gay*, 7 Allen (Mass.) 29.

was a latent defect not discoverable upon inspection, nor until the goods were printed. The consequence was that the goods were unmerchantable. It was claimed that by the usages of the trade there was an implied warranty that the goods were merchantable. The court held that a custom importing a warranty into a contract, where by law none could be implied, was contrary to the rules of the common law upon that subject, and therefore void. In a later case[5] the question was again before the court. In that case a quantity of goat skins—forty bales—were sold by a broker, who, without authority from the principal, put into the memorandum of sale the words, "to be of merchantable quality and in good order." In order to establish the authority of the broker to insert such a warranty into the memorandum of sale, it was claimed that by custom of the trade there was, in all sales of such skins, an implied warranty that they were of merchantable quality; but the court held that such a custom was invalid. Says the court: "It contravenes the principle which has been sanctioned and adopted by this court upon full and deliberate consideration, that no usage will be legal or binding upon parties which not only relates to and regulates a particular course or mode of dealing, but *which also engrafts on a contract of sale a stipulation or obligation which is inconsistent with the rules of the common law upon that subject.*" In a case before the United States Supreme Court[6] this question was reviewed in a careful and able manner. In that case, A., a dealer of wool, in Boston, sent to B., a dealer of wool, in Hartford, Conn., samples of foreign wool in bales, which he had for sale on commission, with the prices thereof. B. offered to purchase the lot at the prices named if equal to the samples sent him. A. accepted the offer, *provided*, B. would come to Boston and examine the wool, and say whether

[5] *Dodd* v. *Farlow*, 11 Allen (Mass.) 426. See also, *Haskins* v. *Warren*, 115 Mass. 514.

[6] *Barnard* v. *Kellogg*, 12 Wall (U. S.) 383.

THE USAGES OF TRADE, THEIR OFFICE.

he would take it. B. accordingly went to Boston, and after having examined a number of bales, and being offered an opportunity to examine the balance and to have them opened for his inspection, which he declined; he purchased the wool. It turned out that the wool, unknown to A., was deceitfully packed, and proved to be rotten and damaged wool, with tags concealed therein, with an outer covering of fleeces in their ordinary state. It was held that this was not a sale by sample, and that, as there was neither an express or implied warranty that the bales not examined should correspond with those which were, the rule of *caveat emptor* applied, and consequently, that proof that by a custom among dealers in wool in bales in New York and Boston, the two principal markets in this country for the sale of foreign wool, there is an implied warranty of the seller to the purchaser, that the same is not falsely or deceitfully packed, is not admissible, *especially, when the parties did not know of the custom.* "It is apparent," said Davis, J., "that the usage in question was inconsistent with the contract which the parties chose to make for themselves, and contrary to the wise rule of law governing the sale of personal property. It introduced a new element into their contract, and added to it a warranty which the law did not raise, nor the parties intend it to contain. The parties negotiated on the basis of *caveat emptor,* and contracted accordingly. This, they had the right to do, and by the terms of the contract the law placed on the buyer the risk of the purchase, and relieved the seller from liability for latent defects. But this usage of trade steps in and seeks to change the position of the parties, and to impress on the seller a burden, which the law said, on making his contract, he should not carry. By this means, a new contract is made for the parties, and their rights and liabilities under the law essentially altered. If the doctrine of *caveat emptor* can be changed by a special usage of trade, in the manner proposed, by the custom of dealers in wool in

Boston, it is easy to see that it can be changed in other particulars, and, in this way, the whole doctrine frittered away." But the learned judge evidently mistook the office of a usage. A usage is never admissible to add *new* terms to a contract, or to make a *new* contract for the parties, *but rather to show what contract was in fact made by the parties, and what their real intention was as to the obligations to be assumed,* and it strikes us as exceedingly erroneous to say that a usage may not be shown, the effect of which is to raise an implied obligation, or add incidents to a contract which the law does not impose, simply because the law does not impose the obligation. If the contract is made relative to matters about which there is a well defined usage, and there is no reasonable doubt that the parties contracted in reference to it rather than in reference to the law, according to that golden rule of interpretation that the *intention* of the parties shall be given effect to if possible, it would seem that the usage might be shown. Upon what principle, or by what process of accurate reasoning, can it be said that the parties may not, by a well settled and known usage, annex an implied obligation of warranty to their contracts? We cannot doubt but that, notwithstanding the loose talk of the courts in some of the States,[7] to the effect that a usage cannot be shown that contravenes the general law, or adds incidents to contracts not raised by the law, that even those courts, would, as was intimated by Davis, J.,[8] hold that parties who *knew* of such usage at the time the contract was entered into, where the usage is shown to be uniform and certain, feel bound to hold that a warranty might be raised thereby. A contrary rule would be repugnant to that sound and well established rule of construction *that requires that the intention of the parties to a contract shall be ascertained and given effect to,* and to that end permits a resort to extrinsic contemporaneous cir-

[7] Massachusetts, New York and Pennsylvania; see cases cited in previous notes to this section.

[8] *Barnard* v. *Kellogg,* ante.

cumstances. In other words, that requires the court to place itself as nearly as possible in the situation of the parties to the contract, and in that light to say what their real intention was. Indeed, in Pennsylvania,[9] where the courts have had considerable to say about usages being inadmissible where they conflict with the general law, and where the courts have held that a warranty cannot be raised by a usage of trade,[1] it has been held that the custom among merchants in Pittsburgh to charge interest on accounts after six months, *having existed for a long time and become uniform and notorious,* had thereby so far become a part of the law that the courts were bound to notice it. So, too, in a later case, the same court holds that the usage and practice of a firm, though not good as a custom, will be binding, if expressly made a part of the contract, *or shown to have been known and assented to* by the person sought to be affected by it, at the time a transaction to which it was applicable was entered into, and that evidence of such a contract, *either direct, or by proving a course of dealing between the parties on such terms, and of such frequency as to justify the inference that the transaction was on the accustomed terms,* is admissible.[2] In Massachusetts,[3] in a case where a note was left with a bank in Boston for collection, and the bank, *conformably with the usage in Boston,* gave notice to the maker *before* the note became due of the day when the note would be payable, and requested him to call and pay it on that day, and the note remained in the bank through banking hours on the day when it became due, it was held that, *if the maker was a trader, and accustomed to transact business at the bank, his consent to the general usage which made such notice sufficient might be shown,* and if shown, rendered any other notice immaterial, and the correctness of this doctrine cannot be questioned. The rule is, as established, both upon principle and by authority, *that*

---

[9] *Watts* v. *Hoch,* 25 Penn. St. 411.
[1] *Cox* v. *Heisley,* 19 Penn. St. 243; *Witherill* v. *Neilson,* 20 *Id.* 448.

[2] *Hursh* v. *North,* 40 Penn. St. 241.
[3] *Warren Bank* v. *Parker,* 8 Gray (Mass.) 221.

evidence of a usage, reasonable, uniform and certain, known to the parties to a contract in reference to the subject matter to which it relates, enters into *and forms a part of such contract, whether in writing or by parol, unless expressly excluded,* as much as though it had been inserted therein,[4] and this too, although its effect is to add incidents to the contract that the law would not otherwise raise.[5] There would seem to be no good reason why a usage, that in the sales of certain kinds of property there is a warranty as to quality, &c., should not be good. Such a usage does not conflict with the law, but simply raises an obligation where the law does not. Can it be said that the doctrine of *caveat emptor* is so sacred that it cannot be encroached upon, except by special contract? We apprehend not, as implied warranties are raised in multitudes of instances, and it would seem that the policy of the law is not trenched upon by admitting a usage to secure the same result, and certainly this is permitted in some of the States. In New Hampshire,[6] it was held that evidence of the usage of a place was admissible to show that a substitute broker, who furnished substitutes for parties, was understood as warranting that the substitutes furnished by him were not deserters, and from that a warranty would be implied. In an earlier case in the same State, it was held that evidence of a custom among manufacturers of iron castings to warrant the quality of the articles made by them, without an express con-

---

[4] *Inglebright* v. *Hammond,* 19 Ohio 337; *Stultz* v. *Dickey,* 5 Binn. (Penn.) 287; *Hursh* v. *North,* ante; *Barber* v. *Brace,* 3 Conn. 9; *Sampson* v. *Gazzam,* 6 Port. (Ala.) 123; *Bank of Columbia,* 1 H. & G. (Md.) 239; *United States* v. *Arredondo,* 6 Pet. (U. S.) 715; *Haven* v. *Wentworth,* 2 N. H. 93.

[5] *Hursh* v. *North,* ante; *Goodnow* v. *Parsons,* 36 Vt. 46; *Steward* v. *Scudder,* 24 N. J. L. 96; *Munn* v. *Burch,* 23 Ill. 35; *Perkins* v. *Jordan,* 35 Me. 23; *Wayne* v. *Steamboat Gen. Pike,* 16

Ohio 421; *Van Ness* v. *Packard,* 2 Pet. (U. S.) 137; *Foster* v. *Robinson,* 6 Ohio St. 90; *Wilcox* v. *Wood,* 9 Wend. (N. Y.) 346; *Alabama R. R. Co.* v. *Kidd,* 29 Ala. 221; *Leach* v. *Beardslee,* 22 Conn. 404; *Cooper* v. *Kane,* 19 Wend. (N. Y.) 386; *Dixon* v. *Dunham,* 14 Ill. 324; *Shaw* v. *Mitchell,* 2 Met. (Mass.) 65; *Naylor* v. *Semmes,* 4 G. & J. (Md.) 274; *Loring* v. *Gurney,* 5 Pick. (Mass.) 15; *Thompson* v. *Hamilton,* 12 *Id.* 425.

[6] *Lebanon* v. *Heath,* 47 N. H. 453.

tract to that effect, was admissible in an action founded on such supposed warranty.[7] The real difficulty about the establishment of a warranty by usage, is the fact that the *prima facie* presumption that the parties contracted with reference to the law rather than the usage, but if the usage and the parties' knowledge of it is established, and there is no provision of the contract that excludes it, it is difficult to see how the courts can exclude it and yet carry into effect the intention of the parties. In England, the rule is, that usage is admissible to show that in the sale of certain articles there is an implied warranty as to quality, or that the words used by commercial usage indicate a certain quality. Thus, in a case[8] where the plaintiff sold to the defendant " fifty tons best palm oil, expected to arrive per the Chalco, at £40 10s. per ton ; curt, dirty and inferior oil, if any, at a fair allowance," and the oil, on arrival, contained only *one-fifth* best oil, whereupon the defendant refused to accept it, it was held in an action to recover the price of the oil, that evidence was admissible to show that by mercantile usage, the contract was satisfied if the oil delivered contained a substantial portion of best oil, and that the question as to whether the usage existed and was met in this case was for the jury. So, where a contract was made,[9] by which the plaintiff sold the defendant, " deliverable in London, ex Ion, from Savannah, 400 loads of pitch-pine timber, the timber warranted of fair average quality, to be taken of fair average of the cargo." Evidence was given that pitch-pine timber is an article which comes from several ports in Central America, and that pitch-pine timber from Darien has more heart in it, being better butted and having fewer holes in it than that from Savannah. It was held that this evidence was admissible to explain the contract and determine the quality of timber to be delivered under it, and that from it the contract must be construed as

---

[7] *Sumner* v. *Tyson,* 20 N. H. 384.   [9] *Jones* v. *Clark,* 2 H. & R. 725.

[8] *Lucas* v. *Bristow,* El., Bl. & El. 907.

for timber of a fair average of Savannah pitch-pine.[1] In another English case,[2] a contract was made at S., by a person residing in London, to sell to a person residing in S., a cargo of St. Giles Marius wheat, free on board, at a French port. The grain was unknown at S., but is known elsewhere in the trade to contain a mixture of barley. Upon the trial at Nisi Prius, evidence of this usage as to the mixture of the grain was rejected, because it was not shown that it was known at S., but upon a motion for a new trial, it was held that if the existence of the usage was proved, it was binding upon both parties, whether in fact known at S. or not.

[1] See also, *Gorrssen* v. *Perrin*, 2 C. B. N. S. 29, where evidence of a usage was admitted to show that on a contract for the sale of bales of gambier, expected to arrive by a particular ship, a bale of gambier is understood as containing two hundred pounds pressed in a particular way.

[2] *Ryder* v. *Woodley*, 10 W. R. 294, Q. B.

CHAPTER V.

USAGES, THEIR OFFICE IN SPECIAL INSTANCES.

As to Amount of Payment—Years as Understood in Theatrical Profession—In Relation to a Charter Party.

SEC. 106. Where there was a custom that the yearly hiring of a clerk is determinable by a month's notice at any time, it was held that such a custom was not inconsistent with a provision in the agreement, that at the end of the year the employer, if satisfied with the amount of business done, would make an addition of £30 to the stipulated salary.(a) Where the agreement in writing contained these words, "to serve B. from 11th Nov., 1815, to 11th Nov. 1817," at certain wages, "to lose no time on our account, to do our work well, and behave ourselves in every respect as good servants," it was held that it was capable of explanation by usage in the particular trade for servants, under similar contracts to have certain holidays and Sundays to themselves.(b) And in a somewhat similar case where the plaintiff had agreed in

(a) *Parker* v. *Ibbetson*, 4 C. B. N. S. 346; 27 L. J. C. P. 236.

(b) *Reg.* v. *Stoke-upon-Trent*, 5 Q. R. 303; see *Phillips* v. *Innes*, 4 Cl. & Fin. 234.

writing to perform at the defendant's theatre, and the defendant agreed to engage her for three years, and pay her a certain weekly salary, evidence was admitted to show that there was a uniform usage in the theatrical profession, that payment was only to be made during the theatrical season, or only during the time that the theatre was open to the public in each of those three years.(c)   Upon a charter party engaging to pay £4 15s per ton for goods shipped at Bombay for London, cotton to be calculated at 50 cubic feet per ton, evidence tendered upon the part of the defendant that there was a usage to pay according to the measurement taken at Bombay before the goods are loaded was held admissible. In this case, too, the plaintiff was allowed to show, in reply, that his captain had objected to receive the goods at Bombay measurement; measured them when on board; and delivered an account of that measurement to the shippers.(d)

Effect of Usage on Liability of Carrier.

SEC. 107. In an action against a carrier for negligence in the method of storing or carrying freight, proof of a usage or custom in that respect, in conformity with the method adopted by the carrier, is admissible to repel any charge of negligence or mismanagement in the absence of an express contract as to the mode of carriage, and in such cases where the contract is silent in that respect, a custom or commercial usage sufficiently ancient and general as to warrant such a presumption, enters into and forms a part of the contract, and both parties are bound by it.[1]   Thus, where a quantity of gin, in hogsheads, was put on board the defendant's sloop to be transported from Hartford to Boston at customary

(c) *Grant* v. *Maddox*, 15 M. & W. 737.
(d) See also *Benson* v. *Schneider*, 7

Taunt. 272; *Gould* v. *Oliver*, 2 Scott, (N. C.) 241.

[1] *Parr* v. *Anderson*, 6 East 202; *Coit* v. *Commercial Ins. Co.*, 7 John. (N. Y.) 385; *Crosby* v. *Fitch*, 12 Conn. 422. In an action for damages caused by the upsetting of a stage-coach, the defendant cannot prove the practice on his own line, but may prove a general custom as to the number of passengers conveyed. *Maury* v. *Talmadge*, 2 McLean (U. S.) 157.

freight, dangers from the sea excepted. The gin was stored on deck, and the weather being tempestuous was necessarily cast overboard. The plaintiff insisted that the defendant had no right to stow the gin upon deck, but should have put it in the hold of the vessel, and having failed to do so, although the *jettison* might have been justifiable, he was liable by reason of his negligence in trusting the freight on deck. The defendant proved that it was the usage of the trade between Hartford and Boston to transport gin on the vessel's deck, and the court held that such usage operated to exculpate the defendant from the charge of negligence.[2] But

[2] *Barber* v. *Brace*, 3 Conn. 9. A custom or usage, to be admissible and valid, must be certain, reasonable and sufficiently long continued to afford a presumption that it is generally known, or that the parties in fact knew of it. *U. S.* v. *Buchanan*, 8 How. (U. S.) 83; *Coxe* v. *Heisley*, 20 Penn. St. 246. It must be general and uniform, but need not be universally acquiesced in. *Desha* v. *Holland*, 12 Ala. 513; see *Maitland* v. *Ins. Co.*, 3 Rich. (S. C.) 331. And it may be established by the testimony of a single witness, if his means of knowledge are abundant, and his testimony full and satisfactory. *Vail* v. *Rice*, 5 N. Y. 156. The usage of a class or trade is good evidence to ground an argument of negligence in one belonging to it. *Sampson* v. *Hand*, 6 Whar. (Penn.) 311. Or to repel fraud or negligence. *Maxwell* v. *Eason*, 1 S. & P. (Ala.) 514; *Cook* v. *Champlain Trans. Co.*, 1 Den. (N. Y.) 92; *Bradford* v. *Drew*, 5 Met. (Mass.) 188; *Chenowith* v. *Dickinson*, 8 B. Mon. (Ky.) 156. And this is probably the true ground of *Barber* v. *Brace*, 3 Conn. 9. It may be stated as a general rule, that evidence that it is usual for people engaged in a

certain business to do a certain act, which amounts to negligence, is never admissible to excuse a person from the consequences of such act. In other words, the fact that negligence in certain respects is habitual in a certain business, does not excuse it. Thus, in *Miller* v. *Pendleton*, 8 Gray (Mass.) 547, an action against a ferryman for the loss of a horse and wagon by his neglect to put up the chain at the end of his boat, it was held that he could not give in evidence a custom at other ferries on the same river to put up the chain *at the request of passengers*, and not otherwise. In *Hill* v. *Portland, &c., R. R. Co.*, 55 Me. 438, the court held that the fact that all the railroads in the country had adopted a rule or custom which is unreasonable and dangerous, and productive of injury to third persons, would not legalize the act, and that the fact of its generality cannot in any degree excuse an act done in conformity with it. But while a usage cannot be admitted to excuse a person from the consequences of an act in fact negligent, yet such evidence is admissible upon the question as to whether or not the act *is* negligent, and the fact that it

while proof of a partial usage may be sufficient to shield a party from liability for negligence, because it has the effect

is generally adopted in a certain business, is a strong circumstance against the claim of negligence, because it shows what men of ordinary prudence do under similar circumstances. In *Myers* v. *Perry*, 1 La. An. 372, it was held that in the absence of any statutory regulation, an established usage among those engaged in navigating the Mississippi river with steamers must be considered in determining questions of fault or negligence in the management of steamers on that river. Indeed, such a usage may become a law of the business. Thus, in *Drew* v. *Chesapeake*, 2 Dougl. (Mich.) 33, it was held that a general custom of navigation, as, for vessels in passing to keep to the right, may be proved by the testimony of persons skilled in navigation; and if satisfactorily proved, such custom is a part of the law of the land, and a departure from it, occasioning collision, will render the party liable, unless the other party, by reasonable effort, might have prevented it. In *Bolton* v. *Calder*, 1 Watts (Penn.) 360, in an action for an injury by the collision of carriages passing in the same direction upon a highway, it was held that the defendant could not justify a forcible driving against the plaintiff's carriage by showing a custom for the leading carriage to incline to the right, and that the plaintiff did not conform to the custom. The reason why such a custom cannot operate as a justification, is, because the law requires persons traveling along the highway to pass without collision, *if possible*, and no custom which authorizes a person by negli-

gence or violence to injure another can have any validity. It is unreasonable, and, therefore, invalid. If a barge or other vessel was improperly loaded, the owners will not be discharged from liability for damages to the freight, because she was loaded as barges usually are, but such evidence is competent to show that for the safety of transportation, such method of loading was a proper and safe mode of stowing the load, and the force of the evidence must be overcome by proof that the method of loading was unsafe and improper; but it is, nevertheless, a question for the jury, whether the method of loading was safe or not. *Stepens Co.* v. *Tuckerman*, 33 N. J. L. 543. In *Cayzer* v. *Taylor*, 10 Gray (Mass.) 274, in an action against the owner of a steam-boiler for damages caused by its explosion, it was held that evidence was not admissible by the defendant to show that it was not customary to use the fusible safety plug which the statute required to be used. Nor to avoid the consequences of a negligent act, and as tending to disprove negligence on his part, is it competent to prove that the defendant is habitually careful and cautious. *Tenney* v. *Tuttle*, 1 Allen (Mass.) 185, but, when an attempt is made to prove that a person, through whose alleged negligence, an injury has occurred, it is competent to prove that he is careful, prudent, cautious, &c., and this may be proved by persons who have seen his conduct in discharging similar duties, and need not be proved by experts. *Gehagan* v. *Boston and Lowell R. R. Co.*, 1 Allen (Mass.) 187. If the station house

of showing that he did what prudent men often do under the same circumstances, yet nothing short of a well established general usage will be permitted to control in actions upon a contract. A general usage, unless excluded in express terms, or by fair inference is presumed to enter into and form a part of all contracts to which they relate, such as the usages of carriers, insurers, &c., but a partial usage cannot be said to enter into the contract, and evidence thereof, instead of showing what the actual intention of the parties was, operates to interpose a new contract for that already made.[3] In the case first cited in the last note, it was shown that the usual route from New York to Norwich, Conn., was through Long Island Sound, and that in an action for the loss of freight by reason of perils of the sea while pursuing another and more dangerous route, it was not competent for the defendant to show a usage for such vessels when the same is obstructed by ice, to perform their voyages on the south side of Long Island instead of waiting in New York until

of a railroad company is separated by a side track from a platform provided for passing to the trains, and there are no regulations or directions as to when or how passengers shall pass to them, the question whether a passenger is bound to wait in the station house until the arrival of a train at the platform, or may go to and stand on the platform during its approach, depends on what is a reasonably safe and prudent course for him to adopt; in determining which it is proper for a jury to consider what is the usage of passengers there, and whether such usage is known to and permitted by the company. *Caswell* v. *Boston and Worcester R. R. Co.*, 98 Mass. 194. A usage of a port that, in order to constitute a delivery of goods by a carrier by water, a receipt for them must be given to the carrier by the consignee or his agent, is a bad usage, and inadmissible as a defence to an action against the consignee for loss of the goods through his negligence. *Reed* v. *Richardson*, 98 Mass. 216.

[3] *Crosby* v. *Fitch*, 12 Conn. 410. Proof of a few instances, not amounting to a general practice, cannot be held to establish an usage. Uniformity is an essential requisite. *Martin* v. *Del. Ins. Co.*, 2 Wash. (U. S. C. C.) 254; *Lawrence* v. *Stonington Bank*, 6 Conn. 521; *Gabay* v. *Lloyd*, 3 B. & C. 793; *Gibson* v. *Culver*, 17 Wend. (N. Y.) 305. The usage of a particular port, for consignees, during the quarantine season, to receive shipments at the quarantine grounds, as a compliance with the engagement of the bill of lading, to deliver at such port, is valid and binding. *Bradstreet* v. *Heron*, 1 Ab. (U. S.) 209.

the usual navigation is free, unless such usage is shown to be general and of such long standing as to have become generally known.

Distinction Between Varying Contract and Adding Incident to.

SEC. 108. A few other cases will show under what circumstances evidence of this nature has been admitted, and the line between "varying" and "adding an incident," is so very fine and so difficult to discover, that the more cases which can be accumulated with reference to this question of admissibility the easier will it be for the practitioner to decide in any case whether a custom is admissible in evidence or not. We shall find that the courts have not been quite consistent as to this matter, and although we ought always to weigh and not count our authorities, still, the majority in such cases must rule, and it is important to ascertain what the real intention of the majority of the judges has been.[4]

[4] The statement in the text may be well illustrated by reference to the cases covering the effect of usages upon contracts of insurance. Thus, evidence of a local usage among insurers which is not communicated to the assured, or which is not so notorious as to warrant a presumption that he knew of it, is not admissible to affect the insurer's liability to the assured. *Hartford Ins. Co.* v. *Harmer*, 2 Ohio St. 452. But evidence of a local usage is binding upon the insurer, because he is presumed to be familiar with all the usages incident to a risk, which he assumes, as of the existence of a custom exempting the assured from providing a branch pilot in a certain coasting trade in which a vessel insured is employed. *Cox* v. *Charleston &c. Ins. Co.*, 3 Rich. (S. C.) 331. In an action on a policy where the claim was for damages sustained by perils of the sea, and on the arrival of goods at New York, they were landed before the wardens of the port had held a survey upon them, the defendants were not permitted to prove, either as an objection to the preliminary proofs, or in bar of the action, that, by the usage of trade in the port of New York, the master of the vessel is responsible for damages sustained by goods delivered by him to the owner or consignee, unless there has been an actual survey on board the vessel, by the port wardens, by which it shall have been found that the goods were properly stowed, and were damaged on the voyage by perils of the sea; and that, by a similar usage, as between assurers and assured, the survey so made must be produced, in order to charge the assurer, and that the preliminary proof is deemed insufficient, unless the survey is exhibited as a part of it. *Rankin* v. *American Ins. Co.*, 1

Usage Adding Incident.

SEC. 109. There is now no doubt that a usage is admissible to add an incident which is not inconsistent with the

Hall (N. Y.) 619. A usage of short continuance is entitled to little if any weight in the explanation of an insurance contract. *Wall v. East River Ins. Co.,* 3 Duer (N. Y.) 264. The rule being that to affect the liability of the parties it must be of such a character that the parties must be presumed to have known of its existence. *Rogers v. Mechanics' Ins. Co.,* 1 Story (U. S.) 603. So, too, it must be reasonable, and it has been held that evidence is not admissible of a custom that when insurance is made on goods with a particular mark, those goods, so marked, must be on board, in order to charge the underwriter with the loss. *Ruan v. Gardner,* 1 Wash. (Va.) 145. It is held that a usage may be shown for the purpose of explaining a clause of doubtful construction in a policy of insurance, it being, in such cases, the safest guide to the intention of the parties. But it can be resorted to only when the language or the law is doubtful or unsettled. *Winthrop v. Union Ins. Co.,* 2 Wash. 7; S. P. *Harris v. Nicholas,* 5 Munf. (Va.) 483; *United States v. Macdaniel,* 7 Pet. 1; *Murray v. Hatch,* 6 Mass. 477; *Coit v. Commercial Ins. Co.,* 7 Johns. (N. Y.) 385; *Allegre v. Maryland Ins. Co.,* 2 Gill & J. (Md.) 136; *Rankin v. American Ins. Co.,* 1 Hall (N. Y.) 619. Parol evidence of a custom cannot be received to show that a marine policy of insurance on goods shipped from New Orleans to Mobile, the language of which is plain and unambiguous, covers the overland transportation of the goods by railroad, because such a custom is ex-

cluded by the terms of the policy. *Smith v. Mobile Navigation &c. Co.,* 30 Ala. 167. Nor where, by the express terms of a policy, an insurance company is bound to pay the ascertained amount of loss sustained by the assured, "without any deduction therefrom," can the company set up a custom or usage on their part to retain, in case of total loss, out of the amount of the ascertained loss, two per cent. per month on the balance of the premium note, from the date of the last assessment thereon, until the expiration of the policy, as the effect of allowing proof of such custom would be to permit a usage to vary and limit the plain and unequivocal terms of an express written contract. *Swanscot Machine Co. v. Partridge,* 25 N. H. 369. Nor where a policy of re-insurance provides for an indemnity to the re-insured, and its terms are not ambiguous, can evidence of a local custom among insurers to pay only such a proportion of the loss as the amount of re-insurance bears to the original policy be received to control the contract, or reduce the amount of a recovery thereon. *Mutual Safety Ins. Co. v. Hone,* 2 N. Y. 235. A policy of insurance against fire, upon a vessel building in the port of Baltimore, and for a specified period, is not controlled in its operation by proof of usage in other parts of the Union; such usage not being considered as entering into the views of the parties in the contract. *Mason v. Franklin Fire Ins. Co.,* 12 Gill. & J. (Md.) 468. Under a policy on copper on board a vessel from New

writing, or that a usage cannot control the clear intention of the parties; but it is most difficult in many cases to say

York to Taunton, a quantity of copper in pigs was laden on deck, and was lost in Long Island Sound. It was held that the insurers were not liable for the loss, notwithstanding the existence of a usage to carry on deck without notice to the shipper, and at the same rate of freight as if under deck, such goods as were not liable to be injured by dampness, it not being proved that insurers had ever paid for losses upon goods so laden, unless under a special contract, or unless, from the nature of the property, they were presumed to have assumed the particular risk. *Taunton Copper Co.* v. *Merchants' Ins. Co.*, 22 Pick. (Mass.) 108. A general usage for the same species of vessels, in various kinds of navigation, and in different seasons of the year, to carry deck-loads, was held to be competent evidence, in ˜connection with the opinion of nautical witnesses, to show that, in fact, the risk was not increased by carrying cotton on deck. *Lapham* v. *Atlantic Ins. Co.*, 24 Pick. (Mass.) 1. In an action on a policy of insurance, which had been filled up and signed, but not delivered, and on which no premium had been paid, evidence of usage that such policies are considered as held for the benefit of the insured, is admissible. *Baxter* v. *Massasoit Ins. Co.*, 13 Allen (Mass.) 320. A commercial usage of long standing, such as that of adding the premiums to the invoice value, in cases of insurance, may be modified and controlled by a local usage, well sustained by proof, and shown by positive testimony or by circumstances to be known to the other

party. *Merchants' Mutual Ins. Co.* v. *Wilson*, 2 Md. 217. So, also, evidence is admissible to establish the fact of a recognized insurable interest upon their part in the goods. Thus in an action on a policy of insurance, that it is the usage of commission merchants in New York to effect insurance on goods consigned to them for sale, without any express orders from their consignors. *De Forest* v. *Fulton Fire Ins. Co.*, 1 Hall (N. Y.) 84. While evidence of usage is inadmissible to vary the application of plain terms in a policy of insurance where there is no ambiguity, or to add terms, conditions or limitations which the terms used clearly exclude—*Rankin* v. *Am. Ins. Co.*, 1 Hall (N. Y.) 619—yet it is admissible to explain words or clauses of doubtful import—*Daniels* v. *Hudson River Ins. Co.*, 12 Cush. (Mass.) 416—and they may be rendered doubtful by the introduction of extrinsic evidence. The rule may be said to be *that if words or phrases have, by usage, acquired a technical meaning variant from that in which they are ordinarily used, the meaning which they have acquired by usage may be shown, unless from the whole instrument it is evident they were used in their ordinary sense.* Wood's Fire Insurance 129; *Allegre* v. *Maryland F. Ins. Co.*, 2 G. & J. (Md.) 136; *Mobile &c. Ins. Co.* v. *McMillen*, 27 Ala. 77; *Bargett* v. *Orient &c. Ins. Co.*, 3 Bos. (N. Y.) 385; *Winthrop* v. *Union Ins. Co.*, 2 Wash. (Va.) 7; *Harris* v. *Nicholas*, 5 Munf. (Va.) 483; *Murray* v. *Hatch*, 6 Mass. 477; *Coit* v. *Commercial Ins. Co.*, 7 Johns. (N. Y.) 385; *U. S.* v. *McDaniel*, 7 Pet. (U. S.) 1; *Merchants'*

whether some particular custom is tacitly included in or tacitly excluded from a written document. This, of course,

&c. *Ins. Co.* v. *Wilson,* 2 Md. 217 ; *Lapham* v. *Atlantic Ins. Co.,* 24 Pick. (Mass.) 1 ; *Smith* v. *Mobile &c. Co.,* 30 Ala. 167. A contract of insurance may be created by usage. Thus, where application was made for insurance for not less than $10,000, and the defendant marked "binding" thereon, it was held that in order to establish a contract between the parties, evidence was admissible to show that a custom existed between the plaintiff and several other insurance companies, including the defendant company; in cases where the value of the property upon which insurance was desired was unknown when application was made, by which applications were made like the one in question, to the numerous companies, for insurance in sums amounting in the aggregate to what the plaintiff supposed might be the actual value of the property at risk, and that such applications were accepted and made binding for such indefinite sums, with the understanding that when the value of the property at risk should be ascertained the amount so insured by the companies should be declared and apportioned so that the amounts actually insured should bear the same proportion to the property actually at risk as they bore to the aggregate of all the indefinite insurance thereon, and that after the amount so ascertained had been fixed, a policy in the form then in use should be issued therefor—was held admissible, and also that it created a liability on the part of the defendant for a proportionate amount of the

loss to the amount insured, notwithstanding a clause contained in the policies used by the defendant to the effect that if the assured made any other insurance upon the property prior in date to the policy, the defendant should only be liable for so much as the amount of prior insurance might be deficient towards covering the loss. *Fabbri* v. *Mercantile &c. Ins. Co.,* 6 Lans. (N. Y.) 446. See also *Audubon* v. *Excelsior Ins. Co.,* 27 N. Y. 216. If it be shown, or may be fairly presumed, that the parties to a policy contracted in reference to a custom existing in the city where they did business, and where the policy was effected, the general law must give way to the custom. In case of partial loss on insured goods, a custom regulating the assessment of damages must be general, known and acted upon in the port, town or city where the policy is effected, and there is no necessity for its extending over the whole State. The custom in the city of Mobile to pay the difference between the sales price of the injured article and the price stipulated in the policy of insurance is binding between parties residing and contracting in that city. *Fulton Insurance Co.* v. *Milner,* 23 Ala. 420. In *Parsons* v. *Manufacturers' Ins. Co.,* 16 Gray (Mass.) 463, in an action upon a marine policy upon a vessel laden with guano at the Chinca Islands, it appeared that having stopped at Callao for a clearance, and then started on her homeward voyage, she sprung a leak and put back to Callao in distress, when it was found that a part of the guano

is a purely legal question. "We take it," said the court in a case already referred to, "that the acknowledged distinction is this: If the evidence offered at the trial by either party is evidence by law admissible, for the determination of the question before the jury, the judge is bound to lay it before them and to call upon them to decide upon the effect of such evidence when offered, whether that evidence is of that character and description which makes it admissible is a question for the determination of the judge alone, and is

had been so damaged by sea water that it was utterly worthless and could not be kept on board with safety to the vessel, and if it could have been landed the cost of drying it would have been greater than its value when dried, and it was thrown overboard. The rest of the cargo was necessarily discharged in order to repair the vessel, a freight paid thereon and it was transshipped by its owner into another vessel bound for a different port, and the vessel after being repaired, and by consent of its charterers, went back to the islands and took in another cargo of guano under the original charter, which she delivered safely at its port of destination. It was held that evidence that the course thus taken was the usual and prudent course for vessels in such a situation, and the testimony of an insurance broker, that in the adjustment of losses, under these circumstances, the usage had been to treat the usage as one and the same, and the substituted cargo as if it were the original cargo landed and re-shipped, and that before the date of the policy on the freight of this vessel, he had adjusted losses in one case, and he thought in others accordingly, were insufficient to prove a custom which would affect the rights of the parties; and that going back to the islands and taking in a cargo after the repairs of the vessel, must be treated as a *new* voyage and not a resumption of the old one. A custom that underwriters are not, under the ordinary form of policy, liable for general average respecting the jettison of goods stowed on deck, is valid, and is generally recognized. *Miller* v. *Tetherington*, 6 H. & K. 278; *Taunton Copper Co.* v. *Merchants' Ins. Co.*, 22 Pick. (Mass.) 108. But it is competent for the assured to show a usage for the same species of vessels in various kinds of navigation, and in different seasons of the year to carry deck loads, especially if the usage is supplemented by the testimony of nautical men, that in fact the risk is not thereby enhanced. *Lapham* v. *Atlas Ins. Co.*, ante. So it is competent to show a usage to carry certain kinds of property on deck, and insurers, unless expressly excepting against it, are liable for a loss although such goods are so stowed, because they are presumed to be familiar with and to contract in reference to this usage. *Taunton Copper Co.* v. *Mechanics' Ins. Co.*, ante.

left solely to his decision."(e)   Hence the importance of the following cases to members of the legal profession.   In the case of *Mackenzie* v. *Dunlop*,(f) it was decided that if A. gives an iron scrip order to B. and B. sells it to a third party, that third party may prove that the document has in the usage of trade an import not expressed on the face of it. Here, then, we have the general principle laid down in the House of Lords.   In *Lockett* v. *Nicklin*,(g) where it appeared that the defendant ordered goods by letter which did not mention any time for payment, and the plaintiff sent the goods and the invoice, parol evidence to show that the goods were supplied on credit, the letter not being a valid contract within the Statute of Frauds, was held to be admissible.   So where the plaintiff contracted in writing to build for the defendant the front and back walls of a house, "for the sum of 3s per superficial yard of work nine inches thick, and finding all materials, deducting for lights."   The lower part of the walls, to the height of eleven feet, was of stone two feet thick, the remainder of brick fourteen inches thick.   In this case it was held that evidence of the usage of builders at the place to reduce brick work for the purpose of measurement to nine inches, but not to reduce stone work unless exceeding two feet in thickness, was admissible, and that the proper construction of the contract was that it provided only for the price of the brick work, leaving the stone to be paid for on a *quantum meruit.*(h)

Weight of Usage.

Sec. 110. These principles are also shown in the case of *Fawkes* v. *Lamb*,(i) which is interesting as showing the

(e) *Lewis* v. *Marshall*, 7 M. & G. 729; see *Parker* v. *Ibbetson*, 4 C. B. N. S. 346. When the jury have decided on the meaning of the terms by the assistance of the usage, it is still for the court to construe the entire contract or document. *Hutchinson* v. *Bowker*, 5 M. & W. 5, 35, the judg-

ment in *Neilson* v. *Harford*, 8 M. & W. 806.

(f) 3 Macq. H. of L. Cas. 22; 2 Jur. N. S. 957; see also *Fox* v. *Parker*, 44 Barb. (N. Y.) 541.

(g) 2 Exch. 93.

(h) *Symonds* v. *Lloyd*, 6 C. B. N. S. 691.

(i) 31 L. J. Ex. 168; 8 Jur. N. S. 385.

254 USAGES, THEIR OFFICE IN SPECIAL INSTANCES.

greater weight of evidence of usage than that of any other species of parol evidence. There a written contract for the sale of goods was silent as to the time for which warehouse room rent was allowed by the seller to the purchaser, and it was held that it was competent to either party to show by parol evidence what time is allowed in such transactions by general custom, but that it was not competent to prove that the parties themselves agreed by word of mouth that certain time should be allowed.

Sales by Sample—Custom in Timber Trade.

SEC. 111. In an action for the price of tobacco sold, evidence is admissible to show that by the established usage of the tobacco trade all sales are by sample, although the bought and sold notes said nothing to that effect.(*k*) In another case, proof that by a custom of trade when timber is sold in bond at a sale by auction in London the buyer contracts to buy at a price including the duty payable, and he may, by giving notice on the following day so to do, elect to take the timber in bond, and if he does so he is then only bound to pay the price less the duty, was admitted under the following circumstances : On the 10th February, 1860, the defendant bought timber in bond at a sale by auction, at a price including the duty; the contract to be completed within fourteen days, and the Chancellor of the Exchequor, on the evening of that day, gave notice that a resolution would be moved in Parliament to reduce the duty on timber, and carried out that resolution on the 8th March. An act of Parliament passed to that effect on the 5th May, and the reduction of the duty was thereby made to date from the 8th March. On the 11th February the defendant gave notice to the seller that he elected to take the timber in bond, and on the 24th February offered the price less the then duty, which the seller refused to take, and he also refused to give a delivery order for the timber. He subsequently brought an

(*k*) *Syres* v. *Jones*, 2 Exch. 111.

action for the price of the timber, in which judgment was given for the defendant on the ground that the usage which was admitted added a term to the contract.(*l*)

Usage as to Measurement.

SEC. 112. In *Bottomley* v. *Forbes*,(*m*) which was an action upon a charter party for freight upon goods shipped at Bombay for London, stating that cotton was to be "calculated at five cubic feet per ton," a usage was held admissible to prove that the measurement was to be calculated when the cotton was taken from a screw at Bombay, though it appeared that it afterwards expanded considerably before it was put on board, and that it would have given a third measurement after it had been unloaded. In that case it was also shown on the part of the plaintiff that the captain of the vessel refused to receive the cotton according to the admeasurement it had after it left the screw; that he measured it when on board, and delivered an account of such admeasurement to the shippers. Here we find that not only was usage admitted to add an incident to a written instrument which was silent as to where the measurement was to be calculated, and which, to be full and explicit, ought, under the circumstances, to have given some indication as to the intention of the parties, but evidence that the captain had at the time refused to be bound by such usage, and had taken such steps as lay in his power to defeat the efficacy of the usage, were both properly admitted—the one on the one side, and the other on the other.[5]

Introducing Broker-Usage—Custom Unreasonable.

SEC. 113. Where the defendant, a ship owner, being desirous of chartering a vessel, and the defendant, a ship broker, introduced him to S., another broker, who intro-

---

(*l*) *Clark* v. *Smallfield*, 4 L. T. N. S. 405.

(*m*) 6 Scott, 816; 5 Bing. (N. C.) 121.

[5] See Sec. 95, ante.

duced him to L., who made known to B. that the charter
was wanted, and through the negotiations of B. with the
defendant D., chartered the vessel. The plaintiff sued for
commission, alleging that the "introducing broker" was
entitled by custom to a share of the commission. The
plaintiff's counsel in this case proposed to ask a witness
the question, "What is the custom with regard to payment
of broker's commission where a broker introduces another
broker to a ship owner, who subsequently negotiates with
the broker introduced?" and this evidence was rejected, the
court held it was properly so.(n)   Bramwell, B., in consid-
ering the question of the propriety of the rejection of the
evidence, said he thought it was properly rejected, "because
the custom, if proved, would be unreasonable, and secondly,
because it would not apply to the case." In another case,
where the question of the rights of "introducing brokers"
was discussed, a custom among ship brokers, that the "introducing broker" should receive commission on every renewal
of a charter originally effected through him was received, and
held to be admissible.(o)

As to Varying Contracts by Usage.

SEC. 114. We have now to note some of those cases in which
evidence of usage has been held to be admissible on the
ground that it varied the document to the interpretation of
which it was to be applied.[6] "In a certain sense," as Lord

(n) *Gibson* v. *Crick*, 1 H. & C. 42.
(o) *Allan* v. *Sundius*, 1 H. & C. 123;

31 L. J. Exch. 307 ; see also *Currie* v.
Smith, 4 N. Y. Leg. Obs. 343.

[6] The rule that usage is not admissible to vary the terms of a contract,
is well illustrated in *Read* v. *Del. &
Hud. Canal Co.*, 3 Lans. (N. Y.) 213.
In that case the defendants sold the
plaintiffs a quantity of coal and
agreed to deliver it in October, upon
boats to be provided by the defendants, but failed to deliver it until late
in November, although the defendants furnished the boats and demanded the coal. Upon the trial
the defendant attempted to excuse
his non-performance by showing
that according to usage the time
from which the detention was to be
reckoned was the time when the
boats were at their loading places in
their order, and not from the time
of their arrival in the port. The

Campbell well remarked, "every material incident which is added to a written contract varies it, makes it different from what it appeared to be, and so far it is inconsistent with it. If by the side of the written contract *without* you write the same contract *with* the added incident, the two would seem to import different obligations and be different contracts."(*p*) And in another case, Mr. Justice Blackburn truly remarked : " You do not need the evidence of custom unless it varies the contract, and makes it so far inconsistent with and different from that which it would be without the evidence of the custom."(*q*) Where a certain custom exists in a certain trade or business as to the case of a certain kind of property under certain circumstances, a person purchasing it under a warranty, which, if kept, would not require such care, is nevertheless, if he retains the property, bound to conform to the custom, and can recover the expenses thereof in an action upon the warranty, but if he fails to do so, whereby the property is seriously damaged, or totally destroyed, the loss is his. Thus, in a Connecticut case,[7] the plaintiff sold the

court held that the usage could not avail, because the contract was specific—to deliver the coal within a specified time. "I think," said *Miller, P. J.*, "this cannot be done where there is a specific agreement to deliver the coal within a specified time, and the plaintiffs were ready to perform at the time named. * *

(*p*) *Humfrey* v. *Dale*, 7 E. & B. 266. Evidence is admissible to give effect to a contract by carrying out the presumed intention of the parties. *Margum* v. *Furrington*, 1 Daly (N. Y. C. P.) 236 ; *Heartshorne* v. *Union L. Ins. Co.*, 36 N. Y. 172 ; *Bissell* v. *Campbell*, 54 *Id.* 353 ; *Fox* v. *Parker*, 44 Barb. (N. Y.) 441 ; *Dalton* v. *Daniels*, 2 *Hilt.* (N. Y.) 472 ; *Casper* v. *Kane*, 19 Wend. (N. Y.) 386 ; *Staunton* v. *Small*, 3 Sandf. (N. Y.) 230. But if the usage

The agreement must control, and, where an express contract is made the parties must be held to its terms strictly, and no excuse is generally available for delay, even if it be without the fault of the party, which is not stipulated in the contract."

[7] *Hitchcock* v. *Hunt*, 28 Conn. 343.

is local or pertains to a particular trade, the presumption that the parties knew of and contracted in reference to it, may be rebutted. *Walls* v. *Bailey*, 49 N. Y. 464 ; *Johnson* v. *De Peyster*, 50 *Id.* 506 ; *Farmers', &c. Bank* v. *Sprague*, 52 *Id.* 605 ; *Duguid* v. *Edwards*, 52 Barb. (N. Y.) 217 ; *Sipperly* v. *Stewart*, 50 *Id.* 62 ; *Halford* v. *Adams*, 2 Duer (N. Y.) 471.

(*q*) *Myers* v. *Sarl*, 3 L. J. Q. B. 9, at p. 15.

16

defendant a quantity of salt pork put up in barrels, with a warranty that the barrels would not leak. The plaintiff stored the pork in a suitable place, but found afterwards that some of the barrels were leaking. He gave no notice to the plaintiff that the barrels were leaking, but from time to time filled the barrels up with new brine. It was shown upon the trial that it was the established practice among persons dealing in pork, when barrels continued to leak after putting in new brine, to take out the pork and repack it in new brine. It did not appear whether the defendant knew of this practice or whether he knew of the necessity for this course, but it did appear that, upon reasonable inquiry, he could have ascertained it, and, therefore, that it should be presumed that he knew of it, and consequently that the only deduction to which he was entitled from the price of the pork, was what he would have been compelled to pay for new barrels in place of those which leaked and for the expense of repacking them.

Addition of Term by Usage.

SEC. 115. It may be added that truly every incident which is sought to be attached by proof of usage is a material incident, and that in fact it is really the addition of a term to the contract as it existed in ink. Yet the law has gone on laying down the dictum that any usage which would have the effect of varying or contradicting either expressly or by implication the terms of a written contract is inadmissible as evidence.(r) The difficulty of understanding how a usage which adds an incident to a written contract is to do so without varying it or without contradicting it to the extent that the assertion of something concerning which it is silent is a contradiction, is to our minds very great. That it has been the means of throwing an element of uncertainty into the minds of many judges will appear from the nature of some of the decisions which we have noted above, and from those

(r) *Menzies* v. *Lightfoot*, 40 L. J. Chan. 561; 11 L. R. Eq. 459.

to which we must now refer. The dictum to which we have just referred was definitely laid down in a case in which it was attempted to set up evidence of usage in contradiction of a written instrument.

Contradiction by Usage Not Allowed—Inconsistent Principles —Addition of Term Inadmissible.

SEC. 116. This was an action on warranty of "prime singed bacon," and evidence was offered of a usage in the bacon trade that a certain latitude of deterioration called "average taint" was allowed to subsist before the bacon ceased to answer the description of prime bacon.(s) There is scarcely any question more difficult to answer than that with reference to the principles upon which certain usages have been held to contradict, while very similar usages have been regarded only as explaining. The above case, in which there was an effort made to explain that the terms "prime singed bacon" included in the trade bacon which was to some extent deteriorated, seems to differ very little from that in which "Calcutta linseed" was held to describe a linseed which had 15 per cent. of inferior material mixed with it. But there are other cases which strike one as anomalous, and suggest the defectiveness of the legal principles under which they were decided. Thus, a declaration stated that by charter party it was agreed between the owner of a ship called the *Maggie*, being in the London Docks, that the ship would load a cargo and therewith proceed to Hong Kong and deliver the same on being paid freight, "the ship to be conveyed to the charterer's agents in China free of commission on the charter." Averments that according to the custom of merchants in London, whenever a ship chartered in London for China is agreed to be conveyed to the charterer's agents, whether consigned free of commission on that charter or not, it is the right and duty of such agents, as the consignee of the ship, to procure a charter or cargo for the ship for any

(s) *Yeates* v. *Pym*, 6 Taunt. 445.

voyage from such port, and they are entitled to be paid the usual broker's commission on the amount of the freight payable under such contract; but in case the owners of the ship procure a charter or a cargo for the ship for the consignees, the consignees are entitled to the broker's commission on any freight payable under such charter party, unless such right is excluded by special contract-breach, that although the ship was loaded, and arrived in China, and the plaintiff's agents, as consignees, performed their duty free of commission on the outward voyage and cargo, and were ready to procure a charter or a cargo from Hong Kong, and although the plaintiff performed all conditions precedent, the defendant, without any default of the plaintiff's agents, procured a cargo for voyage from Hong Kong, and without any such default procured a cargo to the United Kingdom, the usual broker's commission on which amounted to a large sum; yet the defendant has not paid or allowed the same to the plaintiffs or their agents, whereby the plaintiffs were obliged to pay their agents a compensation in respect thereof. It was held under these circumstances that the declaration was bad, since the custom did not explain or annex an incident to the contract, but added a term to it.(t) In this case the court (Pollock, C. B.,) said, " Here it is sought not to explain the contract by the custom, or to add to it some incidental matter not inconsistent with what is expressed, but to impose on the party who has entered into one contract another and a different obligation, and because he has agreed to consign the ship to the charterer's agents on the outward voyage, to make him liable to pay the agents' commission on the homeward cargo. If that could be done, where is it to stop?"

Universal Custom and General Law.

SEC. 117. In *Myers* v. *Dresser*,(u) in which it was decided

(t) *Phillips* v. *Briard*, 1 H. & N. 21; 25 L. J. Exch. 233; see also *Hudson* v. *Clementson*.

(u) 16 C. B. N. S. 646, at 660. Evidence is admissible on the part of carriers of freight by water to show that the consignee of goods under a bill of lading has no right to deduct from the freight, payable on delivery of goods,

that certain usages exist as to the mode of stowage, &c., and as to the kinds of goods that are to be stowed together, and unless the shipper gives special directions in this respect, or the contract provides a different mode, if the carrier follows the usage, and the goods are injured on the voyage in consequence of the mode of stowage, the shipper cannot charge the carrier with liability therefor. *Barber* v. *Bruce*, 3 Conn. 9; *Baxter* v. *Leland*, 1 Blatch. (U. S. C. C.) 526; *Sturges* v. *Bulkley*, 32 Conn. 265. In an action against the owners of a steamboat, as common carriers, for failing to deliver goods at the place specified in their bill of lading, evidence of a custom among the steamboat men to ascend the river as high as the stage of the water in it permitted, and then to land their cargo and deposit the goods in warehouses, is not admissible for the defendants. *Cox* v. *Peterson*, 30 Ala. 608. So, too, it has been held that evidence is admissible to show that, by a custom existing on a particular river, flat boatmen were not responsible for a loss caused by dangers of the river, although the bill of lading contained no such exception. *Steele* v. *McTyer*, 31 Ala. 667. So an owner of a steamboat, when sued for the loss of goods by fire, may show that the exceptive words "dangers of the river," in the bill of lading, by custom and usage include dangers by fire. *McClure* v. *Cox*, 32 Ala. 617; *Hibler* v. *McCartney*, 31 Ala. 501. In an action on a receipt for a quantity of corn in store "on freight," it is competent for the defendant to prove a custom of the place, which had continued forty years, to pay for corn so left, after the owner had ordered it to be freighted, and not before, and that this custom was known to the plaintiff, and that he had been in the habit for many years of leaving grain at the same place, to be freighted on the same terms. *Outwater* v. *Nelson*, 20 Barb. (N. Y.) 29. Evidence of a custom of merchants in Connecticut, that the freight of money received on board a ship by the master is his perquisite, and that he, and not the ship owner, is liable on the contract, was held admissible in a suit against such owner for money taken on freight by the master at a West India island. *Halsey* v. *Brown*, 3 Day (Conn.) 346. A local custom at one port, regulating the mode of delivering goods there, is not binding on shippers at another port, unless known to them. *The Albatross* v. *Wayne*, 16 Ohio 513. A contract for a general lien may be raised from usage, that is, it may be inferred from the general dealings of other persons engaged in the same business, but the dealings must be so general and so long continued, and of such notoriety, that they may be presumed to have been known to the party at the time of his dealing with the other, and from this it may be presumed that the parties dealt upon the same footing as all others with reference to the known usage of the trade. *Rushforth* v. *Hadfield*, 519. See as to commercial usages generally, notes to *Wigglesworth* v. *Dallison*, 1 Smith's Leading Cases. Such proof as the foundation for a lien is required to be much

the value of articles which, though mentioned in the bill of
lading, turn out not to have been put on board, the defendant gave evidence of a usage prevailing in the mercantile
world to allow a deduction for missing goods, whether shown
to have been put on board or not; and the court intimated .
that such evidence was inadmissible, Erle, C. J., remarking,
"If the general law be as I have suggested, this usage cannot avail the plaintiff. It is a self-evident contradiction to
my mind to say, that the general law does not allow the deduction, and that there is a universally established usage to
allow it. A universal usage, which is not according to law,
cannot be set up to control the law."

Direct Variance of Usage and Contract.

Sec. 118. In *Blackett* v. *Royal Exchange Insurance Co.,*(v)
which was an action upon "ship and boat and other furniture," evidence was offered that it was not the usage of underwriters to pay for boats slung on the davits or the larboard
quarter; but this evidence was rejected at Nisi Prius, and
the decision of the judge was held to have been correct by
the Court of Exchequer. "The objection," said Lord Lyndhurst, delivering judgment, "to the parol evidence is, not
that it was to explain any ambiguous words in the policy, or
any words that might admit of doubt, or to introduce matter
upon which the policy was silent, but that it was at direct
variance with the words of the policy, and in plain opposition to the language it used, *viz.*, that whereas the policy imported to be upon ship furniture and apparel generally, the
usage is to say that it is not upon furniture generally, but

stronger in some cases than in
others; in the case of carriers, for
instance, stronger evidence is required than in the case of wharfingers, because the rights of the latter
have been more frequently recognized in the courts. *Naylor* v. *Man-
gles,* 1 Esp. 110; *Holderness* v. *Colli-
rum,* 7 B. & C. 216; *Richardson* v.

Goss, 3 B. & P. 119; *Spears* v. *Hartley,*
3 Esp. 81. The claim of a carrier
for a lien is not founded on the common law, and is watched with great
jealousy. *Oppenheim* v. *Russell,* 3 B.
& P. 42; *Wright* v. *Snell,* 5 B. & Ald.
353; *Butler* v. *Walcott,* 2 N. R. 54.

(v) 2 Tyrwh. 266.

upon part only, including the boat. Usage may be admissible to explain what is doubtful, but it is never admissible to
contradict what is plain."(w)

Evidence of Usage Rejected.

SEC. 119. It has been held, too, that in an action against
the drawer of a bill of exchange, drawn and indorsed in
England and payable abroad, and dishonored, evidence is
not admissible to prove a usage among merchants here to entitle the holder at his option to demand from the drawer the
amount of re-exchange, or the sum which he gave for the
purchase of the bill, this being a usage which in terms contradicts the written instrument.(x)   Again, when at the request of M., the defendant, a proprietor of railway time
tables, signed an order (which M. also signed), which was in
these terms: "Insert my advertisement for one year in 'Hotson's Local Time Table,' the Great Northern (and six others
named), charge for insertion to be 10s. each monthly book."
The plaintiff's time tables consisted of separate books, published monthly, one for each of the seven railways. The
plaintiff did not employ M. to obtain orders for him, but on
such as he obtained allowed him a commission. M. brought
the defendant's order to the plaintiff, who approved it, and
allowed M. his commission, and having inserted the advertisements for a whole year in each of the seven books, brought
an action against the defendant to recover at the rate of sev-
enty shillings a month. At the trial it was pressed on the

(w) See also *Howell* v. *Knicker-
bocker Life Ins. Co.*, 19 Abb. Pr. (N.Y.)
217; compare *Boehen* v. *Williamsburg
Ins. Co.*, 35 N. Y. 331. The decision
in this case was spoken of with dis-
proval in *Humfrey* v. *Dale*, E. B. &
E. 1,004, and it is certainly difficult
to distinguish the principles of its
decision from that which actuated
the court in other instances. Thus
in *Miller* v. *Tetherington*, 30 L. J.

Exch. 217, in which a custom in the
timber trade between British North
America and England, that underwriters under the ordinary forms of
policy are not liable to pay general
average on account of the jettison of
any timber stowed on deck, was held
to be a defence on an action for
general average.
(x) *Suse* v. *Pompe*, 8 C. B. N. S. 538;
30 L. J. C. P. 75.

part of the defendant what representations M. had made to
him to induce him to enter into the written contract, the defendant's contention being that he was only liable for ten
shillings per month, in respect of one advertisement in one
book. It was held that the effect of such evidence would be
to vary a written contract, and that, therefore, it was not admissible.(y)   When a written contract is susceptible, on its
face, of a construction that is reasonable, evidence of usage
is not admissible to explain its language;[8] and this general
rule applies to an instrument so loose as an open or running
policy of insurance, and even to one in which the phrases
relating to the matter in contest are scattered about the
document in a very disorderly way.[9]   Thus, evidence of
usage has been held not admissible to show that the words
"*current funds*" have acquired a peculiar meaning,[1] but it
would seem that, if a well settled and known usage is established, giving to the phrase a peculiar meaning different from
its ordinary signification, evidence thereof *is* admissible.[2]   So
it is not competent to show what is meant by the words "more
or less" in a broker's note for the sale of goods. Thus, where
a note of that kind was "sold to N. W. for account of S. C.,
five hundred bundles 'more or less' gunny bags," it was
held, that no latent ambiguity existed such as would justify
evidence outside the note to explain their signification.[3]   Nor

(y) *Brown* v. *Hotson*, 9 C. B. N. S.
442; 30 L. J. C. P. 106. In this case
it was also expressly held, as we
should have expected, that (assuming M. to have been the plaintiff's
agent) if the issue had been whether
the defendant was induced to sign
the contract by M.'s fraud, the evidence would have been admissible.
See also *Reading* v. *Newnham*, 1 M.
& Rob. 234, at p. 236.

[8] *Lomardo* v. *Case*, 49 Barb. (N. Y.)
95; *Sanford* v. *Rawlings*, 43 Ill. 92;
Ehle v. *Chittenango Bank*, 24 N. Y.
548; *Cabot* v. *Winsor*, 1 Allen (Mass.)
546. Parol evidence of a custom in
contemplation of which a deed was
actually made to run the courses by
the magnetic meridian is admissible
to explain the meaning of the word
"north" in the deed. *Jenny Lind
Co.* v. *Bower*, 11 Cal. 194.

[9] *Insurance Co.* v. *Wright*, 1 Wall.
(U. S.) 456.

[1] *More* v. *Kupfer*, 34 Ill. 287.

[2] *Ehle* v. *Chittenango Bank*, 24 N.
Y. 548.

[3] *Cabot* v. *Winsor*, 1 Allen (Mass.)
546.

is evidence ever admissible to show that the parties to an instrument placed upon a certain word or phrase a peculiar meaning controlling the whole effect of the instrument. The evidence must be such as discloses a scientific or popular meaning; or it must be construed in its ordinary sense.[4] Such evidence is not admissible to show what the words "to erect a marble monument" in a contract is understood to mean by those engaged in the trade.[5] Nor will evidence of the sense which words have acquired by usage be admitted, when the attendant circumstances of the transaction plainly show that the words were used in their *ordinary* sense. Thus, in an action on a contract to deliver stocks, it was held, that the plaintiff would not be permitted to show that by the general custom of brokers and dealers in stocks in New York, the words "dividends, or surplus dividends," in the contract, were intended to mean dividends declared on the stocks, whether they had been announced before or after the date of the contract; *provided, that on the day the contract was made, the stock was selling in the market, dividend on,* and not ex-dividend, for the reason that effect could not be given to the custom without making a new contract between the parties.[6] In an English case, not referred to by the author,[7] the defendant entered into an agreement to "even stones, &c., for the purpose of building" certain cottages, and it was held not admissible to show by parol that the term "building," in such contracts, by usage, included tile pointing and plastering. Creswell, J., said, the construction of the contract being for the court, he was of the opinion that the term building, as used therein, did not include the matters in question. Without entering into any lengthy discussion of the question, yet upon principle, and, as we believe, upon the weight of authority, however well settled the ordinary meaning of a

---

[4] *Hartwell* v. *Camman*, 10 N. J. Eq. 128; *Evansville &c. R. R. Co.* v. *Meeds*, 11 Ind. 273.

[5] *Sanford* v. *Rawlings*, 43 Ill. 92.

[6] *Lombardo* v. *Case*, 45 Barb. (N. Y.) 95.

[7] *Charlton* v. *Gibson*, 1 C. & K. 541.

word may be, *if it has acquired a peculiar sense by the usage
of a certain business, and the usage is well established, certain,
uniform and reasonable,* we entertain no doubt but that our
courts would admit the evidence and permit its meaning so
acquired by usage, to be shown.[8] It will be observed that
in the cases where such evidence was rejected, no well-established usage was shown to exist. In an English case,[9] it was
held that, while the fact that words had by usage acquired a
technical sense might be shown, yet that such evidence was
not admissible to contradict or vary that which is plain.
But if in fact a word has acquired a technical or peculiar
meaning in a trade and the usage is proven to the satisfaction of the jury,[1] and is shown to be uniform and invariable,
it will be admitted, although it entirely changes the ordinary
sense of the word and makes the contract entirely different
from what it appears to be.[2] In the case of *Hall* v. *Janson,(z)* which was an action on a policy of marine assurance
in the ordinary form, in which the interest was declared to
be "on money advanced on account of freight," and the
court alleged the interest to be in the ship owner, and that
it became subject to a general average contribution, a plea to
the court stating a custom of London, where the policy was
made, that assurance upon "money advanced on account of
freight" should not be liable for a general average, was held
bad, the custom alleged being inconsistent with the terms
of the policy.(a)

[8] *Daniels* v. *Hudson River Ins. Co.*,
12 Cush. (Mass.) 416; *Mobile &c. Ins.
Co.* v. *McMillan*, 27 Ala. 77; *Whitmarsh* v. *Conway Ins. Co.*, 16 Gray
(Mass.) 657 ; *Steward* v. *Scudder*, 24
N. J. L. 96; *McClure* v. *Cox*, 32 Ala.
617; *Hibler* v. *McCartney*, 31 Ala.
501.

(z) 4 E. & B. 500; see also *Foster*
v. *Mentor Ins. Co.*, 4 El. & Bl. 8;
Clarke v. *Westrope*, 18 C. B. 765.

[9] *Beacon L. & F. Ins. Co.* v. *Gibb*, 1
Moore P. C. N. S. 73.
[1] *Ashworth* v. *Belford*, L. R., 9 C. P. 20.
[2] *Taylor* v. *Briggs*, 2 N. & M. 28 ;
Hills v. *Evans*, 31 L. J. Ch. 437 ; *Clayton* v. *Gregson*, 4 N. & M. 602; *Kirchner* v. *Venus*, 5 Jur. N. S. 395 ;
Kinglake v. *Bivess*, 18 L. J. C. P. 628.

(a) *Bogert* v. *Canman*, Anth. N.
P. 97.

Words of General Import.

SEC. 120. In *Cross* v. *Eglin*,(b) evidence had been offered for the purpose of showing that the plaintiffs, who had contracted for 300 *quarters* (*more or less*) *of foreign rye*, could not, consistently with the usage of trade, be required to receive so large an excess as 45 quarters over 300. The question as to the admissibility of the evidence was ultimately withdrawn from the attention of the court; but Littledale, J., remarked that where words were of such general import, he should feel much difficulty in saying that evidence ought to be received to ascertain their meaning.

Terms Added Must be Incidental.

SEC. 121. It would appear further that terms which are not only not inconsistent with, but which are not really incidental to those expressed in the written contract, are to be held inadmissible of annexation by oral evidence of the particular usage of a trade. In a case above referred to, where the charterer of a vessel for a voyage from England to China—the ship to be conveyed to his agents there free of commission—endeavored to add to the charter party a term that the agents in China should be entitled to procure charters for the return voyage from China, and be paid on commission an amount of freight mentioned in such charters, by means of proof of a particular custom, he was prevented on the ground of the inadmissibility of such proof.(c) These very numerous and varying decisions are apt to confuse rather than direct the mind in reference to this most difficult question of evidence. We are, however, not left without assistance in relation to this matter. In some recent cases the point has been fully argued and the question fully discussed. The ruling in these cases must be held to be conclusive as to this matter, and it will be seen that these have the effect of giving to parol evidence of custom as modifying

(b) 2 B. & Ad.   25 L. J. Exch. 233; *Fawkes* v. *Lamb*,
(c) *Phillips* v. *Briard*, 1 H. & N. 21;   31 L. J. Q. B. 98.

written agreements very considerable force. To our thinking, the true rule was stated in one of these cases by Lord
Campbell, where he said that "to fall within the exception
of repugnancy the incident must be such as *if expressed in
the written contract* would make it insensible or inconsistent." Addison advised young authors who were indulging
in metaphors, to see whether they could be painted. It
might be a safe rule for those who have to see whether a
usage will attach an incident to a written contract or not, to
see whether they can be written down together without pro-
ducing a contradiction or nonsense.

Contracts for Services.

SEC. 122. When a person enters into the employ of a
person who has adopted a printed table of rules requiring
workmen to give two weeks', or any other, notice of an intention to quit the service, the burden of establishing knowledge on the part of the servant of such regulations is upon
the master, and this requires him to show such knowledge
at the time when the contract was entered into[3] or assent
thereto afterwards, and mere proof that he subsequently
became aware of them and kept on working without objection, is not sufficient to show that he assented to the rules
as a part of his contract. It is competent evidence tending
to show such assent, but is not sufficient, of itself, to establish it.[4] And proof that a printed copy of the rules was
placed in the hands of the servant at the time when he was
employed, does not establish knowledge thereof on his part,
unless it is also shown that he could read, as the law does
not presume that every one can read, but rather the reverse.[5]
Actual knowledge of the rules, or of the custom if it is relied
on as such, must be shown.[6] But where knowledge of the

---

[3] Wood's Master and Servant, 187.
[4] *Collins* v. *N. E. Iron Co.*, 115 Mass. 23.
[5] *Bradley* v. *Salmon Falls Co*, 30 N. H. 487.

[6] *Dodge* v. *Faver*, 15 Gray (Mass.) 82; *Stevens* v. *Reeves*, 9 Pick. (Mass.) 198.

rule at the time of employment is shown, assent thereto is presumed, and it becomes a part of the contract.[7] The question as to whether a contract is made into a local custom is for the jury, and mere proof of the prevalence of such a custom in the community is not sufficient to establish the fact. Both proof of its existence and knowledge of it by the party sought to be affected by it, or circumstances which fairly raise a presumption of knowledge must be established.[8] But if the custom is general and applies to all the class of laborers referred to, and is not confined to a particular locality or district, from the existence of the custom the law will presume that the contract was made in reference to it. But *special* customs, or customs of a single individual, corporation or firm, must not only be proved, but it is also always a question of fact whether a contract was made in reference to it,[9] and if the contract is express in all its provisions, a custom cannot be proved, as the contract is presumed to have been made to avoid the custom.[1] Where the compensation is fixed by the contract, evidence of further compensation by way of customary privileges is inadmissible,[2] but where the rate of compensation is not fixed by the contract, or is left indefinite, evidence of the usual rate of compensation allowed for similar services in that locality is always admissible.[3] So where no special contract as to duration of a term exists, it is proper for the servant, if he can, to show a custom in the business that persons employed as he was are not to be dis-

---

[7] *Harmon* v. *Salmon Falls Mfg. Co.*, 35 Me. 447.

[8] Wood's Master and Servant, 188.

[9] *Littledale, J.*, in *Clayton* v. *Gregson*, 5 Ad. & El. 315; *Powell* v. *Horton*, 2 N. C. 1668; *Studdy* v. *Sanders*, 5 B. & C. 628.

[1] *Peters* v. *Stanley*, 15 L. T. N. S. 275. In *Bedford* v. *Flowers*, 11 Humph. (Tenn.) 242, where by a written contract for the hiring of slaves, it was expressly stipulated that the services

in which they were to be employed was "to cut cord-wood on the Mississippi river, at or near Mills' Point, and for no other purpose." It was held that by the terms of the contract the custom of wood-choppers on the Mississippi river was excluded, the contract negativing any reference to such usages.

[2] *Bogert* v. *Canman*, Arth. (N. Y.) 70; *Phillips* v. *Starr*, 26 Iowa 349.

[3] *Pursell* v. *McQueen*, 9 Ala. 380.

missed until the end of the season, and what the end of the season is by that custom.[4]   In all cases where a person is hired for a term, in the absence of any agreement in that respect, full performance is a condition precedent to his right to recover any part of the compensation therefor,[5] unless he can show a custom applicable to the business to pay weekly, monthly or at other stated periods.   If such a custom exists, it enters into the contract and regulates the time of payment.[6] So, too, the usages in that respect, if there are any, regulate the duties incident to a particular service, and evidence of such customary duties are admissible in a case where the question is involved.[7]   A usage that persons employed in a certain trade are entitled to certain holidays and Sundays to themselves, is admissible.[8]

Principal and Agent.

SEC. 123. It is a well settled principle that evidence is not admissible of a usage that authorizes a factor, or agent, to violate the instructions of his principal,[9] but, if it is shown that the agent has been accustomed to violate such instructions in a particular respect, and the principal has apparently acquiesced therein, the agent, as to those with whom he has so dealt, becomes by usage, clothed with authority to so deal, and the principal is liable for his acts.[1] Where the principal gives his agent no definite instructions, the agent is warranted in pursuing the usual course in reference to the business or duties with which he is entrusted, and is not answerable to his principal if he keeps within the scope of the usages of the business. Thus, if a person entrusts cattle

[4] *Given* v. *Charron*, 15 Md. 502. It is for the court to say whether the custom is reasonable, *Id. Bodfish* v. *Fox*, 23 Me. 90.

[5] *Larkin* v. *Burk*, 11 Ohio St. 561 ; Wood's Master and Servant, 273.

[6] *Thayer* v. *Wadsworth*, 19 Pick. (Mass.) 349.

[7] *Vaughn* v. *Gardner*, 7 B. Mon. (Ky.) 326.

[8] *Reg.* v. *Stoke-upon-Trent*, 5 Q. B. 303.

[9] *Barksdale* v. *Brown*, 1 N. & M. (S. C.) 519.

[1] *Perkins* v. *Washington Co. Ins. Co.*, 4 Cow. (N. Y.) 645 ; *Houghton* v. *Emback*, 4 Camp. 88 ; *Dickinson Co.* v. *Ins. Co.*, 41 Dana 286.

or other property to a person to sell for him, with no positive instructions as to how the sale shall be made, the agent
is warranted in pursuing the usual course of those engaged
in that business, and if it is usual to sell on credit, he will
be justified in so doing; and if he is guilty of no *laches* or
fraud in giving the credit, he will not be responsible,
although the purchaser becomes insolvent before the credit
expires.[2] So, although instructions are given, if they do not
necessarily exclude a usage in regard to the transaction of
the business, the usage will protect the agent or factor. Thus,
where the principal directed a person to whom he sent grain
for sale on commission, to sell for " cash," it was held that he
might show, if he could, that by the usage among such dealers, a short credit, as in this case, three or four days was regarded as a sale for " cash."[3] But if the instructions are
positive and exclude the usage, it affords no protection. Thus,
where the instructions were to " sell for cash, *and not on
credit*," a usage to treat sales on a short credit as a sale for
cash, was held not admissible.[4] Where an agent purchases
property for his principal, he cannot show a usage to sell
such property and return other property similar in kind,
quality and value, because under such a custom the property
could not be identified if the agent should fail; and after a

[2] *Leach* v. *Beardslee*, 22 Conn. 404.
See statement of the case, ante, pp.
168–169.

[3] *Steward* v. *Scudder*, 24 N. J. L.
96. In *Wallace* v. *Bradshaw*, 6 Dana
(Ky.) 382, the defendants, commission merchants in New Orleans, received goods from the plaintiffs,
merchants in Kentucky, for sale,
upon which they made advances.
In an action against them to recover
the proceeds or value of the goods,
it was held admissible for them to
prove that by the custom of New
Orleans, merchants making advances
on goods, to ship them to foreign

ports for sale, if deemed necessary,
and by such proof to offset the
amount of recovery, or even defeat
the action if the proceeds of the
sales did not exceed the advances,
commissions, expenses, &c. See also
Kuhtman v. *Brown*, 4 Rich. (S. C.) 479.

[4] *Catlin* v. *Smith*, 24 Vt. 85. In a
New York case, *Greaves* v. *Hendricks*,
16 Haz. Penn. Reg. 344, it was held
that a commission merchant who
had been instructed to sell for cash,
could not shield himself against a
sale on short credit on the ground
of a usage to consider a sale for six
days, as a sale for cash.

sale in violation of orders, his interest becomes adverse to that of the principal.[5]

Custom Qualifying Meaning—Undisclosed Principal Usage.

SEC. 124. In the recent case of *Hutchinson* v. *Tatham*,(d) the law with regard to the admissibility of the parol evidence of custom to qualify the meaning of a written document has been carried to a very considerable exent. In that case the defendants acting as agents for a person of the name of Lyons, with his authority chartered a ship for the conveyance of a cargo of currants from the Ionian Islands. The charter party was expressed to be made, and was signed by the defendants, as "agents to merchants," the name of the principal not being disclosed. At the trial evidence was tendered on the part of the plaintiff and admitted, of a trade usage, that, if the principal's name is not disclosed within a reasonable time after the signing of the charter party, in such case the broker shall be personally liable. The jury found that there was such a custom, and that the name of the principal had not been disclosed within a reasonable time. The question for the court was as to the admissibility of the parol evidence; and the judges, while restating the doctrine that no such evidence would be admissible to contradict the plain terms of a document, held that it was the law, that you might by evidence of custom add a term not inconsistent with any term in the contract, and that the evidence which was admitted at the trial was rightly admitted.

---

[5] *Foley* v. *Bell*, 6 La. An. 760. In *Allen* v. *Dykers*, 3 Hilt (N. Y.) 593, it was held that evidence of a usage among brokers to sell stock hypothecated, and return the same kind of stock on the payment of the sum for which it was hypothecated, could not be shown. If a broker is employed to purchase stock upon a margin, all transactions to be subject to the usages of their offices, this incorporates into the contract a custom of the office, on failure to furnish a sufficient margin, to sell at the stock exchange, without notice to the customer, of the time and place of sale. *Baker* v. *Drake*, 66 N. Y. 518.

(d) 8 L. R. C. P. 482.

Undisclosed Principals, Agent's Liability—Agent's Liability Modified—Qualification of Usage Introduced.

SEC. 125. As the case last referred to was decided upon the authority of *Humfrey* v. *Dale*(e) and *Fleet* v. *Murton*,(f) this may be the most convenient place to state the effect of these cases. In the case of *Fleet* v. *Murton*, it appeared that the defendants were fruit brokers in London, and were employed by the plaintiffs, who were merchants, also in London, to sell for them. The defendants gave to the plaintiffs the following contract note: "We have this day sold for your account to our principal." Then followed a statement of the number of tons of raisins, (signed) Murton & Webb, brokers, 25 Mincing Lane. The defendants' principal having accepted part of the raisins, and refusing to accept the rest, the plaintiffs brought an action on the contract against the defendants, and endeavored to make the defendants personally liable by giving evidence that in the London fruit trade, if the brokers did not give the names of their principals in the contract, they were held personally liable, although, in fact, they contracted as brokers for a principal. It was held that the evidence of the custom was not inconsistent with the written document, and Cockburn, C. J., said :(g) "For, although where a party contracts as agent, there would not, independently of some further bargain, be any liability on him as principal. Yet, if a man, though professing on the face of the contract to contract as agent for another, and to bind his principal only, and not himself, chooses to qualify that contract by saying that he will make himself liable, though he is contracting for another, and giving to another rights under the contract, he himself will incur the same liability as the principal. Now, although where a party professes to contract as broker, it might, *prima facie*, be taken that he contracts without the intention of incurring liability on his own part, yet, if by the custom of the particular trade,

(e) 7 E. & B. 266.   (f) 7 L. R. Q. B. 126.   (g) At p. 129.

there is that qualification of the contract (which, if written into the contract *in extenso*, would undoubtedly bind him), that qualification may, I think, be imported into the contract by evidence of the custom."

Tacitly Implied Incident.

SEC. 126. In the earlier but ruling case of *Dale* v. *Humfrey*,(h) which was very similar in many respects to the cases above alluded to, the plaintiff, a broker, who brought an action against the defendant, a broker, upon a written note of the sale of oil in which neither of the principal's names were set forth, proved a custom in the trade, that when a broker purchased without disclosing the name of his principal, he was liable to be looked to as principal, and the Court of Exchequer Chamber affirming the judgment of the Court of Queen's Bench,(i) held that evidence of the custom was admissible, on the ground that it did not contradict the written instrument, but explained its terms, or added a tacitly implied incident. In relation to the decision of this case, the reader would do well to read the words used by Mr. Justice Blackburn in the case of *Myers* v. *Sarl.*(k)

Repugnancy the Test—Varying Decisions.

SEC. 127. In any case it would seem that evidence of a custom will be admissible unless it introduces something repugnant to or inconsistent with the tenor of the written instrument; and it seems, from all the cases, that the qualification introduced into a written contract by the proof of a custom, is a qualification of construction, and that as a construction never can be a contradiction, any custom which would negative or contradict the plain words of a written document would be inadmissible in proof. That there has been a considerable amount of vacillation in the minds of various judges as to the extent to which usages should be admitted in this connection is certain. Lord Eldon in one

(h) E. B. & E. 1004.
(i) 7 E. & B. 266.

(k) 30 L. J. Q. B. 9, at 14, quoted ante, pp. 65 and 80.

case(*l*) expressed a decided opinion in favor of the enlargement of the scope of usage in relation to the explanation of written contracts, but as one of the editors of one of the editions of Smith's "Leading Cases," observes,(*m*) "the tendency of the Court appears now to be the other way." Since that was written, however, the decisions in two of the three recent cases we have above referred to have been given, and we cannot see that the principles of the law have suffered by the greater breadth which is thus given to interpretation of documents which have a decided tendency to be too narrow for the intentions of the parties, who from their great familiarity with the incidents to the contracts they are daily in the habit of entering into, are apt to leave a great part of the contract understood, and put only a little of the less familiar matter into writing. Were the law to refuse to give effect to these understandings, it would really be refusing to give effect to the real intentions of the parties at the time the contract was entered upon. It would likewise be throwing difficulties in the way of important transactions which are often too urgent to be fully expressed in lengthy documents, and would be doing something to prevent the regenerative effects on law which may be looked for from custom. There is a possibility of too lax an admission of custom as a force, in such cases. The common business relations of others must not be regarded as so stringent as to bind anyone to perform his business in the same way. Each man is to be left free to contract in what way he pleases, but when the interpretation of a usage is possible in connection with a written agreement, it is as fair to conclude—on the side of one of the parties, that the contract was made with reference to it—as on the other side to infer that it was made without any reference to it, and with the intention of excluding its effect. Thinking thus, we cannot see that the law has suffered in any respect

(*l*) *Anderson* v. *Pitcher*, 2 B. & P. 168.   A. & E. 589 ; and *Johnstone* v. *Us-*
(*m*) See also *Trueman* v. *Loder*, 11   *borne, Ibid.* 549.

from the extension which has been allowed to the common conduct as interpreting the common transactions of men. Guarded by the consciousness that these customs are apt to push their way into the statute book—and we believe that it is well to be careful how they attain that position—little evil can arise.

Modern Dictum.

SEC. 128. Hence we find that the modern dictum where a phrase is used in a document, has two senses, one common to language, the other peculiar to the trade or business in connection with which the writing has been executed, it is to be understood as used in its peculiar meaning unless upon construing the whole contract you can see that either in express terms or by necessary implication the parties intended to use it in a different sense, is to be approved of and acted upon.(n)

Definite Rule.

SEC. 129. To us it seems that a definite rule has been reached, and that a guiding principle has been attained. Everything, however, depends upon the consistency with which our judges follow the precedents to which we have alluded. A timid, retrograde policy is not impossible in the future. Judges are only too apt to prefer the narrow gauge of written words to the broad gauge of uncertain evidence of custom, and some there are who have expressed doubt as to the expediency of the recent policy, and hesitation as to carrying it legitimately into practice.

(n) See *Myers* v. *Sarl*, 30 L. J. Q. B. 9, *per* Blackburn, J., at p. 15.

•

CHAPTER VI.

PRIVATE USAGES, CUSTOM OF BROKERS, &C.

Private Usages.

SEC. 130. Private usages, or the usages of an individual or corporation in a particular matter, are only binding upon those who have knowledge thereof, so that they can be presumed to have assented thereto.[1] Thus a custom among banks to transmit bills and notes from each to the other for collection, and, when paid, of passing the avails to the credit of the bank transmitting them, and to the debit of the bank so receiving them, cannot affect the claims of a third person, to the avails of a bill which he has committed to one of them for collection.[2] But where a private usage in a particular

[1] *Lawrence* v. *Stonington Bank*, 6 Conn. 521; *Osborne* v. *Sisture*, 14 *Id.* 366; *Halsey* v. *Brown*, 3 Day. (Conn.) 346; *Crosby* v. *Fitch*, 12 Conn. 410; *Kilgore* v. *Buckley*, 14 *Id.* 362.

[2] *Lawrence* v. *Stonington Bank*, ante. When it becomes necessary to prove or disprove certain acts, evidence of the usages of the parties in reference to such matters may be given, as tending to show how the act was done in a given case. Thus, where the question at issue was whether the plaintiff's attorney in a former action directed an officer to take the receipt of a certain person for property attached by him, evidence that it was the uniform habit of the attorney *not* to give instructions to an officer as to whom he should take as receiver, was held admissible. *Hine* v. *Pomeroy*, 39 Vt. 211. In an action against a bank to recover a sum of money sent to it in a package directed to the cashier thereof, through an express company, where

matter exists, as to the mode in which an individual, firm or corporation transacts certain business, a person dealing with

the defence was that the package was not delivered to the cashier or the bank, but to the assistant receiving teller, while he was at the receiving teller's desk, and that he never delivered it up, evidence was held admissible to show a usage of delivering packages at the receiving teller's desk, and that a package was delivered to the assistant receiving teller on a previous occasion, and was received by the bank. *Hotchkiss* v. *Artisans Bank*, 42 Barb. (N.Y.) 517. In another case C., one of the plaintiffs, who testified to the delivery of a certain check; fixed the time of such delivery at nearly a quarter past 2 P. M. On his cross-examination he testified that he took no receipt for the check, and did not get the defendant's check for the amount of the gold draft which he had delivered. To meet the effect of this fact with the jury, on the question of delivery or non-delivery of the gold check in question, the plaintiffs were permitted by the judge to prove that other persons who were late in their delivery of checks payable in gold were sometimes accustomed to leave the checks and take no check for currency in payment until afterwards. It was held that this was error ; that the question was, did he deliver this check in the manner and at the time he testified he did; and it was not proper evidence on this issue that persons about whose deliverances of stock no question was made, were sometimes accustomed to deliver checks and receive neither evidence nor payment, when such custom was neither known to the witness nor

stated by him as a reason why he omitted to take either receipt or payment. *Kinne* v. *Ford*, 52 Barb. (N. Y.) 194. If, however, it had been shown that the *plaintiffs* had been accustomed to leave their checks in the manner stated, the rule would have been different. Thus, in a case where the question was as to whether or not the plaintiff, a broker, was entitled to certain commissions not specified in the charter party, proof that on several other occasions the defendants had paid him similar commissions to those now claimed, was held admissible, as being some evidence either that the defendants knew and assented to plaintiff's custom to make such charge, or knew that the charges were in conformity to the usage of trade. *Weber* v. *Kingsland*, 8 Bosw. (N. Y.) 415. But see *Park* v. *Miller*, 27 N. J. L. 338, when a factor offered on trial to show that he hid not guarantee all sales made by him, and for that purpose offered to show that he was in the habit of making entries in his books designating what sales were guaranteed and what not, and the evidence was held not admissible. In a case where it became important to show that an insurance company had waived notice of a transfer of a policy, the plaintiff offered to show that they had done so in other cases, but the evidence was held inadmissible. *Bunger* v. *Farmers*, &c., *Ins. Co.*, 71 Penn. St. 422; *Fogle* v. *Lycoming*, &c., *Ins. Co.*, 3 Grant (Penn.) 77. So in *Hursh* v. *North*, 40 Penn. St. 241, it was held that evidence of the practice of a particular firm to sell on a certain credit is not admissible to

PRIVATE USAGES, CUSTOM OF BROKERS, &C.   279

them in that respect, *and knowing of such usage*, is bound by it as much as though it was a general usage and so notori-

take a case out of the statute of limitations, *unless it is also shown that the parties dealt with reference to it.* See also S. P. *Goodman* v. *Parsons,* 36 Vt. 46, and *Searson* v. *Heyward,* 1 Spear (S. C.) 249, where it was held that the custom of particular firms to charge interest on sales after a certain time is not admissible, unless it is also shown that the parties in a given case *knew* of such custom. The rule may be said to be that a usage of an individual, *which is known to the person who deals with him,* may be given in evidence, as tending to prove what was the contract between them in a matter to which such usage relates. *Loring* v. *Gurney,* 5 Pick. (Mass.) 15. See also *Naylor* v. *Semmes,* 4 G. & J. (Md.) 274. Thus, where a person who purchases goods knowing that the vendor has an established usage by which orders for goods are filled in the order in which they are received, he is bound by such usage, and in order to maintain an action against the vendor for a breach of the contract by the vendor in not reasonably filling the order, he must establish a special contract, or that the vendor did not follow the usage in his case, or he cannot recover, nor complain that he has not been treated fairly. *N. E. Screw Co.* v. *Bliven,* 4 Blatchf. (U. S. C. C.) 97. But a private usage that is contrary to the express or implied provisions of a contract cannot be set up. Thus, where a bank had kept posted a notice that all endorsers of notes to the bank would be required to waive demand and notice, and a note was endorsed to the bank by one who had been for

several years a customer of the bank, but no such waiver was written upon the note, it was held that parol evidence of this usage of the bank, and of the assent of the endorser, could not be shown to change the contract implied in law from the endorsement. *Piscataqua Exchange Bank* v. *Carter,* 20 N. H. 246. Nor one that is unreasonable or that sanctions an immoral act. Thus, a usage of a board of directors to permit its cashier to misapply its funds, is bad. *Minor* v. *Mechanics' Bank,* 1 Pet. (U. S.) 46. In *Grinnell* v. *W. Un. Tel. Co.,* 113 Mass. 199, it was held that evidence of a usage in a local office of the company was inadmissible to vary the terms of a contract under which a message was sent. In *Nanatuck Silk Co.* v. *Fair,* 112 Mass. 354, in an action to recover the price of goods sold, there was a clause upon the bill of parcels accompanying the goods—a clause, "Terms five per cent. off for cash." The defendants introduced evidence of the plaintiff's usage to allow other parties, upon similar sales, a credit of thirty days, but testified himself that, at the time of the purchase, he was ignorant of the custom, and it was held that, as he did not know of, the custom could not be regarded as a part of the contract, and consequently was not admissible in evidence. Again, even though a private usage in a certain respect may be proved, yet if it appears to be one that the party must necessarily exercise his discretion about acting upon, it is not obligatory. Thus, a usage among manufacturing corporations in Lowell to give an hon-

ous as to be binding upon any of the public. Thus, where a person procured a bank to negotiate a bill of exchange for him on parties in New York, and *knew* that it was the custom and usage of the bank to send packages of money, checks, bills, &c., to New York by the captain of a steamer plying between the place where the bank was located and New York, only once a week, and generally Thursdays, although the steamer ran every day, and the bill so negotiated, which was discounted on Monday, was sent to New York, in conformity with such custom, the following Thursday, and duly presented for payment, and protested on the succeeding Saturday, it was held that the defendant could not relieve himself from liability as endorser upon the ground that the bank had not used proper diligence in presenting and protesting the bill, because he must be presumed to have assented to have the bill sent iu that mode, and to have waived the usual rule of law regarding the transmission of such paper.[3] But in order to be operative in a given case,

orable discharge to an operative who had worked faithfully with them for twelve months, and has given a fortnight's notice of his intention to leave, whereby such operative may obtain employment in other mills in Lowell, was held not obligatory although all the conditions had been complied with, as the giving of such a discharge is a matter of discretion and judgment with the corporation. *Thornton* v. *Suffolk Mfg. Co.*, 10 Cush. (Mass.) 376. In *Sweeting* v. *Pearce*, 7 C. B. N. S. 449, it was held that the usage of Lloyd's coffee house, that persons insuring there are bound to admit payment of a loss to them made by way of set off, made between their broker and underwriter, of the premiums due to the underwriter, against the loss, does not apply where they are not shown to be personally cognizant of such usage.

[3] *The Bridgeport Bank* v. *Dyer*, 19 Conn. 136. In this case it was shown that the defendant was a merchant in the city where the bank was located, and had for several years kept his account there, and during *one* year at least, was a director of the bank, and from this evidence it was held that the jury were warranted in finding that the defendant knew of the usage. "No principle of law," said *Ellsworth, J.*, in delivering the opinion of the court, "is better settled than that a known practice, or one belonging to a particular branch of business, is sufficient evidence of the understanding of the parties when contracting in relation to that business, unless there is evidence to the contrary." *The Schooner Reeside,*

actual knowledge on the part of the person to be affected thereby, or circumstances from which such knowledge can be presumed must be shown, because otherwise his assent thereto could not be inferred. This is well illustrated in a Connecticut case.[4] In that case the plaintiff deposited money with

2 Sum. (U. S.) 567; *Bodfish* v. *Fox*, 23 Me. 90; *Clark* v. *Baker*, 11 Met. (Mass.) 186; *Dwight* v. *Whitney*, 15 Pick. (Mass.) 179; *Gibson* v. *Culver*, 17 Wend. (N. Y.) 305; *Renner* v. *Bank of Columbia*, 9 Wheat. (U. S.) 588.

[4] *Eaves* v. *People's Savings Bank*, 27 Conn. 228. A custom, to be binding, must be general and well understood. If the usage is clearly established that the factor has a right to charge commissions on purchases and on acceptances, when not in funds to meet drafts at maturity, such items ought to be allowed. But commissions and interest both cannot be charged on advances. *Smetz* v. *Kennedy*, Riley (S. C.) 218. In a case where A. advanced to B. a certain sum on cotton shipped to Bremen, and brought an action to recover the amount in which the net proceeds fell short of the sum advanced. In the amount rendered by A. against B. were a multitude of small charges besides commissions, such as bill brokerage and interest thereon, for mending, handling, delivering, &c., &c. A verdict was rendered for the whole amount. It was held that the right to make such charges depended so much on commercial usage that the question was properly submitted to the jury. *Kuhtman* v. *Brown*, 4 Rich. (S. C.) 479. So where A. consigned property to B. to sell on commission, with instructions to "sell for cash, or not on credit," and B. sold and delivered the goods to C., who said he would pay for them in

a few days, which promise he renewed from time to time for a few weeks, when he failed. In an action by A. against B. for the value of the goods it was held that B. could not show, in defense, a custom by which such sale was considered a cash sale. *Catlin* v. *Smith*, 24 Vt. 85. The custom of railroad companies to allow their contractors the free use of their own roads cannot be extended so as to bind a company to pay the expenses of its contractors on the road belonging to another corporation. *Colcock* v. *Louisville R. R. Co.*, 1 Strobh. (S. C.) 329. That a railroad company had been for about a month in the habit of storing cotton consigned to their agent at the warehouse of A. without any proof that this was generally known, or any other evidence that the shipper had notice of it, is not sufficient to bind him. *Alabama &c. R. R. Co.* v. *Kidd*, 35 Ala. 209. An isolated instance is not sufficient to prove a custom, nor will evidence of the custom of one person be sufficient to establish a general course of trade. *Burr* v. *Sickless*, 17 Ark. 428. Where a special custom at the place of shipment is proved, and the question is whether the purchaser had knowledge of the special custom, and contracted in reference to it, the previous course of dealing between the same parties—such as the order, shipment and receipt of several invoices of goods, without any charge for insurance—is sufficient

the defendant bank. His bank book was stolen, and an order for the money represented by it was forged, and upon presentation to the bank with the book, was paid by it. It was held that the usage of the bank, or of savings banks generally, to pay money to a person presenting a deposit book and order, could not avail the defendant, unless knowledge of such usage was brought home to the depositor, so that his assent thereto could be presumed.

Customs of Stock Exchange, How Far They Bind a Principal Ignorant of Them.

SEC. 131. We have now to consider, as naturally connecting itself with the cases last referred to, the questions of principal and agent in relation to this principle of the admissibility of evidence of custom. We have seen that the principle of the law is that parties who make a bargain in connection with a particular trade must be taken to have contracted subject to or with reference to the known usages of that trade. It was laid down in the case of *Sutton* v. *Tatham*,(a) that a person employing a broker on the stock exchange impliedly gives him authority to act in accordance with the rules there established, though the principal himself be ignorant of them ; and in a case in which *Sutton* v. *Tatham* was expressly approved of (Parkes, B.), the law was stated generally in these words : "A person who deals

evidence from which the jury may infer knowledge of the special custom. *Walsh* v. *Frank*, 19 Ark. 270. To establish a shipping usage on a certain river, the witness may state his habit and custom in shipping on boats on the river. *Berry* v. *Cooper*, 28 Ga. 543. Proof of the usage of the clerks of steamboats to receive and carry packages from one port to another, without hire, in the expectation that such boat would be preferred by the parties in their shipments of freight, is insufficient to bind the owners—first, because no certain or fixed standard of remuneration is shown, nor that the consignee of the package would be liable to make any return for the risk and labor incurred; and, second, because it is not shown that such usage had grown up with the consent of the owners of vessels, or that it was more than a mere accommodation usage. *Cincinnati &c. Co.* v. *Boal*, 15 Ind. 345.

(a) 10 A. & E. 27.

in a particular market must be taken to deal according to
the custom of that market, and he who directs another
to make a contract at a particular place must be taken as
intending that the contract may be made according to the
usage of that place."(b)   That this is a correct view of the
law has been over and over again decided.   In an action
where the plaintiffs, stock brokers and members of the London stock exchange, had, it appeared, on the 28th of August,.
1856, at the request of the defendant, bought for him twenty
shares in a joint-stock bank, called "The Royal British
Bank," to be paid for on the "settlement day," which was
on the 15th of September, and duly forwarded to him the
usual broker's contract note.   The bank stopped payment
on the 3d September, and ultimately became bankrupt.   On
the 11th, the defendant repudiated the transaction, and gave
the plaintiffs notice not to pay the price on his account.
The plaintiffs, having been compelled, according to the rules
of the stock exchange, to pay for shares on the settlement
day, sent the defendant the certificates and transfers, and,.
upon his declining to accept them, sued him for the money,
and it was decided that they were entitled to recover it.(c)

**Notice to Broker Good Where Notice to Vendee was Neces-
sary—Usage.**

SEC. 132. So in the case of *Graves* v. *Legg*,(d) the defendants, London merchants, employed a broker in Liverpool to
purchase some wool.   The broker negotiated a sale by the
plaintiff to the defendants of certain bales deliverable at
Odessa, "the names of the vessels to be declared as soon as
the wools were shipped."   In this transaction the broker
acted for both plaintiff and defendants.   By the custom of
Liverpool, where a contract contained a stipulation that

(b) *Bayliffe* v. *Butterworth*, 1 Exch.   587; *Stray* v. *Russell*, 29 L. J. Q. B. 279;
425, *per* Alderson, B., at p. 429.   *Lloyd* v. *Gilbert*, 35 L. J. Q. B. 74.

(c) *Taylor* v. *Stray*, 2 C. B. N. S. 175;   (d) 11 Exch. 642, affirmed 2 H. &.
see also *Smith* v. *Lindon*, 5 C. B. N. S.   N. 210.

notice of an event should be given by the vendor to the vendee, it was usual for the vendor to give the notice to the broker, who communicated it to the vendee. In this case it was held, both in the Court of Exchequer and in that of the Exchequer Chamber, that the defendants were bound by such usage, and, therefore, that a notice by the plaintiff to the broker of the names of the vessels on which the wools were shipped was a performance of that stipulation, although the broker omitted to communicate them to the defendants.

This Rule Reconciled with General Principle—Rules in Other Cases—Customs at Lloyd's Coffee House—Bayliffe v. Butterworth.

SEC. 133. But the rule expressed might seem irreconcilable with the general principle which we stated above, that it was only to be presumed that the parties contracted according to the terms of an ·existing custom, and that that presumption was capable of rebuttal; for here we see that a usage may make a man liable to certain incidents of a contract, although he can satisfactorily prove that he was in ignorance of the custom. It also seems to be in almost direct opposition to the rules laid down in *Gabay* v. *Lloyd(e)* and *Bartlett* v. *Pentland.(f)* In the first of these it was found in special verdict that a certain usage with respect to policies prevailed amongst the underwriters subscribing policies at Lloyd's coffee house, in London, and merchants and others effecting policies there, and that the policy in question was effected at Lloyd's coffee house; but it was not found that the plaintiff was in the habit of effecting policies at that place, and it was held that this usage was not sufficient to bind the plaintiff. And in the latter a custom was proved to be in force at Lloyd's coffee house, to consider a set off as payment between underwriter and broker, and it was held that such custom was not binding on one who was not shown

(e) 3 B. & C. 793.   (f) 10 B. & C. 760.

to be cognizant of it, or to have assented to it. Yet these cases were decided before the case of *Bayliffe* v. *Butterworth*—in which the general principle, that the usage of a particular market binds him who buys or sells in it, whether he is aware of it or not, was laid down—came before the Court of Exchequer, and Parkes, B., while he did not question the authority of these cases, distinguished them from the one before the court, which was one in which a person had been authorized to make a contract for a principal, and he remarked that it appeared to him "that a person who authorizes another to make a contract for him, authorizes him to make the contract in the usual way," and that "the question here was as to the authority which the plaintiff received."(*g*)

The Scope of Authority.

SEC. 134. This seems a perspicuous distinction. The scope of authority is to be ascertained by the necessities which are incident to the act which an agent has to do. His action in the matter will be estimated by the possibilities of the trade in connection with which he transacts, and those possibilities are modified by the usages of the trade. It is in the power of the principal to define the agent's authority with a strictness which will prevent the operation of the customs of the place or trade. If he fails to do so, he must not complain if his authority is interpreted by the ordinary usages of the trade, and if he finds himself bound by these, even although he is ignorant of their existence. In the cases to which reference has been made above,(*h*) it was, as in the case of *Bayliffe* v. *Butterworth*, always a question of authority, and it cannot, therefore, be matter for wonder that the principle enunciated in *Gabay* v. *Lloyd* has been confirmed, and that the dictum in *Scott* v. *Irving*,(*i*) that a usage to substitute

(*g*) 1 Exch. pp. 428, 429.
(*h*) *Taylor* v. *Stray*, 2 C. B. N. S. 175; *Stray* v. *Russell*, 29 L. J. Q. B. 279; *Graves* v. *Legg*, 11 Exch. 642; 2 H. & N. 216, ante p. 91.
(*i*) 1 B. & Ad. 606.

another person as debtor to the principal can only bind those who have notice of it, has been adopted.(*k*)

Nature of Usage to be Considered.

SEC. 135. The character of the usage and its effect upon the inter-relation of parties must be considered before it is admitted to affect a contract entered into by persons who were ignorant of it. Some usages are so evidently technical that it would be wrong to suppose that persons contracting without knowing them could reasonably anticipate their existence, or the existence of any in that factual connection. Many, on the other hand, are so palpably matters of general convenience, and belonging to a trade in such rapid growth, that it must be presumed to be making its own laws in the establishment of customs, that it is right to presume that the individual contracting, although ignorant of the particular custom, must have been aware of the existence of usage, may have surmised their nature, and even if he did not, was at least willing to enter into a contract, the precise terms of which were unknown to him, because the incidents were to be attached by a usage of which he was ignorant.

Confidence in the Usages of a Trade.

SEC. 136. Just as one man trusts another to work for him with general authority as an agent, trusting to the honor and honesty of the individual, so may one trust a usage to regulate one's rights—for a usage is the outcome of the honor, honesty, fair dealing, and convenience of a class of men. The admissibility of proof of a usage as against one who was ignorant of it is a question which might well be left to be decided in each individual case. There could, it seems to us, be little reason for dissatisfaction in the admission of a rule of the Liverpool Stock Exchange, in evidence between parties not members of it, when the question was, what is a

(*k*) *Sweeting* v. *Pearce*, 7 C. B. N. S. 449; see also *Adams* v. *Peters*, 2 C. & K. 723.

reasonable time for the completion of a sale of shares made at Liverpool through the agency of brokers?(*l*)

Incidents Annexed by Common Law—As to Title.

SEC. 137. It may be well to remark here that the way in which usage is permitted to annex incidents to written contracts, is another proof of its relationship to the common law. Law annexes various incidents to contracts, and these differ from those annexed by usage only in the circumstance that they claim their own recognition without proof, while the others have to be evidenced. It may be useful shortly to allude to some of these, although many may be in the immediate memory of the reader. In contracts for the sale of estates, whether freehold or leasehold, the law, in the absence of express stipulation, it will be remembered, implies an undertaking on the part of the vendor that he will make out a good title,(*m*) and an undertaking on the part of the vendee that if the title prove defective, the damages to which he shall be entitled shall be limited to the expenses actually incurred in the investigation, and shall only be nominal for the loss of the bargain.(*n*)   So, in a demise of real property, the law annexes a condition that the lessor has a good title to the premises, and that the lessee shall not be evicted during the term;(*o*) but it does not imply from the nature of the contract a warranty that the property leased, whether it be a house or land, shall be in a proper state to admit either of habitation or cultivation, or that in other respects it shall be reasonably fit for the purposes for which it is taken.(*p*)

(*l*) *Stewart* v. *Canty*, 8 M. & W. 160; see also *Stewart* v. *Aberdein*, 4 M. & W. 211.

(*m*) *Souter* v. *Drake*, 5 B. & Ad. 992; 3 N. & M. 40; *Doe* v. *Stanion*, 1 M. & W. 695, 701, *per* Parke, B.; *Hall* v. *Betty*, 4 M. & Gr. 410. These cases overrule *George* v. *Prichard*, *Reg.* v. *Moo.* 417.

(*n*) *Flurean* v. *Thornhill*, 2 W. & Bl. 1,078; *Walker* v. *Moore*, 10 B. & C. 416; *Robinson* v. *Harman*, 1 Ex. R. 855, *per* Parke, B.; *Wordington* v. *Warrington*, 8 C. B. 134.

(*o*) *Per* Parke, B., in *Sutton* v. *Temple*, 12 M. & W. 64.

(*p*) *Sutton* v. *Temple*, 12 M. & W. 52; *Hart* v. *Windsor*, *Id.* 68. But see, as to letting of furnished house, *Smith* v. *Marrable*, 11 M. & W. 5.

Effect of Usage on Insurance Contracts.

SEC. 138. In all cases of fire insurance, the insurer is presumed to know of all the customs and usages incident to any business or class of risks he undertakes to insure,[5] as well as all the risks usually incident thereto, and consequently is presumed to contemplate all the perils connected with it, to the minutest detail, so far as they arise or exist in the ordinary and usual methods of conducting the business,[6] and this extends not only to the character of the risk, but also to the matter covered by the policy. Therefore, when the stock is insured, although nothing is said in the policy in reference thereto, yet it being understood that the stock insured is to be manufactured and sold, and replaced by other stock, the policy covers the stock on hand at the time of the loss, although no part of it was on hand when the policy issued, because it being in accordance with the usual course of business that the stock shall constantly change, the policy is impliedly issued to cover any stock on hand when a loss occurs.[7] Thus, a policy issued upon merchandise in a store, does not cover any special or particular property, but property comprising such a stock as is on hand when a loss occurs, although nothing is said in the policy concerning the matter. This is implied from the nature and usages of

[5] Wood's Fire Insurance 327; *May v. Buckeye Ins. Co.*, 25 *Wis.* 291.

[6] *Sims* v. *State Ins. Co.*, 47 Mo. 54; *Livingston* v. *Maryland Ins. Co.*, 7 Cranch (U. S.) 506; *Citizens' Ins. Co.* v. *McLaughlin*, 53 Penn. St. 485; *Fulton Ins. Co.* v. *Milner*, 23 Ala. 420; *Glendale Woolen Co.* v. *Protection Ins. Co.*, 21 Conn. 19; *Hancox* v. *Fishing Ins. Co.*, 3 Sumn. (U. S.) 132; *Niagara Ins. Co.* v. *De Graff*, 12 Mich. 124; *Archer* v. *Merchants' &c. Ins. Co.*, 43 Mo. 434; *Franklin Ins. Co.* v. *Updegraff*, 50 Penn. St. 350; *Leggett* v. *Ins. Co.*, 10 Rich. (S. C.) 292.

[7] *Peoria &c. Ins. Co.* v. *Annapaw*, 51 Ill. 283. In *New York Gaslight Co.* v. *Mechanics' F. Ins. Co.*, 2 Hall (N. Y.) 108, the policy covered gasmetres and fixtures belonging to and rented by the assured, placed or to to be placed in the buildings, stores or dwellings of subscribers, for seven years. It was held that the liability of the insurers was not limited to such property in building at the time when insurance was made, but to all such property placed and remaining in such buildings at the time when the loss occurred.

the risk and the usual course of the business.[8]   A policy insuring a certain class of property or business, covers all articles incident to or usually or necessarily used in the prosecution of the business.[9]   So, too, a policy may be extended to cover goods not strictly within the premises named, if a usage is shown to regard contiguous places as within the description.   Thus, a policy covering a stock " of ship timber in a ship yard," was held to embrace timber lying on the sidewalks near the yard, a usage being shown to regard the street as a part of the yard,[1] and the same rule was adopted in a Massachusetts case before referred to as to the word "room" used in an application for insurance.[2] Not only is the insurer bound by all customs or usages prevailing in reference either to the business or property insured, but also by all general or special usages incident to the risk,[3] and all the usages of a trade are considered as a part of the contract and are to be regarded in construing it.[4] The insurer is bound to know that certain hazards are incident thereto,[5] and that certain practices exist among those engaged in it.[6]   If the policy is ambiguous, evidence is admissible to explain it, and this may be done when necessary, by proving the course of business and the incidents thereof,[7] even though it does not establish or amount to a

---

[8] *Lane* v. *Maine L. Ins. Co.*, 12 Me. 44; *Sawyer* v. *Dodge Co. Mu. Ins. Co.*, 37 Wis. 504; *Draper* v. *Hudson River Ins. Co.*, 17 N. Y. 424; *Den* v. *Hope Ins. Co.*, 1 Hall (N. Y.) 166.

[9] *Spratley* v. *Hartford Ins. Co.*, 1 Dill (U. S. C.) 392; *Seaney* v. *Central L. Ins. Co.*, 111 Mass. 540; *Lichenstein* v. *Baltic F. Ins. Co.*, 45 Ill. 301.

[1] *Webb* v. *Nat'l F. Ins. Co.*, 2 Sandf. (N. Y.) 447.

[2] *Daniels* v. *Hud. River Ins. Co.*, ante.

[3] *Harper* v. *Albany Ins. Co.*, 17 N. Y. 194. Thus it is competent to show that among insurers and owners of

whaling ships, an insurance upon an outfit covers one-fourth the catching.   *Mary* v. *Whaling Ins. Co.*, 9 Met. (Mass.) 354.   Also a custom that in case of re-insurance, the warranty is confined to the condition of the risk at the date of the original policy. *Foster* v. *Mentor Life Assn.*, 3 Cl. & Bl. 48.

[4] *Hancox* v. *Fishing Ins. Co.*, ante.

[5] *Harper* v. *Albany Ins. Co.*, ante.

[6] *Citizens' Ins. Co.* v. *McLaughlin*, ante.

[7] *Fabri* v. *Phenix Ins. Co.*, 55 N. Y. 133.

18

general usage,[8] for a contract may be affected by proof either of a general usage or by similar acts of the parties in like cases,[9] but neither custom nor usage can be set up to overcome a plain provision in a policy which fairly excludes a usage, as when the contract provides a mode of payment and delivery, a custom to pay and deliver in a different mode cannot be shown,[1] nor can it be shown to put an interpretation upon a contract inconsistent with its language,[2] nor to vary it.[3] But even though inconsistent with the *printed* conditions of a policy, a usage or custom may be shown, not to alter or vary the contract, but to give effect thereto by showing that the conditions were waived because when a usage or custom incident to a risk is shown the insurer is presumed to know of and contract in reference to it, and the only proof requisite to charge them therewith is simply the fact that the usage existed, for they are bound to know of it, and the law imputes knowledge thereof to them.[4]   Although a policy provides that a night watch shall be kept in the building, unless the proviso is specific as to the kind of watch to be kept, it is held that the condition is not of such a watch as is *suitable* according to the *usages* of the business, is kept,[5] and at such times and during such periods as a watchman is *usually* kept in such establishments, and evidence of the usage of other similar establishments is admissible to determine whether the condition has been kept.[6]   Thus, where the policy contained a clause, " a watchman kept upon the premises," it was held that the assured was entitled to recover,

---

[8] 1 Duer on Ins. 57 ; Wood on Fire Insurance, 848.

[9] *Green* v. *Farmer*, 5 Burr. 2221 ; *Rushforth* v. *Hadfield*, 6 East. 619.

[1] *Duncan* v. *Green*, 43 Iowa 679.

[2] *Marks* v. *Elevator Co.*, 43 Iowa 337.

[3] *Partridge* v. *Ins. Co.*, 15 Wall (U. S.) 373 ; *Ins. Co.* v. *Wright*, 1 *Id.* 456 ; *Barnard* v. *Kellogg*, 10 U. S. 383 ; *Cash* v. *Hinkle*, 36 Iowa 623.

[4] *May* v. *Buckeye Ins. Co.*, 25 Wis. 291 ; *Citizens' Ins. Co.* v. *McLaughlin*, 53 Penn. St. 485 ; *Fowler* v. *Ætna Ins. Co.*, 7 Wend. (N. Y.) 270 ; *Finley* v. *Lycoming Ins. Co.*, 31 Penn. St. 311.

[5] *May* v. *Buckeye Ins. Co.*, ante ; *Priegen* v. *Exchange L. Ins. Co.*, 6 Wis. 89 ; *Crocker* v. *People's Ins. Co.*, 8 Cush. (Mass.) 79.

[6] *Crocker* v. *People's Ins. Co.*, ante.

although there was no watchman on the premises when the
fire occurred, and had been none for ten days previous, the
shop having been unused during that period, and it being
shown that in such establishments it was usual *not* to keep a
watch when the shop was not in operation.[7] " What is common and usual," said Shaw, C. J., in the last named case,
" under given circumstances, is evidence tending to show
what is reasonable."   But the language may be such as to
exclude the usage.   Thus, where the question in the application was, " Is there a watch kept nights?" and the answer
was, " There is a watchman nights," the court held that this
clearly bound the assured to keep a watchman *every* night,
including Sunday nights, and excluded evidence of a usage
in similar establishments *not* to keep a watch Sunday night.[8]
Where a stock of goods are insured, as " a stock of goods
such as are kept in a country store,"[9] or simply " a stock of
groceries,"[1] the terms carry with them the right to keep any
article or class of articles *usually* kept as a part of such
stocks, whether the keeping of such articles is expressly prohibited in the printed portion of the policy or not.[2] Thus,
in a New York case,[3] the policy covered a printing press,
types, negatives, " and their stock as photographers, including engravings and materials used in their business."   The
policy also contained a clause prohibiting the keeping or
use of kerosene in a building containing the property
insured, except by consent in writing.   The plaintiffs used
in their business as photographers, a portable kerosene
stove, such as was *generally* employed in the business, and

[7] *Crocker* v. *People's Ins. Co.*, ante.
[8] *Glendale Manufacturing Co.* v.
Protection Ins. Co., 21 Conn. 19 ; *First
National Bank* v. *Insurance Co. of N.
America*, 50 N. Y. 45 ; *Ripley* v. *Ætna
Ins. Co.*, ante. *Contra*, see *May* v.
Buckeye Ins. Co., ante.
[9] *Prudar* v. *Continental Ins. Co.*, 47
N. Y. 114.

[1] *Niagara Ins. Co.* v. *De Graff*, 12
Mich. 124.
[2] *Archer* v. *Merchants' Ins. Co.*, 43
Mo. 434; *Whitmarsh* v. *Conway F. Ins.
Co.*, 16 Gray (Mass.) 657; *Pindar* v.
Kings Co. Ins. Co., 36 N. Y. 648.
[3] *Hall* v. *Ins. Co. of N. America*, 58
N. Y. 292.

while so using the stove, *and from its use*, the premises
were set on fire and the loss occurred. It was proved that
a portable *gas* lamp or stove might as well have been used
in the business, but that a *kerosene* stove was *customarily*
used. The company was held liable for the loss, Grover, J.,
remarking: "When a policy is issued upon a stock of goods
in a specified business, *the underwriter is presumed to know
what goods are usually kept in that business.* When a policy
is issued as in the present case, upon the materials used in
the business of photography, *it includes all such as are in
ordinary use,* although some other things might be substituted therefor.[4] In a Missouri case[5] the effect of the usages
of a business upon the conditions of the policy, was well
illustrated. In that case a policy was issued upon a wagon
maker's shop and materials. The policy prohibited the use
of camphene, benzine, &c. The plaintiff had a paint shop
in connection with his business where the wagons were
painted, and had a half barrel of benzine in the shop for
mixing the paints. A loss occurring, payment was resisted
on the ground that the keeping of benzine was in violation
of the conditions of the policy. But the court held that if
a paint shop was a usual part of a wagon maker's shop, and
paints were used for manufacturing wagons, and were customarily kept in the building and used for that purpose,
and benzine was customarily used for mixing paints, the
printed conditions were plainly in opposition to the written
clause, and should be rejected.[6] In a Pennsylvania case

---

[4] *Harper* v. *New York Ins. Co.*, 22
N. Y. 444; *Steinbach* v. *La Fayette Ins.
Co.*, 54 *Id.* 90; *Elliott* v. *Hamilton Ins.
Co.*, 13 Gray (Mass.) 139.

[5] *Archer* v. *Merchants' L. Ins. Co.*,
43 Mo. 434.

[6] In *Phenix Ins. Co.* v. *Taylor*, 5
Minn. 492, the same rule was adopted
as to gunpowder. In that case the
plaintiff procured an insurance upon
a stock of goods described in the
policy as "dry goods, groceries, &c,"
such as are usually kept in a general
retail store. The policy prohibited
the keeping of gunpowder, saltpetre,
or phosphorus. The plaintiffs kept
gunpowder for sale, and the company set up the breach of this condition in defence. The court held
that, if gunpowder and the articles

which is referred to elsewhere[7] and the main facts in which are there given, the effect of a usage of a trade upon the condition of a policy was strikingly illustrated. In that case the policy provided that benzole, in quantities not exceeding *five* barrels, might be kept in "a small shed entirely detached from the other buildings, situated on the rear end of the lot, about one hundred feet from the main building, *and no where else on said premises.*" The policy covered "*the buildings of their tannery and patent leather manufactory.*" Benzole was an indispensable article in the prosecution of the business, and, while it was stored in the building referred to, yet, it was the custom of the workmen to carry it into the building in open pails as often as wanted, and on the morning of the fire a workman carried a pail of it into the building, when it almost instantly ignited and produced the loss. The insurer insisted that this method of carrying benzole into the factory operated as a breach of the condition of the policy, and excused them from liability. The plaintiff proved that the method adopted by him, was the *customary* method in similar establishments, and, the fact of custom being found, the court held that there was no breach of the condition, as the insurer was bound to know of such custom, and, in the absence of anything in the policy excluding it, must be regarded as having waived the condition to the extent of

prohibited were *usually* kept in general retail stores, there was no breach. In *Niagara Ins. Co.* v. *De Graff*, 12 Mich. 124, it was held that where a policy covered a stock of "groceries" and contained a condition prohibiting the keeping of alcohol and spirituous liquors, the latter articles were kept by the assured. In an action for a loss the insurer set up this breach in defence. The plaintiff showed that such articles "usually" formed a part of such stocks. The defendant insisted that this usage of the trade could not affect the policy, because

the statute in Michigan prohibited the keeping of liquors. The court held that if the liquors usually formed a part of a stock of "groceries," the policy was not avoided, and that the fact that the statute prohibited their being kept, would not aid the defendants, citing as to the effect of the statute, *Armstrong* v. *Tolen*, 11 Wheat. (U. S.) 258; *The Ocean Ins. Co.* v. *Palleys*, 13 Pet. (U.S.) 157; *Hibbard* v. *People*, 4 Mich. 125.

[7] *Citizens' Ins. Co.* v. *McLaughlin*, 53 Penn. St. 485.

the custom. Woodard, J., in delivering the opinion of the court, said: "The argument on behalf of the company is, that the policy, both in letter and spirit, meant to confine the benzole to the shed on the rear of the lot, and to exclude it from any other part of the premises; that in carrying it from the shed across the yard in open buckets, and setting it down in a room with the door open, was an abuse of the privilege granted by the company, which, if it could have been anticipated, would have prevented their taking the risk; and that such use of it was *keeping it elsewhere than in the shed*, and was, therefore, a palpable violation of the covenant." The answer which the learned judge made to this argument was substantially as follows: "You insured a patent leather manufactory; you knew, *for you were bound to know, that benzole was ordinarily used in such factories;* you stipulated that five barrels of it might be kept on hand near to the factory, and the necessary presumption is that you meant that it might be kept for use in that factory, *as the article is ordinarily used in similar factories.* If, therefore, it was kept in the place stipulated, *and used according to the custom of trade*, it was one of the risks covered by the policy."[8] Another striking illustration of the effect of *usage* upon a policy of insurance is to be found in a Connecticut case,[9] in which it was held that, although a certain use of premises might increase the risk, yet if it was temporary, and only an *ordinary use*, and one that the insurer must have known was incident thereto, the policy was not avoided. Thus, the buildings were described as barns, to which was added, "all the above described barns are used for hay, straw, grain unthreshed, stabling and shelter." The night before the fire, the assured had placed

---

[8] *Girard Ins. Co.* v. *Stephenson,* 1 Wright (Penn.) 198; *Harper* v. *Albany City Ins. Co.*, 1 Bos. (N. Y.) 520; app'd, Court of Appeals, 17 N. Y. 194; *Buchanan* v. *Exchange F. Ins. Co.*, 61

N. Y. 26; *Washington F. Ins. Co.* v. *Davidson,* 30 Md. 91.

[9] *Billings* v. *Tolland Co. Ins. Co.*, 20 Conn. 139.

two bushels of lime in one of the barns, and six or eight pails of water, both the water and lime being placed in a large tub, for the purpose of preparing the lime for rolling in it some wheat which he was about to sow upon his farm. A short time previous to the fire, he had commenced painting his house, and the painter had mixed his paints in the same room, and at the time of the fire there were in it, an oil barrel containing about a gallon of oil, a keg of white lead and a pot with about a pint of mixed paint. The insurer held that by this use of the premises, the risk had been increased and consequently that he was absolved from liability under the policy. Waite, J., in commenting upon the effect of usage in the ordinary use of property in construing warrantees or conditions in policies, said: "The acts done by the plaintiff are set forth in the motion, so that one can see what they were, and whether they were a departure *from the common and ordinary use of such buildings.* We very well know that farmers in this State are in the habit of using their barns for a variety of purposes, connected with their agricultural business, besides that of storing their hay and stabling their cattle. Their barns are frequently used as a shelter for their wagons, plows, sleds and other farming implements. When the plaintiff procured the insurance to be effected on the buildings, it is not to be presumed that he meant to deprive himself *of their common and ordinary use,* or that the defendants by their policy intended any such thing. And, excepting so far as there is an express prohibition in relation to the use of them, the understanding of the parties undoubtedly was, that the common and ordinary use of them was to be continued in the same manner as if the policy had never been issued."[1] In all cases, in determining whether or not there has been an increase of the risk such as avoids the policy, the court will ascertain so far as possible what the parties must be presumed to have contem-

[1] *Dobson* v. *Sotheby,* 1 Mac. & M. 90.

plated when the insurance was made, *and this involves a consideration of the usages and incidents of the risk*, because if the use was warranted by the usages or ordinary incidents of the risk, it does not come within the prohibition, for the parties must be presumed to have contemplated the use.[2]

As to Marine Insurance—Voyage Commenced.

SEC. 139. In relation to marine insurance, we have an instance of this legal annexation of incidents. One of these is that in every voyage-policy, whether it be on a ship or on goods, a warrant of seaworthiness at the commencement of the risk is implied. These further conditions are also understood as forming a tacit part of the contract—that the voyage is to be commenced in a reasonable time, that all material circumstances are to be disclosed. If these conditions are not performed, this omission will render the policy void, whether the omission has been due to fraudulent motives or not.(*q*) These decisions are only given by way of illustrating the method by which usage annexes incidents to written contracts. It will be understood that the method of such annexation is precisely the same, and that there is a close analogy in this respect between the usages of trade and the Common Law—an analogy which we have endeavored to keep before

[2] *Washington F. Ins. Co.* v. *Davidson*, 30 Md. 91; *New York* v. *Hamilton Ins. Co.*, 10 Bos. (N. Y.) 537. The rule is well expressed in *Hall* v. *Ins. Co. of N. America*, ante, that, where a policy is issued upon the materials used in a business, it includes and authorizes the use of all such materials as are in ordinary use in the business, although by the printed clauses of the policy, the keeping or use thereof is prohibited, and although other materials might as well be substitued therefor. *Langdon* v. *Equitable Ins. Co.*, 1 Hall (N. Y.) 226; *Duncan* v. *Sun Ins. Co.*, 6 Wend. (N. Y.) 488; *Archer* v. *Merchants' L. Ins. Co.*, ante; *Harper* v. *Albany City Ins. Co* , ante; *O'Neill* v. *Buffalo Ins. Co.*, 3 N. Y. 122; *Buchanan* v. *Exchange F. Ins. Co.*, 61 N. Y. 26; *Phenix Ins. Co.* v. *Taylor*, 5 Minn. 492; *Harper* v. *N. Y. F. Ins. Co.* 22 N. Y. 441; *Franklin Ins. Co.* v. *Updegraff*, 43 Penn. St. 450; *Steinback* v. *La Fayette Ins. Co.*, 54 N. Y. 90; *Whitmarsh* v. *Conway F. Ins. Co.*, 16 Gray (Mass.) 359; *Bryant* v. *Poughkeepsie Ins. Co.*, 17 N. Y. 200.

(*q*) *Gibson* v. *Small*, 4 H. of L. Cas. 398, *per* Parke, B.

the reader's mind, as it seems, in our opinion, to explicate the real nature of each.

Necessity for Usage.

SEC. 140. It will be remembered, too, that the incidents which are annexed by the Common Law are very few in number, and that there may be innumerable useful incidents in relation to every trade and business, and every transaction which is made in the course of these, which might well be annexed, and which, therefore, fall within the province of that handmaid of the Common Law—usage—to supply. The nature of these may be understood from what has already been said, and the scope of the authority of usage will also be appreciated from the various cases of treating the admissibility of evidence of such customs.

Usage and Legal Enactments—Usage Cannot Control a Statute.

SEC. 141. One other matter may be alluded to in relation to usage, and that is its relation to legal enactments. We have already seen that customs which are an invention for the convenience of those who are employed in trade, and are, in fact, the natural growth of law in organization, when they are judicially recognized cease to be customs, provable by evidence; but rise to the level of laws evidenced by the legislative authority, which resides in the judges or by the existence of a statute which has embodied the former usage.(r) It follows, therefore, that when the courts have ascertained and declared a usage, it is alterable only by legislature, and it will not affect such a recognized usage to prove that a usage of trade which varies its terms actually exists. Hence it is that we have the well known rule that a custom opposed to a statute is bad,(s) and that no usage or custom can be set up for the purpose of controlling the rules of law.(t)

(r) Ante, p. 2, 5, et seq.
(s) Ante, p. 26 and 27, and see Walker v. Transportation Co., 3 Wall (U. S.) 150; Winter v. United States, Hemps. (U. S.) 344.

(t) Hinlon v. Locke, 5 Hill (N. Y.) 437; see Thomson v. Ashton, 14 John. 316; Beirne v. Doed, 5 N. Y. 95; Wheeler v. Newbold, 16 N. J. 392; Huggins v. Moore, 34 N. J. 417; Du-

298 PRIVATE USAGES, CUSTOM OF BROKERS, &C.

Instances in which Usages are Bad.

Sec. 142. Where the statute provides what a certain officer shall do, and how he shall do it, so far as his duty is dependent upon the statute, evidence of a usage or custom to discharge this duty in another or different manner is not admissible.[3] Thus, where by statute a note must be presented for payment and protested by a notary, a presentment by a clerk is not good, although such a usage among notaries may have existed for a long time. None of the official duties of an officer (as a notary) can be delegated to another, except when so provided by statute, and neither a custom or usage can confer any such power.[4] Nor can the custom or usage of a trade be shown to control a statute that conflicts therewith,[5] and it is said that a *local* usage cannot be shown to control the well settled rules of the common law relating thereto.[6] In an English case,[7] it was sought to introduce evidence of a custom among merchants to treat an indorsement of a bill of exchange without the words " or order " as restrictive, when by the courts such indorsements had been treated as negotiable when the bill itself was negotiable. Lord Mansfield said, " The point now in question has already been solemnly settled, both in the Court of King's Bench and in Common Pleas, and therefore witnesses ought not to have been examined as to the usage, after such a solemn determination of what was the law." In a New York case,[8]

guid v. *Edwards*, 50 Barb. (N. Y.) 288; *Woodruff* v. *Merchants' Bank*, 25 Wend. (N. Y.) 674; *Frith* v. *Baker*, 2

[3] *The Commercial Bank of Kentucky* v. *Varnum*, 3 Lans. (N. Y.) 86; *Supervisors* v. *Van Clief*, 1 Hun. (N. Y.) 454.
[4] *Onandago Bank* v. *Bates*, 3 Hill (N. Y.) 53.
[5] *New York Firemen's Ins. Co.* v. *Ely*, 2 Cow. (N. Y.) 678; *Bank of Utica* v. *Wager*, Id. 712.
[6] *Minnesota Cent'l R. R. Co.* v. *Morgan*, 52 Barb. (N. Y.) 2171; *Bissell* v.

John. (N. Y.) 327; *Bowen* v. *Newel*, 18 Barb. (N. Y.) 391.

Campbell, 54 N. Y. 353; *Higgins* v. *Moore*, 34 Id. 417; *Dewees* v. *Lockhart*, 1 Tex. 535; *Schiefflin* v. *Harvey*, Auth. (N. Y.) 56; *Strong* v. *Bliss*, 6 Met. (Mass.) 393; *Home* v. *Mutual L Ins. Co.*, 1 Sandf. (N. Y. Superior Ct.) 137.
[7] *Edin* v. *The East India Co.*, 2 Burr. 1216.
[8] See *Thompson* v. *Ashton*, 14 John. (N. Y.) 316.

the court say, "No custom in the sale of any particular
description of goods can be admitted to control the *general*
rules of law ; such a principle would be extremely perni-
cious in its consequences, and render vague and uncertain all
rules of law.[9] The reason for this doctrine is, that after a
rule has been recognized at law, it is no longer under the
control of usage or custom, and the adjudication is the proper
evidence of it.[1] But I apprehend that the rule seemingly
established by these cases is, after all, to be taken subject to
qualifications, and instances may certainly arise where even
a usage of trade may control the rules of the common law.
It is certainly competent for the parties to make a usage a
part of any contract, except where it is prohibited by statute
or contrary to sound public policy, by express agreement to
that effect. If a rule of the common law can be renounced
by an *express* agreement, can it not also be renounced by an
implied agreement? It would be absurd to say that it could
not be, and the instances are quite numerous where long continued and well settled usages have been held to be good,
although in direct conflict with the rules of the common law.
Thus, the custom of Gavelkind and Borough-English grew
up and became valid in spite of the fact that they were contrary to the rules of the common law. When it is said that
a mere usage cannot be shown to control or vary the rules
of the common law, the courts almost daily act upon a contrary rule, as we shall show hereafter, and the rule may be
stated thus: Where the rules of the common law relating to
a particular transaction are well settled, it will be presumed
that the parties contracted in reference thereto, but this presumption may be overcome by proof of a well established

[9] *Wheeler* v. *Newbold*, 16 N. Y. 392;
Duguid v. *Edwards*, 50 Barb. (N. Y.)
288; *Higgins* v. *Moore*, 34 N. Y. 417;
Bierne v. *Dord*, 5 N. Y. 95; *Allen* v.
Merchants' Bank, 22 Wend. (N. Y.)
215; *Haskins* v. *Warren*, 115 Mass.
514. A well settled rule of commercial law cannot be overcome by
proof of the usage or understanding
of banks contrary thereto. *Security
Bank* v. *Bank of the Republic*, 67 N.
Y. 458.

[1] *Nelson, J.,* in *Allen* v. *Merchants'
Bank*, 22 Wend. (N. Y.) 215.

usage of the trade or business to which the transaction, of such long standing and uniform application, as to leave no doubt that the parties contracted in reference to it, rather than in reference to the rules of the common law, and it then becomes a question of fact for the jury to find whether the parties intended to adopt the usage or the general law,[2] and the question turns upon the *quantum* of proof rather than upon its conflict with the common law,[3] and where they vary the presumption is undoubtedly *prima facie* in favor of the intention to adopt the general law, but this may be overcome by proof that unmistakably shows a contrary intention. The proof to establish the adoption, or rather the presumption of the adoption, of a usage in opposition to the general law, must of course be strong. The usage must be shown to be uniform and well known to both parties, or of such long standing and notoriety as to warrant a presumption of knowledge, and show that the parties must have had it in view when they entered into the contract.[4]   This rule necessarily

[2] *Gordon* v. *Little*, 8 S. & R. (Penn.) 583; *Halsey* v. *Brown*, 3 Day (Conn.) 346; *Wild* v. *Gotham*, 10 Mass. 366. In *Horton* v. *Beckman*, C. T. R. 760, it was held to be no objection that a custom is not conformable to the common law.

[3] *Blanchard* v. *Hilliard*, 11 Mass. 85; *Middleton* v. *Haywood*, 2 N. & McCord. (S. C.) 9; *Renner* v. *Columbia Bank*, 9 Wheat. (U. S.) 581.

[4] In *Isham* v. *Fox*, 7 Ohio, 317, the most sensible view of this question was taken. In that case the court held that, in the absence of any statutory regulation, a rule of commercial law has been adopted by the courts of last resort in a State, the usage will henceforth be held to conform thereto throughout the State, *and this can only be rebutted by clear proof of a uniform and settled local usage*

to the contrary. Again in a Georgia case, *Latimer* v. *Alexander*, 14 Ga. 259, the court say, "A *mere local usage* in a small part of the country cannot change the law and give a person a remedy against a person, when the law does not, and generally it will be found that the idea that crops out in some of the cases that a usage or custom that conflicts with the common law, cannot prevail, is after all nothing more than a well recognized rule that the common law will prevail against a mere usage, unless the usage is of such a character and of such long standing and notoriety as to indicate that the parties must have contracted in reference to it." *Dewees* v. *Lockhart*, 1 Tex. 535; *Schiefflin* v. *Harvey*, Anth. (N. Y.) 56; *Strong* v. *Bliss*, 6 Met. (Mass.) 398; *Home* v. *Mutual Ins.*

results from that salutary and inflexible rule of construction
that gives effect to the true intent of the parties to a contract, and leads the courts, for the purpose of ascertaining
it, to look to the subject-matter of the contract and the
attendant circumstances and surroundings, and as a custom
or usage is only allowable as a means of arriving at the real
intention of the parties, and never to thwart it, it follows as a
matter of course that where a usage and the common law conflict, effect is to be given to the one or the other as the weight
of the evidence bearing upon the question preponderates, and
the fact that a conflict exists between the usage and the common law does not, if the usage is reasonable and not opposed
to public policy, necessarily render the usage inoperative.[5]
"A custom used upon a certain reasonable cause, depriveth the common law."[6] A custom *known and acquiesced in*
by a party affected by it, will excuse the performance of a
duty prescribed by law.[7] If it is shown, or may fairly be
presumed, that the parties contracted with reference to a
custom existing in the place where the transaction was
entered into, the general law must give way to the custom.[8]
The rights of parties are to be determined by the law, and
not by any local custom or usage, *unless there is proof that
such custom or usage is certain, general, frequent and so
ancient or notorious as to be generally known and acted upon,*

Co., 1 Sandf. (N. Y.) 137. As sustaining the proposition advanced in the
text, see *Leach* v. *Perkins*, 17 Me. 462;
Caldwell v. *Dawson*, 4 Met. (Ky.) 121;
Governor v. *Withers*, 5 Gratt (Va.)
24.

[5] *Isham* v. *Fox*, ante; *Von Scmidt*
v. *Huntington*, 1 Cal. 55. There is a
disposition in some of our courts to
limit the effect of usages and their
office, on the ground that they often
arise from mistaken notions of the
rights of parties, and are dangerous
innovations upon the law. But, to

the extent of determining the true
intent of the parties in a matter in
which the contract itself is silent, or
where a doubt arises from the language used therein, the courts all
hold them admissible, if clearly
proved uniform and reasonable.
The Schooner Reeside, 2 Sumn. (U. S.)
567.

[6] Co. Lit. 113–115.

[7] *Govenor* v. *Withers*, 5 Gratt.
(Va.) 24.

[8] *Fulton Ins. Co.* v. *Milner*, 23 Ala.
420.

and unless it shall be adjudged reasonable.[9] Usage is evidence of the construction given to the law, and, when it is established and uniform, it regulates the rights and duties of those who act within its limits,[1] and ought to be respected by the courts.[2] It will be found by reference to the cases where proof of usages has been denied, and the courts have spoken of the usage as conflicting with the general law, that the rejection was based upon the unreasonableness of the usage, or its lack of uniformity or notoriety, rather than upon the circumstance that it conflicted with the common law. In other words, the usage was really insufficient in its elements to override the legal rule,[3] either because it was local and not sufficient to charge the parties with knowledge of it,[4] or because it was unreasonable and lacking in those elements of justice and fair dealing which are requisite to warrant the courts in giving effect to it, rather than to. the general rules of law ;[5] or because its existence was not estab-

[0] *Leach* v. *Perkins*, 17 Me. 462; *Caldwell* v. *Dawson*, 4 Metc. (Ky.) 121.

[1] *United States* v. *Richardson*, Crabbe (U. S.) 563.

[2] *Wilcocks* v. *Phillips*, 1 Wall., Jr. (U. S.), 47.

[3] *Dwight* v. *Boston*, 12 Allen (Mass.) 216; *Eagar* v. *Atlas Ins. Co.*, 14 Pick. (Mass.) 141; *Stover* v. *Whitman*, 6 Binn. (Penn.) 416; *Frith* v. *Barker*, 2 Johns. (N. Y.) 335.

[4] *Higgins* v. *Moore*, 34 N. Y. 417; *Bissell* v. *Campbell*, 54 *Id.* 353; *Minnesota &c. R. R. Co.* v. *Morgan*, 54 Barb. (N. Y.) ——; *Murlatt* v. *Clary*, 20 Ark. 251.

[5] In *Dodd* v. *Farlow*, 11 Allen (Mass.) 426, this was well illustrated. In that case it was sought to set up a usage that in the sale of certain kinds of goods there is an implied warranty that they are merchantable, and that, if they are sold by a broker, he may bind his principal by an express warranty that the goods are merchantable, although he had no express authority to give such warranty, and the court held that the usage was invalid, because it was unreasonable to extend the powers of a broker in that manner. In *Reed* v. *Richardson*, 98 Mass. 216, an attempt was made to extend the liability of a common carrier by proof that, by the usage of the port, in order to constitute a delivery of water-borne goods by the carrier, it is necessary for a receipt to be given by the consigner or his agent, and that until such receipt was given the liability of the carrier continues. The court very justly held that this usage was unreasonable, and consequently invalid. See also *Tremble* v. *Cramell*, 17 Mich. 493; *Freary* v. *Cook*, 14 Mass. 488. If a usage or custom be never so general or uniform, yet if it is unreasonable it will not be

lished as a uniform rule in the particular matters to which it related;[6] or because, being local, its existence was in fact unknown to one of the parties ought to be affected by

upheld; and a custom, although adopted by every person in the country engaged in a certain business, if it is unreasonable, dangerous or productive of injury, the fact of its generality cannot in any degree excuse an act because in conformity to it. *Hill* v. *Portland &c. R. R. Co.*, 55 Me. 438. Thus, where a person is sued for negligence he cannot set up a custom or usage for parties to be negligent engaged in that business if the act complained of is really negligent. Thus, where an action was brought against a ferryman for the loss of a horse and wagon because of his failure to put up a chain at the end of his boat, it was held that he could not be permitted to show a custom at other ferries to put up the chain *at the request of passengers*, and not otherwise—*Miller* v. *Pendleton*, 8 Gray (Mass.) 547—because such a custom is not only unreasonable, but also opposed to the policy of the law. While, however, such proof is not admissible to excuse liability absolutely, yet it is admissible upon the question of ordinary prudence as one means of determining what prudent men do under similar circumstances, but is by no means decisive. In *Barber* v. *Brace*, 3 Conn. 14, in commenting upon this question, *Hosmer*, J., said: "The gist of the complaint is, that the defendant mismanaged in the stowage and did not exercise ordinary care. Now," he added, "proof that he did what prudent men *usually* do, repels every imputation of neglect, want of care and inattention to the obligations of

the contract. Thus the rule of the common law and the usages of merchants are in entire harmony on the subject under discussion, and both of them coincide with the charge to the jury." *Baxter* v. *Leland*, 1 Blatchf. (U. S.) 526. The general rule is that a custom or usage is not legal if contrary to morality, religion or the law of the land (*Holmes* v. *Johnson*, 42 Penn. St. 159), and a custom of the country which sanctions that which by statute is made unlawful, as taking usurious interest, &c., is unreasonable and invalid. *Greene* v. *Tyler*, 39 Penn. St. 369; *N. Y. Fireman's Ins. Co.* v. *Ely*, 2 Cow. (N. Y.) 678; *Dunham* v. *Dey*, 13 Johns. (N. Y.) 40; 16 *Id.* 367. Nor can a usage be set up to establish that which is *malum in se*. *Bryant* v. *Commercial Ins. Co.*, 6 Pick. (Mass.) 131. Thus, it would not excuse a tailor for keeping all the cloth furnished by a customer for a suit of clothes because such is the custom, nor a miller for taking twice the amount of grain allowed as toll because such is the general practice, &c., &c., because such acts are *malum in se*, and prohibited by law, and for that reason the custom is bad. See *Snowden* v. *Warder*, 3 Rawle (Penn.) 110.

[6] *Halls* v. *Howell*, 1 Harp. (S. C.) 427; *Bowen* v. *Newell*, 8 N. Y. 190; *Adams* v. *Otterback*, 15 How. (U. S.) 539; *The Albatross* v. *Wayne*, 16 Ohio 513; *Flynn* v. *Murphy*, 2 E. D. S. (N. Y. C. P.) 378; *Leach* v. *Perkins*, 17 Me. 462; *Taylor* v. *Ketchum*, 5 Robt. (N. Y.) 507.

it.[7] In an English case[8] will be found the groundwork for the doctrine, that a usage can never be received that is contrary to a settled rule of law.[9] The doctrine as applied in that case was undoubtedly correct, because the custom set up was unreasonable. In that case, upon the trial at Nisi Prius, Lord Mansfield received evidence of the custom of merchants, that, in the case of a bill of exchange payable to order, the endorsement was restrictive, unless that also contained the word order. Upon a motion for a new trial, it was held that, the law being settled, the custom of merchants could not control it; that is, could not be permitted to subvert the law of the land, not that the parties might not make the endorsement restrictive by special agreement, or by the customary course of some particular business, making an exception in their own case, leaving the general law to take its course. In that case the bill was drawn in the East Indies, and the evidence came mainly from bankers in London. Their opinion was admitted to overturn a rule of law which prevailed in the whole British Empire, but throughout the whole commercial world. In a later English case[1] the true doctrine was advanced. In that case the court agreed that evidence of usage was admissible to enlarge the rights of carriers. The defendant claimed a lien of the goods carried, not only for the price of their carriage, but also for a balance due from the parties for freight upon goods previously carried. The common law

---

[7] *Halford* v. *Adams*, 2 Duer. (N. Y. Superior Ct.) 471; *Duguid* v. *Edwards*, 50 Barb. (N. Y.) 62; *Sipperly* v. *Stewart, Id.* 288; *Minnesota C. R. R. Co.* v. *Morgan*, 52 *Id.* 217. Aff'd by Court of Appeals.

[8] *Edie* v. *East India Co.*

[9] See for such propositions *Frith* v. *Barker*, 2 John. (N. Y.) 335; *Winthrop* v. *Union Ins. Co.*, 2 Hall (N. Y.) 9; *Eagan* v. *Atlas Ins. Co.*, 14 Pick. (Mass.) 141; *Schiefflin* v. *Harvey*,

Auth. (N. Y.) 56; *Dewees* v. *Lockhart*, 1 Tex. 535; *Strong* v. *Bliss*, 6 Met. (Mass.) 393; *Harris* v. *Carson*, 7 Leigh (Va.) 632; *Winder* v. *Blake*, 4 Jones (N. C.) L. 362; *Henry* v. *Risk*, 1 Dall (U. S.) 265; *Barksdale* v. *Brown*, 1 N. & McCord. (S. C.) 517; *Brown* v. *Jackson*, 2 Wash. (U. S. C. C.) 24; *Horner* v. *Dorr*, 10 Mass. 26; *Stoever* v. *Whitman*, 6 Binn. (Penn.) 626; *Newbold* v. *Wright*, 4 Rawle (Penn.) 195.

[1] *Rushforth* v. *Hadfield*, 7 East 225.

denies to carriers a lien for a general balance, but a large amount of evidence was received to show that custom and a particular course of trade, among a particular class of carriers—including those in question—to overcome the law. The jury found against the defendants, but the evidence was so formidable that they moved for a new trial. Chambre, J., who tried the cause, put it to the jury, whether the usage was so general as to warrant them in presuming that the parties who delivered the goods he carried, knew of it; if not, the general rule of law would entitle the plaintiffs to a verdict. All the judges concurred that a custom of this kind which is *quoad hoc* to supersede the general law of the land, *should be clearly proved*, and the interested encroachments of persons engaged in a particular trade, watched with great jealousy. Not one of them disapproved the rules under which the case went to the jury, and Lord Ellenborough and Grose, J., put it on the ground of *a usage so general and so uniformly acquiesced in for a length of time, that the jury would feel themselves constrained to say it entered into the minds of the parties and formed a part of the contract.* On the whole, it would seem that usage may change the rules of the common law, but that in such cases it is hard to establish it so that a court will feel warranted in saying that the parties contracted in reference to *it*, rather than in reference to the general rules of law, but there seems to be no good foundation for a rule that would prevent parties from making the attempt.[2] In reputable courts in this country proof of a usage among banks has been permitted to be shown, to demand payment of an endorsed note or bill on the *fourth* day after it became due, and an endorser has been held liable under such usage, when by the common law he was discharged because the demand was not made upon the *third* day.[3] Local usage has

---

[2] *Cowen, J.*, in *Gibson* v. *Culver*, 17 Wend. (N. Y.) 308. As to bills of exchange. *Yeates* v. *Pim*, 1 Holt 95.

[3] *Renner* v. *Bank of Columbia*, 9 Wheat. (U. S.) 581; *Loring* v. *Gurney*, 5 Pick. (Mass.) 16; *Bank of Col-*

been held admissible to show that, by the custom of a certain city, certain kinds of negotiable securities, as a certificate of deposit, is not entitled to grace, and that, when it falls due upon Sunday, it becomes payable on the preceding Saturday, and this too, although the general law of the State as to negotiable paper is otherwise.[4] The ground upon which evidence of such usage is admitted, is, that it aids in ascertaining and carrying into effect the real intention of the parties. So too it has been held competent to show that, by the custom of a certain bank at which a note is negotiated, four days of grace are allowed, although by the general laws it was entitled to but three. Thus in a case heard in the United States Supreme Court,[5] in which the question was very carefully considered, it was held that, where by the custom of a bank, notes negotiated by it were presented for payment and protested upon the *fourth* day after they became due, the indorser is bound, although by the general law but three days of grace are given. In this case the custom was *known* to all the parties to the note, but it has been held in the same court that where such à usage of a bank is established and shown to be invariable, all the parties to the note are bound by it, whether they had personal knowledge of such usage or not.[6] "In the case of such a note," says the

umbia v. *Magruder's Heirs*, 6 H. & J. (Md.) 172; *Bank of Utica* v. *Smith*, 18 Johns. (N.Y.) 230; *Bank of Washington* v. *Triplett*, 1 Pet. (U. S.) 25; *Leavitt* v. *Simes*, 3 N. H. 14; *Kennebec Bank* v. *Page*, 9 Mass. 155; *Weld* v. *Gorham*, 10 *Id.* 356; *Blanchard* v. *Hilliard*, 11 *Id.* 85.

[4] *Kilgore* v. *Bulkley*, 14 Conn. 362. But see *contra, Merchants' Bank* v. *Woodruff*, 6 Hill (N. Y.) 174.

[5] *Renner* v. *Bank of Columbia*, 9 Wheat. (U. S.) 582. But it is held that proof of the usage of a certain bank for two years to hold notes until the fourth day of grace, and if

that day fell on Sunday to demand payment and give notice to the endorser on Monday, is not sufficient to change, as to such bank, the general law requiring demand to be made on Saturday. *Adams* v. *Otterbach*, 15 How. (U. S.) 539.

[6] *Mills* v. *Bank of United States*, 11 Wheat. (U. S.) 430. In *Jones* v. *Fales*, 4 Mass. 245, it was held that where, by the general law, a note is entitled to three days of grace on demand made upon the maker on the first day, and a notice of non-payment upon the last day of grace is sufficient to hold the endorser if such

court, "the parties are presumed by implication to agree to be governed by the usage of the bank at which they have chosen to make the security itself negotiable. The doctrine of these cases has been extended to bills of exchange, drawn on a person residing in a place where such a usage is established, and placed in a bank for collection which has established such a usage, although not in terms made payable at such bank.[7] So evidence of a usage in New York city, has been held admissible to show that a check drawn upon a bank and made payable on a day subsequent to its date, is not entitled to grace, and therefore that a demand and protest upon the day mentioned in it for payment, is sufficient to charge the endorser.[8] While, in the absence

is shown to be the usage of the bank at which it is payable. " This usage," says *Parsons, C. J.*, in the course of his opinion, "is evidence of the defendant's agreement, proper to be submitted to the jury to infer from it the agreement of the defendant. Evidence of this kind, and for this purpose, is not to establish new law, but to prove that the defendant has waived a condition implied by law for his benefit, and has consented to other terms, to which, without question, he might have expressly agreed." See also, sustaining this doctrine, *Widgery* v. *Monroe*, 6 Mass. 459; *Whitwell* v. *Johnson*, 17 Id. 452; *Lincoln &c. Bank* v. *Page*, 9 Id. 155, and *Blanchard* v. *Hilliard*, 11 Id. 85. In *Warren Bank* v. *Parker*, 8 Gray (Mass.) 221, a bank in Boston, with whom a note was placed for collection, gave notice to the maker, *before the note fell due*, according to the usage in Boston, of the day when the note would be payable, and requested him to come and pay it, and the note remained in the bank through-

out the banking hours of the day on which it became due. It was held that if the maker was a trader and accustomed to transact business at the bank, his consent to the general usage which made such notice sufficient might be shown, and if shown rendered any other demand immaterial.

[7] *The Bank of Washington* v. *Triplett*, 1 Pet. (U. S.) 25.

[8] *Osborne* v. *Smith.* N. Y. Superior Court decided in 1837 (*Mss.*) *Jones, C. J.*, in delivering the opinion of the court in this case says, "The objection to the custom drawn from its supposed collision with the common law cannot, in our view of it, be sustained without impugning some of the best settled principles applicable to mercantile law usages that constitute a large portion of commercial rules, and to that source solely the allowance of days of grace on mercantile paper is to be traced. No rule of common law or statutory provision impressed that feature upon the character of commercial paper. It had its origin in usage, and to usage

of any statute regulating the matter, the usages of a locality, or of a bank, may control in the matters stated, yet a usage dispensing with the requirements of the law as to demand of payment and protest is bad, because it impairs the implied contract raised by indorsement. Thus, in a New Hampshire case,[9] where it was shown that the bank kept

it owes its existence. It has now become, it is true, where it is applicable, parcel of the contract, and is no longer an indulgence of grace, but is, and long has been, a matter of right. A bill or a note payable at sixty days is in legal effect payable in sixty-three days; but this custom does apply to every species of commercial paper; in its application to bills it does not exist at all places, and it varies moreover at different places in the time or grace it allows; and this case shows, I think, that it does not embrace checks on banks, though made payable at a day certain subsequent to their date, and notwithstanding their resemblance to inland bills of exchange. In *Bowen* v. *Newell*, 8 N. Y. 190, a usage by banks in Connecticut to treat drafts as checks, and so not entitled to grace, was held bad as contravening the general law.

[9] *Piscataqua Exchange Bank* v. *Carter*, 20 N. H. 246. That usage cannot be resorted to, to contradict the plain terms of an express contract, is illustrated by numerous cases. In *Curtis* v. *Brewer*, 17 Pick. (Mass.) 513, it was stipulated by contract that a vessel should be built, caulked, finished and ready for the rigger to complete his work, launched and delivered afloat in the harbor at a specified time. It was the custom to rig vessels on the stocks. It was held that the builder was bound to have the vessel ready for the rigger, so that she

might be completed and launched at the day specified. In *Atkins* v. *Howe*, 18 Pick. (Mass.) 16, upon the sale of certain property, it was stipulated that all claims for damages must be made within three days. Evidence was held not admissible that, according to the custom of the trade in Boston, goods were returned by purchasers at auction and received by the owners, and an allowance made after the expiration of three days, if within a reasonable time after the sale. In *Snelling* v. *Hall*, 107 Mass. 134, in an action on a written contract for the sale of coal, providing for the shipment of the coal at the buyer's option, between certain dates, evidence is not admissible of a usage in the coal trade that under like contracts, the option must be exercised in time to allow all the coal to be shipped between the dates named in the contract. And, even though the parties agreed by parol, at the time the written contract was executed, that it should be subject to a certain usage, conflicting therewith, such evidence is not admissible, in the absence of fraud, or mistake, because it is irrebuttably presumed that the parties embraced in their contract their intention in reference to the subject matter, and that they did not intend that anything *different* from what is expressed therein, should be done or omitted to be done. *Oelricks* v. *Ford*, 23 How. (U. S.) 49. This rule does not exclude

posted a notice that all indorsers of notes to the bank would
be required to waive demand and notice, it was held that the

evidence to show that by the usages
of the business to which the contract relates certain terms employed
therein, have acquired a *peculiar*
meaning, different from that ordinarily attached thereto. *Senett* v.
Shumway, 102 Mass. 365; *Miller* v.
Stevens, 100 *Id.* 518; *Keller* v. *Webb*,
125 *Id.* 88. Thus it may be shown
that it is the usage among owners
of whale ships and underwriters to
treat an insurance upon "outfits" as
covering one-fourth of the catchings.
Macy v. *Whaling Ins. Co.*, 9 Met.
(Mass.) 354. So where goods are sold
"with all faults," it may be shown
that by the usage of the trade these
words have acquired a peculiar
meaning, and what that meaning is.
Whitney v. *Boardman*, 118 Mass. 242.
Evidence has also been admitted in
a libel suit to show that the words
"State cop" is a slang expression
meaning a deputy State constable.
Cann v. *Morgan*, 107 Mass. 199. So to
show, where a contract is for a certain article of which there are several kinds, which kind was intended.
Bradford v. *Manly*, 13 Mass. 139;
Hogins v. *Plympton*, 11 Pick. (Mass.)
97; *Woods* v. *Sawin*, 4 Gray (Mass.)
322. But this is only the case, when
the evidence is explicatory of the
contract and does not contradict it.
The rule in this regard was well expressed by *Allen, J.*, in *Lawrence* v.
Maxwell, 53 N. Y. 21. "Evidence,"
said he, "may be given of a custom
or usage in explanation and application of particular words or phrases,
and to aid in the *interpretation* of the
contract, but not to derogate from
the rights of the parties or to import
into the contract *new* terms and con-

ditions, or vary the legal effect of the
transaction." See also *Robinson* v.
United States, 13 Wall (U. S.) 365.
Coleridge, J., in *Brown* v. *Bryne*, 3 E.
& B. 703, perhaps gives the clearest
and best illustration of this rule.
"In *all* contracts," says he, "as to
the subject matter of which a known
usage prevails, parties are found to
proceed with the tacit assumption
of those usages; they commonly reduce into writing the special particulars of their agreement, but omit
to specify those known usages which
are included however as of course,
by mutual understanding; evidence
therefore, of such usage is receivable. The contract in truth is partly
express and in writing, partly implied or understood and unwritten.
But in these cases a restriction is
established on the soundest principles, that the evidence received,
must not be a particular which is
repugnant to, or inconsistent with,
the written contract. *Merely that it
varies the apparent contract*, is not
enough to exclude the evidence; for
it is impossible to add any material
incident to the written terms of the
contract without altering its effect
more or less; neither in the construction of a contract among merchants, tradesmen or others, will the
evidence be excluded because the
words are, in their ordinary meaning, unambiguous, for the principle
of admission is, *that words perfectly
unambiguous in their ordinary meaning are used by the contractor in a
different sense from that*. What words
more plain than 'a thousand,' 'a
week,' 'a day?' Yet the cases are
familiar in which 'a thousand' has

fact that a person who had procured a note indorsed by him to be negotiated there, had been a customer at the bank for

been held to mean twelve hundred; 'a week' only a week during the theatrical season; 'a day' a *working* day. In such cases the evidence neither adds to, nor qualifies, nor contradicts the written contract; *it only ascertains it by expounding the language.*" See upon this point, and admitting and adopting the rule, *Stewart v. Smith,* 28 Ill. 397; *Wallo v. Bailey,* 49 N. Y. 467; *Baron v. Plaide,* 7 La. An. 229; *Grant v. Maddox,* 15 M. & W. 737; *Cochran v. Ritberg,* 3 Esp. 121; *Jolly v. Young,* 1 Jd. 186; *Myers v. Sarl,* 3 E. & C. 306; *Simpson v. Margitson,* 11 Q. B. 32; *Lowe v. Lehman,* 15 Ohio St. 179; *Whitney v. Boardman,* 118 Mass. 242; *Schneider v. Heath,* 3 Camp. 506; *Henshaw v. Robbins,* 9 Met. (Mass.) 83; *Shepherd v. Kain,* 5 B. & Ald. 240; *Miller v. Stevens,* 100 Mass. 518; *Bottomley v. Forbes,* 5 Bing. N. C. 121; *Mason v. Skurry,* Park. Ins. 245; *Buckle v. Knapp,* L. R. 2 Exchq. 125; *Spicer v. Cooper,* 1 Q. B. 424; *Mackenzie v. Dunlap,* 3 Macq. 26; *Miller v. Letherington,* 6 H. & M. 278; *Bowman v. Horsey,* 2 M. & Raf. 85; *Shove v. Wilson,* Cl. & F. 355; *Rushford v. Hatfield,* 7 East. 225; *Wilson v. Randall,* 67 N. Y. 338; *Barnum v. Gatliff,* 11 Cl. & F. 45; *Falbri v. Ins. Co.,* 55 N. Y. 133; *Jaurnu v. Borden,* Park. Ins. 245; *Kidston v. Ins. Co.,* L. R. 1 C. P. 535; *Ober v. Carson,* 62 Mo. 209; *Gray v. Harper,* 1 Story (U. S.) 574; *Carter v. Coal Co.,* 77 Penn. St. 286; *Neighan v. Bank,* 25 Jd. 288; *Da Costa v. Edwards,* 4 Camp. 143; *Ganson v. Madigan,* 15 Wis. 144; *Peisch v. Dickson,* 1 Mas. (U. S.) 11; *Whitmarsh v. Conway Ins. Co.,* 16 Gray (Mass.) 359; *Barton v. McKelway,* 22 N. J. L. 165; *Gossler*

v. Eagle Sugar. Refinery, 103 Mass. 331; *Noyes v. Canfield,* 29 Vt. 79; *Shepherd v. Kain,* 5 B. & Ald. 240; *Cuthbert v. Cumming,* 11 Exchq. 405; *Wait v. Fairbanks,* Brayt. (Vt.) 77; *Johnstone v. Usborne,* 11 Ad. & El. 549; *Vallance v. Dewar,* 1 Camp. 503; *Cowles v. Garrett,* 30 Ala. 341; *Drake v. Goree,* 22 Id. 409; *Moran v. Prather,* 23 Wall. (U. S.) 499; *Johnson v. Ins. Co.,* 39 Wis. 87; *Taylor v. Satalinge,* 6 La. Ann. 154; *Lamb v. Klaus,* 30 Wis. 94; *Eldredge v. Smith,* 13 Allen (Mass.) 140; *Soutier v. Kellerman,* 18 Mo. 509; *Locke v. Rowell,* 47 N. H. 46; *Barnes v. Ingalls,* 39 Ala. 193; *Farrar v. Stackpole,* 6 Me. 154; *Fitch v. Carpenter,* 43 Barb. (N. Y.) 401; *Stone v. Bradbury,* 14 Me. 185; *Noyes v. Canfield,* 27 Vt. 79; *Broadwell v. Broadwell,* 1 Gill. (Md.) 599; *Carey v. Bright,* 58 Penn. St. 70; *Stroud v. Frith,* 11 Barb. (N. Y.) 300; *Williams v. Wood,* 16 Md. 220; *Bowen v. Brooks,* 25 Penn. St. 210; *Hart v. Hummett,* 18 Vt. 127; *Colwell v. Lawrence,* 24 How. Pr. (N. Y.) 324; *Ehle v. Chettenango Bank,* 24 N. Y. 548; *Marc v. Kupfer,* 34 Ill. 287; *Jenny Lind Co. v. Bower,* 11 Cal. 194; *Hite v. State,* 9 Yerg. (Tenn.) 357; *Cahat v. Winsor,* 1 Allen (Mass.) 146; *Bean v. The Belfast,* 40 Ala. 184; *Sampson v. Gazzam,* 6 Port. (Ala.) 123; *Ins. Co. v. Wright,* 1 Wall. (U. S.) 156; *Sanford v. Rawlings,* 43 Ill. 92; *Collins v. Driscoll,* 34 Conn. 43; *Reynolds v. Jourdan,* 6 Cal. 108; *Sturgis v. Cary,* 2 Curtis (U. S. C. C.) 382; *Webb v. Plummer,* 2 B. & Ald. 746; *Hudson v. Ede,* L. R. 3 Q. B. 412; *Myers v. Walker,* 24 Ill. 133; *Barnard v. Kellogg,* 10 How. (U. S.) 270; *Spicer v. Hooper,* 1 Q. B. 424; *Elton v. Larkins,*

several years, did not warrant the admission of parol evidence of this usage, because the effect of it was to change the contract implied by law from the indorsement. It may be said that in the absence of an express provision in the note itself, a custom or usage that deprives a party thereto of the benefits of a statutory provision relating thereto cannot be set up. Thus, in a Massachusetts case,[1] it was held that a usage among banks to regard a bank post note, payable at a future day certain, as payable without grace, there being no express stipulation to that effect in the note itself, was

8 Bing. 198; *Chaurand v. Ankerstine,* Peake 43; *Planché v. Fletcher,* 1 Doug. 521; *Merrick v. McNally,* 26 Mich. 374; *Hughes v. Gordon,* 1 Bligh. 287; *Leidman v. Schultz,* 14 C. B. 287; *Clinan v. Cooke,* 1 Sch. & L. 22; *Whittemore v. Weiss,* 33 Mich. 348; *George v. Jay,* 19 N. H. 544; *Patch v. Ins. Co.,* 44 Vt. 481; *New Jersey Co. v. Boston Co.,* 15 N. J. Eq. 418; *Dent v. S. S. Co.,* 49 N. Y. 390; *Astor v. Ins. Co.,* 7 Cow. 202; *Dudley v. Vose,* 114 Mass. 34; *Elliott v. Secor,* 60 Mo. 163; *Martin v. Union Pacific R. R. Co.,* 1 Wy. Ter. 143; *Kirkpatrick v. Bowen,* 59 Ga. 450; *Eneas v. Hoops,* 42 N. Y. Superior Ct. 517; *Stewart v. Smith,* 59 Tenn. 231; *Carmichael v. White,* 11 Hus. R. (Tenn.) 262; *Hearn v. Equitable Safety Ins. Co.,* 3 Cliff. (U. S. C. C.) 328; *Singleton v. Mutual Ins. Co.,* 66 Mo. 63; *Miller v. Burke,* 68 N. Y. 615; *Farmers' &c. Bank v. Erie R. R. Co.,* 72 Id. 188; *Rankin v. American Ins. Co.,* 1 Hall (N. Y.) 619; *Harris v. Rathbun,* 2 Keyes (N. Y.) 312; *Wilcox v. Wood,* 9 Wend. (N. Y.) 346; *Collender v. Dinsmore,* 55 N. Y. 200; *Dickinson v. Water Commissioners,* 2 Hun. (N. Y.) 615; *Arthur v. Roberts,* 60 Barb. (N. Y.) 580; *Sturm v. Williams,* 6 J. & S. (N. Y.) 325; *Fowler v. Ætna*

Ins. Co., 7. Wend. (N. Y.) 270; *Dow v. Whitten,* 8 *Id.* 160; *Gorrissen v. Perrin,* 27 L. J. C. P. 29; *Brown v. Brooks,* 25 Penn. St. 210; *Dana v. Fielder,* 13 N. Y. 40; *Allan v. Comstock,* 17 Ga. 554; *Russian Steam Nav. Co. v. Silva,* 13 C. B. N. S. 610; *Bliven v. N. E. Screw Co.,* 23 How. (U. S.) 420; *Falkner v. Earle,* 3 B. & S. 360. In construing wills, the courts will regard the technical meaning of certain words acquired by usage, and this *must* be done to carry into effect the intention of the testator. *Hawley v. Northampton,* 8 Mass. 3; *Needham v. Ide,* 5 Pick. (Mass.) 510; *Ide v. Ide,* 5 Mass. 500; *Myers v. Edely,* 47 Barb. (N. Y.) 263. And in determining whether the technical or ordinary sense was intended by the testator, the court will consider which would best effectuate the testator's intention. *Den v. McMurtie,* 15 N. J. L. 276. But where the meaning attached to words can be ascertained from the will itself, that meaning should be given to them in construing the will, although contrary to correct usage. *Carnagy v. Woodcock,* 2 Munf. (Va.) 234.

[1] *Perkins v. Franklin Bank,* 21 Pick. (Mass.) 483.

invalid, because it conflicted with the statute of the State, which provides that all notes payable at a future day certain shall be allowed grace, unless otherwise stipulated in the note. In a New York case,[2] it was held that a usage among banks that a bill of exchange drawn upon a bank and accepted by the cashier and payable at a day certain is not entitled to grace, is invalid because it deprives the parties of certain legal rights that are implied in all such transactions. In a later case, before the Court of Appeals,[3] it was held that a usage of banks in another State to regard drafts drawn upon them and payable at a day certain, as checks, and therefore not entitled to grace, could not be shown, because contrary to the general rules of law.[4] Where the statute confers certain rights upon the parties to negotiable paper, as that certain days of grace shall be allowed, and how and when demand and protest shall be made, this right cannot be overcome by a mere custom or usage, so as to make a demand or protest made in a different manner from that provided by statutes operative, at least, unless such facts and circumstances are shown as to establish the fact that the parties impliedly contracted in reference to such usage;[5] therefore it was held in the last case that evidence that notaries in New York city, in their protests and registers usually state a demand made upon a firm, to have been made upon one of the firm, without naming him, was inadmissible. There is no question but that the parties to a note or bill may expressly waive the statutory or common law requirements as to demand, protest, &c., and unless the statute otherwise provides, they may do so impliedly, and in such cases proof of the usages of a bank at which it is discounted, or at which it is made payable, varying the

---

[2] *Merchants Bank* v. *Woodruff*, 6 Hill (N. Y.) 174.

[3] *Bowen* v. *Newell*, 8 N. Y. 190.

[4] See also same case, *Bowen* v. *Newell*, 5 Duer. (N. Y. Superior Ct.)

584, where the facts are fully set forth, and the rules applicable in such cases are well stated.

[5] *Otsego County Bank* v. *Warren*, 18 Barb. (N. Y.) 291.

legal method, is admissible, and if brought home to the knowledge of the parties, so far as to establish their assent thereto, it is binding upon them.[6] Where a note is made payable in specific articles "at wholesale prices at the factory," or other place of manufacture or production, it is competent to show that by the usage of the trade a price other than the wholesale *market* price was meant.[7] The usages of a business have been held admissible to show the intention of the parties under a covenant in a lease over ten years, and to excuse a party from a literal performance thereof. Thus, where A. leased to B. a tract of land in a mountainous country, and B. stipulated to allow and pay to A. as part of the rent, for a quantity of bark to be taken by him from the timber on the premises, "*not less than* 800 *nor more than* 1000 *cords a year*," during the continuance of the term, the sum of one dollar for each cord taken, and that he would take "at least 800 cords of bark each year." B. actually took much less than 800 cords of bark each year, but A. insisted that B. was bound to pay him for at least 800 cords each year, and produced evidence to show that there was more than enough bark left upon the premises to make up that amount. B. showed, however, that he had taken all the bark upon the premises that was accessible, and which *by the usual and customary means which are employed for the purpose of taking bark from such lands by those who carried on that business in the section of country where it was situated*, except about 50 cords, and that the balance was upon or near a high peak of the Catskill mountains, about 1000 feet higher than the surrounding land, and was wholly inaccessible to teams of any kind, and that the bark thereon could not by any reasonable or practicable means be taken therefrom. The court held that the defendant was only liable for what bark he had actually taken, and such a quantity in

---

[6] *The Hartford Bank* v. *Stedman*, 3   Mass. 85.
Conn. 489; *Blanchard* v. *Hilliard*, 11   [7] *Avery* v. *Stewart*, 2 Conn. 69.

excess thereof not exceeding 800 cords a year, as was accessible and could have been taken by the use of the usual and customary means employed for the purpose of taking bark from such land by those employed in that business in the section of country where it was situated.[8] " This covenant," said Church, J., "is to receive either a literal or a practical construction. . . The defendant was bound to pursue a reasonable and prudent course in fulfillment of his contract, having reference to the situation of the timber, the purposes and uses for which the bark was intended, and the general usage of persons employed in such business in that region." In a South Carolina case,[9] a usage of the river

[8] *Livingston* v. *Tyler*, 14 Conn. 493.

[9] *Middleton* v. *Haywood*, 2 N. & M. (S. C.) 9. Evidence of a usage as to the payment of commissions is, in the absence of a special agreement, admissible not only to show that payment should be made, but also to fix the amount. Thus in *Turner* v. *Yates*, 16 How. (U. S.) 14, in an action of debt against the sureties on a bond conditioned for the repayment of money advanced for the purchase of packed meats for shipment, and which were sent to London, evidence of a usage to charge a commission on advances on shipments made to that port was held admissible, and the usage, if proved, was held to bind the parties. *Goodenow* v. *Tyler*, 7 Mass. 36; *Cooke* v. *Fiske*, 12 Gray (Mass.) 491. So evidence of a usage is admissible to show that certain parties are entitled to certain deductions. Thus in an action for freight by a ship-owner against the indorsee of a bill of lading, to whom goods had been delivered at L., and who had accepted them, the bill of lading making them deliverable, " he paying freight for them five-eighths of a penny sterling per pound, with 5l. per cent. primage and average accustomed," it was held that evidence was admissible that by the custom of L. the plaintiff was entitled to a deduction of three months' discount from the freight; though such custom applied only to goods coming from certain ports in the Southern States of America. *Brown* v. *Byrne*, 3 El. & Bl. 703. Where a usage to charge commissions for certain services is established, mere proof by others engaged in the same business that it is not their custom, and, so far as they know, not the custom of others to charge commissions for such services, is not sufficient to defeat the application of such usage or prevent a recovery for such commissions. *Cooke* v. *Fiske*, ante, nor can such a usage be operative if it is unreasonable or unjust. Thus, where goods are consigned to a merchant to sell, and he consigns them to another merchant to sell, a custom for each merchant to charge the commission usually charged for a sale, is void, as being against common reason and common justice. *Spear* v. *Newell*, Rutland Co., cited by

trade for the carrier of goods to look to the producer and consignee alone for freight, was set up as a defence by the person who sent them, and it was held that the usage might be proved. Grant, J., in delivering the opinion in the case, conceded that it would be difficult to make out a usage in such cases, but that the matter of difficulty had nothing to do with the question of competency. As to the question of the reasonableness of such a usage, he said: "Although at the first blush, the custom alleged may appear unreasonable and such as ought not to prevail, this is by no means conclusive that the usage is not a good one in law. In such cases, recourse is had to artificial and legal reason, and thus considered the usage may be shown to be beneficial to the boatmen themselves. . . . *It is competent for a man or a body of men to renounce a common law right if they think proper.* And if, in relation to the river trade, either from views of interest on the part of boat owners, or other politic considerations, expediency has pointed out the propriety, and usage has sanctioned it, then it might become

Redfield, J., in *Burton* v. *Blin*, 23 Vt. 151. The same rule was applied. *Strong* v. *Grand Trunk R. R. Co.*, 15 Mich. 206. In that case it was held that an alleged mercantile custom by which an intermediate consignee is authorized to deduct from the back freight earned any deficiency in the cargo, as shown by a comparison of the bill of lading with the measurement of the carrier receiving it, was not to be a custom that the courts would recognize, as it would prevent the carrier from showing that there was error in the bill of lading, and would enable the intermediate consignee to deduct for discrepancies between the bill of lading and amount delivered, which occurred owing to erroneous measurement or count when the bill was signed; and because it would deprive the carrier of his lien upon the cargo for freight to the extent of the amount thus improperly deducted. In *Kuhtman* v. *Brown*, 4 Rich. (S. C.) 479, A. advanced to B. a certain sum on cotton shipped to Bremen, and brought this action to recover the amount in which the net proceeds fell short of the sum advanced. In the amount rendered by A. against B. were a multitude of small charges besides commissions, such as bill brokerage and interest thereon, for mending, handling, delivering, &c., &c. A verdict was rendered for the whole amount. Held, that the right to make such charges depended so much on commercial usage that the question was properly submitted to the jury.

the law by which the contract should be surrounded."[1]
Without pursuing the inquiry farther, it may be stated as a
result of the authorities that a usage may be proved to influence the construction of the law, or to explain it,[2] and that
it may be proved to influence the construction of a contract,
although contrary to some rule of general law, and when
proved it then becomes a question of fact whether the parties contracted in reference to it, or, in other words, whether
they adopted it as a part of their contract in preference to
the general law as the rule for its interpretation, and this is
properly a question for the jury.[3] While, as we have before
stated, we think that upon principle as well as upon high,
and, we may say, the great weight of authority, evidence of

[1] See *Haywood* v. *Middleton*, 3 Mc-
Cord. (S. C.) 121. In *Barksdale* v.
Brown, 1 N. & M. 521, it was intimated by *Cheves, J.*, that the very
fact that a particular thing had been
sanctioned by usage so general, uniform and extensive as to raise the
presumption that all who deal in
reference to its subject are presumed
to have knowledge of it, and to contract in reference to it, would in itself
afford very cogent evidence of its reasonableness in the particular trade or
business to which it related, and that
if it was not objectionable in any other
point of view, the simple question
should be, *is it a usage?* In other
words, are not the persons to be
affected by the usage, better able to
judge as to its expediency and reasonableness than a jury or the court?
But it may be said that this notion
does not prevail, and the question
of reasonableness is open to inquiry.
Eager v. *Atlas Ins. Co.*, 14 Pick.
(Mass.) 141.

[2] *Frith* v. *Barker*, 2 John. (N. Y.)
327; *Markham* v. *Jaudon*, 41 N. Y.
235; *Ewing* v. *Dunbar*, 1 Daly (N. Y.

C. P.) 408; *Bowen* v. *Newell*, 8 N. Y.
190; *Schiefflin* v. *Harvey*, Auth. (N.
Y.) 76; *Sewall* v. *Gibbs*, 1 Hall (N. Y.)
602; *Jones* v. *Bradner*, 10 Barb. (N.
Y.) 193; *Gibson* v. *Culver*, ante; *Out-
water* v. *Nelson*, 20 Barb. (N. Y.) 29;
Mackenzie v. *Schmidt*, 22 Am. Law
Register 448; *Ruan* v. *Gardner*, 1
Wash. (Va.) 145; *Austin* v. *Williams*,
2 Ohio 64; *Winthrop* v. *Ins. Co.*, 2
Wash. (Va.) 7.

[3] *Gordon* v. *Little*, 8 S. & R. (Penn.)
533; *Snowden* v. *Warden*, 3 Rawle
(Penn.) 101; *Halsey* v. *Brown*, 3 Day
(Conn.) 346; *Renner* v. *Columbia
Bank*, 9 Wheat. (U. S.) 581; *Middle-
ton* v. *Haywood*, 2 N. & M. (S. C.) 9;
Jones v. *Fales*, 4 Mass. 245; *Weld* v.
Gotham, 10 *Id.* 366; *Wood* v. *Wil-
cox*, 9 Wend. (N. Y.) 349; *Kennebec
Bank* v. *Page*, 9 Mass. 155; *Widgerley*
v. *Maunar*, 6 *Id.* 449; *Blanchard* v.
Hilliard, 11 *Id.* 85; *Kennebec Bank* v.
Hammott, 9 *Id.* 159; *Leach* v. *Perkins*,
17 Me. 462; *Caldwell* v. *Dawson*, 4
Met. (Ky.) 121; *Fulton Ins. Co.* v.
Milner, 23 Ala., 420; *Isham* v. *Fox*, 7
Ohio St. 317.

a usage is admissible even though it conflicts with the general law, yet limitations upon this right exist, and instances must often necessarily arise where the court must adjudge a usage void. It may be stated as a rule, that *if that which is sought to be incorporated into the contract, by way of usage, would be void as an express stipulation, it gains no additional virtue because it has become a general practice*,[4] consequently a usage sanctioning that which is *malum in se*,[5] or is prohibited by statute, as the taking of usurious interest, is without validity.[6] So also are those which contravene the policy of the law, as those in restraint of trade,[7] or which sanction that which is immoral, dishonest, fraudulent or unjust, as a usage of a bank not to rectify a mistake in counting money unless discovered before the person leaves the bank;[8] or that permits a person to recover for services never performed, or materials never furnished;[9] or which deprives a person of his title to property without authority of contract or law;[1] or which

[4] *Coleman* v. *McMund*, 5 Rand. (Va.) 51.

[5] *Snowden* v. *Warden*, 3 Rawle (Penn.) 107; *Bryant* v. *Ins. Co.*, 6 Pick. (Mass.) 131; *Holmes* v. *Johnson*, 42 Penn. St. 159.

[6] *New York Firemen's Ins. Co.* v. *Ely*, 2 Cow. (N. Y.) 278; *Bank of Utica* v. *Wager*, 2 Id. 712; *Dunham* v. *Day*, 13 John. (N. Y.) 40; *Greene* v. *Tyler*, 39 Penn. St. 361.

[7] *Williams* v. *Gilman*, 3 Me. 281.

[8] *Gallatin* v. *Bradford*, 1 Bibb (Ky.) 209.

[9] *Whitesides* v. *Meredith*, 3 Yeates (Penn.) 318. In *Kendall* v. *Russell*, 5 Dana (Ky.) 501, the plaintiff sued to recover for laying brick in a building. The covenant under which he performed the work compelled him to lay as many brick as the defendant might need to complete the building, for which the defendant bound himself to pay a certain sum

per thousand for each thousand of brick laid. On the trial the plaintiff claimed to recover according to a local custom, allowing the quantity of brick laid to be ascertained by assuming as a basis of calculation that the walls of the building were solid, and making no allowance for openings therein, such as doors, windows, &c. The court held that the usage was not admissible. In *Jordan* v. *Meredith*, 3 Yeates (Penn.) 318, a custom among plasterers to charge for *one-half* the size of the windows, at the price agreed upon per foot or yard, was held unreasonable and void. But a custom permitting a person to charge a day and a quarter for twelve and a half hours' work, has been held valid among carpenters. *Hinton* v. *Locke*, 5 Hill (N. Y.) 437.

[1] In *Macomber* v. *Parker*, 13 Pick. (Mass.) 175, a brick yard was let to

•

releases an employee from the duty of giving his entire and
exclusive attention to the business of his master, and allows
him to carry on business in competition with his employer;[2]
or one which releases a party from joint liability with a party
with whom he has become jointly liable under a contract;[3] or
excusing a manufacturer of articles from the implied warranty against latent defects, raised by the law;[4] or which
permits a factor to violate the positive instructions of his
principal;[5] or indeed any custom which contravenes a statute,
the policy of the law or the express provisions of a contract.[6]
From what has been said, and the general tenor of the
authorities cited, it may be fairly stated *that, prima facie, all
contracts are to be understood as containing an implied reference to the general law, but that this presumption may be
overcome by proof of such a state of facts as fairly rebuts this*

H. by two persons who were the
owners thereof, under a contract
that he should hire the workmen
and manufacture bricks, give his
own time and services and pay a
certain sum for every thousand
bricks made, as rent. The owners
were to attend to the sale of the
bricks, purchase necessary materials
for their manufacture, and collect
the bills. The profits and losses
were to be shared equally by the
parties, the owners of the yard to
have the right to retain the brick,
or the money collected for those
sold to the value of all sums advanced by them from time to time
to H. The court held that the
bricks made under the contract became the joint property of all the
parties, and that a usage which
tended to show that H. had no
property in the bricks, but only an
interest in the profits to the extent
of his share, was bad, and therefore
inadmissible. In *Delaplane* v. *Cren-*
shaw, 15 Gratt. (Va.) ——, it was held
that a custom for a flour inspector
to use the draft flour drawn out to
be examined, was bad, as being
against the policy of the law.

[2] *Story* v. *Farmers' Trans. Co.*, 17
Hun. (N. Y.) 579.

[3] *Leach* v. *Perkins*, 17 Me. 462;
Ripley v. *Croaker*, 47 Me. 370.

[4] *Whitmore* v. *South Boston Iron
Co.*, 2 Allen (Mass.) 52.

[5] *Barksdale* v. *Brown*, 1 N. & M.
(S. C.) 519.

[6] *Cadwell* v. *Meek*, 17 Ill. 220;
Meaghar v. *Lufkin*, 21 Tex. 383;
George v. *Bartlett*, 22 N. H. 496;
Sweet v. *Jenkins*, 1 R. I. 147; *Renner*
v. *Bank of Columbia*, 9 Wheat. (U.
S.) 581; *Wadsworth* v. *Allcott*, 6 N. Y.
64; *Sleight* v. *Rhinelander*, 1 Johns.
(N. Y.) 192; *Cooper* v. *Purvis*, 1
Jones (N. C.) L. 141; *Barlow* v. *Lam-
bert*, 28 Ala. 704; *Bank of Commerce*
v. *Bissell*, 72 N. Y. 615; *Farmers' &c.
Bank* v. *Logan*, 74 *Id.* 568.

presumption, and shows that the parties really intended to adopt a particular usage, which is reasonable and contains the elements requisite to give it validity, as the rule for its interpretation.[7] What will be deemed a sufficient expression of an intention to overcome the general law and adopt the usage, necessarily depends upon the circumstances of each case. First, the usage itself, its uniformity, certainty and reasonableness, and secondly upon the knowledge of its existence by the parties contracting, or its notoriety and the probability that the parties knew of and contracted in reference to it. It is held by some of the courts, that a usage is not admissible to confer a right upon parties where such right is in conflict with the general law, but this question has been variously decided by our courts, and the weight of authority would seem to favor the doctrine that such a right *may* be conferred by usage.[8] But however this may be so far as the general law is concerned, there seems to be no doubt that a usage or custom is wholly inoperative to confer validity upon a con-

[7] *Renner* v. *Bank of Columbia,* 9 Wheat. (U. S.) 581; *Gordon* v. *Little,* 8 S. & R. (Penn.) 583; *Halsey* v. *Brown,* 3 Day (Conn.) 346; *Snowden* v. *Warden,* 3 Rawle (Penn.) 101; *Wadd* v. *Wilcox,* 9 Wend. (N. Y.) 349. There are some usages of trade and commerce that have been proved so often, and have so far incorporated themselves into the general law, that courts will take judicial notice of them. *United States* v. *Arredondo,* 6 Pet. (U. S.) 715; *Consequa* v. *Willings,* 1 Pet. (U. S. C. C.) 230. But particular usages must always be proved, and the circumstance of its being of recent origin, unreasonable, local, against the general law, restricted within narrow limits, &c., always come in to enhance the difficulty of making it clearly appear that the parties con-

tracted in reference to it, and intended to make it controling in their contract. *Kendall* v. *Russell,* 5 Dana (Ky.) 501; *Gibson* v. *Culver,* 17 Wend. (N. Y.) 307; *Allegre* v. *Maryland Ins. Co.,* 2 G. & J. (Md.) 136; *Thomas* v. *O'Hara,* 1 Const. (S. C.) 306. If parties engaged in the business to which the usage relates, and therefore having the means of knowing of its existence or non-existence, testify that they have no knowledge of its existence, or that it has been resisted by some and is not uniformly acted upon, this is very material, as tending to dispense with the effect thereof. *Parrott* v. *Thatcher,* 9 Pick. (Mass.) 426; *Kendall* v. *Russell,* ante.

[8] See Section 105, ante, entitled "Proof of Usage to Establish a Warranty."

tract which the statute declares invalid, or to give a right of
action, upon a contract where the statute provides that no
action shall be maintained. Consequently proof of a custom
or usage, can never give validity to a contract within the
statute of frauds, or to take a case out of the operation of the
statute of limitation.[9]

Where Meaning is Given to Word by Statute - "Bushels"— "Hobbett"—Custom as to Weight—As to "Lumps."

SEC. 143. It follows, therefore, necessarily from these
rules, that the admissibility of the evidence of custom to
explain the meaning of a word used in any contract whatever is subject to the qualification that, if a statute has given
a definite meaning to any particular word, it must be understood to have used it with that meaning, and no evidence of
custom will be admitted to attach any other meaning to it.
The words to which statutes have given a definite meaning
are for the most part those which denote weights, measures
or numbers. Thus, in one case, "bushels" were held to
mean only statute bushels.(u) In another, "quarters of
corn" was understood to mean legal quarters.(v) In *Hughes*
v. *Humphreys*,(w) the statute 5 & 6 Will. 4, c. 63, s. 6,
which abolishes all local or customary measures, and imposes
a penalty on every person who shall sell by any denomination or measure other than one of the imperial measures, or
some multiple or aliquot part thereof, was held to apply only
to the sale by measure of capacity, and not to sale by weight
estimated in pounds. And that, therefore, it did not extend
to sale by any local term designating a given number of
pounds' weight. As to sale of wheat by Welsh hobbett, it
appearing by evidence that this designated 168 pounds'
weight, and that a sale by hobbett entitled the purchaser to
so many pounds of wheat. And in another case, a contract

---

[9] *Dunham* v. *Gould*, 16 Johns. (N. Y.) 367.

(u) *Hockin* v. *Cooke*, 4 T. R. 314.   *Howard de Walden*, 6 T. R. 338.
(v) *The Master of St. Cross* v. *Lord*   (w) 3 E. & B. 954.

for the sale of a certain number of tons of iron, "long weight," was held not to be a contravention of the statute, and that consequently such a contract was valid. It appeared in that case that the 15th section of 5 Geo. 4, c. 74, is not repealed by the act alluded to, and that, therefore, contracts by local weight may be lawfully made if the proportion to the standard is expressed.(x) It has been held that a custom that every pound of butter sold in a particular market town shall weigh eighteen ounces is bad; but it was a question whether a custom to sell butter *in lumps* might not be supported.(y)

As to Importance of Subject.

SEC. 144. Little remains to be added in this place. It may be objected that, after all, undue importance has been given in the foregoing pages to what is, after all, only one branch of the Law of Evidence. We cannot, however, admit that that is so. It is true it is a branch of the law of evidence, but it is one of the most important branches, and it is doubly important to the real student of jurisprudence, by reason of the fact that it is, as it were, the connecting link between the science of evidence and the science of law. The fact that questions in relation to usage have been so frequently litigated, shows the importance of the subject and the importance of having the main questions in connection with it definitely settled. If we could feel that our work had contributed to this end we should feel that this book was not insignificant, but of very great practical worth. If we have not that consciousness, our failure is due to the execution, and not to the purpose.

(x) *Giles* v. *Jones*, 11 Exchq. 393.   see also *Wing* v. *Earle*, Cro. Eliz.
(y) *Noble* v. *Durrell*, 3 T. R. 271;   267.

INDEX.

324 INDEX.

332   INDEX.

M.

N.